D0913020

THE ADMINISTRATIVE
PROCESS IN BRITAIN

The Administrative Process in Britain

R. G. S. BROWN

METHUEN & CO LTD

First published in 1970
Reprinted with an additional chapter 1971
by Methuen & Co Ltd
11 New Fetter Lane, London EC4

First published as a University Paperback 1971

Hardback SBN 416 15200 7
Paperback SBN 416 150200 9

© 1970 and 1971 by R. G. S. Brown

Printed in Great Britain by
The Camelot Press Ltd, London and Southampton

Distributed in the USA
by Barnes & Noble, Inc.

'The money to be earned is the solitary attraction. A clerk in a Public Office may not even dream of fame to be acquired in that capacity. He labours in an obscurity as profound as it is unavoidable. His official character is absorbed in that of his superior. He must devote all his talents, and all his learning, to measures, some of which he will assuredly disapprove, without having the slightest power to prevent them; and to some of which he will most essentially contribute, without having any share whatever in the credit of them. He must listen silently to praises bestowed on others, which his pain has earned for them; and if any accident should make him notorious enough to become the suspected author of any unpopular act, he must silently submit to the reproach, even though it be totally unmerited by him. These are indeed the indispensable disadvantages of the position of a clerk in a Public Office, and no man of sense and temper would complain of them. But neither will any man of real mental power, to whom the truth is known beforehand, subject himself to an arduous examination in order to win a post so ill paid, so obscure, and so subordinate or should he win it, no such man will long retain it.'

SIR JAMES STEPHEN, 1854

'That is the way I think a permanent secretary should behave, with a rather consistent attempt to consider what the Minister really needs. But I think no man of spirit can do this for long.'

SIR EDWARD PLAYFAIR, 1965

For Gordon and Stuart

CONTENTS

PREFACE

We are at a watershed in the development of public services in Britain. New functions of government have made it necessary to create new administrative machinery. New departments and agencies have grown up piecemeal over a quarter of a century, with increasing prolixity since the early 1960s. The experimental phase must soon be followed by one of consolidation. There is enough evidence, if we can read it aright, to devise a workable administrative machine, each part of which is tailor-made for the purpose it serves.

There has also been a long period of argument, to which the Fulton Report[1] has contributed, about the structure, the morale and the performance of the higher civil service. The culmination of this discussion must be a new pattern of organization and staffing which is as well suited to the needs of the time as the great reconstructions of the past – the implementation of the Northcote-Trevelyan Report in the last century, the introduction of the executive class after the First World War and the assimilation of specialists after the Second.

The subject has already attracted such a spate of writing that some apology may be needed for adding to it. This essay was conceived while the writer was directly involved in the machinery of government. It seemed obvious that there were serious weaknesses in the central policy and decision-making machine. Skills and energies were being frittered away on relatively trivial matters, while there was a failure to seek out dynamic solutions to major problems. People of very considerable ability seemed unable to break out of an inhibiting organization structure that no longer reflected contemporary priorities. Many suggestions were being made to improve matters, but none of them appeared to offer a

[1] *Report of the Committee on the Civil Service 1966–68*, Cmnd. 3638 (1968) vol. 1 'Report of the Committee'; vol. 2 'Report of a Management Consultancy Group'; vol. 3 'Surveys and Investigations'; vol. 4 'Factual, Statistical and Explanatory Papers'; vol. 5 'Proposals and Opinions'.

complete and adequate solution. Some criticized the civil service for not achieving the impossible, others for not doing a job that it was not allowed to do by the government it served. There was a gap between the assumptions and objectives of efficiency experts, who often paid no regard to the way the civil service was embedded in the political system, and those of political theorists, who tended to give little or no weight to the practical difficulties of organizing a large and complex body of men and functions. There was also a gap between official studies of administrative procedures and academic accounts of the general growth and functioning of public bodies (which often failed even to distinguish between the roles of administrator and politician). Although more material was becoming available about the working of central government machinery, much of it was discursive and imprecise or else – a point that applies particularly to the invaluable evidence collected by parliamentary committees – badly in need of interpretation and assimilation.

The most promising method for a systematic analysis of these problems seemed likely to emerge from a growing body of theory and research about organizations which was attracting interest on both sides of the Atlantic. The twenty years since Simon published the first edition of his *Administrative Behavior* had seen increasingly successful attempts to refine the original crudities of management theory and to apply it to different sorts of organizational problems. In this country, Burns, Lupton, Joan Woodward and members of the Tavistock Institute of Human Relations had made considerable additions to the available knowledge, which had become familiar stock in trade of the better management training schools. But there had been little or no attempt to apply their methods of analysis to the problems of British public administration. The purpose of this essay is, therefore, to try to move away from the 'common-sense' approach that still colours much analysis of public administration and to see whether an application of the methods developed by Simon and later social scientists might not provide a more satisfying rationale for proposed changes in central administrative machinery.

In the meantime the Fulton Committee has published its report on the civil service, accompanied by voluminous evidence from official bodies and private individuals and a more slender quantity of research. The supporting material contains a mass of information about the civil service in a relatively convenient form. The writer has drawn on it gratefully. The report itself is less helpful: it is imbued with a 'business-managerial' philosophy, but fails to make any effective contribution to the theoretical understanding of public administration; its recommendations are on the whole opportunist and seem likely to solve some problems at the price of making others more intractable, particularly those concerned with co-ordination and political accountability. The main Fulton recommendations are described and discussed below, but they do not provide anything like a complete answer.

This book is in three parts. The first is a brief account of the changing role of the civil service since the Northcote-Trevelyan Report, its present structure and the political framework within which it operates. The Fulton recommendations about recruitment, training and career paths are included here for convenience. Part Two contains a brief introduction to organization theory. The first two chapters (VI and VII) are elementary, and are included only for the benefit of readers with no previous knowledge of the subject. Chapters VIII and IX, on the other hand, attempt to pick out the distinctive characteristics of the public sector from an organization theory point of view. In Part Three these theoretical concepts are applied in an experimental way to a number of current problems in the machinery of government, executive management, policy and planning, and the recruitment and training of administrators. One of the main arguments, about the most appropriate structure for carrying on the processes of public administration, runs through several chapters and comes to a head in Chapter XIII. The final chapter deals with the separate questions of motivation and morale in the public sector.

The main immediate lessons of the analysis are two. First, that general solutions are likely to have limited relevance to the complex and varied problems facing the future architects of British central administration. The trend of current thinking is that an organizational structure cannot sensibly be described as good or bad, but only as appropriate or inappropriate to the task to be performed. There is a great need to disentangle various criteria of the administrative process in order to test, as rigorously as possible, the relevance for the achievement of different tasks of different suggestions for reform and to see whether they are likely to be practicable and at what cost. For example, those who wish to strengthen the apparatus of political control often seem to assume that administrative initiative is unnecessary or undesirable – and vice versa. In practice different parts of the machinery may need to be structured in different ways according to the nature of the job they are required to do.

The second conclusion is that it would be foolish to adopt the Fulton Committee's advice to jettison the general administrator: some equivalent to the present administrative class *élite* will still be required alongside the new (and needed) public service managers and administrative specialists.

These conclusions underline the need for research. There has been a surprising absence of research on the administrative implications of planning (such as the integration of research and development into a policy-making framework). There have been hardly any studies of crucial questions about the relationship between human factors and performance in public employment. Problems urgently requiring investigation, using social science techniques, include: (a) problems of internal structure, communication and sensitivity to change in the political and technological environment; (b) the implications of increasing size and complexity for organizational structure and relationships between generalists and specialists; (c) the reaction of people to structural change; (d) the effect of conditions of service on efficiency and allegiance. Some more detailed suggestions for research are contained in an appendix.

Two limitations of the study should be admitted at the outset. It does not deal with the civil service as a whole. The focus for discussion is the fairly small group of administrators (including some of those who are now senior members of the executive and specialist classes as well as the administrative class) who are concerned with the formulation and implementation of policy, the operation of the top-level policy-making machine and the major questions of public sector management. These are the senior administrators who work in a near-political atmosphere, who contribute directly to policy decisions and on whose ability in some measure depends the quality with which we as a nation govern our affairs. There are important questions about the middle ranks, who are charged with the detailed working out of policy decisions, including the operation of regional and local offices, and about the junior staff who are in contact with the public; but they are not examined here.

Second, nearly all the illustrative material is concerned with the administration of social and economic services. There are only passing references to important aspects of government activity in defence, production, trade and external affairs. This bias reflects the experience as well as the interests of the writer. Moreover, the economic and social service departments offer a reasonable range of the problems to be met by modern government, and it is these areas particularly that have given rise to much of the current controversy.

This book is not intended as a comprehensive account of organization theory, nor as a complete picture of the problems facing public administration in contemporary Britain; its purpose is the more tentative one of exploring the territory common to both. Much objective research on which a development of this subject must depend still has to be done; this essay will have been successful largely to the extent that it identifies areas in which such research is carried out in the future.

ACKNOWLEDGEMENTS

This book could not have been written without the generous assistance of friends and former colleagues in the civil service. Unpublished documents have readily been made available and have provided useful source material. Individual civil servants have been kind enough to read and comment on parts of the manuscript. I cannot thank them all by name, but I must record my particular gratitude to K. E. Couzens and Norman Dugdale for their frank but always constructive criticisms. Responsibility for errors of fact and of judgement is, however, my own.

Academically, my debts to H. A. Simon, D. K. Price and V. Subramaniam will be obvious from footnotes. I am personally indebted to Rodney White, then of Cornell, for his introduction to the administrative theories which he has played an important part in developing, to T. E. Chester for advice and encouragement at several stages of a mixed university-civil service career, and to colleagues and students at the University of Hull for various forms of advice and forbearance. My family has endured a great deal so that this book could be written. So has Lynda Wright, who has tackled successive drafts with unfailing enthusiasm.

Extracts from Crown Copyright documents are reproduced by permission of the Controller of Her Majesty's Stationery Office.

PART ONE: Background

I. The Century of Northcote-Trevelyan

A permanent civil service, in the sense of 'full-time salaried officials, systematically recruited, with clear lines of authority, and uniform rules on such questions as superannuation', emerged in Britain early in the nineteenth century.[1] In the eighteenth century there was no clear distinction between political and administrative offices. The civil service of the Crown became established as the growing volume of parliamentary and administrative business made it necessary to place more of the latter in the hands of officials. Civil servants owed their permanent status, at a time when the development of party politics was making their political chiefs less secure, to parliamentary jealousy of Crown patronage: the opportunities for patronage could be reduced by granting security of tenure to officials already in post. The alternative to a career service – a spoils system in which officials were replaced as their political sponsors demitted office – never took root in Britain.

The watershed between politics and administration became fairly clear as posts immediately below the Secretaries of State in the great departments separated into temporary ones held by Parliamentary Under Secretaries (the junior Ministers of today) and those of Permanent Under Secretaries, held by career civil servants who took no part in politics. The office of Permanent Under Secretary (Assistant Secretary in the Treasury, and Permanent Secretary in other departments not headed by a Secretary of State) became established in most departments between 1800 and 1830. The first Assistant Secretary to the Treasury was appointed in 1805. At this stage vacancies were still filled by patronage. The 'Campaign for Economical Reform' initiated by Burke and Fox had reduced the number of sinecures, but it was not until the 1850s that Northcote

[1] H. Parris, 'The Origins of the Permanent Civil Service 1780–1830', *Public Administration*, vol. 46 (1968) p. 143.

and Trevelyan showed the way to a modern career service, immune from nepotism and jobbery.[1] It took the rest of the nineteenth century for their ideas to be fully worked out.

Sir Stafford Northcote (later Chancellor of the Exchequer under Disraeli) was a politician who had been private secretary to Gladstone. The real author of the famous Northcote-Trevelyan Report was Sir Charles Trevelyan, Assistant Secretary to the Treasury, a former member of the already reformed Indian Civil Service and son-in-law of Lord Macaulay, whose ideas permeate mid-nineteenth-century discussions about administrative reform. Their report was the culmination of a series of enquiries into the organization and staffing of government offices. Professor Wheare described it in 1954 as 'this premature vision in the middle of the nineteenth century of the sort of Civil Service we need in the middle of the twentieth century'.[2] Less enthusiastically, the Fulton Committee on the Civil Service, 1966–8, started its report with these words: 'The Home Civil Service today is still fundamentally the product of the nineteenth-century philosophy of the Northcote-Trevelyan Report. The tasks it faces are those of the second half of the twentieth century. This is what we have found; it is what we seek to remedy.'[3]

Northcote and Trevelyan made four main recommendations:

1. There should be a clear separation between 'intellectual' work, performed by graduates, and 'mechanical' duties allocated to a 'lower class' of lesser ability. (It was not until 1876, however, that a real attempt was made to establish a separate lower division by Order in Council. Subsequent enquiries showed that it took a long time to distinguish clearly the work appropriate to each division. After several refinements, the present system of administrative, executive and clerical 'classes' was introduced in 1920.)

2. Entry to the service should be at an early age through competitive examinations, the highest being set at the level of a university degree. (The Civil Service Commission was established in 1855 to test the suitability of candidates nominated by departments; from

---

[1] *Report on the Organisation of the Permanent Civil Service* (Northcote-Trevelyan Report) C. 1713 (1954). Reprinted in *Report of the Committee on the Civil Service 1966–68* (Fulton Report) Cmnd. 3638 (1968) vol. 1, app. B.

[2] K. C. Wheare, *The Civil Service in the Constitution* (a lecture given to mark the centenary of the Northcote-Trevelyan Report) (London, 1954).

[3] *Fulton Report*, vol. 1, par. 1.

1859 only persons approved by the Commission were entitled to superannuation. It was 1870 before an Order in Council provided that all vacancies should be filled by open competition – and even then posts in the Foreign Office and the Home Office were exempted.)

3. Separate departments should be made part of a unified service, in which transfers and promotions could be made between departments. (Although service-wide conditions of service were introduced for some grades before 1900, real unification did not come until Warren Fisher, as Permanent Secretary of the Treasury, assumed the title of Head of the Civil Service in 1919 and obtained the right to advise the Prime Minister on senior appointments throughout the service.)

4. Promotion should depend on merit, assessed by reports from superiors. (It is harder to identify stages in the implementation of this principle. The growth and recognition of staff associations has made promotion at lower levels subject to rules, negotiated with the staff themselves, in which seniority has inevitably and perhaps defensibly played a large part. But nepotism has long since ceased to be a factor in promotion.)

THE CIVIL SERVICE OF 1854

By 1854 the permanent civil service was firmly established. Northcote and Trevelyan took its importance for granted.

> It cannot be necessary [they said] to enter into any lengthened argument for the purposes of showing the high importance of the Permanent Civil Service of the country in the present day. The great and increasing accumulation of public business, and the consequent pressure upon the Government, need only be alluded to; and the inconveniences which are inseparable from the frequent changes which take place in the responsible administration are matters of sufficient notoriety. It may safely be asserted that, as matters now stand, the Government of the country could not be carried on without the aid of an efficient body of permanent officers, occupying a position duly subordinate to that of the Ministers who are directly responsible to the Crown and to the Parliament, yet possessing sufficient independence, character, ability, and experience to be able to

5

advise, assist, and to some extent, influence, those who are from time to time set over them.

But the service was still very small. The 1851 census tables show over 40,000 civilians directly employed by central government, but two-thirds were accounted for by the revenue departments and the Post Office. The Poor Law Board employed 84 persons, including 12 inspectors and a clerk apiece. The Public Works Loan Office employed 4 people (disregarding office keepers, messengers and porters), the General Board of Health 26, the Treasury 70, and the Board of Trade 79, compared with nearly 12,000 in the Customs Service.[1]

This was the age of Bentham and of *laissez-faire*. The conventional view was that governments should not interfere with the operation of natural economic laws, and there was little reason to challenge the assumption that these laws were, on the whole, beneficent. Trade conditions were favourable and apparently stable. There were no major wars to upset the equilibrium in the period between the Crimean and Boer Wars, both of which were associated with administrative change. True, Bentham had taught that the State should intervene to protect the weak (as in the case of children in factories) and to maintain uneconomic institutions of social value, but until the publication at the end of the century of the social surveys of Booth and Rowntree, these categories had not begun to be identified, far less understood. So there was little intervention by governments in social and economic affairs. When they did intervene, as in factories legislation or in the centralized administration of the Poor Law, it was usually to set limits to acceptable economic activity rather than to exert positive influence.

Nineteenth-century administration was primarily regulatory: Parliament said what was to be done and Parliament's wishes were carried out by inspectors (who watched for infringements) and by lawyers (who prosecuted them); the typical job of an administrator was therefore the simple one of preparing legislation and briefing the Minister when the need arose; he had little need for drive or initiative but could spend his life sitting waiting for papers. Compared with the position even at the turn of the century, the functions

[1] Parliamentary Papers 1854–55, vol. XX, *Papers on the Re-organisation of the Civil Service*, app. 'Census 1851 – Supplementary Tables on the Civil Service'. See also M. Abramovitz and V. F. Eliasberg, *The Growth of Public Employment in Great Britain* (Princeton, N.J., 1957) pp. 16–18.

of government were narrow, both in theory and in practice. Ministers did more of the actual policy work themselves, and civil servants less, because there was altogether less to do. Central co-ordination was weak and functions of the State could be administered in watertight compartments. The administration of any particular field or service was relatively simple, because there was little in the way of specialized knowledge and techniques. Finally, most government departments were so small that internal management did not present serious problems.[1]

Consequently, it was easy for senior men, commenting on the Northcote-Trevelyan Report, to pour scorn on the capacity of the service to provide work for good university men. Here, for example, is Arbuthnot, Trevelyan's immediate subordinate at the Treasury:

> The officers of our Civil Service cannot in ordinary cases aspire to become statesmen, and to carry out systems of policy. Their humble but useful duty is, by becoming depositories of departmental traditions . . . to keep the current business in its due course; to warn Ministers of the consequences of irregular proceedings into which they might inadvertently fall; to aid in preparing subjects for legislation; and possibly to assist by their suggestions the development of a course of reform. [Their function is to obtain] that intimate acquaintance with details, and the bearing of those details upon general principles, which constitute the distinction between the permanent executive officers and the members of Government who are charged with the duty of administration.[2]

This sounds like work that clerical or executive officers would carry out today. There were already some posts comparable to those of the present-day administrative class. In evidence to a Select Committee, Trevelyan had described the work of the eight Principal Treasury Officers – each of whom had to decide, within the section of the work for which he was responsible, when to bring matters forward to the Treasury Board and later to prepare appropriate

---

[1] There are useful summaries of the development of the civil service in: Abramovitz and Eliasberg, ibid.; E. M. Cohen, *The Growth of the British Civil Service* (London, 1941); H. R. G. Greaves, *The Civil Service in the Changing State* (London, 1947). For the period of the Northcote-Trevelyan Report see M. W. Wright, *Treasury Control of the Civil Service, 1854–1874* (London, 1969).

[2] *Papers on the Re-organisation of the Civil Service*, p. 411.

7

minutes – in terms which would not serve too badly as a description of the work of a junior Principal working with a committee in many departments today.[1] Because there was less complexity and less need for co-ordination, we can probably say that there were no equivalents to the modern Under Secretary or above. But there were at least a few Assistant Secretaries, able and willing to discharge the kind of positive role that some writers consider to have emerged only in the twentieth century. The most outstanding was Trevelyan himself, whose part in the Irish Famine, for example, was certainly not that of a 'humble but useful . . . depository of departmental tradition'. Another was Edwin Chadwick, Secretary to the General Board of Health, every inch a technocrat, impatient of parliamentary control and anxious to see the development of professionalism, both in administration itself and in supporting fields like structural engineering. Like many other distinguished nineteenth-century civil servants, Chadwick enjoyed great power as secretary of a semi-autonomous board. His comments on the Northcote-Trevelyan Report are considerably longer than the report itself, partly irrelevant, but wholly worth reading because of the insight they give on the outlook of a thoroughly modern administrator in the middle of the nineteenth century.[2]

The administration of 1854 was not *purely* regulatory. Professor Greaves has commented that, in a sense, the nineteenth-century state never existed: the social service democracy of the twentieth century was born before the maladministration and paternalism of the eighteenth century had wholly disappeared.[3] The principle of administering social services through local agencies under the supervision of a central department was introduced by the Poor Law Amendment Act of 1834 and extended by the Public Health Act of 1848. By 1851 the Government was a substantial employer of artificers and labourers: nearly 15,000 of them were employed in the ordnance factories and naval dockyards. The Post Office had become a large commercial enterprise with the introduction of the penny post in 1840 and employed another 15,000 people. In 1829, the Home Secretary had become responsible for the Metropolitan Police Force. The Board of Trade was given the duty of collecting and producing statistics in 1832. Although, therefore, it lacked the

[1] *Select Committee on Miscellaneous Expenditure 1847–48*, XVIII, p. 151, quoted in Cohen, p. 88.

[2] *Papers on the Re-organisation of the Civil Service*, pp. 135–228.

[3] Greaves, op. cit., p. 9.

machinery and the will to control much of the economy, the Government had begun to take on some functions characteristic of a modern state. The civil service that emerged from the 'premature vision' in the Northcote-Trevelyan Report was an essential instrument in its development.

DEVELOPMENT AND GROWTH 1900–39

The principal Northcote-Trevelyan reforms had been implemented and consolidated by the end of the nineteenth century. In the highest administrative classes, at least, there were men of calibre ready to carry out the 1905 Liberal Government's programme of social and economic intervention and to deal with the administrative aspects of the First World War.

The Old Age Pensions Act of 1908, the Labour Exchange Act of 1909 and the National Health Insurance Act of 1911 established government social services of a wholly new kind. The employment and pensions services (augmented in the 1930s by new schemes for supplementary benefits and employment assistance) brought civil servants into direct contact with the public. The National Health Insurance scheme, administered by the new Ministry of Health after 1919, brought the medical profession irrevocably within the Government's sphere of interest. Other health services were established and entrusted to local authorities, whose educational services, including the school medical service, were also expanding under the Board of Education (established in 1899). The development of these services required an intimate relationship between government departments and local authorities which would have been recognized by Chadwick, although not perhaps by many of his contemporaries. Sir George Newman wrote that they 'enlarged the purpose of the Civil Service, as guide, philosopher and friend to the Local Authorities and the auxiliary voluntary movements associated with them'.[1] The task of government became one of participation and encouragement and not merely of regulation and restraint.

In the field of trade and industry, government intervention was more reluctant and change was less continuous. During the 1914–18 war, the Government became involved in the regulation of economic activity, and particularly with the distribution of manpower, on a very large scale. New Ministries were set up including a Ministry

[1] Sir George Newman, *The Building of a Nation's Health* (London, 1939) p. 103.

of Food and a Ministry of Mines. Some of them, like the Ministry of Labour and the Department of Scientific and Industrial Research, were to become permanent. But the main policy objective after the war was to return to 'normal conditions' as soon as possible. This meant eliminating many of the regulatory agencies in industry and trade. Retrenchment and economy were also the orthodox reaction to the great depression.

Thereafter, however, there were stirrings of interventionism, accompanying a change in the general economic climate. There were a number of moves to encourage investment in the depressed areas, to rationalize hard-hit industries like shipbuilding and to set up cartels in industry and marketing boards in agriculture. In 1930, the Government appointed an Economic Advisory Council (to replace a Civil Research Committee appointed in 1925) with a high-level composition of Ministers and outside experts. But (as Lord Bridges points out in his book *The Treasury*[1]) there was no consensus of economic opinion about a remedy for the major current evil of unemployment and this body made relatively little impact on actual policy. The Government was not yet in a position, or possessed of the necessary techniques, to attempt a systematic management of the economy.

All this was reflected in the numbers of central government employees. In absolute figures, the number of non-industrial civilian staff rose from 229,000 in 1914 to 285,000 in 1928 and 387,000 in 1939. Within this total the staff of the social service departments more than doubled by 1928 and trebled (to 25,000) by 1939, mainly as a result of the expansion of insurance and assistance schemes. Those concerned with trade, industry and transport had also doubled in number by 1928 and nearly quadrupled (to 43,000) by 1939, three-quarters of this increase being attributable to Ministry of Labour functions. Over the same period, the staff of the revenue departments doubled and that of the Post Office went up by only a third.[2]

One effect of the steady growth in the functions of government was increasing pressure on the time of Ministers and of Parliament. The pressure on parliamentary time was eased by an increase in the amount of business handled by subordinate legislation. In 1929 the Committee on Ministers' Powers was set up 'to consider the

---

[1] Lord Bridges, *The Treasury* (2nd edn., London, 1968) p. 90.
[2] Abramovitz and Eliasberg, op. cit., pp. 40–4 (table 4).

powers exercised by or under the direction of the Crown by way of (a) delegated legislation and (b) judicial or quasi-judicial decision, and to report what safeguards are desirable or necessary to secure the constitutional principles of the sovereignty of Parliament and the Supremacy of the Law'. In its report the Committee agreed that it was necessary to use delegated legislation, partly to save parliamentary time, partly as a speedy and flexible way of getting things done and partly because the scope of legislation now extended to technical matters which it was difficult to include in a Bill 'since they cannot effectively be discussed in Parliament'.[1] The amount of delegated legislation has increased enormously since the Committee reported, and more and more business has come to be subsumed under these categories. Quantitatively, most decisions of a legislative character have been taken out of Parliament. There has been some anxiety that they should not, in practice, be left to civil servants. The Committee suggested a number of safeguards, one of which was that Parliament should set up a committee to keep an eye on rules and orders submitted for formal approval. This was not implemented until 1944.

The increased work of government also implied more delegation from Ministers to civil servants. Although new Ministries were set up during and after the war, and Boards were converted into Ministries, there was a limit both to the number of able politicians and to the time they could give to departmental matters. The rest had to be done by professional administrators. A Reorganization Committee in 1920 described the duties of the administrative class ('those concerned with the formation of policy, with the co-ordination and improvement of Government machinery, and with the general administration and control of the Departments of the Public Service'[2]) in terms that would, not much earlier, have been thought more appropriate to the Minister himself. The 1929–31 Royal Commission on the Civil Service accepted this definition without modification, saying that the need for civil servants to carry out such work had not been challenged in the evidence given to them, and dismissing the whole question of the administrative class in three or four pages.[3]

[1] *Report of the Committee on Ministers' Powers*, Cmd. 4060 (1932) pp. 21–4.

[2] Civil Service National Whitley Council, *Report of the Joint Committee on the Organisation of the Civil Service* (London, 1920).

[3] *Report of the Royal Commission on the Civil Service 1929–31* (Tomlin Report) Cmd. 3909 (1931).

But this did not mean that civil servants were usurping the Minister's ultimate function of deciding on policy. Sir Warren Fisher told the Commission:

> Determination of policy is the function of Ministers, and once a policy is determined it is the unquestioned and unquestionable business of the civil servant to strive to carry out that policy with precisely the same energy and precisely the same goodwill whether he agrees with it or not. That is axiomatic and will never be in dispute. At the same time it is the traditional duty of civil servants, while decisions are being formulated, to make available to their political chiefs all the information and experience at their disposal, and to do this without fear or favour, irrespective of whether the advice thus tendered may accord or not with the Minister's initial view.[1]

The relationship between a Minister and his civil servants is discussed in detail by H. E. Dale, a retired Principal Assistant Secretary, in a classic account of the higher civil service just before the war. Of the daily work of a department he says:

> Only a tiny proportion of the mass would embody decisions of importance, taken by the Permanent Secretary or other high official: and those decisions would every one of them be applications of the policy determined by the Government and the Minister, or adaptations to fit into a change of circumstances. The higher the rank of a civil servant and the more closely he is acquainted with the Minister's mind, the more he feels himself at liberty to modify the detailed application of the policy: but no civil servant, whatever his rank, would think it compatible with his duty to take any step inconsistent with it. If he thought such a step to be imperatively required, he would represent his difficulties and ask for instructions. There are now many more officials and they do many more things than forty or fifty years ago: but in reality they do no more without the authority of Parliament and Ministers. Bureaux have grown, but not bureaucracy . . . This view I think, will be contested by few who know the inside workings of Government Departments.[2]

---

[1] *Report of the Royal Commission on the Civil Service 1929–31, Minutes of Evidence*, p. 1268 (evidence from Sir Warren Fisher).

[2] H. E. Dale, *The Higher Civil Service of Great Britain* (Oxford, 1941) pp. 38–9. Dale's description of the relationship between a senior civil servant and his

The administrator appears in Dale's account as a rather ingenious secretary: 'A good official commands the terse and simple style appropriate to a memorandum for the Cabinet or the easy style appropriate to a private letter as readily as he commands the stately language of a circular to Local Authorities.'[1] On a tricky parliamentary question, the Permanent Secretary 'will be satisfied when a draft reply has been framed which is brief, completely accurate, courteous, exhibits the Minister as modestly surprised to find his own attitude so clearly right, and gives no opening for awkward "supplementaries"'.[2] His entire job is to serve his Minister. To do this he needs broad experience, and a mastery of the government machine that can come only with time. Civil service training must be geared to producing this in the officials closest to the Minister:

> The ultimate criterion of the system is whether it produces a sufficient supply of men fit for great office. Assistant Secretaries are important in themselves as administrators and advisers of the Minister on their own subject, but it is much more important that they should provide men fit to be Permanent Secretaries and Second Secretaries.[3]

Some people argued that the administrators were not fit for their new responsibility. Some put the blame for the political inertia of the 1930s on the shoulders of a civil service alleged to be lacking in vitality and in social consciousness. This view was expressed polemically by Laski in his last lectures after the war (my italics):

> They never met, with any *imaginative insight*, the problems of a society with never less than one million unemployed, and, more often, as many as two million or more. They never *pushed forward* the plans so urgently needed . . . They showed no sense of the *urgent need* for re-education at a far higher level . . . They did not *compel attention* to the very serious problem of monopolies . . . They did not *press the cabinet* into any serious grasp either of the scale of the housing problem or of the *impossibility* of leaving it to be dealt with by private enterprise . . . Not all the devotion the Civil Service brought to its work was a compensation for

Minister agrees almost point for point with Lord Morrison's post-war account of the relationship from a Minister's point of view in *Government and Parliament* (3rd edn.) (Oxford, 1964) ch. XIV.

[1] Ibid., p. 121.   [2] Ibid., p. 37.   [3] Ibid., p. 220.

the absence of *imaginative enterprise* on its part at a time when this quality was vital to the national future.[1]

At less exalted levels of policy making, also, new needs were emerging. The Government's responsibility for providing services such as labour exchanges and unemployment assistance schemes called for new qualities of management and drive of a type not previously associated with central administration. Although the report of the 1929–31 Royal Commission on the Civil Service was generally complacent, the Commission felt that in the Post Office, at least, there were special administrative requirements that needed further investigation. The subsequent report of the Bridgeman Committee put the Post Office on a different basis from other government departments and can be seen in retrospect as the first official questioning of the generalist tradition. Its recommendations included the devolution of powers to regional directors, training in the regions for headquarters administrators and the establishment of a Board system in which responsibility for advising the political head was shared between administrative and technical officers.[2]

To sum up, government had by 1939 taken on many new services of a different character from those of the previous century. The increase of work alone led to some delegation of functions from political heads of departments to professional administrators. Many of these functions were primarily political in character, and could be discharged by a generalist whose mind was tuned to the politician's. Some, however, called for new kinds of ability which the generalist did not necessarily possess. It was coming to be recognized that special training (and sometimes special forms of administration) were needed in these areas. Both at senior and at middling levels, the criteria by which civil servants were judged were beginning to change.

NEW DEMANDS : THE POST-WAR PHASE

The Second World War provided an opportunity for rethinking the responsibilities of government and for absorbing some of the economic theories that had been gaining currency in the 1930s.

[1] H. J. Laski, *Reflections on the Constitution* (Manchester, 1951) pp. 164–5.
[2] *Report of the Committee of Inquiry on the Post Office* (Bridgeman Report) Cmd. 4149 (1932). The Report had not been fully implemented by the outbreak of war in 1939.

Two decisions of the 1940–5 Coalition Government entailed lasting changes in the role expected of central government. First came the acceptance of the general principles expressed in the Beveridge Report. This put social insurance firmly in the context of a comprehensive social policy, including national assistance, family allowances and other measures to combat disease, ignorance, squalor and idleness.[1] These ideas finally took shape in plans for improved services, whose impact was summed up by Greaves in 1947:

> The regulatory state has given place to the social service state. Public responsibility is now admitted for the securing to every citizen of an important body of his fundamental needs. Free and enforced educational provision is made for him, with much assistance for further training in technical institutes and universities. His care is organized through a national health service. There is local and central responsibility for housing him. An elaborate insurance system has been constructed to meet the contingencies of sickness, accident, and old age. When he is unemployed the community recognizes a responsibility for his maintenance and for assisting him to obtain and train for work.[2]

These activities were not, of course, all carried out by organs of central government under the direct responsibility of a Minister. The National Health Service, for instance, was administered partly by local authorities and partly by *ad hoc* local bodies appointed and financed by the Minister. But the scale of the new services, and the magnitude of the problems they had to tackle, involved local agents in a continuous dialogue with the responsible central departments.

The second major decision of the Coalition Government was the acceptance in 1944 of government responsibility for maintaining full employment after the war.[3] This commitment implied a continuing intervention in economic affairs. During the war, a high proportion of economic activity had been regulated from the centre through controls, licensing and rationing. Some resources were controlled directly by the Government through the bulk purchase and allocation of raw materials. Others were controlled indirectly through restrictions on investment, manpower and prices. To allow

[1] *Social Insurance and Allied Services, Report by Sir William Beveridge*, Cmd. 6404 (1942).

[2] Greaves, op. cit., pp. 221–3.

[3] *Employment Policy*, Cmd. 6527 (1944).

the controls to be operated, the Government collected a great many statistics about industry and trade. The 1945 Labour Government decided to maintain a large part of this machinery as an instrument of peace-time planning. It faced many economic and financial problems and had to deal with conflicts between social and economic priorities. The situation seemed to demand centralized economic planning. It was decided to place parts of certain key industries, particularly transport and fuel, under public ownership.[1]

Direct physical controls were unpopular. Most of them were gradually abandoned as shortages eased. The election of a Conservative Government in 1951 hastened the process, but derestriction and decentralization had already started. Restrictions on the movement of manpower, other than miners and agricultural workers, were taken off very quickly after the war. Building licences were abandoned in 1954 (although not the attempt to control the location of industry through industrial development certificates). The last traces of war-time rationing of consumer goods, and most price controls, had disappeared by 1955.

In place of direct controls, the Government attempted to regulate the economy through financial management of taxation levels and public expenditure. The necessary machinery for economic intelligence and planning was already in embryo. During the war, the Cabinet Office had included an Economic Section charged with presenting 'a co-ordinated and objective picture of the economic situation as a whole and the economic aspects of projected Government policies'.[2] This section remained in existence after the end of the war. Herbert Morrison, as Lord President of the Council, became generally responsible for economic co-ordination and in 1947 Sir Edwin (now Lord) Plowden was appointed Chief Economic Planning Officer, with a mixed staff of businessmen, civil servants, statisticians and economists, in the Lord President's Office. Later in the same year, the central planning staff joined Sir Stafford Cripps in the new Ministry for Economic Affairs and followed him to the Treasury six weeks later when he became Chancellor of the Exchequer. The Treasury then took on a responsibility for economic co-ordination that it retained until 1964. The Economic Section

[1] The factors influencing economic planning in the late 1940s and the structure of nationalized industries are discussed by Lord Morrison in *Government and Parliament*, chs. XII and XIII.

[2] Sir John Anderson, 'The Machinery of Government', *Public Administration*, vol. 24 (1946) p. 153.

of the Cabinet also reported to Sir Stafford Cripps, but was not formally transferred to the Treasury until 1953.

There were at least two other ways in which the Government began to influence economic activities. One of these mainly affected food and agriculture. In an attempt to stimulate home production, farmers were guaranteed a market and a price for some of their main products. For a time, too, certain foodstuffs were directly sub-sidized. The operation of this and similar schemes involved the Government in negotiations about the detailed structure of the industry.

The other source of influence was the State's own economic activity. The expansion of central and local government and the nationalization of key industries gave the public sector a leading position in the labour market. In 1938 less than 10 per cent of the working population had been employed in the public sector, most of it in local government. By 1950 the public sector, including the armed forces, employed over five and a half million people, or nearly a quarter of all employed workers. The nationalized industries and services alone accounted for over a tenth of the total working population.[1] The number of persons paid from public funds of one sort or another became a significant factor in attempts to influence incomes in the country as a whole. The high proportion of graduates employed by public bodies gave the Government a direct interest in the deployment of highly-trained manpower. Moreover, the size of the public sector placed a new instrument in or near the hands of a Chancellor of the Exchequer who wished to influence national levels of investment and employment.

The nationalized industries and services (from house coal to hospital care) constituted a very large field where market forces could, if the occasion demanded, be replaced by political decisions about prices and the level of supply. Public enterprises also had a tremendous potential influence on the market as purchasers of commodities. Some departments, like the Ministry of Health, were practically in a monopsist position and had to develop a new relationship with suppliers of drugs and equipment. This situation created new opportunities and new problems which had not been solved by the 1960s, when the need for more effective management of these enormous resources in the interests of the economy as a whole was at last fully recognized.[2]

[1] Abramovitz and Eliasberg, op. cit., p. 25.

[2] See, for example, Sir Richard Clarke, *The Management of the Public Sector of the National Economy*, Stamp Memorial Lecture (London, 1964).

The implementation of these new social and economic responsibilities entailed an expansion of statistical and intelligence services
and the development of new consultative machinery. Each of the
new social services had its apparatus of consultative, advisory and
executive committees, representing professions employed in the
services as well as local interests and consumers. In the economic
field, consultative machinery was established to provide links
between government and industry, including the National Production Advisory Council on Industry, the National Joint Advisory
Council and the Economic Planning Board. The last was set up in
1947, comprising six officials from the departments mainly concerned with finance and industry, three employers' nominees and
three nominees of the trade unions, to exchange views on economic
problems. It was in some ways the precursor of the National
Economic Development Council (1962).

The changes were reflected in the size and structure of the central
administrative machine. Between April 1939 and April 1950 non-
industrial staff directly employed by central government departments, including the Post Office, increased by over 75 per cent
from 387,000 to 684,000. The departments concerned with social
services and with trade, industry and transport had more than
tripled in size.[1]

We have a fairly clear picture of the civil service at this time. The
rules about publication by serving civil servants were relaxed and
there are several first-hand accounts of the work of departments in
the 1950s, notably those by Critchley, Campbell, Dunnill, Sisson
and Walker.[2] Many of the academics who came into the service
during the war, like Franks and Devons, had already written of their
experiences.[3] Later still, valuable information became available in
the published evidence to parliamentary committees. By comparing
these accounts with Dale's pre-war study, certain trends became
discernible.

[1] Abramovitz and Eliasberg, op. cit., pp. 40–5 (table 4).

[2] T. A. Critchley, *The Civil Service Today* (London, 1951); G. A. Campbell, *The
Civil Service in Britain* (2nd edn.) (London, 1965); Frank Dunnill, *The Civil Service:
some human aspects* (London, 1956); C. H. Sisson, *The Spirit of British Administration:
and some European comparisons* (London, 1959); Nigel Walker, *Morale in the Civil
Service: a study of the desk worker* (Edinburgh, 1961).

[3] Sir Oliver (now Lord) Franks, *The Experience of a University Teacher in the Civil
Service*, Sidney Ball lecture (Oxford, 1947); E. Devons, *Planning in Practice* (Cambridge, 1950).

Delegation to Officials

In the first place, it is clear that political chiefs were forced to devolve even more responsibility to their senior administrators. From merely administering legislation, civil servants began to interpret it and to prepare schemes for its implementation. Here, to contrast with Dale, is what Lord Franks had to say about his work as a temporary member of the administrative class in the Ministry of Supply during the war. Although this particular job was abolished after the war, it had its permanent counterparts in many corners of the 'new look' departments:

> Once he was clear about what in general was desirable, he would normally go on to find out, through enquiry, consultations, and meetings with experts, what was practicable in the circumstances, establishing the main heads of the workable schemes and identifying the agents, whether members of the Civil Service or of the public, who must carry out the plans, explaining the policy and the steps worked out to realize it, to make sure that each main agent knew his part and its general context and was convinced that his part and the whole scheme was practicable. Having thus established agreement based on understanding, he would give the word to start operations, satisfied at least that action would not be held up by failures of will or intelligence. Even so, he would arrange for progress reports so that difficulties or delays could be ascertained and dealt with before they grew to proportions which would wreck the scheme or its timing and relevance to wider plans.[1]

Immediately after the war the administrative class was reorganized 'to facilitate speedy and efficient transaction of public business by the maximum devolution of responsibility and by the reduction of steps in the administrative structure to the minimum consistent with the needs of sound organization'.[2] The Permanent Secretary remained the official head of the department and, with the assistance of one or two deputy secretaries, remained responsible to the Minister for all its activities. A new grade of Under Secretary was created, with the responsibility of advising Ministers on major questions of policy, and, generally, for co-ordinating very large

[1] Franks, op. cit.
[2] *The Administrative Class of the Civil Service*, Cmd. 6680 (1945).

19

blocks of administrative work. Below the Under Secretaries came the Assistant Secretaries, in charge of divisions and supported by Principals or senior executive officers in charge of branches. All day-to-day work was to be done within the division and only questions of major policy were normally to be referred above Assistant Secretary level.

The 1953–55 Royal Commission on the Civil Service described 'the most significant function' of the administrative class as follows:

> The members of the class must be able to work from a very broad Government aim, first to thinking out a policy for the execution of that aim and satisfying Ministers that it correctly interprets the aim, secondly to putting that policy into legislative form and thirdly to its translation into action, frequently on a national basis . . . These duties have to be carried out in ways compatible with Ministerial control, the accountability of Ministers to Parliament and their accountability, in a less direct but very real sense, to public opinion.[1]

What this means in practice varies from department to department according to tradition, the type and volume of its work and the calibre of its staff. In some departments, Assistant Secretaries acting under very broad authority will issue circulars, handle discussions with pressure groups and present subordinate legislation to Parliament on their own initiative. In others, there is a tradition of consulting the Minister to 'keep him in the picture' even on matters of detail. But it must be rare for a Minister to wish to see much of the more technical or the more routine aspects of his department's work. The assumption is that he will hear soon enough through conventional political channels if something wrong, or inconsistent, is being done in his name.

Sometimes this happens, as in the Ministry of Agriculture and Fisheries in 1954. After persistent complaints about the way some requisitioned land at a place called Crichel Down had been restored to agricultural use, the Minister (Sir Thomas Dugdale) appointed an independent Q.C. to find out how his officials had reached their decision. Sir Andrew Clark's report found that some officials had

---

[1] *Report of the Royal Commission on the Civil Service 1953–55* (Priestley Report) Cmd. 9613 (1955), par. 413. The Commission was prevented by its terms of reference from discussing reorganization and was therefore at some pains to define jobs as it found them, in order to recommend fair pay scales.

acted less fairly than they ought (though there was no question of personal advantage to them) and that they had failed to explain to the Minister what they were doing.[1] The Minister took steps internally to prevent the same sort of thing happening again, but the matter was not allowed to end there. The Prime Minister appointed a committee of two ex-civil servants and a distinguished industrialist to advise whether the officials concerned should be transferred to other duties,[2] and Sir Thomas Dugdale himself resigned.

Following this incident, it was felt necessary to reconsider a Minister's formal position in relation to acts of his officials. The Home Secretary (Sir David Maxwell-Fyfe) defined it in the following terms:

1. Where a civil servant carries out an explicit order by a Minister, the Minister must protect the civil servant concerned.

2. Where a civil servant acts properly in accordance with the policy laid down by the Minister, the Minister must equally protect and defend him.

3. Where a civil servant makes a mistake or causes some delay, but not on an important issue of policy and not where a claim to individual rights is seriously involved, the Minister acknowledges the mistake and he accepts responsibility, although he is not personally involved. He states he will take corrective action in the department.

4. Where action has been taken by a civil servant of which the Minister disapproves and has no prior knowledge, and the conduct of the official is reprehensible then there is no obligation on the Minister to endorse what he believes to be wrong, or to defend what are clearly shown to be errors of his officers. The Minister is not bound to approve of action of which he did not know, or of which he disapproves. But, of course, he remains constitutionally responsible to Parliament for the fact that something has gone wrong, and he alone can tell Parliament what has occurred and render an account of his stewardship.[3]

[1] *Report of the Public Enquiry into the Disposal of Land at Crichel Down*, Cmd. 9175 (1954).

[2] *Report of a Committee Appointed by the Prime Minister to consider whether certain Civil Servants should be transferred to other duties*, Cmd. 9220 (1954).

[3] *H.C. Debs.*, vol. 530 (20 July 1954), cols. 1284–7.

Perhaps the most serious risk is that a civil servant, through ignorance, malicious intent or misunderstanding of the Minister's mind, will put up proposals which do not in fact exhaust the viable alternatives. This raises important questions of training and attitude as well as of political responsibility. The best comment may be Lord Morrison's:

> What the reader can be sure of is that the British Civil Service is loyal to the Government of the day. The worst that can be said of them is that sometimes they are not quick enough in accustoming themselves to new ideas, but then it is up to the Minister to educate them. The greatest danger in the running of a Government Department is a Minister who does not know how to handle civil servants; who does not possess a mind of his own; or who is lazy and finds life easier and pleasanter by blindly taking the advice of his civil servants without considering and criticizing it.[1]

Co-ordination

The second feature of the post-war service was a vast increase in the complexity of its work. The new responsibilities which government had taken on could not simply be aggregated in separate compartments like the nineteenth-century boards or even the *ad hoc* social services of the 1930s. The emphasis on economic management implied qualitative changes in the way the individual functions of government were discharged. So, to a lesser extent, did the attempt stemming from Beveridge to see social policy as a whole. The increasing scale of government activity would in any case have meant that decisions taken in one field had significant repercussions in others. If a programme of factory construction is large enough, it implies a shortage of labour and materials for building houses, schools and hospitals. The Central Electricity Generating Board can cause massive problems for the National Coal Board and ultimately for the Ministry of Labour if it miscalculates its requirements. Lord Bridges put the point clearly in his 1950 Rede lecture:

> But it is economic factors more than anything else which have compelled Departments to work more closely together. No government can today discharge its responsibilities unless it has a coherent economic policy, and such a policy must be framed

[1] Morrison, op. cit., pp. 335–6.

after bringing together the views of separate Departments, while
its execution demands constant consultation between them.[1]

This, of course, meant that individual decisions had to be taken
in the light of incessant consultation, within and across departmental boundaries. Part of the load fell on Ministers and on their
immediate advisers as members of interlocking Cabinet and official
committees. But perhaps the greatest burden of consultation fell
on officials at about Assistant Secretary level in the course of their
day-to-day work.

After 1947 the Treasury became particularly significant as a co-
ordinating department concerned with the adoption of uniform
standards throughout the public service as well as with the impact
of financial and economic policies on one another. Perhaps it
should be said that this was co-ordination of a rather special kind.
The objectives of economic policy were negative rather than
positive: it was necessary to *avoid* inflation, to *avoid* excessive unemployment and to *avoid* expenditure not absolutely necessary for
the purpose determined by Ministers. In regional planning, too,
the tests were negative: factory development in congested areas
must be restrained; but new building elsewhere must not make more
than a limited demand on national resources of materials and manpower. This approach fitted well with the traditional regulatory
functions of the Treasury.[2] In circumstances of acute shortage,
perhaps it was inevitable. But post-war writers like Greaves and
Munro claimed that the Treasury mistook economy for efficiency
and never understood the need to find criteria for the developing
public services (like health, education and job-finding) different
from those appropriate to a nineteenth-century regulatory department. Much later, when positive planning for economic growth
had become an agreed objective of all parties, Brittan echoed a
fairly general feeling that the Treasury was an unsuitable agent
for such growth, because of its departmental philosophy.

It is largely a well-justified suspicion that the projects of other
Departments will cost much more than appears at first sight, and
that total Government spending has an inherent tendency to get
out of control. This philosophy has been carried over into the

[1] Sir Edward (later Lord) Bridges, *Portrait of a Profession*, Rede Lecture (Cambridge, 1950) p. 23.

[2] The Treasury had other functions, e.g. in relation to civil service training, where
a more constructive approach was sometimes permissible.

Treasury's newest responsibilities, where it has become a perennial fear that the whole economy is likely to become overstrained, that as a nation 'we are trying to do too much'.[1]

Morale

A third feature of the post-war situation was a sharp drop in the public estimation of civil servants. Although not easy to substantiate or quantify, there is a very strong impression that the civil service enjoyed a status and reputation before the war which it lost afterwards. The service became less attractive to potential recruits. Salaries and conditions of service tended to fall behind; other opportunities were opened to school and university leavers and the Civil Service Commission found it progressively more difficult to satisfy its appetite.

The enlarged functions of government must have affected the situation. The civil service was an obvious target for the frustration caused by restrictions and shortages. Moreover, there were more points at which the service impinged on the lives of the public; inevitably, more mistakes were made and they were more visible. With the volume of criticism and the size of their work-load rising in step, it would not be surprising if many civil servants began to feel their job to be thankless and unrewarding.

Heterogeneity

The fourth characteristic which, if not new, became more pronounced in the post-war period, was variety and versatility. The new range of services brought civil servants at all levels into contact with a greater variety of people. New patterns of consultation brought representatives of the professions, industrialists, trade unionists, scientists and pressure groups of all kinds into the penumbra of government. Administrators found themselves working with new kinds of specialists, as colleagues and as advisers, and having to learn something of their language and techniques.

Their range of activity also became wider. Some were still engaged in the kind of quasi-political work described by Dale – preparing briefs to be inserted at the right time and the right place in the government machine. At the same time (perhaps in the same department) a colleague might be considering what light social survey techniques could throw on a problem which a committee was

[1] S. Brittan, *The Treasury under the Tories 1951–64* (London, 1964) p. 38.

investigating. Another might be handling judicial work of rare complexity, like the Principal in the Civil Service Commission who sat for four years with a staff of over a hundred to decide what candidates were eligible for special examinations on the ground that they had received a number of years' 'full time continuous and systematic education'.[1] Others would be more concerned with horizontal relationships, collaborating with people in other departments and outside the civil service to get things done. Others, again, were beginning to look downwards, at management and organization, applying new managerial techniques to the business of conducting large enterprises like the hospital service without waste of resources.

And yet, as one reads not what outsiders said the civil service ought to be doing but what civil servants and Ministers say they actually were doing, the overall impression is one of continuity. Critchley's account of an Assistant Secretary's day, written about 1950, is almost identical with Dale's account of his pre-war equivalent, with one conspicuous exception. The pre-war Assistant Secretary tended to work from 10.30 a.m. to 7 p.m. on weekdays and 1 p.m. on Saturdays. Ten years later his successor's hours were 9.30 a.m. to 7 p.m. or 8 p.m. on weekdays, with a few files taken home for good measure, and possibly 3 p.m. or 4 p.m. on Saturday. Both writers were worried about the effect on quality of increasing work-load.[2]

[1] Civil Service Commission, *86th Report* (*covering the Reconstruction period*) (London, 1954) p. 11.
[2] Dale, op. cit., pp. 27–32; Critchley, op. cit., pp. 71–3.

II. The Sixties: a Decade of Doubt

By the early 1960s leaders of British opinion had begun to seek remedies for disorders in the economic and financial management of their affairs. The wage-price spiral continued to rise. Economic growth was checked by stop-go policies. Problems such as imbalance between the regions seemed to be becoming worse. At the same time there was no overall plan to settle priorities within the growing total of public expenditure. There was a feeling that national prestige was waning and it was natural to look for a scapegoat.

Labour supporters blamed the Conservative Government. Academic economists blamed that Government's advisers. Many felt obscurely that part of the trouble lay in the weakness of Parliament. But the main targets of criticism were administrative methods and institutions and the quality of civil servants themselves. Controversies about the civil service that had been smouldering for half a century were re-ignited. It was claimed that senior civil servants were selected and trained in a way that discouraged vitality and creativity. Their social origins, their university subjects and their lack of outside experience combined to make them a narrow *élite* from whom not much could be expected. They were not interested in management and had no feeling for technology. They were secretive and used the doctrine of ministerial responsibility to conceal their (apparently negative) use of power. As for the real experts, there were not nearly enough of them, and the administrators were careful to keep them away from any position of real influence. 'In sum, there are new functions to be performed. They require new forms of organization and new men with new skills.'[1]

At the centre of the permanent apparatus of government was an

---

[1] It would be tedious to give detailed references for all these comments. They are derived from B. Chapman, *British Government Observed* (London, 1962); Fabian Tract No. 355, *The Administrators* (London, 1964); S. Brittan, *The Treasury under the Tories* (1964); M. Nicholson, *The System* (London, 1967); H. Thomas (ed.), *Crisis in the Civil Service* (London, 1968). The last quotation is from R. Neild, 'New Functions: New Men?', *The Listener*, vol. LXXII (27 August 1964) p. 304.

enormously powerful Treasury, controlling the budget and all public expenditure, controlling the civil service, influencing pay throughout much of the public sector, responsible for exchange control, short-term financial regulators and, since 1947, for economic co-ordination and such economic planning as existed. Inevitably, the Treasury was at the centre of most of the storms.

THE PLOWDEN AND FULTON ENQUIRIES

In 1957–8 the Estimates Committee of the House of Commons looked at 'Treasury Control of Expenditure' and found it inconsistent and haphazard. There was no system of control – rather a shapeless bundle of procedures and precedents. The Treasury was solemnly authorizing the loan of naval flags to churches while apparently lacking any means of supervising hospital expenditure running into hundreds of million pounds.[1] The Committee's recommendations led eventually to a largely internal study under the Lord Plowden who had been Chief Planning Officer to Morrison and Sir Stafford Cripps in 1947. The published Plowden Report is a rather unsatisfactory summary of the main points in a series of confidential reports to departments, which provided a framework for a new look at our institutions for controlling public expenditure. Although the main problem was 'how to bring the growth of public expenditure under better control, and how to contain it within such limits as the Government think desirable', the Committee's approach was very broad. 'The kernel of the matter' was 'what the machine of government is trying to do, what its attitudes are, what it regards as important, and its approach to its work on all matters involving public expenditure'.[2] The Plowden Committee was assisted by a well-known management consultant (Mr. E. F. L. Brech) and its report stresses the importance of management. This was defined to include:

1. The preparation of material on which decisions are based.
2. The technical efficiency with which larger administrative operations are carried out.
3. The cost-consciousness of staff at all levels.

---

[1] *Sixth Report of the Estimates Committee 1957–58* (H.C. 254–1) 'Treasury Control of Expenditure'.

[2] *Control of Public Expenditure*, Cmnd. 1432 (1961).

4. The provision of special skills and services (e.g. organization and methods, training, and the quantitative techniques of statistics, costing, accountancy and operational research).
5. The awareness and effectiveness with which these are used.
6. The training and selection of staff for posts at each level of responsibility.

The Committee found that heads of departments did not give enough time to management compared with their other duties of advising on policy and accounting for expenditure. Nor was management experience shared between departments. The Treasury should therefore build up a management service and develop techniques to help departments, among other things, to relate the value of an activity to the cost of carrying it out. (The consequences of this recommendation will be described in later chapters; they include some notable achievements. But when an official described the Treasury's management functions to the Royal Institute of Public Administration in the year following the report his examples were mainly concerned with office machinery.[1])

The most important outcome of the Plowden enquiry, however, was the 'forward look' at commitments for several years ahead, so that major decisions could be taken 'in the light of surveys of public expenditure as a whole . . . and in relation to the prospective resources'. In 1963 the Government published the results of an early survey in the first of a series of White Papers.[2] It became apparent that the country was committed to a level of expenditure that could not be met painlessly unless the whole economy was expanding. Faster economic growth became a major policy objective and a new task for the civil service.

But not for the Treasury. In 1962, as a result of the Plowden enquiry, the Treasury had been reorganized into two 'sides', one responsible for the pay and management of the civil service and the other, under a separate Permanent Secretary, for finance and economics. But many people felt that the Treasury outlook was too geared to passive co-ordination and regulation. A new central agency was needed to carry out a positive planning role. At the end of 1964 the Treasury lost its responsibility for long-term economic planning to the new Department of Economic Affairs,

[1] W. W. Morton, 'The Management Functions of the Treasury', *Public Administration*, vol. 41 (1963) p. 25.
[2] *Public Expenditure in 1963–64 and 1967–68*, Cmnd. 2235 (1963).

which published the optimistic and ill-fated National Plan early in the following year.[1] The D.E.A. was a very 'modern' department, with unconventional staffing patterns giving great weight to temporary experts. It was fairly small, with no executive responsibilities of its own, but powerful enough under its first Secretary of State (Mr George Brown) to challenge the Treasury on its own ground.

Whatever was right or wrong with the Treasury, it had become a convenient symbol for all that was supposed to be stuffy and out-of-date in the civil service. It was soon to lose its dominating position in civil service management also. This position had been under intermittent attack for a long time. In 1964 a Fabian group which included many serving civil servants argued that the Treasury was bound to bring a restrictive, uncreative attitude to its personnel work because of its primary concern with economy. Establishment work should be transferred to a reformed Civil Service Commission.[2] Although the 1963–64 Estimates Committee had taken a fairly kindly view of the way the Treasury had gone about its job since the Plowden reforms,[3] a report on recruitment in the following year hinted at some serious deficiencies and recommended that 'a committee of officials, aided by members from outside the civil service on the lines of the Plowden Committee, should be appointed to initiate research upon, to examine, and to report upon the structure, recruitment and management of the Civil Service'.[4] When the Fulton Committee was appointed in February 1966, with four serving civil servants and two Members of Parliament among its twelve members, its terms of reference were 'to examine the structure, recruitment and management, including training, of the Home Civil Service, and to make recommendations'.

The Fulton Committee reported in June 1968.[5] Its main finding was that the structure and practices of the service had not kept up with its changing tasks: 'Despite the recent improvement in its management services the Treasury had failed to keep the Service up to date.' One of its main recommendations, among three that were accepted by the Government on the day of publication, was

[1] *The National Plan*, Cmnd. 2764 (1965).

[2] Fabian Tract, *The Administrators*.

[3] *Fifth Report of the Estimates Committee 1963–64* (H.C. 228) 'Treasury Control of Establishments'.

[4] *Sixth Report of the Estimates Committee 1964–65* (H.C. 308) 'Recruitment to the Civil Service', p. xxxv.

[5] *Report of the Committee on the Civil Service 1966–68* (Fulton Report) Cmnd. 3638 (1968).

that responsibility for central management of the service should be given to a new Civil Service Department under the Prime Minister, largely although not solely, 'to demonstrate that a fresh start is being made'.[1] (The other reasons provided by the Committee are pretty weak. For example, it is suggested that personnel work calls for a different expertise from control of expenditure. But this problem would have been overcome by the Committee's own proposal for specialization within departments. It is also surprising, if the argument about special expertise is sound, to find that Sir William Armstrong, the popular and obvious choice as first head of the new department, should a year or two earlier have been in charge of the finance and expenditure 'side' of the Treasury – the change seems to be largely symbolic.)

To discover how far the sacrifice is purely ritual, and how far the service is really in need of a new image we must, like the Fulton Committee itself, take a look at the changing task. The Committee asked a group of management consultants to examine what civil servants actually did in selected parts of twelve departments. The consultants' general findings are made available separately in Volume 2. Their report is valuable partly for its descriptive content, and partly because it explains the logic behind parts of the main report. Blocks of work are assessed from a management point of view and, although the consultants (including a Treasury organization and methods man) were forced to acknowledge the effect of political environment, their recommendations reflect an industrial rather than a public service outlook. Their findings have to be supplemented by first-hand accounts from senior civil servants and politicians.[2]

CIVIL SERVICE TASKS

When all the available material is taken into account, we cannot help noticing that new responsibilities have not replaced the old ones. Public interest shifts from one aspect of public administration to another as new functions of government create new

[1] *Fulton Report*, vol. 1, par. 253.
[2] For example, Lord Morrison, *Government and Parliament;* H. Wilson, Enoch Powell and others *Whitehall and Beyond* (London, 1964); Sir Edward Boyle, Sir Edward Playfair and others 'Who are the Policy-Makers?', *Public Administration*, vol. 43 (1965) pp. 251 ff.; T. D. Kingdom 'The Confidential Advisers of Ministers', *Public Administration*, vol. 44 (1966) p. 267.

demands. In the debate about the Northcote-Trevelyan Report the main concern was about how to reconcile intellectual qualities with loyalty, integrity and discretion. The Haldane Committee of 1918 was concerned that administrators should reflect and think ahead.[1] Between the wars, there were doubts about the ability of 'conservative' civil servants to understand the needs of radical social policies and to serve a Labour Government. During and after the 1939–45 war, the expansion of services directly affecting the public brought anxieties about training and public relations that are reflected in the Assheton Report.[2] Twenty years later, questions were very properly being raised about the drive, the breadth of understanding and the technical expertise of administrators who might be required to make far-sighted proposals, going beyond the life of a parliament or even of a government, in areas of great technical complexity. But as new requirements appear, the old ones are still there – even the nineteenth-century regulatory and office-maintenance functions for which Northcote and Trevelyan tried to recruit the best available material. The demand for effectiveness and competence does not mean that economy and accountability can be neglected. Indeed, practically all that has been lost over the century is the need for the laborious copying of letters before the invention of the typewriter and its female accompaniment. The Fulton Committee does not suggest that any of the traditional skills and knowledge of the administrator can be dispensed with. The new requirements are additional:

> It must be accepted that for the administrator to be an expert in running the government machine is not in itself enough. He must in future also have or acquire the basic concepts and knowledge, whether social, economic, industrial or financial, relevant to his area of administration and appropriate to his level of responsibility. He must have a real understanding of, and familiarity with, the principles, techniques and trends of development in the subject-matter of the field in which he is operating.[3]

The following analysis of the work falling on the higher civil service is drawn from many sources. It is tentative and can no doubt be improved upon, both by including additional categories

[1] *Report of the Machinery of Government Committee* (Haldane Report) Cd. 9230 (1918).
[2] *Report of the Committee on the Training of Civil Servants*, Cmd. 6525 (1944).
[3] *Fulton Report*, vol. 1, par. 41.

and by making them more specific, but it will do for our immediate discussion.

Working the Machine

Someone in a department has to run the Minister's office. In the narrower sense, this is a job for a private secretary. The Minister has to be supplied with papers when he needs them, including material for speeches and letters; he also needs help in deciding which claims on his time have priority. In a broader sense, running the office is the job of the Permanent Secretary and his administrative staff. Before the Minister makes an executive decision, somebody must check that he is statutorily empowered to do so and has not forgotten the precedents of similar cases. If the Minister has ideas about new legislation, he will have to obtain authority from a Cabinet committee, after making sure that the Chancellor of the Exchequer is aware of the financial implications and that there will be no objections from other Ministers about repercussions affecting their territories. This, in essence, is how the system of collective responsibility works. To make it work, and to handle the related consultative and legislative machinery, requires a body of people who have expert knowledge and skill in the machinery of government, who know their own part intimately, several other parts nearly as intimately and have a general knowledge of the whole machine and the principles on which it works. This 'telephone exchange' function of the administrator, stripped of some of its present-day complexity, would be easily recognized by the administrators of the mid-nineteenth century. It has no real counterpart elsewhere.

Representing the Minister

The Minister cannot personally discharge even that part of his duties which involves him as a political figure. He needs representatives who will present his view to interested groups in contact with his department, to subordinate agencies and to representatives of other Ministers at inter-departmental meetings. He needs people who will argue, persuade and bargain on his behalf and apply his general line of thought to detailed issues with which he will never have time to make himself familiar. Such a function can be carried out only by a group of people who, in Sisson's words, 'specialize in the awareness of Ministerial responsibility'.[1] These people do not

[1] Sisson, *The Spirit of British Administration*, p. 13.

only speak, write and think in his name; it will often be necessary that they should usurp part of his personality and prepare a speech or a letter for him as he himself would have prepared it.

Formulation of Major Policy

Once, perhaps, the function of advising Ministers meant little more than the kind of office support described above. Nowadays it means suggesting what action the Minister should take. The process of formulating policy is distinct from taking decisions. It can be described as 'analysing the problems, defining the issues they present, and finding out what methods might be used to deal with them'.[1] This entails making available to the Minister all the special knowledge and techniques that are thought most relevant to the issue under consideration. Since no decisions would be made if *all* relevant considerations had to be sought and taken into account, it also involves the selection and evaluation of different aspects of a problem.

Deciding Minor Policy

Nearly all observers agree that, in practice, all major issues (and many that are not major) are brought before the Minister personally. Nor does it rest entirely with his staff to decide which are major and which are minor. Discretion, however, is involved in the detailed implementation of his decisions. Anyone who has worked in a government department knows of questions of minor policy which are settled by civil servants at about Assistant Secretary or Under Secretary level on their own responsibility. Sir Edward Playfair provides two examples from his own experience:

I was in charge of the arrangements for what had to be said to everybody in every part of the world about the devaluation of the pound, and I never enjoyed anything so much. It was important, urgent, tied in to great matters, yet not so big and vital that I could not manage it myself . . .

For an example of an independent piece of minor policy one needs a situation where something ought to be done by the machinery of politics which arouses no political feelings. You get your Minister's general blessing and go ahead with it. I had a good example of that. It was quite clear that the constitution

[1] N. Johnson, 'Who are the Policy Makers?', *Public Administration*, vol. 43 (1965) p. 282.

of the National Gallery and the Tate Gallery wanted bringing up to date, so I asked the Chancellor if I might go ahead with it. He agreed: I negotiated with the Trustees of both bodies, I got everybody squared, I got a Bill drafted, I got it introduced and it all went marvellously.[1]

This sort of activity is different from those already discussed because of the increasingly technical issues involved. It is a significant element in the work-load of higher civil servants.

Management

There are many definitions of management. The Plowden Committee's definition (pp. 27–8) was very wide. What is meant here is something narrower: management in the sense of getting things done – and getting them done with the human, financial and physical resources available. Policy has to be implemented at various levels. The Minister's own department has to be organized, equipped and staffed. This may involve decisions about the recruitment and training of people with special skills or about statistics and the use of computers to help in formulating policy for a decision. Policy may also have to be implemented through agents, and management skills may be involved in helping them to do something that they do not particularly want to do and may even believe to be impossible with the resources they have. Or the Minister may be directly responsible for a large executive service (for example running social security offices) in which day-to-day service decisions have to be taken in much the same way as in commercial industry. The parallel with industry can never be exact. It is just possible, although rather misleading, to compare a Permanent Secretary with a managing director and his Minister with the chairman of a company. (In departments where they are responsible for substantial blocks of executive activity some Ministers, for example successive Postmasters General, tend to be the real managing directors. In other departments, like the Home Office or the Treasury, management in any ordinary sense is a relatively small part of even the Permanent Secretary's work-load.) But a body of shareholders normally has a simple and direct interest in one aspect of the company's activities and does not, if things are going well, take the same delight as Members of

[1] Sir Edward Playfair, op. cit., p. 263.

Parliament in spotting errors of detail. Nevertheless, the modern civil service does have management responsibilities which are perhaps closer to those of industry and commerce than its other functions. The Fulton Committee rightly pointed out that 'the management of the department's executive activities' constitutes the work of most (that is to say not necessarily the top) civil servants.

Taking these functions as a starting point, we can start to translate them into specifications for the composition and design of the administrative machine. It then becomes possible to study problems in public administration as special cases of general problems in organizations and to consider the relevance of research and experience in quite different contexts. We can also identify problem areas where more research is needed and see the lines on which this might be carried out. (In some cases, this may not amount to much more than repeating in a public institution an investigation that has already proved fruitful elsewhere.) Most importantly, it gives us the opportunity to distinguish different components of the public administrative machine and to examine them, as far as possible, both in isolation and as parts of a whole. The tendency in the past (this is in some ways true of the Fulton Report) has been to try and find general solutions for particular problems without taking the trouble to study their repercussions.

It is convenient to distinguish the human implications from the structural implications of this analysis. An organization consists of people arranged in a particular way. The people and the structure interact to produce a form of behaviour. But it is helpful to focus separately on the individuals and on the way they are organized.

A government department which is designed to meet the five main functions described above seems to need personnel who *collectively* possess the following characteristics (the order is not important): personal loyalty to the Minister; easy familiarity with all aspects of the government and parliamentary machines; reluctance to act on proposals until they have been tested from every possible point of view; unwillingness to take risks that might cause embarrassment to the Minister; detachment from any particular policy and willingness to change direction after a change of Government; a scrupulous approach to the *mode* of administration (for example above-board contract procedures) and to record-keeping against subsequent challenge; a legalistic awareness of

35

precedent and principle; literary and presentational skills; negotiating and persuasive ability; a sensitive awareness of political mood and climate; the resilience necessary to meet short-term pressures: intellectual and synthesizing ability of a very high order; imagination and far-sightedness; knowledge of modern data-handling techniques; specialist knowledge in depth of each field of administration; knowledge of and sympathy with other people's problems; good judgement; interest, involvement and perseverance in a current field of work; vigour and readiness to initiate, and to press new ideas on political leaders; courage to take decisions and stand over them; cost-consciousness; the ability to lead junior staff.

The list is, of course, an impossible one. It includes personality attributes (intelligence, imagination) as well as knowledge, skills and attitudes that can be cultivated by training and experience. Some qualities, like vigour and caution, or personal loyalty and commitment to the job in hand, are opposites. Others, like imagination and detachment, are on the whole unlikely to co-exist in the same person. It is also clearly impossible that one person would possess all the special knowledge relevant to the consideration of a problem of any complexity. The whole list suggests a need to cast a fairly wide net in order to ensure that all the qualities are to be found among a Minister's senior staff. Instead of looking for the impossible all-rounder, attention has to be given to the organization that links people together.

But similar problems emerge from a list of the structural requirements for such an organization. There are many alternative ways of grouping individuals in an organization, with differing effects on their relationships, behaviour and communication patterns. It is again possible to deduce some particular requirements from the five main functions. The following list is not claimed to be unique or exhaustive. With the possible exception of (6), each pattern is directly or indirectly advocated at some point in the Fulton Report.

1. The organization should be stable: stability and continuity will maximize the benefit of past experience and ensure that proper attention is given to the future implications of a policy.

2. Waste and delay should be eliminated by encouraging specialization, avoiding overlaps, and locating particular knowledge, authority and skill clearly in one part of the organization; each department should be organized along the most effective lines for

its particular function and as few people as possible should be involved in each decision.

3. The communication system should be designed to ensure that all available knowledge and skill, from outside as well as inside the organization, is made available as and when the relevant problem is under consideration; consultation should be extensive (and decision-making must therefore be slow); authority patterns should not be so rigid as to inhibit contributions from all participants.

4. Career-patterns should be broad, so that experience is pooled and inter-departmental co-ordination made easier; all departments, therefore, should be organized along similar lines; and finance and personnel work should be centralized.

5. The organization should be designed to respond rapidly to change, whether political, economic, social or technological.

6. The organization must be designed so that political decisions are transmitted quickly and accurately to the point at which they are implemented.

7. To encourage new ideas and the acceptance of responsibility, the organization should be supportive, and encourage both originality and bold decision-making even if mistakes are made in the process.

8. Unless every question is going to the top, the department should be designed in a way that incorporates some device for resolving disputes; there must be a clear line of authority.

Here again, perhaps less obviously, there are inconsistencies. A system that encourages creativity is unlikely to be either tidy and economical or good at transmitting instructions and resolving disputes. Similarly, an organization designed to assemble all possible material bearing on a problem is unlikely to be designed for speedy action. Nor is it easy to combine centralized finance with the devolution of authority, or to combine short, clearly-articulated lines of command with a flexible use of specialist knowledge. We shall return to these points in Part Two.

III. 'Enlightened Amateurs'

This chapter outlines the main features of the British civil service as it was about the time of the Fulton Report. There are notes on numbers, selection, training arrangements and the career structure for the 'general' classes. Specialists are discussed separately in the next chapter.

SIZE AND COMPOSITION OF THE SERVICE[1]

At 1 January 1968 the non-industrial staff in the home civil service numbered about 760,000 (including 200,000 temporary staff and 45,000 part-timers). If the Post Office is excluded (since its staff were paid out of postal revenue, although at that time legally civil servants) the total for the non-industrial home civil service was 465,000.

This is about three times the size of the civil service in April 1939, excluding the Post Office, and about a quarter more than in April 1960. Civil service numbers expanded rapidly during the war and then gradually ran down as those who had been administering controls and rationing were released. After a nadir in 1958–60 the numbers began to rise again, with great rapidity from 1964–5 to

[1] The Fulton Committee, like two previous Royal Commissions on the civil service, adopted the definition 'Servants of the Crown, other than holders of political or judicial offices, who are employed in a civil capacity and whose remuneration is paid wholly and directly out of moneys voted by Parliament'. This definition excluded staff of such bodies as the Research Councils whose organization, pay and conditions are similar to the civil service. It also excluded the Post Office. *Fulton Report*, vol. 1, app. A.

Unfortunately it is not possible to apply this definition consistently in statistics. Those quoted in the text are taken from official evidence submitted to the Committee (*Factual, Statistical and Explanatory Papers*, vol. 4). Particularly in comparison with earlier years, they do not always show Diplomatic and Post Office staff separately. Precise comparisons are made difficult by reclassifications (e.g. engineering staff previously classified as industrial) and by inconsistencies between figures collected in different ways for different purposes. Nevertheless, the broad trends are clear enough.

early 1968, when the Prime Minister announced that special measures would be taken to arrest the growth in the number of people employed in the public service.[1] A large part of the increase can be attributed directly to new departments and new services introduced by the Labour Government. Of the increase of 32,000 between January 1964 and January 1967, 6,000 was in the Ministry of Social Security, 4,000 in the Ministry of Labour, 2,600 in the Board of Trade, 2,500 in Inland Revenue, 1,500 in Customs and Excise, 1,000 in the Ministry of Housing and Local Government (mainly due to setting up new Rent Assessment Panels) and 1,000 in the Land Registry (to cope with a programme for the compulsory purchase of land). In each case there were new schemes, grants, taxes or benefits to administer.

These figures include all non-industrial staff, including typists, messengers and cleaners. They can be broken down, as in Appendix I, into staff groups which are roughly equivalent to the 'classes' into which civil servants are divided for recruitment and career purposes. (They are not identical. The 'administrative' group of 2,800 includes about 300 civil servants who are not members of the administrative class proper.) Most controversies about the civil service are concerned with three groups – administrative, executive, and senior professional – amounting in all to less than a sixth of the total. With the inspectorate (concerned nowadays with rather more than detecting infringements of the law) they are the key decision-makers in the permanent civil service, and most of the Fulton Report is about them. It is therefore interesting to see how their respective numbers have been changing over recent years.

The administrative group hardly increased at all between 1956 and 1966, when it was still about 2,500 strong, compared with 3,000 in 1950 and 1,300 in 1937. In the same decade, the executive group increased from 68,200 (practically the same as in 1950) to 83,600; the 1937 figure was 17,700. The senior professional group grew from 22,400 in 1956 to 25,200 in 1966 compared with 23,100 in 1950 and 9,600 before the war.[2]

Most of the overall increase in civil service numbers during this period was not at decision-making levels but in the infrastructure of

---

[1] *Fulton Report*, vol. 4, 'Civil Service Manpower Statistics' etc., pp. 195–289. For the announcement about special measures to limit expansion see *Public Expenditure in 1968–69 and 1969–70*, Cmnd. 3515 (1968) par. 53.

[2] Ibid., vol. 4, pp. 271–3.

clerical and supporting staff. To some extent the large increase in executives also reflects the greater volume of routine work. The administrative group was declining in relative size, if not in importance, and some posts previously held by administrators were assigned to senior executive officers. In the early 1960s, the number of chief executive officers increased by nearly 40 per cent, partly to fill posts for which administrators were not available.[1] The rate of growth in the top professional group is slower than might be expected, considering the number of new professions established towards the end of the period. The really large categories here, however, are the traditional public service professions like architects and engineers. The 11,556 professionals in the 'Works Group' (at 1 April 1967) obscure substantial increases among economists (106), statisticians (190) and research officers (268).[2] Many of the professional group are more concerned with the prosecution of scientific research, or with building army barracks, than with advising on policy. Nevertheless, it is clear that the civil service had been becoming more specialist (in the conventional sense) and more 'executive' rather than 'administrative', before the Fulton Committee started work.

These figures are for the numbers actually in post, and in some cases are affected by recruitment difficulties. In April 1967 the Treasury estimated, with some reservations about the usefulness of such estimates after a long period of deficiency, that there were shortages varying from 1 per cent in the executive class through 7 per cent in the administrative class (Principal and above) and 9 per cent in the Works Group to 17 per cent among research officers, 23 per cent among economists and 27 per cent among statisticians.[3]

RECRUITMENT

Non-specialist civil servants are recruited through a system developed in the late nineteenth century mainly in order to discourage patronage. Traditionally it rested on open written examinations set by the Civil Service Commission in academic subjects. The

[1] *Sixth Report of the Estimates Committee 1964–65* (H.C. 308) 'Recruitment to the Civil Service', app. 11.

[2] *Fulton Report*, vol. 4, 'Introductory Factual Memorandum', part II, pp. 32–168, pars. 291, 448, 483, 564.

[3] Ibid., pars. 104, 298, 310, 492, 570.

underlying assumption was that administrators needed general abilities similar to those called for by academic study. Such abilities could be recognized early, by the time prospective entrants had reached the highest point of the educational ladder open to them, and could be tested by an examination in the subjects studied in school or university. The candidates who did best in such examinations could be appointed to a secure career in the reasonable confidence that they would be able to meet any demands likely to be placed upon them in the class of posts for which they had been recruited.

Class Structure

For nearly fifty years, most non-specialist desk civil servants have been recruited into one of three 'classes':

1. An administrative class recruited primarily from university graduates.

2. An executive class recruited at roughly matriculation standard at about the age of 18, whose responsibilities 'may be summarized as the day-to-day conduct of government business within the framework of established policy including, for instance, the higher work of accounts and revenue collection, and the management of regional and local offices'.

3. A clerical class, recruited about the age of 16 at the level of the first major school examination, who 'deal with particular cases in accordance with well-defined regulations, instructions or general practice; scrutinize, check and cross-check straightforward accounts, claims, returns, and statistics in prescribed forms; undertake simple drafting and précis work; collect material on which judgements can be formed; supervise the work of clerical assistants; and deal with members of the public in person, interviewing them about their problems or answering their enquiries on the telephone.'[1]

This class structure developed from two of the main ideas in the Northcote-Trevelyan Report about (a) division of labour and (b) service-wide careers for persons at each level of ability. Professor Chapman has pointed out that a similar three-class sytem, with a fourth group of supporting staff, and with specialists standing outside, applies in most countries in Europe.[2] Although the Fulton Committee criticized the class system as such, its recommendations

---

[1] Ibid., pars. 123, 302.
[2] B. Chapman, *The Profession of Government* (London, 1959) pp. 76–7.

about recruitment do not depart from a three-tier pattern (ignoring specialists and the supporting grades) based on stages in the educational system.

Methods of Selection

In practice, the open written examination has never enjoyed quite the importance ascribed to it. Although an Order in Council in 1870 laid down that all vacancies, except in the Home Office and Foreign Office, should be filled by open competition, a Royal Commission reported in 1914 that only a third of appointments (including professional posts) were being filled strictly on this principle.[1] About this time, the first of many modifications was made in the written examination by introducing an interview for administrative class appointments.[2]

The Civil Service Commission has gradually abandoned its own academic examinations in the last few years. The last – the administrative class 'Method I' – was abandoned after ninety-eight years in 1969 (only 50 candidates sat the 150 optional papers in 1967). But this does not mean abandoning an academic criterion – entry qualifications for direct entrants normally specify an appropriate level of performance in school or university examinations.

After the Second World War, a new method ('Method II') of recruitment for the administrative class was introduced which placed a great deal of stress on the possession of specific administrative abilities, measured in a series of tests at the Civil Service Selection Board. This non-academic selection method was normally available only to candidates who already possessed a satisfactory university degree.[3]

A more fundamental departure from the nominal basis of classification has resulted from the impossibility of staffing the service solely with people possessing the 'normal' educational qualifications. When new examinations were established (e.g. for the executive class in the 1920s) concessions were, of course, given to those already in the service. Rapid expansion and the suspension of normal

[1] *Fourth Report of the Royal Commission on the Civil Service 1912–15* (Macdonnell) Cd. 7339 (1914).

[2] *Report of the Royal Commission on the Civil Service 1929–31* (Tomlin) Cmd. 3909 (1931) pars. 253–6. On the history of interviews, see also the *84th Report of the Civil Service Commission* (1950) covering the period 1941–9, pars. 31–4.

[3] *Fulton Report*, vol. 4, 'Selection Procedure for Civil Service Appointments', p. 297.

recruitment during two world wars brought in many temporary staff who were subsequently absorbed. Special concessions had to be made after each war to ex-servicemen whose education had been interrupted. The run-down of the armed forces and the displacement of British officials from the former Colonial Service brought further special schemes in the late fifties and early sixties. On top of this, a proportion of places in each higher class has always been reserved for 'limited competition' among members of the class below (although it has not always been possible to fill them). But the most important factor of all has been the service's inability to attract the number of entrants it needed at the nominal starting age in each category.

The basic qualification for the clerical class is now five passes at Ordinary level in the General Certificate of Education (or equivalent) in prescribed subjects. The minimum age is 15, but recruits are accepted up to age 59. In the early 1960s there was an annual shortfall of about 5,000 recruits against vacancies.[1] This was made up largely by promoting existing civil servants with lower qualifications. In 1966, for example, there were 11,000 new entrants to the class. Only 1,450 of these were direct entrants and only 850 of these were under 20; the others were existing civil servants who were successful in a limited competition in general subjects, or simply obtained promotion, often late in their careers.[2]

At first sight, the executive class was more successful in holding its own. Until 1954 recruitment mainly by written examination at the ages of $17\frac{1}{2}$ to 19 produced a surplus of acceptable candidates. But in that year it was necessary to go down to the minimum standard in order to fill the places. Two years later the conventional examinations were supplemented by a competition, consisting only of an interview, for young people with five G.C.E. passes, including two at Advanced level, or a higher qualification. This was very successful. The written exam was finally abandoned in 1963. Age limits were progressively raised to 27 in 1966. By these means, it proved possible to attract about 1,400 successful candidates a year, including a hundred graduates, and to fill all the vacancies until 1964, when increasing requirements again overtook the number of suitable candidates.[3] But places in the executive class are also filled

[1] Ibid., 'Introductory Factual Memorandum', p. 49, par. 130.

[2] Ibid., 'Civil Service Manpower Statistics', p. 238.

[3] Ibid., 'Introductory Factual Memorandum', p. 91; 'The Quality of recent Executive Class Recruitment', pp. 343–5.

by older candidates from H.M. Forces, by limited competition among clerical officers and by promotion from members of that class aged 25 and over. In 1966 approximately 2,000 of all entrants to the basic executive officer grade (against 4,000 available posts) came from open and limited competitions and 2,500 by promotion from the clerical class. 80 per cent of the competition entrants were under 25. Nearly two-thirds of the promoted clerical officers were over 40.[1]

The Administrative Class

It is in the administrative class that the difference between the traditional and the true picture is most striking. 'Normal' recruitment to the training grade of Assistant Principal is of newly-qualified graduates. For a period after the war the age limits were $20\frac{1}{2}$ to 24. The upper limit has since been raised, largely to accommodate people who did not consider the civil service immediately on graduating, and now stands at 28. Those admitted at this stage have consistently possessed certain social characteristics which have attracted adverse comment over the years. A thorough investigation of this aspect was made by the Estimates Committee in 1965. Its report showed that over the period 1957–63, 85 per cent of successful candidates came from Oxford and Cambridge, 37 per cent had been at boarding schools, 46 per cent had fathers in Social Class I and 54 per cent had degrees in classics or history. These trends are very well-established: the proportion of Oxford and Cambridge successes had been 82 per cent in 1904–14, 78 per cent in 1925–37 and 78 per cent again in 1948–56. The administrative class intake had not gained much from the increase in the output of provincial and 'redbrick' universities during this time.[2]

There are many reasons for this. The kind of person who is likely to succeed in the competitions may also be the kind of person who seeks and obtains a place at Oxford or Cambridge. Graduates at other universities are often committed to other careers and are not

[1] *Fulton Report*, 'Civil Service Manpower Statistics', p. 235.

[2] Estimates Committee, *Recruitment to the Civil Service*, pp. vi–vii, 27, 29–31. Follow-up figures for 1964 and 1965 are provided in the *Fulton Report*, vol. 4, 'Selection Procedures for Civil Service Appointments', pp. 321–6; they show a slightly decreasing dominance by Oxford and Cambridge – possibly associated with a lowering of the threshold of acceptability (see final comment on p. 311, par. 5.10) – but do not otherwise differ markedly from the earlier trend. By 1968, however, the intake of successful candidates from Oxford and Cambridge had been reduced to about 60 per cent.

given so much encouragement by their tutors to consider the civil service. They may genuinely not like what little they know about it. Many potentially good candidates prefer the familiar world of research and teaching.[1] A table prepared for the Fulton Committee showed that the proportions of graduates competing for the administrative class, and the proportions of those who succeeded, were very unbalanced between subjects and universities. In 1965, 13·5 per cent of Oxford and Cambridge arts graduates applied (including over 20 per cent of the historians and over 25 per cent of the classicists) compared with 3·2 per cent of the arts graduates of all other universities. 22·6 per cent of the Oxford and Cambridge applicants were successful (33 per cent of the historians and 27 per cent of the classicists) compared with 7·9 per cent of the applicants from other arts faculties. The rates for social science and natural science graduates are generally lower than in arts but show the same trends.[2]

Similarly, the disproportionate representation of those with middle-class origins may simply reflect the willingness of middle-class children to consider and compete for civil service posts, or the combination in such candidates of skills and qualities – verbal ability, educational background, family interest in administration and so on – which the civil service needs. A similar trend is found in countries with such differing social, economic and political structures as Denmark, Turkey, the United States, France and India.[3]

The possibility of bias in the selection procedure itself must also be considered. In 1967, two researchers concluded from statistical analysis that each stage – written, interview or selection board tests – tended to reject the same type of candidate and that the most important variables were concerned with the *class* of degree obtained and the *type* of university attended.[4] The Davies Committee reported two years later that there was no evidence at all of social or educational bias in the civil service interview and selection procedures for administrative entrants.[5]

[1] See the discussion of student attitudes to the civil service in ch. XIV below.
[2] *Fulton Report*, vol. 4, 'Applications for the Administrative Class compared with University Output', p. 335.
[3] V. Subramaniam, 'Representative Bureaucracy: a Re-assessment', *Amer. Pol. Sci. Review*, vol. LXI (1967) p. 1010.
[4] C. H. Dodd and J. F. Pickering, 'Recruitment to the Administrative Class, 1960–4', *Public Administration*, vol. 45 (1967) pp. 55, 169.
[5] *Report of the Committee of Inquiry on the Method II System of Selection* (Davies Report) Cmnd. 4156 (1969).

But it is necessary to look beyond the 'normal' channel of recruitment to assess the flavour of the administrative class as a whole. Roughly two-fifths of those serving in mid-1967 had originally been members of another class in the civil service. This was partly the effect of the war, at least in the older age groups (among those born before 1921, over 46 per cent were 'indirect entrants') but it also reflected the number of routes into the administrative class other than the graduate open competitions:

1. One-fifth of the Assistant Principal vacancies are in theory reserved for limited competition among members of other classes. In practice, only half the places are filled, often by graduates who just missed the administrative standard in the open competition and took up posts temporarily in the executive class or 'special departmental' classes, such as the tax inspectorate, which recruit graduates. Some executive officers (about 20 candidates in 1966) are also 'tried out' as Assistant Principals in their departments with a view to transfer.

2. Members of the executive and other classes are eligible for departmental promotion to Principal or higher grades. Special efforts have been made to offer a transfer to scientists who wanted it; this produced 5 candidates in 1966, two of whom later decided that they wanted to return to scientific work.

3. In recent years, persons with suitable external experience have been recruited direct to the grades of Principal and Assistant Secretary. The Assistant Secretary posts have been specific ones, calling for expertise not normally available in the service (for example a post in the Ministry of Housing requiring wide experience of administration in local government, housing or large-scale planning). For the more numerous posts at Principal level, candidates were required to have held a responsible post in industry or commerce, at a university, or in some professional field.[1] By 1969, the Civil Service Commission was advertising for a Welsh-speaking educationalist to be Under Secretary in charge of the Department of Education and Science office in Cardiff.

The reason for some of these developments was undoubtedly the failure of the traditional open competition to bring enough recruits into the class. Not since 1951 has the Civil Service Commission been

[1] *Fulton Report*, vol. 4, 'Introductory Factual Memorandum', pp. 39–40 and Estimates Committee, *Recruitment to the Civil Service*, p. 262.

able to fill all the vacancies offered to young graduates. In some years the gap has been substantial, and throughout the 1950s the Commissioners' annual reports express concern about the lack of really outstanding material ultimately suitable for the highest posts. In the mid-sixties there was a consequent shortage of about 13 per cent in the basic Principal grade. Clearly some steps had to be taken to close the gap, which could not be done entirely by opening posts previously held by administrators to members of other classes. In 1966, there were 159 appointments to the grade of Principal. Only 44 of them were former Assistant Principals recruited through the open competition; 49 came from other classes in the service (41 by immediate promotion from the executive grades); 66 were appointed direct from outside.[1] Of all new entrants at any level to the administrative class during the same year, 130 were new civil servants and 132 entered by one means or another from other grades in the service.[2] Commenting on a similar situation some years earlier, Professor Chapman had said:

It may be that the proportion of ex-executive class officials now serving in the British administrative class has weakened its intellectual calibre and collective imagination. No other country has anything like the same proportion of ex-middle-ranking officials in the highest class, nor such elaborate methods for ensuring a continual flow of such people.[3]

The effect of these modifications is that the class is much less homogeneous than might appear from the recruitment figures quoted earlier. Many of the class-to-class promotees, of course, are graduates, as are many of the late entrants. But they have all enjoyed experience outside the class itself. In April 1967 about a quarter of the class were non-graduates, a proportion which was being maintained for new entrants from all sources. 47 per cent held degrees in arts, 19 per cent in social science and 9 per cent in natural science.[4] And recruitment from outside was taking place at all ages from 20 to 51. The notion of a career service recruited from a homogeneous group at an early age had been virtually abandoned.

[1] Ibid., vol. 4, 'Introductory Factual Memorandum', p. 40, par. 100.
[2] Ibid., 'Civil Service Manpower Statistics', p. 233.
[3] Chapman, *The Profession of Government*, p. 173.
[4] *H.C. Debs.*, vol. 747 (31 May 1967) col. 33 (written answer to David Marquand).

Even at the top the myth did not hold: of the 29 Permanent Secretaries, only 13 had attended a public school; admittedly 23 were Oxford or Cambridge graduates, but two held no degree at all.

Fulton Committee recommendations

In this context, we can look at the Fulton Committee recommendations. The Committee disliked three aspects of civil service structure which had a bearing on recruitment:

1. The philosophy of the generalist or all-rounder. 'The ideal administrator is still too often seen as the gifted amateur who, moving frequently from job to job within the Service, can take a practical view of any problem, irrespective of its subject-matter, in the light of his knowledge and experience of the government machine . . . The cult is obsolete at all levels and in all parts of the service.'[1]

2. The division into classes, which on the surface determines civil servants' career prospects and the range of jobs in which they may be employed. This 'rigid and prolific compartmentalism . . . prevents the best use of individual talent, contributes to the inequality of promotion prospects, causes frustration and resentment, and impedes the entry into wider management of those well fitted for it'.[2]

3. Insufficient contact with the rest of the community, partly because the service offers a career for life, but also because of its social and educational composition. A graduate entry drawn from a wider range of universities 'should help to ensure that graduate recruits to the Civil Service become more representative, geographically, educationally and socially, of the nation at large than they have been in the past; we regard this as a desirable objective in itself'.[3]

The Committee also had to deal with the problem that graduates of middle quality, needed in the civil service but not outstanding enough to qualify for the administrative class, were not attracted by an executive career designed for the A-level school leaver.

Its solution was to abolish the distinction between classes – but not between graduates or specialist fields of work. All graduate entrants would be placed on a training grade (some of the more

[1] *Fulton Report*, vol. 1, par. 15.   [2] Ibid., par. 16.
[3] Ibid., pars. 19, 95.

outstanding being recognized with special increments and placed in posts 'appropriate to their ability') in which they could show their fitness for higher posts. Recruits would be selected for work in a definite field of administration (for example finance or social affairs) and specialize in it at least for the early part of their career.[1]

The Committee recommended by a majority that the selection procedure should be modified to give more weight to the qualifications, aptitudes and qualities appropriate to these specified ranges of jobs. The old written examination in academic subjects should be replaced by one in which papers were 'restricted entirely to those with a direct relevance to the problems of modern government' (that is to say, economics and business studies, social and administrative studies, science and technology); a minority argued that it should be abolished altogether. The Civil Service Selection Board method should be made more 'objective'. Candidates with degrees in relevant subjects should have an advantage over those without. This would not prevent the admittance of 'outstandingly able' men and women from any discipline, but those with 'wrong' degrees would be further handicapped by an extension of their training period.[2]

If the majority recommendations had been implemented in full, they might have made the service more attractive to some types of graduates, particularly social scientists at provincial universities who find it difficult to see themselves as general administrators. But after consulting university appointments boards the Government came down in favour of the minority group on the Committee, who had argued that the majority proposals over-estimated the importance of first degree subjects and that a bias in favour of certain academic disciplines would be more likely to reduce than to increase the number of acceptable candidates. It would be better to modify the selection process to identify candidates with relevant personal qualities and to give any necessary training after entry. In the meantime a committee was appointed to see how the Method II selection procedure could be improved and the Civil Service Department began to study the long-term needs that should govern any change in the arrangements for graduate recruitment.[3]

[1] Ibid., pars. 42–51, 74–86 and app. F.
[2] Ibid., pars. 75–80, 106 and app. E.
[3] Civil Service National Whitley Council, *Developments on Fulton* (London, 1969) pars. 24–33. The main decisions were announced by the Prime Minister in the Commons debate on the Fulton Report, *H.C. Debs.*, vol. 773 (21 November 1968) cols. 1542–65.

A CLOSED CAREER

The staffing pattern which evolved from the Northcote-Trevelyan Report placed great weight on the accuracy of pre-entry selection. Once appointed to the permanent civil service ('temporaries' are not so lucky) the new civil servant can look forward to a secure career with a pension at the end of it. He is unlikely to be dismissed and can reasonably look forward to several more or less automatic promotions in accordance with the normal expectations of his class. At the very top, promotions are made on merit; but at lower levels it is assumed that all members of a class are equally qualified and have the same claim for consideration, so that promotion tends to take place in accordance with seniority rules agreed with the staff associations. An official is therefore protected from the effects of an unlucky posting early in his career – perhaps to an unsympathetic superior or to a field of work which is declining in importance. Conversely, he must be ready to move into any vacancy that is open to members of his class, even if the work is unfamiliar (and perhaps uncongenial) to him. Almost every aspect of this system was criticized by the Fulton Committee.

In general terms, it felt that civil servants enjoyed too much security. The service as a whole was too insulated from the outside world. These characteristics contributed to what the Committee saw as failure to adapt to changing needs.

There is some evidence to support this diagnosis. New civil servants have to complete a period of probation. But 221 of the Assistant Principals who entered from 1961 to 1965 passed their probation and only four failed.[1] Either the selection is unusually accurate (which the selection board method, at least, probably is) or assessments at the end of two years of probation are made too lightly. Over the same period about five Assistant Principals a year were leaving voluntarily with an average of just over two years of service and a very few others left voluntarily in anticipation of probation failure.[2]

Assistant Principal is primarily a training grade, so that the qualities tested at the end of two years in it are perhaps not very different from those tested by a highly specific selection process.

[1] *Fulton Report*, vol. 1, par. 132.
[2] *Fulton Report*, vol. 4, 'Wastage of Principals and Assistant Principals', p. 593.

The Civil Service Commission Research Unit followed up successful candidates for up to sixteen years and reached the conclusion that Method II had as high a validity as could be expected from a field of candidates of this kind. As between different sorts of entrants, comparison showed that 'Method II entrants fare best; that Limited Competition and Method I entrants are the next best; and that Direct-Entry Principals and Departmental Promotees did least well, expecially those who were 35 or more when they became Principals'.[1]

Civil servants who are inefficient or unsuitable can be dismissed, but the provisions are used sparingly. Only about 500 permanent non-industrial civil servants a year (less than one per thousand at risk) left for such reasons between 1963 and 1966.[2] In the grades of executive officer and above, the number varied from 20 to 25; the 1967 figure (22) was 0·015 per cent of the permanent staff in these groups.[3]

Nor is there much voluntary resignation. At one time it was difficult for a civil servant to move into other employment without losing his pension rights, but this has been becoming progressively easier in recent years. Pension rights can be transferred without difficulty to teaching and a fairly wide variety of other public employment. A civil servant can leave at 50 for any employment and draw at 60 the pension he has earned from his earlier service. Since 1964, Assistant Secretaries and above have been able to exercise this right and go into industry and commerce at any age.[4] (The main restriction at this level is a long-standing rule that Under Secretaries and above must obtain special permission before taking up business appointments with government-assisted firms. The rule is designed to maintain public confidence in the integrity of the service. In practice permission is hardly ever refused.[5]) But the provisions are not widely used. In 1966 the administrative staff group lost 3·5 per cent of its male members and the executive group 2·5 per cent. Half the administrators and two-thirds of the executives left as a result of natural causes – age, ill-health, or death in service. A fifth of the administrators and a quarter of the executives left

[1] *Fulton Report*, vol. 3(2), 'Administrative Class Follow-up 1966', p. 111, par. 19 (iv).
[2] *Fulton Report*, vol. 4, 'Civil Service Manpower Statistics', p. 222.
[3] *Fulton Report*, vol. 1, par. 123.
[4] Ibid., app. H, par. 6.
[5] *Fulton Report*, vol. 4, 'The Acceptance of Business Appointments by Civil Servants', p. 393.

without pension rights (normally after a fairly brief period of service, so that the number who took advantage of the pension transfer or preservation rights was a very small proportion of the total class.[1] Separate tables for junior members of the administrative class show that, on average, about five Assistant Principals and four Principals left voluntarily each year in the early 1960s. Over half of them went into teaching and university work, where they would be able to maintain their pensions rights.[2] The vast majority of civil servants go on to normal retirement ages, which in 1964 averaged 62 for administrators, 64 for executives and 65 for members of the clerical classes.[3]

The Treasury advised Fulton that the security given by 'established' (that is to say, permanent and pensionable) status was necessary to protect a civil servant, whose skills might not be readily marketable in the outside world, from the contraction or winding up of his department: without such protection it might be difficult to staff organizations like the Land Commission which might be closed down after a change of government. At higher levels, security of tenure also helped to secure independence of advice to Ministers.[4] The Fulton Committee broadly accepted these arguments, and added that the long experience and accumulated knowledge of many civil servants was an important aspect of professionalism. But at the same time it wanted to encourage more movement in and out of the service in mid-career. Accordingly it recommended that pension arrangements should become still more flexible and added the corollary that the civil service should be more ruthless in dispensing (on fair terms) with the services of members who were no longer needed or useful. In summary, its view was that 'it should remain a career service in the sense that most civil servants should enter at young ages with the expectation, but not the guarantee, of a lifetime's employment; and that the great majority of those who come to occupy top jobs will in practice be career civil servants'. Specifically, new entrants who completed two years' probation should be offered an indefinite contract which could be terminated on, say, six months' notice.[5]

---

[1] *Fulton Report*, vol. 4, 'Introductory Factual Memorandum', pp. 181–2 and 'Civil Service Manpower Statistics', pp. 220–5, particularly table 19.

[2] Ibid., 'Wastage of Principals and Assistant Principals', pp. 593–4.

[3] Ibid., 'Retirement Policy', p. 380, par. 3.

[4] Ibid., 'Establishment', p. 362 and 'Establishment Procedure', p. 365.

[5] *Fulton Report*, vol. 1, pars. 123–144 and app. H. These proposals were still under discussion with the staff associations at the end of 1969.

CAREER STRUCTURE

Prospective candidates for the civil service are offered the prospect of one or two promotions. Thus, new Assistant Principals expect promotion to the rank of Principal at about 28, and to Assistant Secretary in their late thirties.[1] Promotion to Under Secretary, if it comes at all, will tend to be in the mid-forties and to Deputy Secretary or Secretary about five years after that.[2] Direct entry executive officers, apart from the really able ones who have transferred to the administrative class, expect to become higher executive officers in their early thirties and senior executive officers about eight years after that.[3] Further promotion is difficult to predict as it depends on uncertain opportunities and to some extent on the possession of relevant skills, for example in automatic data processing.

Some executive officers will spend their entire careers in a special field of administration, becoming specialists in the management of local offices, in the interpretation of a tax or insurance code, or in the application and development of management techniques.[4] But other executive and nearly all administrative civil servants will move among a succession of posts, sometimes fairly rapidly, gaining general rather than specific experience. The service follows a deliberate policy of interchanging administrative staff, particularly those who are likely to reach the highest levels, so that they can widen their experience. At the end of 1966 the Assistant Principals in the Home Office, the Ministry of Housing and Local Government and the Ministry of Power had held approximately one post for each year in the grade, the Principals had been moved about every two years and the Assistant Secretaries about every three.[5]

The Fulton Committee felt that movement on this scale reflected poor personnel management:

> Civil servants are moved too frequently between unrelated jobs, often with scant regard to personal preference or aptitude.[6]

[1] *Fulton Report*, vol. 4, 'Civil Service Manpower Statistics', pp. 234–6.
[2] Ibid., 'Promotion in the Administrative and Executive Classes', pp. 562–4.
[3] Ibid.
[4] There are some good examples in the *Fulton Report*, vol. 2, 'Report of a Management Consultancy Group', pp. 26–7.
[5] *Fulton Report*, vol. 4, 'Patterns of Administrative Class Careers', pp. 582–91.
[6] *Fulton Report*, vol. 1, par. 20.

The group of management consultants who surveyed blocks of work in different departments commented more acidly:

> Much of the movement of staff from job to job . . . masqueraded as career planning. This was because in the civil service all movement is thought of as good and contributing to the development of a career . . . Indeed, we frequently met cases where valuable experience was dissipated by the enforced transfer of officers in the alleged interests of their careers.[1]

They judged that many administrators spent too short a period in a job to grasp the subjects they were dealing with: time was wasted learning the essentials; specialist time was wasted in explanation to new administrative colleagues; and the administrator was moved on just when he was acquiring enough knowledge and confidence to start evaluating results and reviewing the policy.[2] Civil servants themselves seemed to believe in the policy (although this confidence was not shared by a number of former administrative civil servants who gave evidence to the Committee).

Two factors impose some sort of order on administrative careers. One is the allocation of staff to departments. Most administrators seem to spend their early years in the department to which they were originally allocated by the Civil Service Commission (or if there is a transfer of functions – say from the Ministry of Transport to the Board of Trade – they follow a block of work to its new home). Of the 37 men who were recruited in 1949, only 4 appeared in the 1965 Imperial Calendar under departments clearly different from those to which they were originally assigned; 7 did not appear at all and the other 26 were in either the same department or its functional successor. Similarly, 36 of the 49 men who entered in 1959 were still shown in their original departments; 9 had disappeared and only 3 had changed departments. This may do something to mitigate the worst effects of mobility: at worst, departments have only a finite number of divisions and some civil servants do in fact spend their careers spiralling among a limited number of fields, keeping within the same system of general purposes, working with the same colleagues and using the same information, without necessarily spending long in any one post.

The second factor is that an attempt is made to sort sheep from

---

[1] *Fulton Report*, vol. 2, par. 240.   [2] Ibid., pars. 67–72.

goats. Civil servants who seem likely to go all the way to the top tend to be identified fairly early and to be given opportunities for really wide experience in different departments. Such breadth of experience is secured by the intervention of the Civil Service Department (formerly the Treasury), which is responsible for career management over the service as a whole and is consulted about filling the highest posts.[1] The career profiles of administrators in a sample of three departments in 1966 indicated a watershed between those up to Under Secretary, most of whose previous experience was internal, and the two highest grades, whose previous posts had been mainly in other departments.[2] Another survey showed that all the 'Treasury group' of 5 Permanent Secretaries had some experience of other departments, while 14 out of the other 24 had some experience of the Treasury or Cabinet Office and less than half had spent more than ten years in their current departments.[3]

The Fulton Committee (like the Estimates Committee three years earlier) did not attach much weight to the kind of ability that was developed by breadth of experience alone. The practical managerial abilities it thought were needed at the top could not be identified in the early twenties or late teens, but would emerge later in a man's career.[4] It was more important to develop expertise in particular areas of administration. The Committee believed that administrators should move within and between departments within a special field and that merit should play a larger part in promotion than seniority. Appointment to particular posts should depend on the possession of specific abilities and experience instead of on membership of a general class.

It accordingly recommended that automatic promotion and indiscriminate job-rotation should cease. All members of a particular occupational group (for example the existing specialist classes and the new administrative specialists, including those at present in the clerical as well as executive and administrative classes) should be put on to a continuous grading structure, within which posts would be graded according to such factors as 'the end-results required, the degree of personal responsibility involved, the importance

---

[1] *Fulton Report*, vol. 4, 'Promotion in the Administrative and Executive Classes', p. 559; 'Management of the Civil Service', p. 602.

[2] Ibid., 'Patterns of Administrative Class Careers', p. 582.

[3] Ibid., 'Previous Histories of Permanent Secretaries', p. 597.

[4] *Fulton Report*, vol. 1, par. 57.

attaching to the work and the qualifications and experience needed in the holder to achieve the prescribed results'.[1] When a vacancy arose, it would be offered to the best man for the job, whether or not he was already a member of the appropriate occupational group. Promotion would not therefore be to a higher grade, carrying the implication that the individual was able to fill any post on that grade, but to a particular post for which he was qualified. In assessing candidates, a good deal of weight would be given to a man's performance on his present job: annual reviews of performance should be much fuller. Once on the job, unusual performance would be rewarded by extra increments of pay, poor performance correspondingly penalized.[2]

The abolition of 'class-distinctions' is always a popular slogan, and the Government announced its acceptance of this recommendation as soon as the Fulton Report was published. This left the Civil Service Department, in consultation with the staff associations, to work out details of the 'occupational groups' that would replace classes. Studies were made of the grading systems used in the American, Canadian and Australian civil services and in some British non-governmental organizations, and a number of practical difficulties began to emerge. As a first step it was decided to concentrate on: (a) the merger of some existing classes carrying out broadly similar work on linked pay scales, (b) easing impediments to movement between classes, (c) the establishment of a common structure for administrators at the very top of the service, where responsibilities tended to be very similar regardless of specialist background. So far as the 'administrative specialities' were concerned, it was decided that the *esprit de corps* generated by departmental loyalties was too valuable to discard, but a review of the work of middling grade posts was set in hand to discover what practical basis there was for career specialization within departments (and incidentally to replace the job-analysis of Assistant Secretaries carried out in 1945 to provide a framework for the Method II selection tests).[3] It seemed increasingly unlikely that a system of 'promotion by merit' would or could be introduced wholesale. The probable consequences for morale of this and other Fulton recommendations affecting the career pattern will be examined in Chapter XIV.

[1] *Fulton Report*, vol. 1, par. 57.   [2] Ibid., pars. 229, 238.
[3] *Developments on Fulton*, pars. 42–55, 70–9.

TRAINING

Not much was done about formal training for civil servants until the Assheton Report in 1944.[1] It was assumed that the main job of the civil servant, running the government machine, could best be learned on an apprenticeship basis. Responsibility increased with promotion, so that experience and authority coincided at the top, while the qualities of breadth, flexibility and adaptability were sufficiently inculcated by the tradition of job-rotation already discussed.[2]

The Assheton Report drew attention to the need to equip civil servants for their new and expanding responsibilities, particularly in dealing with the public. It argued, in terms mainly of the administrative, executive and clerical grades, for the adoption of the best training practices at that time, including induction courses for new entrants, training for supervision and background training. In spite of a setback during an economy campaign in 1951, when the Treasury favoured arrangements that concentrated on helping staff to do their immediate jobs, the Assheton principles were implemented generally. By 1966 there was an impressive variety of training courses, particularly in vocational subjects (for example National Insurance procedures) and in developing new specialities like organization and methods and automatic data processing, which attracted favourable comment from the Fulton Committee.[3]

The present arrangements for members of the administrative class have developed fairly recently and are still fluid. An Assistant Principal currently has a short course on the structure of government in his first year. In his second or third year he attends a course of lectures and seminars on the basic concepts of science. (This course was instituted in 1964 apparently in response to agitation from the parliamentary science lobby; its precise objectives are rather confused.) In his third year he goes to the Civil Service

[1] *Report of the Committee on the Training of Civil Servants*, Cmd. 6526 (1944).

[2] There is a classic pre-war defence of this viewpoint in Dale's discussion of training needs in the higher civil service. H. E. Dale, *The Higher Civil Service of Great Britain* (Oxford, 1941), app. C.

[3] *Fulton Report*, vol. 1, p. 35, par. 97. Current training arrangements are described with examples in vol. 4, 'Civil Service Training' and papers following, pp. 513-50. The history of training up to about 1964 is summarized in a working party report, 'Review of Civil Service Training', *Whitley Bulletin* (London) vol. XLIV (1964) p. 155.

Department's Centre for Administrative Studies for a twenty-two-week course in economic and social administration, followed by one of five six-week extension courses in specialized fields of administration (project appraisal and control; international economics; industrial growth; environmental planning; or social administration II). Economics is the largest single element in the main course, which also includes an introduction to statistics, decision theory and management techniques, including operational research. Its purpose is 'to introduce young administrators to quantitative analytic techniques relevant to the work of Government, to make them familiar with the literature and methodology involved and thus to equip them to understand the advice given by economists and other specialists and to use and question it intelligently'.[1] The C.A.S. courses have been very successful and have played a large part in overcoming the handicap of 'non-numerate' first degrees. Those who have not read economics at university are said to 'show up very well' by the end of it as compared with those who have.[2]

But the Centre was opened only in 1963. The long course does not cater for the specialist or the late entrant to the administrative class. Even Assistant Principals who joined the service before 1961 had no formal training apart from a three-week course on the structure of government. Some have been able to fill the gap later in their careers. Short courses in management subjects have been provided for Principals and Assistant Secretaries, but up to the time of the Fulton Report the number of places was small in relation to the number eligible. A few civil servants have been to the Administrative Staff College at Henley (where since 1946 10 per cent of the places, or eighteen to twenty-four a year, have been reserved for civil servants) and more recently to the Manchester and London Business Schools. A few who are alive to the possibilities and can be spared by their departments have enjoyed sabbatical leave (72 out of 2,400 administrators in 1957–61 but only 12 in the five years 1961–6). But most senior civil servants have had little or no training in economics and management. The Centre is now organizing courses which will help to close the gap more quickly. Administrators in their thirties and early forties are expected to take a series of short (three-

[1] Civil Service Department, *Civil Service Training 1967–68* (1969) p. 5, par. 13. The 22-week course plus extensions is a development of an earlier 20-week course, taken by everyone, without a 'social' element.
[2] *Fulton Report*, vol. 1, par. 80(d).

to six-week) courses in: (a) decisions, techniques and computers (b) organization and staff management and, depending on their department's field of work, either (c) economics or (d) social administration. The courses are attended by professional staff of equivalent grades. There are also one-week residential seminars for Assistant Secretaries, mainly in management and evaluation techniques.[1]

Proposals of a Treasury Working Party and Fulton Committee

In 1966 a Treasury Working Party reviewed the arrangements for management training and made proposals to make them more comprehensive and available to a wider group of staff in the future. Thus it suggested that all the graduate and 18-year-old entrants to the general management grades (equivalent to Assistant Principals and executive officers) should take a short 'Introduction to Management' course at about the age of 25. About this stage, prospective high-fliers would be 'spotted' for more intensive training, divided between the twenty-week course (as it was then) and an additional course of about the same length several years later. The second long course would include the study in depth of a number of aspects of government and public administration, an introduction to social administration, the study of organization and management problems, and a section on scientific and technological developments, as well as some specialist material either for administrators serving in groups of departments (e.g. 'economic', 'social service' and 'defence/international'), or for those practising functional skills of management such as personnel management and financial control techniques. In the meantime, other staff would be taking a shorter course suitable for middle managers. Those who developed well could be offered the longer courses later in their career. Scientists and other professionals could join in appropriate short or long courses as their ability and interest in administration developed.

The Working Party recognized that the success of any such scheme would depend on the service's skill at 'talent-spotting', on a basis of ability rather than on method of entry, at an early age, and that its recommendations about specialized training would have to be linked with better career planning: there was no point in giving specific training in social service administration to a man who was liable to be posted immediately to the Ministry of Defence.[2] Both these

[1] *Civil Service Training 1967–68*, pars. 16–39.

[2] *Fulton Report*, vol. 5(1) Proposals and Opinions, 'Report of a Working Party on Management Training in the Civil Service', p. 60.

arguments are consistent with the constructive part of the Fulton philosophy. As we have seen, an element of specialization has subsequently been built into central training at both Principal and Assistant Principal levels.

The Fulton Committee's own recommendations on training did not go into much detail, and it may be assumed that most of the Working Party's ideas were implicitly accepted.[1] But there were a number of differences in emphasis:

1. The Committee suggested formal training lasting 'up to one year' in the third year of service, covering: (i) the application of economic and financial (*or* social) concepts to practical problems of government in the field in which the individual will be working; (ii) the techniques of modern management; (iii) the machinery and practice of government and administration. These recommendations follow from the Committee's firm commitment to specialization at the outset of an administrative career. They involve a higher investment in training, at an earlier age, and an earlier commitment to specialization than the Treasury Working Party envisaged. At the time of writing, plans are being discussed to provide up to one year of training for the best of the non-specialist graduate and 18-year-old intake, but it has not been decided whether this should all be taken at once.[2] There is of course a risk that training which is too narrowly conceived can impose blinkers. There might also be disadvantages in putting the main weight of training so early that the trainee has not yet become familiar with the practical situation in which he will be deploying what he learns.

2. In the Committee proposals, management replaced economics as the common element for all graduate training. 'Social' administrators would not take the economics course then provided at the Centre for Administrative Studies, but they would all study staff organization and management and the use of numerate analysis as a tool for dealing with management problems. The machinery and practice of government was played down: not all would need to study it in detail. In contrast, the Working Party recognized the force of criticisms that the current pattern of courses did not place enough weight on the special problems of 'public administration' as such. (In 1969, Professor Peter Self was invited to spend a year reviewing the place for public administration teaching in civil service training.)

[1] *Fulton Report*, vol. 1, par. 106.   [2] *Developments on Fulton*, par. 38.

3. The Committee suggested that training should be tailored to suit 'the needs of the individual, the administrative group in which he is working, and the requirements of his department'.[1] The Treasury Working Party felt that it was very questionable whether specialist training linked to career planning of the 'horses for courses' type was a practical proposition.

One recommendation from the Fulton Committee that was accepted at once was that central training should be based on a Civil Service College. It was proposed that the College should provide: (a) major courses in administration and management including those discussed in the foregoing pages; (b) a wider range of shorter courses for a much larger body of staff; (c) a base for research on government organization and major policy problems.[2] This very broad role appears to include the concept of an administrative 'staff college', which could be an important instrument in restoring morale and *esprit de corps* in a more fragmented and diversified service. It is sometimes argued that it is unhealthy for the civil service to arrange the bulk of its own training, but in practice the service provides only the organization for top-level courses – teaching is done mainly by visiting staff from universities and industry. (The programmes of the Centre for Administrative Studies could serve as a list of leading national experts in the fields covered.) The College would have a larger permanent teaching staff, but there is no real danger of the training arrangements becoming inbred.

Finally, the Fulton Committee emphasized the importance of repairing gaps in the training of existing civil servants, and stimulated a very considerable extension in both introductory and refresher courses for senior administrators.[3]

CONCLUSIONS

The old structure of the higher civil service was inadequate in many ways. The role of the generalist was perhaps over-played at the expense of special knowledge and technical skill, e.g. in quantitative evaluation. On the other hand, it was (and is) well suited for some of the continuing functions of government. Notably, it developed a small group of senior administrators with broad experience of

[1] *Fulton Report*, vol. 1, par. 106. [2] Ibid., pars. 97–114.
[3] *Developments on Fulton*, par. 41.

government who were qualified as 'brokers' between the world of politics and the world of specialist techniques. For a larger group, its security fostered the loyalty and integrity needed to extend the arm of the Minister and his top advisers into the details of administration. Its homogeneity, whether the result of common education or of long post-entry socialization and shared experience, promoted a common outlook and allowed the conduct of government business to rest on some unwritten major premises. But it was never as homogeneous as it seemed – indeed a possible criticism is that the administrative class has never been exclusive enough.

It is clear that the appearance and therefore the myths of the service were bound to change. Many of the Fulton recommendations about career structure set the seal on changes which would have occurred anyway, perhaps at a slower pace. Traditional ideas about a lifetime career were being eroded by recruitment difficulties. Developments in training were becoming essential to deal with the increasing complexity and scope of public administration, and the sheer expansion of the service itself. The need for administrative specialization had long been recognized in the higher ranks of the executive class, and was becoming inevitable in the 'administrative' range of posts also. The load placed by the generalist tradition on individual members of the administrative class was becoming unbearable. It was becoming necessary to specialize in a field of administration, or in an administrative technique, or perhaps in a 'layer' of administration (since administrators do different things at different levels) in order to assimilate the great range of special skills and knowledge now available and essential to government. One way to do this would have been to strengthen the executive class and to make the administrators a smaller group of semi-political assistants to the Minister. This would have been difficult, given the need to recruit graduates for managerial posts. So Fulton took the alternative course and recommended abolishing the special position given to the administrative class.

The effect of the Fulton proposals is to 'managerialize' the civil service. In 'pre-Fulton' terms, this means giving priority to the kind of jobs previously done by top-grade members of the executive class.

In the short term, the main sacrifice to the new managerialism may be the work formerly done by junior members of the administrative class in their capacity of 'enlightened amateurs'. The weakness is likely to be felt at the top within a generation or two. For a period, the civil service will be very strong indeed, when its junior members are deploying their technical skills in administration and their superiors, trained in the traditional school, are experts at co-ordinating and relating all these special fields to one another and to the broad stream of political consciousness. When the now numerous group of senior civil servants in their late forties and early fifties retire, they may be replaced by a group who have been brought up in quite different traditions. It is difficult to predict the results.

The alarming point about Fulton is not the move towards specialism, but the distance of the leap. The weight placed on specialization during early training seems particularly questionable. It is doubtful whether administrators should be committed (many of them for life) to a particular range of functions so early in their career. In the past, when the civil service has been under strain and has found difficulty in absorbing new functions, the trend has been to aim at flexibility by broadening the scope of training to encourage the general development of individuals rather than their fitness to perform prescribed tasks. That was the main theme behind the Assheton Report of 1944, the 1962 reports that led to the establishment of the Centre for Administrative Studies and the later reports of the National Whitley Council (1964) and the Treasury Working Party (1967). The Fulton Report seems to aim in the opposite direction. In a time of rapid change, we may find in the future that we have paid a high price in order to get particular jobs done better now. But this is not to understate the need for some change in the traditional pattern.

IV. Specialist and Professional Civil Servants

EMERGENCE OF A NEED FOR SPECIALISTS

The Northcote-Trevelyan Report contained only a passing reference to the recruitment of specialists, saying that so long as there was a suitable choice of subjects the principles of open competition were 'not inconsistent with the appropriation of special talents or attainments to special departments of the public service'. The Superannuation Act of 1859 made special provision for the appointment of officers whose qualifications were 'wholly or in part professional or otherwise peculiar and not ordinarily to be acquired in the Civil Service'.[1] At this time the main groups of specialists were inspectors and surveyors. Half a century later, the MacDonnell Commission found civil service lawyers, doctors, engineers, architects, surveyors and natural scientists in addition to the inspectorates of constabulary, schools etc.[2] The scientists were augmented after the foundation of the Department of Scientific and Industrial Research in 1915. The Institution of Professional Civil Servants was established in 1919, although it did not really become a major organization until the Second World War. By that time, new functions of government were demanding new forms of expertise and inevitably more civil servants with external qualifications were being recruited.

In 1966 there were more 'professional, scientific and technical' civil servants than in the administrative and executive classes combined. Of 6,000 posts above the salary level of administrative Principal, over two-thirds were in the professional classes. Professionals held half the 2,200 posts at Assistant Secretary level and above. Three professional officers held ranks equivalent to Per-

[1] *Superannuation Act 1859*, section IV.
[2] *Fourth Report of the Royal Commission on the Civil Service, 1912–14*, Cd. 7338 (1914).

manent Secretary.[1] The rapidly growing proportion of senior posts, especially in the scientific and 'works group' classes, no doubt reflected pressure from their Institution for higher status and better promotion outlets. But it also reflected the increasing importance of specialist contributions to management and to policy. For example, a Chief Scientific Adviser and an Economic Adviser were attached to the Cabinet Secretariat in 1964; a distinguished academic statistician was later invited to head the Central Statistical Office, which is an integral part of the Cabinet Office.

The increasing complexity of government organization and decision-making was also creating a demand for new specialist skills among the so-called 'general' classes. Executive officers are often specialists in management services (for example O & M and A.D.P.), in stores or contract procedures or in a branch of social security or taxation law. They handle conveyancing and litigation work in the Treasury Solicitor's Office and in the Land Registry, where they 'virtually run practices in their own right'. They also carry out the bulk of government accountancy.[2] Members of the administrative class also may develop competence in a specialized field: there is an Assistant Secretary who has spent nearly twenty years on Organization and Methods and Work Study. The relatively few administrators with degrees in science and technology tend to be concentrated in 'relevant' departments. So do the 300 members of the class (about twice the membership of the Government Economic Service) who have degrees in economics, including at least twenty-five postgraduate degrees.[3] But there is a clear distinction between specialization by a member of the general classes – who has always been liable, at least in theory, to be transferred to other work – and membership of a specialist class whose work in government 'is just one of a number of career opportunities for the exercise of their qualifications and skills'.[4]

Doctors, lawyers, scientists, architects, engineers, economists, statisticians, research officers and many others have been organized in separate classes. The scientists and the 'works group' of engineers,

[1] *Fulton Report*, vol. 5, 'Proposals and Opinions' (Institution of Professional Civil Servants) p. 300, par. 27.

[2] Ibid. (H.M. Treasury) p. 51, par. 14; p. 45, par. 11. See also vol. 2, 'Report of a Management Consultancy Group', pp. 86–98.

[3] Sir Alec Cairncross, 'The Work of an Economic Adviser', *Public Administration*, vol. 46 (1968) p. 7.

[4] *Fulton Report*, vol. 1, par. 35.

architects and surveyors, indeed, are the top layer of a tiered system of classes rather like the clerical, executive and administrative structure discussed in the last chapter. (The Fulton Committee ignored advice from the Treasury that it would be unwise to abolish class differences in these cases, since they reflected externally recognized differences in status and qualifications which it was becoming increasingly difficult to cross.)[1]

STATUS OF SPECIALISTS

For a long time, specialist and professionally qualified civil servants seemed to be outside the main stream of administration. The first serious discussion of their proper place in the administrative system occurs in the report of the 1929–31 Tomlin Commission, to whom the I.P.C.S. had represented (unsuccessfully) that specialist advisers in all departments should have the right of access to the Minister on important questions involving technical considerations.[2] Specialists resented the idea that their views would reach the Minister only through an intermediary who, as a non-professional, might misrepresent them. They also resented the monopoly of senior posts in most departments by the administrative class.

By the 1960s this particular malaise had become acute in places like the Ministry of Public Buildings and Works and the Highways Division of the Ministry of Transport, where large numbers of professional staff are working under the financial and policy direction of administrators. Although there were experiments with new patterns of organization that gave more senior posts to professional officers and integrated them more fully into the 'line' structure, these did not satisfy the I.P.C.S.:

> The role of the specialist, however, is still largely subordinated to that of the administrator . . . Despite interesting developments in some departments, the general position of specialists is still grossly unsatisfactory . . . It would be wrong to perpetuate or deify the wholly unwarranted mystique that it is only a member of

[1] *Fulton Report*, vol. 1, par. 215. See also vol. 5, pp. 20–31. (H.M. Treasury) and 303–7, 335–45 (Institution of Professional Civil Servants).

[2] *Report of the Royal Commission on the Civil Service 1929–31* (Tomlin) Cmd. 3909 (1931) pars. 172–7. Dale indignantly repudiates the notion that any competent administrator would put forward a brief, or take important decisions, which did not reflect the views of the appropriate professional officer. H. E. Dale, *The Higher Civil Service*, p. 16.

the administrative class who can understand the machine and advise on policy . . . No man should be effectively debarred at any level because of his speciality, whether it be science, engineering, medicine, law, administration or any other branch.[1]

The relationship that developed in Britain between the professional and the generalist administrator is unusual.[2] In France, for example, the specialist *technicien* is himself a member of an administrative *élite*: key posts at the Ministry of Transport are filled from engineers in the *Corps de Ponts et Chaussées*. In Australia, the professional enjoys higher status and salary than the general administrator and some posts, like those at the head of the Departments of Health and Works, are reserved for him. In the United States a high proportion of senior posts are held by scientists and engineers; specialist heads of bureaux carry more weight than generalists with Congressional Committees.[3] The higher status of the specialist in these countries is linked with calibre and qualifications. The Australian and American civil services have not, at least until recently, been able to attract general graduates of the standard recruited as Assistant Principals in this country. On the other hand, the French *Ecole Polytechnique* and the *Ecole des Ponts et Chaussées* attract high quality applicants who are aiming at careers in public or private enterprise after a period in the civil service. Their graduates are trained in administrative law, economics and report-writing in addition to their engineering speciality; it is misleading to compare them with a newly-recruited engineer in the British Ministry of Transport. A status pattern which is reinforced by recruitment and training tends to be self-perpetuating.

POLITICAL TRADITION

There are also differences in political tradition among these countries. The key figure in the British tradition is the amateur gentleman-politician, who takes decisions by applying common sense and political judgement to the advice of experts.

In these circumstances the volume of work demands that a Minister should be supported by a body of staff which can bring

---

[1] *Fulton Report*, vol. 5 (Institution of Professional Civil Servants) p. 287, pars. 5–7.
[2] F. F. Ridley (ed.) *Specialists and Generalists* (London, 1968) *passim*.
[3] D. K. Price, *The Scientific Estate* (Cambridge, Mass., 1965) pp. 59–63.

to bear on the work of the Department the same type of considerations that the Minister would himself bring and act for him under his general direction in matters either of a minor policy or quasi-judicial nature.[1]

Sir Ernest Barker suggested long ago that the key to understanding the British system was the historical fact that political reform preceded administrative reform in this country;[2] parliamentary politicians tended to fashion their secretaries and assistants in their own image. On the Continent, in contrast, the administrative machine was developed initially as an instrument for carrying out the will of an absolute monarch (or, later, of the doctrinaire politician) who needed experts, e.g. jurists and engineers, to implement their policies and looked to political friends (in a *cabinet*) rather than to career civil servants for advice on policy itself. In new countries like Australia and the United States, political questions were relatively unimportant at formative periods of administrative history compared with the problem of exploiting and dominating natural resources. It was natural to give senior positions to the possessors of relevant specialist knowledge. These differences and their effects are discussed with insight by Subramaniam:

> Even now, Australian ethos finds it difficult to recognize policy-advising as a special skill, requiring special modes of selection and training. The same compulsions of economic development work in favour of the specialist in the other young democracies such as Canada and New Zealand and in Soviet Russia too, where the engineer administrator is as common a phenomenon as in America.[3]

The main criticism of the British arrangements has been that they are no longer appropriate in modern conditions. The party politician, supported with advice from his party research department and from academic sympathizers, has taken over from the gentleman-amateur. The involvement of government in the social, economic and technological affairs of the nation often demands speedy action by experts rather than appraisal by laymen. The

---

[1] *Fulton Report*, vol. 5 (Association of First Division Civil Servants) p. 105, par. 3.

[2] Sir E. Barker, *The Development of Public Services in Europe 1660–1930* (Oxford, 1944) ch. 1.

[3] V. Subramaniam, 'The Relative Status of Specialists and Generalists', *Public Administration*, vol. 46 (1968) p. 337. See also his 'Specialists in British and Australian Government Services: a Study in Contrast', ibid., vol. 41 (1963) p. 357.

knowledge explosion has encouraged new and esoteric specialisms with which the administrative generalist simply cannot keep abreast. Finally, the diminishing stature of Britain in the world has made it more important to deal with urgent problems on technical grounds alone, without worrying too much about remote political consequences. Consequently the relative positions of the administrator and the professional need to be reassessed. The general administrator must either become professional or make way for those who really know their business.[1] It is, however, interesting that when the special position of the administrative generalist is being attacked in Britain, authorities like Price in the United States and Professor R. S. Parker in Australia should be arguing the need for just such an institution in their own countries.

STRUCTURAL CHANGES

The trend has for some time been towards an enhancement of professional opportunities and status. Following the 1932 Bridgeman Report, technical staff in the Post Office have been given a major voice at policy levels and senior posts in that department have long been filled by promotion of the best man available. During and after the 1939–45 war special consideration was given to providing an attractive career for government scientists, whose position in, say, the Ministry of Defence (under the leadership of a distinguished scientific adviser) has not noticeably been one of inferiority to the administrator. The most important recent development affecting scientists has been in the Ministry of Technology (successor to the Department of Scientific and Industrial Research, in which scientists had always been deeply involved in policy-making). Since 1965 a band of senior posts in the Ministry has been filled either by scientists or administrators according to personal qualifications. Scientists have also been encouraged (without much success) to transfer to the administrative class. Another important group of professional staff, architects and engineers, have been the subject of administrative experiments in the main employing departments, the Ministry of Public Building and Works, the Ministry of Housing

---

[1] See, for instance, Fabian Society, *The Administrators* (London, 1964); Conservative Political Centre, *Change and Decay* (London, 1963); B. Chapman, *British Government Observed* (London, 1963).

and Local Government, the Department of Education and Science and the Ministry of Transport. These merit a brief explanation.[1]

The traditional civil service structure is one of separate, though broadly parallel, hierarchies. Below the Minister, and radiating from the Permanent Secretary, are a number of 'policy' divisions and branches. An administrator in one of these branches who needs advice on a technical problem will refer it to a specialist officer of approximately equal rank. The latter is a member of his own hierarchy, leading up to a chief professional officer who carries general responsibility for the quality of professional advice provided by his staff. For example, the original way of dealing with post-war school building in the Ministry of Education was for the 'policy' (schools) branch to put technical aspects of building plans to an architects branch, consisting solely of professionals, whose job was to advise on specific points and to check that local authority plans conformed to the regulations; the architects had no concern with policy. The 'policy' branch also consulted H.M. Inspectors of Schools on educational aspects and, at that time, another administrative branch which dealt with building controls and priorities. This procedure proved to be cumbersome and frustrating in practice; it could not have coped with the rapid expansion of school building after 1949. In that year, coinciding with the appointment of a new chief architect, the separate branches were combined into a single architects and building branch, headed jointly by the chief architect and an administrator, who shared responsibility for all aspects of school building. Resident inspectors were attached so that the three principal skills needed for control of a national school building programme were represented in the combined branch. The work of the integrated branch was outstandingly successful.

It was nearly ten years before the idea of 'joint responsibility' was applied, on a much larger scale, in the Works Directorate of the

---

[1] The material in the following paragraphs is derived from a number of sources, including an unpublished paper prepared for the Training and Education Division of the Treasury (now Civil Service Department). The most convenient account of the changing philosophy, especially in the Ministry of Transport, is D. E. Regan, 'The Expert and the Administrator: Recent changes at the Ministry of Transport', *Public Administration*, vol. 44 (1966) p. 149. There is also a great deal of relevant material in the evidence to the Fulton Committee from the Institution of Professional Civil Servants (*Fulton Report*, vol. 5, pp. 294 ff., pars. 13–26 and app. I). The position is summarized succinctly in a paper by the Deputy Secretary General of the Institution in Ridley (ed.), *Specialists and Generalists*, pp. 13–56.

War Office. In this case, there were several pairs of architect and administrator 'twins', at different points in the hierarchy. In 1963 army building was transferred to the new, and enormous, Ministry of Public Building and Works. The principle of joint heads was applied to the main divisions of the Directorate General of Research and Development, but there was a further innovation. The entire staff, administrators and all, were originally placed under a single head, the Director General, who was an architect. For a number of reasons, mostly beyond the immediate control of the Director General, relationships between professional and administrative staff proved exceptionally difficult, with adverse effects on staffing and performance. In December 1967 the older pattern of separate but parallel hierarchies was reintroduced.

In the meantime, following comment by the Estimates Committee,[1] the Ministry of Transport had been reviewing the organization of its highway engineering staff. Recruitment difficulties and poor morale seemed to be associated with the engineers' relationship with administrators, which was on traditional lines. A committee recommended that steps should be taken to improve the standing of engineers and to involve them more closely in administrative work. In particular it was recommended that the Ministry's highways organization should be headed by a chief engineer and a deputy secretary jointly (previously responsibility had rested only with the administrative deputy secretary). Below that level, it was envisaged that there would be mixed divisions of administrative and professional staff, some headed by 'twins' and others by an engineer or an administrator alone. These recommendations were implemented in stages from the end of 1963. Two years later the former chief engineer was put in sole charge of the administrative and professional aspects of highways with the title of Director General, Highways. Below him were a number of divisions, some with professional heads, some with administrative heads and some with both. It was made clear when the Director General was appointed that his successor would not always be a professional. This (unlike the Directorate General in the Ministry of Public Building and Works) is directly comparable with the senior posts in the Ministry of Technology which are filled impartially by administrators and scientists.

[1] *Seventh Report of the Estimates Committee 1961–62* (H.C. 227), 'Classified Roads'.

71

MERGER OR TAKEOVER?

One object of these experiments was to remove artificial and restrictive barriers to communication between people engaged on a common task. But the experiments have also been designed quite deliberately to improve the status and morale of professional staff. Their effect has been to blur the distinction between generalist and specialist roles, making it difficult to defend the distinction between classes, at least at the top. In the Ministry of Technology, for example, scientists have had to remain members of their own 'class' even when they were occupying posts indistinguishable from those of administrators. The alternative would have been a clumsy process of 're-certification' by the Civil Service Commission on transfer from a post in one class to another. The Treasury recognized this in its evidence to the Fulton Committee and proposed that existing classes should merge into a common service structure at senior levels which would make it easier for professionals and scientists to move into general management and perhaps back again without having to cross and re-cross class barriers.

The Treasury did not envisage a great deal of additional movement, however:

Most scientific and professional officers would still make their careers in their own field and indeed wish to do so; and most senior scientific and professional posts would still need to be filled by men trained in these disciplines. At the same time, those who had spent their careers in general management and administration would tend to look to the general policy posts in the higher Civil Service. Moreover, at these levels, a high degree of expertise in government administrative processes and the working of a very complex machine is essential. The civil servants concerned have acquired a knowledge in depth of public administration which, as a profession, is as exacting in its demands as any other.[1]

There would be nothing to be gained by introducing more flexibility lower down (that is to say at salary levels below Assistant Secretary's maximum) since professional and scientific officers at intermediate levels could easily transfer to general management posts

[1] *Fulton Report*, vol. 5, p. 5, par. 13 (H.M. Treasury).

if they did not wish to continue to undertake the specific tasks within their own disciplines for which they had been recruited.

The blurring of class distinctions was very acceptable to the Institution of Professional Civil Servants. But it attacked the Treasury proposals as inadequate, admitting that its own proposals for a much wider pattern of integration were 'quite openly designed to open up to professional officers the prospect of promotion to the very top posts in the Service.[1] It argued that the current pattern restricted career opportunities for professionals, gave administrators a monopoly of senior positions, and discouraged recruitment. The I.P.C.S. claimed that senior professionals could not expect to be eligible for top management positions unless they had obtained relevant experience earlier in their careers. The class system prevented this. Professionals were very rarely given a 'general management' post in the course of a normal career and were reluctant to transfer to the administrative or executive class since that would mean abandoning their specialism entirely and render them liable to be posted to work in which they had no interest. Tables were prepared to show the relatively poor career prospects enjoyed by scientists and members of the 'works group' compared with the administrative class: only 9 per cent of posts in the works group and 24 per cent of scientific posts were in grades higher than administrative Principal, compared with 47 per cent of administrative posts.[2] The Institution could see no reason why the career expectations of civil servants with comparable entry qualifications should differ so much. In a reasoned reply, the Treasury pointed to some errors in the calculations. It also argued that comparisons were fallacious, since entry standards were not in fact similar (for example the basic qualification for an engineering post had been at a lower academic standard than a pass degree while administrative entrants needed second class honours plus management potential). There were important differences in career patterns, service requirements and the calibre of individuals in the various groups.[3]

The Fulton Committee accepted almost completely the I.P.C.S. proposals for fuller integration. It was encouraged to do so by the findings of its own management consultancy group. After studying a number of cases of 'parallel' and 'joint' hierarchies the group

---

[1] Ibid., p. 301, par. 33 (Institution of Professional Civil Servants).
[2] Ibid., pp. 359–63.
[3] Ibid., pp. 364–7 (H.M. Treasury).

concluded that there was no case for such complicated arrangements; it was better to have a single head, who should normally be a professional.[1] One of the Committee's six basic criticisms of the civil service was that:

> . . . many scientists, engineers and members of other specialist classes get neither the full responsibilities and corresponding authority, nor the opportunities they ought to have . . . In the new Civil Service a wider and more important role must be opened up for specialists trained and equipped for it.[2]

The need to make more flexible use of specialists, and also to prepare specialists for later promotion to top management posts, were among the arguments behind the recommendations about the abolition of classes and the need to fill posts with the best men available.

But the Fulton recommendations were less revolutionary than they may appear in summary form. Although 'classes' were to be abolished, specialists and generalists would still belong to different occupational 'groups' – a less emotive nomenclature which was actually suggested by the Treasury.[3] The Committee recognized that most specialist civil servants should work in their own field, at least in their early years; thereafter some would continue in a specialized field, while others 'should progress after appropriate training and experience to work that becomes steadily more managerial in character in areas adjacent to their specialism'.[4] In what the Committee called the Senior Policy and Management Group (that is to say, grades equivalent to Under Secretary and above), speciality would become almost irrelevant:

> At these levels an individual's particular occupational group is thus often of less significance than his range of experience, and personal qualities and qualifications should be the main criteria for filling posts with these wider horizons.[5]

[1] *Fulton Report*, vol. 2, 'Report of a Management Consultancy Group', pp. 56–9, esp. par. 203. Compare the report of the main Committee (vol. I, par. 162) which adds only the proviso that it will take time to find and develop the skills required by such responsibilities.

[2] *Fulton Report*, vol. 1, par. 17. The point is further developed at par. 197.

[3] *Fulton Report*, vol. 5, p. 5, par. 15 (H.M. Treasury).

[4] *Fulton Report*, vol. 1, par. 224.

[5] Ibid., par. 222. See also par. 57.

These arguments are not essentially at variance with those expressed in the Treasury's paper. The reason why the Committee took a more fundamental attitude towards interchangeability emerges in an earlier passage about the possibility of classifying jobs as suitable for one class or another.

There are many jobs that can be filled only by qualified doctors or engineers; and many that will require the training and experience of the economic or social administrators . . . But a growing proportion of jobs in the Service require both technical and managerial knowledge and ability, and cannot now be properly classed as either technical (and therefore reserved for the appropriate specialist class), or managerial (and therefore normally reserved for the Administrative or Executive Class). These jobs are to be found not only in the highest reaches of the Service; they exist at much more modest levels . . . especially in the big technological departments. Taking the Service as a whole, they may be a relatively small proportion at present. But as the work of the Service continues to change, and as new specialisms emerge, they are certain to multiply.[1]

The crux of the Fulton recommendations is therefore the unsuitability of 'joint hierarchies' as a means of combining administrative and specialist contributions in work like that described earlier in this chapter.

ROLE OF THE SPECIALIST

At this point it may be helpful to leave out of account the career problems that very properly concerned the I.P.C.S. and the Fulton Committee and to look in general terms at the special contribution which a specialist makes to government administration by virtue of his qualification. The fact that, independently of his qualification, he may develop general administrative ability towards the end of his career is a different point, since it argues for easy transfer into management, not for making managerial posts more professional.

The special problems of public administration are concerned with deciding what to do and getting things done in a political context. There is no difficulty about the role of professional staff who are carrying out strictly professional work at a long remove from the political decision centres. The scientist pursuing research in the

[1] Ibid., par. 212.

National Physical Laboratory, the medical officer conducting clinical examinations in connection with social security benefits and the lawyer undertaking prosecutions for a government department are all doing work which is only fortuitously in the public sector. It would not, in principle, make much difference to the scientist's work if he was employed by an industrial firm; the medical officer and the lawyer could easily be acting in the same way for a private insurance company.

Policy and the Expert

At the other end of the spectrum are civil servants who have been specially recruited, either as a group or as individuals, because their specific knowledge and experience is essential to the formulation or execution of policy at the highest level. Many of these are specialists in the sense used in this chapter. Economists provide a good example. Their importance was symbolized by the establishment of the Government Economic Service in 1965. (Although, of course, there were some economists, especially in the Treasury, long before that.) The actual number of economists has never been large – about 100 to 120, excluding specialists in fields like agricultural economics – but their influence has been considerable. They are concentrated in the 'economic' departments – the Treasury, Department of Economic Affairs, Ministry of Transport, Ministry of Overseas Development – where they have been closely involved in policy and have had much to do with the 'new look' in settling priorities and planning government expenditure. The Permanent Secretary of the Department of Economic Affairs told the Estimates Committee that economists 'tend to be directly concerned with what has become 50, 60 or 70 per cent of the range of activities as a whole'.[1] One of his staff, writing as 'Gagged Economist', wrote that: 'The need is for economists to take day-to-day decisions, rather than merely give general advice as to how decisions should be taken. In D.E.A., outside the industrial divisions, one rather wonders how there could be any policy role for non-economists at all.'[2]

This has not prevented many economists, recruited on short contracts, from saying on return to their universities that they had not been fully used, nor from implying that they had been the

[1] *Sixth Report of the Estimates Committee 1964–65* (H.C. 308), 'Recruitment to the Civil Service', p. 148 (evidence from Sir Eric Roll).
[2] Letter to *The Guardian*, 1 April 1965.

victims of some sort of administrative conspiracy to keep them in the dark.[1] The paradox is explained in a paper by the former head of the Government Economic Service.[2] Sir Alex Cairncross showed how the increasing importance of economic thinking has made it difficult to be a successful administrator without some knowledge of economics; hence the introductory courses at the Centre for Administrative Studies. At the same time, the academic who enters government service as a specialist economist soon learns that economics alone does not take him very far in the complicated issues on which he is expected to advise; he 'has to acquire the ability to judge a situation from limited and uncertain evidence just like any other administrator'. Moreover, there is very often no clear distinction between his role and the administrator's. In economic departments both economists and administrators are functioning as advisers on issues of economic policy, and the final decision rests with the Minister. On the other hand, there may be a difference in approach:

> Inevitably, when economists enter government service their interest tends to be concentrated on policy decisions rather than on the way they are taken. Administrators, on the other hand, are often more interested in the process of getting decisions taken and implemented ... It is, at any rate, not infrequent for the economist to feel that the administrator doesn't even understand the question and is too willing to blur it by considerations of procedure, while the administrator in his turn has to cope with economists who are unaware that the question has already been studied times without number, that their views are irreconcilable with those of the responsible department, or that what they are urging is in flagrant contradiction with some recent ministerial pronouncement.[3]

A two-year secondment is not very long for learning to operate within such a difficult role-system.

The central position of economists could be deduced *a priori* from

[1] For example, S. Brittan, 'The Irregulars', *Crossbow*, vol. 10, Oct.–Dec. 1966, p. 30. The question was raised with varying degrees of resentment and understanding in evidence to the Fulton Committee: *Fulton Report*, vol. 5, pp. 982–93 (D. L. Munby), pp. 1093–1105 (D. Seers) and pp. 856–72 (a group of members of the Economic Planning Staff of the Ministry of Overseas Development).

[2] Cairncross, 'The Work of an Economic Adviser'.

[3] Ibid., p. 8.

the status and quality of senior economists in the policy-making structure. Sir Alec himself joined the Treasury, initially as Economic Adviser to the Government, in 1961 and left in 1968 to become Master of Pembroke College, Cambridge. From 1964 onwards, other well-known economists began to appear in Whitehall, often returning to their universities or moving on to other jobs after much shorter periods – Dr Thomas (later Lord) Balogh, Dr Nicholas Kaldor, Mr Robert Neild, Mr Michael Posner, Mr Keith Berrill and Mr Christopher Foster were among the most eminent. They occupied influential positions. During his three years' absence from Oxford, Dr Balogh served in the Cabinet Office as Adviser on Economic Affairs with direct access to the Prime Minister. Dr Kaldor, Reader in Economics at Cambridge, held a part-time appointment at the Treasury from 1964–8 as special adviser to the Chancellor on social and economic aspects of taxation policy. Mr Foster, joint author of the cost-benefit analysis that persuaded the Government to finance the Victoria Line extension to the London underground,[1] became head of the powerful economic division set up in the Ministry of Transport in 1966. Their arrival brought a new fluidity to the top administrative structure. Posts and duties were re-shuffled to suit personalities. Most were politically sympathetic to the Government and their appointments were seen as largely political. It is impossible to believe that men of such reputation and standing would allow an administrator to intervene between them (or economic staff reporting to them) and the Prime Minister, Chancellor or Minister concerned.

Much the same can be said of the Industrial Advisers who were appointed to the Department of Economic Affairs to provide a bridge between economic planning and private industry.[2] These men are seconded from their companies, where they are normally on the main board, for two years during which the company makes up the difference between their previous salaries and what they get from the Government. From October 1964 to April 1966 (when he became Director-General of the National Economic Development Council) the chief industrial adviser was Mr Frederick Catherwood, formerly Managing Director of British Aluminium. Among other

[1] M. E. Beesley and C. D. Foster, 'The Victoria Line: Social Benefits and Finance', *Journal of the Royal Statistical Society*, Ser. A, vol. 128 (1965) p. 67.

[2] Campbell Adamson, 'The Role of the Industrial Adviser', *Public Administration*, vol. 46 (1968) p. 185. See also Sir Eric Roll, 'The Department of Economic Affairs', ibid., vol. 44 (1966) p. 8.

Industrial Advisers have been Mr Michael Shanks (an economic journalist, author of *The Stagnant Society* and subsequently economic adviser to the Leyland Motor Corporation), Mr Campbell Adamson (Director of the steel firm Richard Thomas and Baldwins) and people of similar status from Shell, I.C.I., Unilever, Tilling, the merchant bankers Morgan Grenfell, the management consultants Urwick Orr and the department store Peter Jones. It would clearly have been impossible to attract such people – perhaps the nearest British equivalent to the American 'in-and-outers' – except on a basis of personal and unrestricted access to Ministers. Any 'administrative' objection to such direct contact between expert and Minister would presumably have been derisively ignored by both.

What goes for economists and Industrial Advisers also applies to senior professional officers like the Chief Scientific Adviser, the Chief Medical Officer (Sir George Godber – more of a career civil servant than the others) and the Director of the Central Statistical Office, Professor Claus Moser. Economists, statisticians and those of the legal officers who are concerned with the preparation of legislation are indeed in rather a special position at all levels, because their work is so closely involved in the formulation of policy. But headquarters scientists, medical and nursing officers, and senior members of the inspectorates share their importance in some measure.

In the social service departments, policy has long been determined in a dialogue between expert and administrator. In these exchanges, administrators have often played a more modest part than might have been supposed. It may be helpful to illustrate this with an example from a field rather different from that of grand economic or industrial strategy.

An Illustration: Police Establishments. The Home Secretary is responsible for approving the number up to which each police force in the country can recruit. This is, in principle, a matter of political judgement. On the one hand there is public concern about a rising crime-rate and a decreasing proportion of crimes cleared up. It is easy to interpret such figures as indicative of a need for more policemen. (It is also an advantage for those who represent the police in pay negotiations if they can point to authorized establishments which are considerably higher than the actual number of policemen willing to serve on current pay and conditions of service.

79

Within police forces, too, promotion is slow and growth may be welcomed because of the new senior posts it implies.) On the other hand, there are obvious objections to over-policing. Policemen are expensive; they are taken out of the productive labour force and paid with public money which could be used for other purposes. Although studies are in progress, there is currently no way of estimating the marginal contribution of an additional policeman to the campaign against crime. The Home Secretary, therefore, has the difficult but essentially political task of assessing the claims of specific demands on a general pool of resources without a great deal of solid factual information to guide him.

In theory, he exercises this judgement with the assistance of administrative civil servants, who formulate a policy based partly on general considerations that are susceptible to lay judgement and partly on advice from the appropriate professional staff – H.M. Inspectors of Constabulary – who inspect each police force annually before certifying that it is 'efficient', and so eligible for police grant. In practice, the Inspector (himself these days a man with long police training and experience) plays a most influential part throughout. It is he who assesses in the first instance what the 'realistic' (that is to say desirable) establishment should be for the forces he inspects. He advises the Chief Constable what scale of increase to apply for. As the Home Office told the Estimates Committee in 1963, 'It would be a very foolish Chief Constable who did not accept advice.'[1]

The Chief Constable still has to persuade his local authority to accept the increase and the local authority then has to persuade the Home Secretary. But in the normal way the question has already been settled at professional level. The Home Office officials routinely check proposals when they receive them, to make sure that they do not violate agreed conventions about, for example, the ratio of senior to junior posts and then refer to the Inspector for 'advice'. As for the local authority share in this procedure, we may quote the address of the Home Secretary (Sir Frank Soskice) to the 1965 annual conference of the Association of Chief Police Officers:

> ... I have officially asked a number of Police Authorities whose existing establishments, in the light of the advice of Her Majesty's

[1] *Eleventh Report of the Estimates Committee 1962–63* (H.C. 292) 'The Home Office', p. 129 (Sir William Johnson).

Inspectors of Constabulary, appear to be substantially below a realistic level, to review the establishment of their Forces in consultation with the Chief Constable and to propose whatever revision appears to be necessary for the adequate policing of the areas . . .

As you know, the initiative for proposing increases in establishment normally comes from the Chief Officer and the Police Authority, and I am glad to say that in most areas Police Authorities loyally support their Chief Officer's needs in this respect. Only in a few cases does financial stringency dissuade the Authority from putting forward necessary proposals for increases in establishments, and then of course it is the function of the H.M. Inspectors of Constabulary to report the facts to me, so that I can consider my own responsibility in the matter, bearing in mind that the Police Act requires me to exercise my powers in such manner and to such extent as appears to me to be best calculated to promote the efficiency of the Police.

Fortunately, a solution is usually found by consultation and it is rarely necessary for me even to consider withholding the Exchequer grant; but it is clearly my duty to go to this length, if need be, to ensure that no Police Force in this country is deprived of essential manpower merely for want of an adequate establishment.[1]

The only meaning that can be given to the word 'essential' in the last sentence is 'essential in the eyes of the Inspector of Constabulary'. If a decision has to be taken in a situation of uncertainty, it is necessary to arrive at a working assumption. The Inspector is at the crucial point where uncertainties harden into 'facts' that are unlikely to be challenged later. The question for the Home Secretary is whether, on other grounds, the 'essential' requirements can be accepted or not. He has to decide whether it is consistent with other objectives of the Government of which he is a member.

One such objective is the orderly management of public expenditure. If public expenditure has to be squeezed, as it was when Mr Callaghan was Home Secretary, an arbitrary limit may be set on the resources allocated to additional policemen. The Home Office administrators are expected to check that the financial implications of any specific proposal can be contained within this total.

[1] *Police Review*, 18 June 1965.

Another test is political acceptability. It is possible, although unlikely, that the Home Secretary might have to defend himself against criticism in Parliament or in the press for authorizing an increase in police establishment. (It is more likely that he would be attacked for turning a proposal down.) Whatever his decision, he would want to be satisfied that it was defensible in political terms and again he would expect his administrators to relate general principles to the particular case. In practice, of course, the H.M. Inspector of Constabulary would normally know of an unfavourable financial or political wind and would not inspire applications at a time when they were certain to be turned down.

The limits to the Inspector's influence are set by the way Ministers carry out their individual and collective responsibilities and not by his formal relationship to administrators. He settles 'technical' aspects of questions regardless of whether he carries executive authority or is merely an 'adviser' – although he must of course be in a position to be consulted, which means having a close working relationship with whoever does carry administrative responsibility.

The Inspector of Constabulary has his equivalent in other social service departments which administer professional services. Within the Home Office there is a separate Child Care Inspectorate working with the administrators in the Children's Division. The Department of Education and Science has its H.M. Inspectors of Schools. The Department of Health and Social Security has its medical, dental and nursing officers. In each case the professional officer is prominent wherever policy is in the making. He is in touch with professional people in the field. He is present when the relevant professional interests come to bargain with the department. He plays an active part in the department's advisory system, preparing papers, guiding discussion and chairing working parties. The true measure of his influence on policy and day-to-day administration will become apparent if and when departmental working files are available for research. Clearly there will be cases where structural arrangements are in need of overhaul, where the professional is too remote or where his calibre is simply too poor. But most of the visible and anecdotal evidence confirms his key role.

A general hypothesis can be formulated that, given reasonable calibre and a workable link with the main channels of communication in his department, the professional officer (whatever his formal status) will effectively decide policy questions within limits set by current conventions about what is financially and politically tolerable.

Technical Management and the Administrator

Most of the enduring quarrels between specialists and general administrators have not arisen where exclusively professional work is being done on the periphery of government business nor at the apex where professional advice is an essential element in the formulation of policy. They are rather at the intermediary levels, where professional officers providing professional services, or managing technical projects, complain that they are not left alone to get on with their job without administrative interference.

In some departments, the system of joint decision-making described on pp. 69–71 has had the desired effect of bringing administrators and professionals closer together. For example, Regan claims that in the Ministry of Transport the new arrangements have given engineers a broader perspective on financial and political aspects of their work, while a closer personal relationship has made it easier for administrators to seek engineering advice without risking loss of face.[1] But the Institution of Professional Civil Servants felt that professional staff were still being allotted an advisory, auxiliary role, with the main policy and financial decisions reserved to the administrative members of the joint hierarchy. It was particularly indignant about the system in the Ministry of Public Building and Works, where administrators were responsible for 'ascertaining the requirements of client Departments and deciding which should be met, when, where and at what cost'. The administrator was thus 'interposed between the professional and his client'.[2]

One of the main jobs of the Ministry is providing and maintaining accommodation for other government departments. It is thus a vast executive building organization. In some ways it is a historical accident that it is a government department at all and not an *ad hoc* agency or even a private contractor. If comparable work was being done outside the civil service, there would almost certainly be a more streamlined organization in which professional staff took executive decisions in their own name. In local government, an

---

[1] Regan, 'The Expert and the Administrator', p. 160.
[2] *Fulton Report*, vol. 5 (Institution of Professional Civil Servants) pp. 327–35, esp. par. 11.

organization of this type would be headed by a professional chief officer who was also chief adviser to the appropriate committee. But the M.P.B.W. situation is repeated in other departments where civil servants are engaged in the supervision and execution of complex technical work. In these areas the traditional civil service command structure may not seem particularly appropriate. It is necessary to ask what the distinctive contribution of administrators to this sort of work is and how far it is associated with factors peculiar to the civil service.

The general administrator's contribution to technical management can perhaps be divided into three aspects, which overlap and are sometimes confused.

Secretarial assistance. Members of the administrative and executive classes are trained to express themselves acceptably on paper. Thus in the development group of the Department of Education and Science it is the administrative member who writes the reports. In the branch that vets school building schemes it is the higher executive officer who conducts the correspondence with local education authorities (a function which the Fulton Committee's management consultants, incredibly, seem to have confused with the right to over-ride technical advice).[1] The secretarial function can be expanded to include the preparation of Ministerial briefs and parliamentary papers or the routine administration of personnel, accounts and common services. It is obviously desirable that professional staff should not be burdened with these details; but there is no obvious need for an administrator who is primarily a secretary to share executive control with a professional head of branch. In the Royal Aircraft Establishment at Farnborough a central administrative unit, headed by an Assistant Secretary, is responsible to the scientific director.[2] The Fulton Committee saw no reason why this pattern should not be adopted more widely.[3]

Financial control. This includes the preparation of estimates and long-term forecasts of expenditure, arguing with Treasury over specific proposals and ensuring that they are covered by available finance, controlling expenditure during the year and providing explanations (ultimately for the Public Accounts Committee of the

[1] *Fulton Report*, vol. 2, par. 200 and app. IV, par. 9. [2] Ibid., par. 152.
[3] Ibid., vol. 1, par. 162.

House of Commons) of any over- or under-spending. Traditionally these functions, stemming from the responsibility of the Minister to Parliament and the personal responsibility of the Permanent Secretary, as Accounting Officer, for the proper spending of all public money, are given to administrators. Professional staff resent the restrictions on their autonomy and claim that administrators are not in a position to evaluate technical projects. Administrators tend to reply that specialists are not noticeably cost-conscious and may give too high a priority to aesthetic or technical frills. Clearly, however, there is no great incentive to economy if someone else is responsible for that side of things – there may even be a temptation to bargain for as much as one can get. There seems no reason in principle why the government professional should not accept financial responsibility for schemes in the same way as his counterpart in local government or private industry, subject to two reservations. One is that he may need specialist help with accounting requirements, as with the other secretarial parts of his work. The other is that he must accept the conventions of public accounting, including the overriding authority of the Public Accounts Committee, the Treasury and the departmental Accounting Officer. Some of the evidence given by the Institution of Professional Civil Servants suggests that its objection is to the restrictions inherent in the system rather than to the part played in it by administrators.[1] The First Division Association evidently had this point in mind when it saw no objection to professional leadership of project teams so long as the leader accepted direct financial responsibility for the project.[2] Financial control procedures would not in themselves justify joint control.

General 'approval'. The administrator's part in giving final approval to a scheme is more difficult to assess. The I.P.C.S. felt that administrators frequently interfered in matters beyond their competence, outside the financial field, causing wasted effort and delays.[3] The

---

[1] For example: 'Professional staff . . . are not used to the maximum capacity because they are still subject to detailed day-to-day control by finance branches and constantly required to refer to the centre for financial authorization in respect of projects they are alleged to control . . . In many cases no commitment may be incurred without the approval of the central finance division which alone may seek Treasury authority for work exceeding such powers as the Treasury may have delegated to the Department.' *Fulton Report*, vol. 5, p. 333, par. 28 (Institution of Professional Civil Servants).

[2] Ibid., p. 110, par. 19 (Association of First Division Civil Servants).

[3] Ibid., p. 299, par. 23 (Institution of Professional Civil Servants).

Fulton Committee supported their point of view.[1] There seems to have been some confusion in discussing this subject. The word 'approval' is ambiguous. It can imply that the person giving approval is a superior, with the right to veto, or it can denote the mere giving of assent by an interested party (for example, a consultative committee) with no hierarchical implications.

Often, when the administrator appears to be approving a scheme he is not assessing its technical merits but confirming that it is financially within the budget – or acting secretarially by making sure that its official acceptance is conveyed to the appropriate people in the appropriate form and noted on the appropriate files. To do either of these things, he may have to ask questions that seem ignorant and trivial to the professional. But sometimes he is doing more than that.

In the public sector, decisions depend partly on technical considerations and partly on economics and politics. Better techniques might be developed for separating broad policy from detailed administration and so for freeing technical administration from day-to-day political accountability.[2] But in a government department, which the Ministry of Public Building and Works is, there is also a constant possibility of parliamentary interest in particular projects on grounds of suitability, extravagance, aesthetic appearance, the rectitude of tendering procedures and so on. Someone must therefore be involved in quite detailed work who is familiar with the principles of lay control and knows the working of the parliamentary machine and the Minister's mind. The strongest argument for joint responsibility at project level is that schemes must, if they are to be viable, command the assent of administrators who apply a lay mind and a knowledge of the administrative machine to match their partner's professional expertise. If two types of skill are needed for the pursuit of an activity, it will probably be more effective if they are applied simultaneously through joint working.

It is clear, however, that great strains may be involved for the partners in joint responsibility. Roles may be easier to define in principle than in practice. Some people may be temperamentally unsuited to joint working. (The Ministry of Education found that it had to select members of its Development Group very carefully.)[3]

[1] *Fulton Report*, vol. 1, pars. 40, 161, 210 and others.

[2] See the discussion of 'accountable management' in ch. XI, below.

[3] See the description of this Group in *Report of the Committee on the Management and Control of Research and Development* (Zuckerman Report) Office of the Minister of Science (1961) app. V, par. 8(8).

It may be unreasonable to expect the advantages of a dual system of control to outweigh the obvious possibilities of delay and friction.

The basic issue is whether, given relevant training and experience, one man could fill both roles. A Treasury working party on the role of the professional engineer said:

> If one brain could provide the expertise of both aspects (i.e. the administrative and professional) it would be the natural arrangement to make one man responsible for both; but failing that two brains must work as one.[1]

Administrators claim that the roles of specialist and administrator are inconsistent, at least at higher levels. It is not only unlikely that the different qualities would be found in the same person but also undesirable:

> What we are saying, however, is that the specialist who becomes fully able to perform the administrative role thereby ceases to be a specialist and will in turn need other specialists to provide the element of expert knowledge that is essential to the dialogue.[2]

It would perhaps be more realistic to think in terms of a series of dialogues, in which Treasury administrators, departmental administrators, senior professional advisers and narrower specialists all play a part, through which technical questions are progressively enmeshed in the general welfare and the political system. To quote the Treasury working party again, the function of administration is:

> the analysis and co-ordination of ideas and proposals, the relation of these to political and economic conditions and the expression of proposals and decisions in a form in which they can be assimilated and carried out by the government machine.[3]

This argument has also been propounded by civil service writers like Sisson,[4] who see government as a process of arbitration among special interests. Administration is a matter of making adjustments

---

[1] *Report of Working Party on the Role of the Professional Engineer* (unpublished) quoted in *Fulton Report*, vol. 5, p. 298, par. 17 (Institution of Professional Civil Servants).

[2] Ibid., p. 109, par. 14 (Association of First Division Civil Servants).

[3] Ibid., p. 328, par. 3 (Institution of Professional Civil Servants).

[4] Sisson, *The Spirit of British Administration.*

where interests conflict. The committed specialist is therefore incapable of filling the administrative role. Others, like the authors of the Labour Party's evidence to Fulton, feel that co-ordination and adjustment are relatively less important in these days than purposive and committed management.[1] Summing up a long, reasoned, argument on the subject of specialists and generalists, Professor Ridley endorsed this view:

> One might . . . expect the professional to be a little more impatient of administrative difficulties and, indeed, public opinion, more anxious to get things done, even at a cost. Perhaps too much emphasis is placed on avoiding friction: it may be less important to have a smooth-running machine than a machine which actually gets somewhere. But that obviously brings one back to one's own philosophy of politics.[2]

The Fulton Committee, in effect, accepted both sets of arguments. It advocated putting one man – the best man for the job and therefore often a professional – in charge of units of administration and giving him undivided responsibility and the authority to implement it. It also followed fashion in discounting the integrating role of the generalist, skilled only in the ways of Whitehall and Westminster. But at the same time it saw the need for some administrative contribution. These ideas are spelt out in detail only for administrators specializing in economics and finance. It was thought necessary that some of their skills should be applied to work of a high scientific and technological content, such as the economic aspects of research or the financial control of advanced technological projects, in fields where scientists and engineers would take the lead. Others would be working side by side with professional economists, but not duplicating them, since they would be working on different aspects of the same problems. The administrators would be more immersed in day to day administration and in serving the needs of the Minister and Parliament than the specialists:

> Our aim is not to replace specialists by administrators, or vice versa. They should be complementary to one another. It is, rather, that the administrator, trained and experienced in his subject-matter, should enjoy a more fruitful relationship with the

[1] *Fulton Report*, vol. 5, pp. 653–4, pars. 10–13 (Labour Party).
[2] Ridley (ed.) *Specialists and Generalists*, p. 209.

specialist than in the past, and that the Service should harness the best contribution from each.[1]

POLICY AND EXECUTION

What the Committee seem to be doing here is drawing a distinction between policy and executive work. In the latter case, they have applied the principles of accountable management – which, for technical work in departments like the Ministry of Public Building and Works and sections of Transport and Defence, means technical management, with administrators in support. In the formulation of new policy, on the other hand, it sees more scope for a contribution by the administrator on something like equal terms so long as he is skilled in a field of administration as well as in the machinery of government.

To a large extent, and particularly when they were in line with existing trends, the Fulton recommendations about specialists have been adopted fairly quickly. The modifications of the class system described in Chapter III[2] will open up wider opportunities for specialists and accelerate the development of an 'open society' at the top of the service. On the training side, major increases have been planned in the provision of management courses for senior specialists. But a more cautious approach has been taken to the proposal that joint hierarchies should be abolished at executive level. It was felt that different departments would need different forms of organization because the nature of their work differed. As a first step, the Civil Service Department began to study how different kinds of hierarchy worked in practice.[3]

CONCLUSIONS

The number of special techniques relevant to government has increased markedly over the last half-century. Decision-making has become more difficult, and governments are engaged in many

[1] *Fulton Report*, vol. 1, pars. 50–2.

[2] Ch. III, pp. 55–6. These included further steps to open the top management of the Ministry of Public Building and Works to professional staff (*The Times* (London) 16 June 1969).

[3] National Whitley Council *Developments on Fulton*, pars. 49, 66.

fields where technical competence is of supreme importance. Consequently more and more specialists have been employed. Over the years they have gradually taken on policy-making and managerial as well as advisory functions and their status has been recognized by creating more specialist posts at senior levels with access to Ministers.

But the general administrative framework in which general administrators represent the lay Minister and are involved on his behalf at every level of administration, except in research establishments, has been slow to change. The Fulton enquiry gave the Institution of Civil Servants a fresh opportunity to press for more status, authority and opportunities for its members. Its case was strongly supported by the Committee's management consultancy group, which was not convinced that the special problems of public administration were such as to justify the differences which were noted between the civil service and private industry. The Institution won (and the Treasury lost) on almost all points where there was a conflict.

But the sweeping terms of the Fulton Report should not exaggerate the extent of the changes the Committee was suggesting. In a quiet way, experts and specialists had enjoyed a great deal of influence behind the façade of 'expert advice; administrative decision'. In the newer departments, like Technology, the façade had been crumbling too. The main skirmishes have been in fields of executive management where administrators, afflicted by over-frequent postings, were uncertain of their role and unable to keep out of matters of detailed technical management. At policy-making levels, at least in the social service and technological departments where technical issues predominate, the administrative role has on the whole been relatively modest and could be best described as secretarial.

It is not possible, without a radical change in our political system, to imagine an administration which has become entirely professional, even if professional training is altered to include more basic administration than it does now and civil service professionals enjoy fuller opportunities to gain administrative experience early in their careers. So long as the doctrines of individual and collective Ministerial responsibility are held, there will be a need to relate different technical fields to one another and to the social and political environment. Professionals can do this, but only at cost of ceasing to be specialist.[1] It is interesting that the only significant points on which the Fulton Committee did not accept the Institution's evidence were on political issues. The I.P.C.S. was opposed to the introduction of political advisers and to changes in the machinery of government which were not justified on grounds of greater efficiency.[2] On these points, and in other places where its evidence ignores differences between the civil service and industry,[3] the Institution can fairly be accused of political naïvety.

The problem about professionals is the same as the problem about excessively 'departmentalized' administrators. Policy and priorities are normally evolved as a result of a dialogue. There may have to be several stages in the dialogue before a sectional pressure (for example, for better quality school baths) can be given its place in the current political scale of values. If the school baths department is staffed by professional educationalists (or by administrators who have spent all their working lives listening to professional educationalists), the settlement of priorities must take place somewhere else, either in the Treasury or in the Minister's private office. And no professional worth his salt is going to be completely satisfied with the share of resources allocated to him as a result of the process!

[1] Bacchus has shown how the substitution of Ministerial for Colonial government in Guyana led almost inexorably to conflict between professionals, committed to the provision of a service, and administrators whose main interest was in the processes of policy-formulation – and to the elevation of the administrator over the professional. M. K. Bacchus, 'Relationships between professional and administrative officers in a government department during a period of administrative change', *Sociological Review*, vol. 15 (1967) pp. 155–78. He argues (as by implication, does the Fulton Committee) that the Whitehall-Westminster pattern of Ministerial government is inappropriate to a situation where central government is directly engaged in the provision of technical services.

[2] *Fulton Report*, vol. 5, p. 292, par. 7, p. 312, pars. 77–9, p. 322, pars. 114–16 (Institution of Professional Civil Servants).

[3] Ibid., e.g. p. 329, par. 56.

V. The Political Environment

'A FUNDAMENTAL FEATURE OF OUR PARLIAMENTARY
SYSTEM'

The public servant works within a framework of political institutions. British civil servants work under the direction of a political
Minister who is in turn accountable to Parliament, to his colleagues
in the Government and, more remotely, to the political party of
which he is a member. Each line of accountability imposes its own
discipline on the Minister and limits his department's scope for
manœuvre. Civil servants are constantly aware of the political
implications of their work and many of them spend much of their
time servicing the political machine by preparing answers to
parliamentary questions, briefs for debates and material for the
Minister's correspondence.[1] They are, of course, exposed to many
influences that do not arise from the central political machine. They
have to deal with the public, and with the interest groups and cause
groups that make up their special 'publics'. They have to bargain
with colleagues in other departments, notably in the Treasury.
These relationships have developed outside the parliamentary
system. But in an important sense they are conditioned by it; in the
last resort a dissatisfied group can appeal to political levels and this
possibility sets the tone for relationships lower down. Without
Parliament there would be no final sanction for the weight given to
impartiality, fairness and consistency in the daily work of government departments.[2]

[1] Members of the administrative class estimated that they spent between a fifth
and a quarter of their time on functions directly related to the parliamentary
system. *Fulton Report*, vol. 5, p. 119 (Evidence from the First Division Association).
The management consultancy group found an Assistant Secretary who spent half
his time on such work and 16 other administrators who spent a quarter of their
time or more. (Ibid., vol. 2, par. 48.)

[2] This is not the place for a discussion of constitutional theory. Birch finds
substantial truth both in the 'Whitehall' view of the constitution, which locates
power and initiative in a strong central government subject only to debate in

The Fulton Committee was not allowed to criticize this framework. Announcing its appointment, the Prime Minister emphasized that the basic relationship between civil servants and Ministers was to be maintained:

> Civil Servants, however eminent, remain the confidential advisers of Ministers, who alone are answerable to Parliament for policy; and we do not envisage any change in this fundamental feature of our parliamentary system of democracy.[1]

The Committee evidently had to keep reminding itself and its readers of this limitation. Both the main report and the report from the management consultancy group (which was strongly impressed with the extent to which parliamentary accountability was an integral part of civil servants' daily life) contain many references to political context and its effects on what civil servants do and the way they do it.[2] But these give an impression of having been inserted as an afterthought. It is difficult to see how some of the Committee's main recommendations (for example, on accountable management) can be implemented without modifying the constitutional arrangements outlined by the Prime Minister.

The Fulton enquiry can be seen as part of a wider review of British institutions. While the Committee was sitting, other investigations were taking place, notably on local government, on trade union law and on law reform. The relationship between government and the nationalized industries was being reviewed by a parliamentary Select Committee and a new financial structure was being worked out for the industries in a succession of White Papers. Arrangements were being made to convert the Post Office into a nationalized industry. Regionalism and federalism were in the air; in the 1968 Queen's speech the Government announced a Commission to study the constitutional and economic relationships between different parts of the United Kingdom. Several witnesses who gave evidence to the Fulton Committee argued the need for a full-scale review of the machinery of government. The Committee recommended a further study to determine the possibility of 'hiving off' some areas of civil service work to autonomous

Parliament, and in the 'liberal' view, which traces the sources of power from the electorate through Parliament to a government which carries out its will. A. H. Birch, *Responsible and Representative Government* (London, 1964).

[1] *H.C. Debs.*, vol. 724 (8 February 1966) cols. 209–14.

[2] *Fulton Report*, vol. 1, pars. 13, 27, 46, 276; vol. 2, pars. 21–7, 303–15, 371.

corporations, which could be made part of a more general review.

Most important of all, there was a continuing debate on the reform of Parliament itself. Although the basic arguments were expressed in many different ways, with differing shades of emphasis, there was a widespread feeling that parliamentary institutions were no longer able to cope with the vast amount of business presented to them nor with controlling the activities of an executive whose planning horizons often had to stretch beyond the life of a parliament. The abortive attempt to make the House of Lords into a smaller and largely nominated assembly was inspired partly by the hope that a reformed upper chamber would make a more effective contribution to the parliamentary system.[1] In the House of Commons, there were a number of changes in procedure. Significant changes affecting the work of the civil service were the appointment of a Parliamentary Commissioner for Administration and a series of experiments with special committees to scrutinize the administration. Before considering their impact on administration, it is necessary to describe the general relationship between civil servants and Ministers.

CIVIL SERVANTS AND MINISTERS

Formally, the Minister *is* the department, whose members are his agents and are appointed only to carry out the functions entrusted to him. The Minister alone is accountable to Parliament, although this no longer means that any substantial part of the department's work is done with his knowledge and specific approval.

In the early years of the 1964 Labour Government it was constantly alleged (for example in the Labour Party's evidence to the Fulton Committee)[2] that civil servants were conspiring to conceal information from their Ministers. When challenged on the point in a Third Programme broadcast, however, the Prime Minister retorted: 'If you'll tell me the names of any Ministers who allow their civil servants to keep back information, or any civil servants who would do it, I think the time has come for a rapid change, whether of the Ministers or of the civil servants or both.'[3]

[1] *House of Lords Reform*, Cmnd. 3791 (1968). The subsequent *Parliament (No. 2) Bill* was withdrawn in April 1969 after considerable opposition in the House of Cmomons, in order to allow time for a Bill on industrial relations.

[2] *Fulton Report*, vol. 5, p. 655 (Labour Party).

[3] 'The Prime Minister on the Machinery of Government' (second part), *The Listener*, vol. LXXVII (13 April 1967) p. 482.

The Minister is not a superior civil servant and is likely to approach problems in a different way. He is recruited, trained and promoted to office through very different channels. He is likely to have little or no knowledge of his post and if he is ambitious he may hope not to remain in it for very long. Mr Kenneth Robinson, Minister of Health from 1964 to 1968, had held the office for longer than any Minister since Aneurin Bevan. The Treasury had eight different Chancellors of the Exchequer between 1947 and 1964. On the whole, a Minister is more likely to be interested in positive action in the short-term than in long-term strategy. He is unlikely to be well-disposed to decisions that are going to be unpopular or difficult to explain. In contrast, the experienced career official is more aware of problems about continuity and more concerned with the risk of a policy going sour in the long-term. Some appearance of conflict between them is therefore unavoidable if advice is to be tendered frankly and Ministers made aware of all the consequences of their proposed actions.

In the last resort, the civil servant must do what he is told. In the last resort too, a Minister who is determined to get rid of a senior civil servant whose advice he finds uncongenial can do so, although it is not easy – he has to persuade the Prime Minister first and would be unwise to attempt it for trivial reasons. In practice, a Minister can depend on habits of loyalty.

The Minister's immediate influence on his department owes a good deal to his strategic constitutional position. Some questions are bound to come to his personal attention, simply because he provides an essential link with the political system. He must concern himself with his department's contribution to his party programme. For this he will have to answer not to Parliament as such but to the Prime Minister, his Ministerial colleagues and the appropriate backbench committee. He must also become aware of any reference to his department in Parliament. He or his Parliamentary Secretary answer parliamentary questions, reply to criticisms in debates and introduce new legislation or statutory instruments. A reply to any letter from an M.P. is also, as a rule, signed by the Minister personally. Through all these means a sample of his department's work is exposed to his attention and possible criticism.

Apart from parliamentary business, the Minister is like the head of any other concern. He sees papers that his senior advisers think he ought to see. A good deal will depend on the training and experience

95

of the civil servants and on their ability to anticipate the Minister's wishes. They know the pressures on his time and see their job partly as protecting him from being deluged with paper. No question of any importance, however, is likely to be settled in the Minister's name before he has seen the papers and had a chance to intervene.

Indeed, most questions of any importance will be referred through him to Cabinet or one of its committees. He will have to be brought in as a final big gun in disputes with other departments or powerful outside interests. He will be informed about fairly minor questions that seem likely to have political repercussions. A new Minister will be consulted on many questions that will be settled much lower down once his mind is known. Finally, the Minister will see papers (and arguments as detailed as he likes) on questions in which he has expressed a particular interest. It is this aspect of the job that tests the calibre of the Minister.

The amount of detail that is given to the Minister on any question will vary for all these reasons. Normally the department will present him with as brief a summary as possible, including a highly compressed description of the problem, a note of the main factors in which he is likely to be interested (including, for example, repercussions in his own constituency) and an outline of the main arguments. Even if the arguments are fairly evenly balanced, the paper will end with a definite recommendation. Usually this summary is the top document on a file which the Minister, if he has time and inclination, can read to see what sort of detailed arguments have been put forward in earlier discussion. If he is busy, he need only read the top document. If he wishes action to proceed as suggested all he has to do is to add his initials. Most Ministers will initial most documents most of the time. But he may disagree with the recommendation. He can ask for fuller information, covering points that seem to him to have been missed out. He may call in the Permanent Secretary and other civil servants and instruct them to look at other possibilities. The process is a subtle one of mutual influence, which it is very difficult to describe except in the context of a particular question and of particular personalities.

The vast majority of decisions, however, will not and cannot be seen by a Minister personally. These are not just routine questions. Many near-Ministerial decisions are given by senior civil servants who decide whether a concession should be made to a pressure group, whether a piece of legislation should be reviewed in consultation with other departments, or whether a problem should be referred to a committee before recommending any particular way of dealing with it. The test of these decisions is not just that the Minister can defend them in Parliament if challenged. The test is that each decision should, as far as humanly possible, be the one that the Minister himself would have taken if he had been able to take it personally. Ministers thus expect their senior assistants to be able to think in terms of their own priorities. They even expect to be warned about political reactions to a proposed policy. Experience of a particular field sometimes makes civil servants more aware of impending trouble than the Minister himself.

When the relationship is examined in detail like this the crude differences between a good Minister and a good civil servant begin to melt away. The Minister is a political animal. But one of the jobs of his administrative entourage is to help him to handle his political business creditably. They are bound to become, in some measure, political animals too and to transmit their political sense through their own subordinates. The administrative system is a mirror of the political one.

This is true to the extent that Ministers and civil servants are interchangeable within broad limits. When a new Parliamentary Secretary is appointed to a department, it is often to take over functions from a career official. Mr Wilson tried to involve junior Ministers in inter-departmental committees that had previously consisted entirely of officials. Ministers and civil servants intermingle on committees of the Cabinet. Posts are held by career officials in this country that in America would be held by political appointees. Conversely, French civil servants were appointed under de Gaulle to many posts normally regarded as political. Paradoxically, the real ground for criticizing British civil servants is not that they are too much at odds with the Minister, but that their approach is too similar to his.

Much of the work of administrators is thus taken up with assisting and representing Ministers in a primarily secretarial capacity. Between a secretary and his chief there can be no disagreement in public. Their relationship would become impossible if those at the receiving end of an administrative decision knew that the person they were dealing with had previously argued against the very policy he was now defending. It would also be impossible for civil servants to provide continuous assistance after a change of Minister, or even a change of government, if they were personally identified with particular policies. Relationships between senior civil servants and

Ministers must be as confidential as those between a solicitor and his client. Ministers themselves would hardly have it otherwise. It is they who take the credit for good ideas and the blame for listening to bad ones.[1]

A special problem is how far confidentiality between Ministers and their immediate advisers should apply to government business as a whole, including work that is primarily managerial or professional. So far as consideration of policy is concerned, some civil servants have taken the view that, since all decisions belong constitutionally to the Minister, official ideas should not be made public until the Minister has announced his decision. The official habit of secrecy has been attacked again and again by critics of British administration, sometimes with scant recognition either of the problems involved in releasing information at critical stages in the formulation of policy or of the politician's desire to maintain the illusion of personal omniscience.

The practice of confidentiality, and the extent to which individual civil servants remain anonymous, varies from department to department and from situation to situation. As part of their normal jobs, civil servants have to consult outside bodies and give evidence to parliamentary committees, although in neither of these cases would they be expected to express personal views where these differed from the Minister's. Professional civil servants are often invited to address meetings as individuals, and some (for example, the Chief Medical Officer of the Department of Health and Social Security and the Chief Inspector of Constabulary) present their own views on policy in published reports. Administrative civil servants lecture to bodies like the Royal Institute of Public Administration. Individual civil servants are generally found both revealing and helpful by an outside enquirer, so long as he is not obviously wasting their time, or trying to penetrate the mysteries of an essentially political decision. Kingdom tells the story of a young American who wanted to study departmental files in order to find out what part the Chancellor of the Exchequer, the Minister of Health and their respective advisers had played in the decision to impose National Health Service charges in 1951, 'Wherever he went in London he received literally nothing but courtesy.'[2]

---

[1] For a witty but penetrating exposition of this point, see T. D. Kingdom 'The Confidential Advisers of Ministers', *Public Administration*, vol. 44 (1966) p. 267.

[2] Kingdom, op. cit., p. 271.

The Fulton Committee recognized the need for confidentiality at some stages in decision-making and also the steps that had already been taken towards wider and more open consultation. (One important experiment was publishing policy ideas for discussion, before the government was committed to them, in the form of a 'Green Paper'. The first Green Paper, issued in 1967, was concerned with regional employment premiums. It was followed by papers on the reorganization of the National Health Service, speed limits, economic growth targets, proposals for road-construction, and the control of public expenditure.) But they felt that more could be done. They were much impressed with the Swedish practice, where Ministerial files are (literally) open to the public except when there is a security risk, and except for working material while policy decisions are actually in preparation. The Committee suggested that the Government should set up a review to make recommendations for getting rid of unnecessary secrecy. In the same context, it argued that the doctrine of Ministerial responsibility, in the literal sense that the Minister had full knowledge and control of all the activities of his department, was no longer tenable and that civil servants 'should be able to go further than now in explaining what their departments are doing, at any rate so far as concerns managing existing policies and implementing legislation'.[1] Here, as elsewhere, the Committee demonstrated the emphasis which it placed on managerial rather than political aspects of the civil service. It is impracticable to give much personal autonomy to civil servants, or to extend their freedom to explain departmental policies in public, so long as Members of Parliament see it as their duty to make political capital out of human errors and to upbraid a Minister with the sins of his servants. It is also difficult in our political system to draw clear distinctions between 'policy' and 'implementation' – Parliament holds the Minister equally responsible for both.[2]

PARLIAMENTARY COMMISSIONER FOR ADMINISTRATION

It was largely the belief that the Minister's own accountability to Parliament was no longer sufficient to protect the victims of

[1] *Fulton Report,* vol. 1, pars. 277–84.

[2] For a considered approach to these problems, see *Information and the Public Interest,* Cmnd. 4089 (1969) in which the Government accepted the case for more openness within defined limits.

departmental error and maladministration that led to the institution of the office of Parliamentary Commissioner in 1967.

In the late 1950s considerable interest began to be taken in the Scandinavian Ombudsman, who investigates complaints by citizens against the administration. In 1961 a private organization, Justice, produced a report on existing procedures for protecting the citizen against arbitrary administration. The report recommended the institution of a Parliamentary Commissioner to deal with complaints of maladministration, as well as greater use of tribunals to allow citizens to appeal against administrative decisions.[1] The idea was taken up by the Labour Party in its election campaign in 1964. A White Paper duly appeared in October 1965. The first Parliamentary Commissioner for Administration took up office in September 1966 (before Parliament had approved the enabling legislation!) and started work on 1 April 1967.[2]

The main objectives of the new office were described by Mr R. H. S. Crossman, then Leader of the House, in the second reading debate on the Bill.[3] The Commissioner's duty would be to investigate cases of alleged maladministration referred to him by Members of Parliament. This 'would provide the back-bencher with a new and powerful weapon' in addition to his existing rights to question Ministers in the House and to raise matters in adjournment debates. The Commissioner and his staff would have the power to call for papers and witnesses, including the Minister himself if he was involved, and would report to the House of Commons (which later set up a Select Committee to consider the reports) as well as to the M.P. who had taken up the complaint. The Bill went beyond the original 1961 recommendations in several ways: Ministers would not be allowed to veto investigations and could prohibit the publication of information only if disclosure would be prejudicial 'to the safety of the State or otherwise contrary to the public interest' – even this could not prevent publication of the findings.

The Commissioner was left to define the term 'maladministration' as he went along, subject to a number of important restrictions:

1. He could not investigate maladministration on the part of

---

[1] *The Citizen and the Administration: the Redress of Grievances* (Whyatt Report) (London, 1961).

[2] *The Parliamentary Commissioner for Administration*, Cmnd. 2767 (1965); Parliamentary Commissioner Act, 1967.

[3] *H.C. Debs.*, vol. 734 (18 October 1966) cols. 42–61.

local authorities, hospital boards, nationalized industries, the police, personnel questions in the civil service and the armed forces, or matters on which a right of appeal was open to the complainant. In the debate Mr Crossman said that local government should be left to work out its own machinery for dealing with complaints, at least for the time being. He also suggested that the question of a Military Commissioner should be considered separately. The possibility of having a separate Hospitals Commissioner was subsequently raised by the Minister of Health, after a series of allegations about the ill treatment of mental patients, in a Green Paper;[1] a 'hospital advisory service' was introduced by Mr Crossman (by this time Secretary of State for Social Services) in 1969. The idea of a Commissioner of Rights to investigate allegations against the police had been suggested in a Royal Commission report in 1962[2] but nothing had come of it. One of the early questions of jurisdiction that the Parliamentary Commissioner had to settle was whether the Metropolitan Police, which come directly under the Home Secretary, were within his scope. He decided that they did not and was supported by the Select Committee.

2. The Commissioner was not allowed to question policy, which remained subject to general parliamentary control. Nor could he question the merits of discretionary administrative decisions, so long as they were taken legally and after an appropriate administrative procedure. Given these restrictions, it is not perhaps surprising that the early work of the Parliamentary Commissioner should have occasioned some disappointment. A good deal of his first two general reports is taken up with points of procedure and jurisdiction.[3] He set out very clearly the grounds on which he decided whether to act in doubtful cases, and also the limitations set by his inability to criticize the substance of discretionary decisions and legislation (an important point since many complainants were really dissatisfied with what they saw as the intrinsic unfairness of regulations and not with the propriety with which they were applied).

[1] *National Health Service: The Administrative Structure of the Medical and Related Services in England and Wales* (London, 1968).
[2] *Report of the Royal Commission on the Police 1960–62*, Cmnd. 1728 (1962), par. 479 and app. V.
[3] *First Report of the Parliamentary Commissioner for Administration 1967–68* (H.C. 6); *Fourth Report of the Parliamentary Commissioner for Administration 1967–68: Annual Report for 1967* (H.C. 134).

His interpretation of these limitations attracted some adverse press criticism. *The Times*, 10 November 1967, had an editorial entitled 'Ombudsman – or Ombudsmouse?' In reviewing his report, the Select Committee accepted that the Commissioner would have to tread carefully if he was not going to cut across Ministerial accountability. For example, the Committee agreed that it would be improper to seek to identify and blame individual officials whose administrative acts were criticized. On the other hand, the Committee felt that, within the terms of the Act, the Commissioner could and should concern himself more with hardships caused by the application of a 'bad rule', which ought to have been reviewed, or by a 'bad decision'. It felt 'that the cases of maladministration found by the Commissioner might have been more in number and less trivial in content if he had allowed himself to find on occasion that a decision had been taken with maladministration because it was a bad decision'.[1] The Commissioner did extend his scope to cover these cases but reported that the effect was slight, at least for the first few months.[2] The extension must, however, have made it harder for him to decide when injustice was the result of administrative incompetence and when of deliberate policy.

These early reports show how the Commissioner set about his business. Between 1 April and 31 December 1967, 1,069 cases were referred to him from 428 Members and 849 were completed. 52·5 per cent of these were rejected on jurisdictional grounds, usually because they related to local authorities or some other body not mentioned in the Act, or because they related to personnel questions. Another 9·5 per cent of these cases were discontinued after partial investigation, mainly because there turned out to be no question of administration involved or because the Commissioner did not feel there were grounds for using his discretion to modify some of the normal restrictions (for example, a time bar) in special circumstances. Similarly, over half of the 1,340 cases dealt with during 1968 were rejected as outside his jurisdiction. Of the 562 valid cases investigated by the end of 1968, the Commissioner discovered instances of maladministration in 57 (or 10 per cent). These occurred mainly in departments where fairly junior staff have substantial dealings with

---

[1] *Second Report from the Select Committee on the Parliamentary Commissioner for Administration 1967–68* (H.C. 350).

[2] *First Report of the Parliamentary Commissioner for Administration, Session 1967–68* (H.C. 6); *Second Report of the Parliamentary Commissioner for Administration 1968–69: Annual Report for 1968* (H.C. 129).

the public. Nineteen cases were discovered in Inland Revenue, twelve in the Department of Social Security and four in the Ministry of Labour. There were also five in the Ministry of Housing and Local Government, four each in the Home Office and the Foreign and Commonwealth Office, three in the Ministry of Transport, and one each in seven other government departments and authorities. Most of the complaints that were upheld related to delay, failure to apply rules, inadequate correspondence, wrong advice or decisions made without taking account of the available evidence. The reports gave details of all such cases that arose in the first year and also of others in which no evidence of maladministration was found. Remedies applied by departments after the maladministration had been pointed out varied from an apology (to a taxpayer whose file was lost) to an extra statutory payment (to a lady who had lost pension rights as a result of wrong information about her national insurance position). In none of these cases did the Commissioner have any criticism of the action taken by the department to remedy any injustice caused by maladministration.[1]

The Commissioner presented Parliament with two special reports dealing with exceptional cases during 1967. One became a *cause célèbre*. It concerned the way the Foreign Office had handled certain claims for a share in £1 million made available under the Anglo-German agreement for British victims of Nazi persecution. The Foreign Office had turned down claims on behalf of twelve survivors of ill-treatment in parts of the Sachsenhausen concentration camp on the ground that the areas where the claimants were held were not part of the main concentration camp. The Commisioner found that the Foreign Office had ignored some relevant information and, by casting doubts on the claimants' stories, had cast slurs on their veracity and on their distinguished war records. The Commissioner had no power to recommend financial compensation, and the original £1 million had already been disbursed, but he suggested that the Foreign Office should reach a fresh decision and consider then whether a financial award was appropriate.[2] This was done, and an ex-gratia sum was made available for the survivors early in 1968.

[1] *Fourth Report of the Parliamentary Commissioner for Administration, 1967–68: Annual Report for 1967* (H.C. 134); *Second Report of the Parliamentary Commissioner for Administration 1968–9: Annual Report for 1968* (H.C. 129).
[2] *Third Report of the Parliamentary Commissioner for Administration, 1967–68* (H.C. 54).

The Sachsenhausen case is perhaps one in which it would have been almost impossible to obtain redress, against the opposition of the Foreign Office, without the intervention of the Parliamentary Commissioner. But most of the other cases he discovered were of a fairly trivial sort that would probably have been put right departmentally regardless of the means by which they had come to light. The main achievement of the Commissioner has been to reassure the informed public that the administrative machine was not characterized (as Mr Crossman had darkly hinted in 1966) by bias, neglect, inattention, perversity and turpitude.

As for its effects on Ministerial responsibility, there is not much risk that the Commissioner's direct line to Parliament will by-pass the Minister so long as he resolutely avoids criticism of policy and discretionary decisions that are taken in a proper way with due regard to the evidence. Indirectly, indeed, the Commissioner's work should make the Minister's task easier by exposing irregularities that the Minister himself would want to put right and by adding another element to the apparatus of sanctions that obliges administrators to bear in mind in all their actions how they will look if exposed to parliamentary scrutiny. This may have been the thought in Mr Crossman's mind when he suggested that the Parliamentary Commissioner and the Select Committee 'would in due course evolve a doctrine of ministerial accountability that took account of the real relations between the political head of a department and the civil servants under him'.[1]

PARLIAMENTARY COMMITTEES

Mr Crossman had introduced the office of the Parliamentary Commissioner as 'a potent instrument for the protection of the good name of the Civil Service, *the restoration of parliamentary authority* and the redress of individual grievances'.[2] The decision to make the new office available only through Members of Parliament made it a logical extension of their traditional job of securing redress of grievance. (Compare the New Zealand version, established in 1962, which allows any citizen to approach the Commissioner direct on payment of a £1 fee.) The establishment of a Select Committee on the Parliamentary Commissioner for Administration (to give it its

---

[1] *H.C. Debs.*, vol. 738 (14 December 1966) col. 489.
[2] *H.C. Debs.*, vol. 734 (18 October 1966) col. 61 (my italics).

full title) may be expected to consolidate the link with Parliament and to involve some backbenchers more closely in problems of administration.

The move was well-timed. An informal group of academics and House of Commons officials calling themselves the Study of Parliament Group had been looking at ways of bridging the gap that separated backbenchers from the mainstream of government administration. The young and enthusiastic new Members elected in 1964 and 1966 were anxious to have something to do and eagerly adopted one of the main proposals of the Group, that Parliament should establish a number of specialist committees to review particular blocks of administrative work.

There are three well-established committees through which Members of Parliament are able to interrogate civil servants and enquire into details of administration. They are the Public Accounts Committee, the Estimates Committee and the Select Committee for Nationalized Industries. The Public Accounts Committee is the traditional watchdog of public money. It considers reports from the Comptroller and Auditor General on irregular and unusual features of government expenditure and makes recommendations after examining papers and witnesses if it chooses to do so. The scope of its work is indicated by a debate on three P.A.C. reports towards the end of 1967.[1] This covered: (a) the recommendation, accepted by the Government, that the books of universities and the University Grants Committee should be open to inspection by the Comptroller and Auditor General;[2] fears that Bristol-Siddeley Engines Ltd. had been allowed to make excessive profits on a defence contract; (c) criticisms of expenditure on new headquarters for the Metropolitan Police which had cost more than four times the estimate; (d) a number of minor questions about particular items of expenditure.

Whereas the P.A.C. looks at expenditure already incurred, the Estimates Committee has to 'examine and report' on matters connected with a particular head of estimates. Its influential report on recruitment to the civil service which led to the Fulton investigation was theoretically based on an examination of the estimates of the Civil Service Commission. From a shaky start after the war,

[1] *H.C. Debs.*, vol. 754 (13 November 1967) cols. 36–165.
[2] Committee of Public Accounts 1966–67, Special Report, *Parliament and the Control of University Expenditure* (H.C. 290). In considering this subject the Committee took the unprecedented step of hearing evidence from university witnesses who were not civil servants.

the Estimates Committee has become an important source of information and ideas about the administration of government departments.[1]

The Select Committee on Nationalized Industries is a more recent addition. It was set up in 1956 to give Members some means of informing themselves about the affairs of public industries whose day-to-day management was not subject to the normal processes of parliamentary scrutiny.[2] From examining each industry in turn it has recently moved on to more general questions, such as the use Ministers make of their powers to give directions and the case for establishing a separate Ministry for Nationalized Industry.[3]

Shortly before the 1964 election, Mr Harold Wilson outlined his own ideas about consitutional reform, which included a larger place for backbench M.P.s in the formation of policy and the development of more all-party committees, not only to investigate but also to draft non-controversial social legislation.[4] After the election, the Select Committee on Procedure invited evidence from academic members of the Study of Parliament Group[5] and recommended that the Estimates Committee should be replaced by a Select Committee with wider powers 'to examine how the departments of State carry out their responsibilities and to consider their Estimates and Reports'. The Committee would have operated mainly through specialist sub-committees covering fields like social services or defence.[6] But the Leader of the House (then Mr Herbert Bowden) felt that such a committee was bound to get involved in political discussion and would impinge an the responsibility of Ministers to the House of Commons as a whole.[7] The Estimates Committee's terms of reference remained unchanged. But it could, and for a time did, divide into sub-committees covering fields of activity – technological and scientific affairs, defence and overseas affairs, economic affairs,

---

[1] The work of the Estimates Committee is discussed very fully, with a list of subjects covered since the war and notes on the more important enquiries, in N. Johnson, *Parliament and Administration; The Estimates Committee 1945–65* (London, 1966).

[2] For a critical account see D. Coombes, *The Member of Parliament and the Administration. The Case of the Select Committee on Nationalized Industries* (London, 1966).

[3] *Select Committee on Nationalized Industries 1967–68.* 'Ministerial Control of the Nationalized Industries' (H.C. 371-I).

[4] Speech at Stowmarket, Suffolk, 3 July 1964.

[5] Professor P. A. Bromhead, Professor A. H. Hanson and Professor H. V. Wiseman.

[6] *Select Committee on Procedure, Fourth Report 1964–65* (H.C. 305).

[7] *H.C. Debs.*, vol. 718 (27 October 1965) cols. 182–5.

building and natural resources, and social affairs. It was at one time thought that the Committee might need to increase its membership to man all these sub-committees. Instead, the experiment was soon abandoned and in 1967 its membership was in fact cut from 43 to 36. In the meantime, however, there had been other developments.

After his party's position in the House of Commons had been strengthened by the 1966 election Mr Wilson again (but this time more cautiously) raised the possibility of setting up one or two all-party committees. He excluded foreign affairs and defence and stipulated that they should not develop into imitations of the powerful Congressional Committees in the United States.[1] With enthusiastic encouragement from the new Leader of the House, Mr Crossman, the Select Committee on Procedure again deliberated and recommended that two new Select Committees should be set up, one to deal with a subject, science and technology, and the other to cover a single department, the Ministry of Agriculture and Fisheries. This time the proposals were accepted. Mr Crossman made a memorable speech about the changing relations between Parliament and the executive. It was not possible to hark back to ancient days. But the transfer of power to the executive had gone too far; a strong healthy executive was all the stronger and healthier if it was stimulated by responsible investigations and criticism.[2]

For the next few months, it seemed as if all the traditional objections about strong parliamentary committees encroaching on the executive had been forgotten. No serious attempt was made to keep them away from 'policy' issues. Ministers announced their willingness to give evidence in person, not only to the new Committees but to the older Committee on Nationalized Industries as well.[3] It was agreed that the Committees could take evidence in public. By April 1967 a delighted press was reporting evidence from the chairmen of the National Coal Board and the Electricity Council about the 'arm-twisting' tactics of Ministers of Power and the incoherence of their policies.[4] The press also quoted a benign Mr Crossman telling the Nationalized Industries Committee that he would welcome the extension of its activities to the Bank of England,

[1] *H.C. Debs.*, vol. 727 (21 April 1966) cols. 75–9.
[2] *H.C. Debs.*, vol. 738 (14 December 1966) cols. 477–94.
[3] *The Times* (London) 28 March 1967. It was later announced (24 June 1967) that a list of points was being prepared on which Ministers need not answer questions, e.g. on security grounds; but details never became available.
[4] Ibid., 7 and 17 April 1967.

the B.B.C., the Independent Television Authority and the Industrial Reorganization Corporation, among others (a suggestion which bore fruit in a special report in July 1968 but was accepted by the Government only in part); and that it might be a good idea to have a Select Committee on private industry, with powers to summon businessmen to justify their actions.[1] Early in 1968 a committee on education and science was set up; within a few weeks it had examined the role of H.M. Inspectors of Schools and decided to study the troubled field of staff-student relations in universities and colleges. Yet another new committee had as its remit race relations and immigration.

But all was not sweetness and light. The Agricultural Committee turned out to be troublesome and was disbanded at the end of February 1969. This Committee decided that its first task should be to look at the quality of the Ministry of Agriculture's assessment of the effect on agriculture if Britain joined the Common Market. This raised questions, previously regarded as confidential, about the basis on which a Minister reached decisions. Indeed, as J. P. Mackintosh (himself a political scientist interested in parliamentary reform and a member of the Committee) has made clear, such was the main purpose of some of its members.[2] Moreover, the Committee came into conflict with the Foreign Office over its wish to go to Brussels to see if the official picture was correct and to see in detail why the Foreign Office had declined to approve an extra assistant for the agricultural attaché to the British delegation there. The Foreign Office refused to grant the second request but eventually agreed to a meeting in Brussels on a basis that did not compromise official negotiations. The Committee's report on all this did not, in the end, make major criticisms, but it claimed (probably rightly) that it had succeeded in getting information published about the Common Market that would not normally have been available.[3]

[1] *The Times* (London) 13 July 1967. See also H.C. 298, 1967–68, and H.C. 142, 1968–69.

[2] J. P. Mackintosh 'Failure of a Reform', *New Society*, vol. 12 (28 November 1968) p. 791.

[3] *Report from the Select Committee on Agriculture 1966–67* (H.C. 378–XVII) 'British Agriculture, Fisheries and Food and the European Economic Community'. A letter from Mr Crossman explaining the difficulties about meeting the Committee's wishes is included in the official reply to criticisms in the Report. Cmnd. 3479 (1967). See also *Special Report from the Select Committee on Agriculture 1968–69* (H.C. 138) which is devoted to the practical difficulties experienced by the Committee and the issues of principle which they raise.

According to Mackintosh, the Government reappointed the Committee in 1967 only after considerable delay and after 'press-ganging' nine new members to restrain the original sixteen. The Committee then turned its attention to the equally difficult subject of import replacement and had not completed its work when the Government peremptorily ordered it to close down. After a struggle an extension was granted which allowed the review to be completed.

The original hope had been that two new committees would be appointed each year until all the main departments were covered. But by November 1967 Mr Crossman was arguing that committees should spend one session on a department and then move on. This, of course, defeated the original object of allowing a group of M.P.s to become specialists in the affairs of a particular department. The Agriculture Committee was replaced by one on the Scottish Office and the Education and Science Committee by one on overseas aid.[1] It seemed likely that a committee on the most difficult area of all – defence planning and administration – would be the next to be established in the 1969–70 session.

The Science and Technology Committee was more successful. Its chairman was a chartered engineer, chairman of the Parliamentary and Scientific Committee and an experienced member of the Nationalized Industries Committee. Nearly all the original eight Labour, five Conservative and one Liberal members had some previous connection with science or technology. It was authorized 'to consider science and technology and to report thereon'. Its first report dealt in great detail with the nuclear reactor programme and was welcomed by the Minister of Technology in the debate which eventually followed – although the debate seems to have been sparsely attended except by Ministers and members of the Committee. The members seem to have been less than enthusiastic about a suggestion from the Government that they should study the problem of coastal pollution after the damage caused by the stranding of the giant tanker 'Torrey Canyon'. This additional remit made it necessary to expand the Committee from fourteen to seventeen members.[2]

One reason for the partial failure of the experiment with special-

[1] J. P. Mackintosh, 'Dwindling Hopes of Common Reform', *The Times*, 13 March 1969.

[2] The early work of the Science and Technology Committee is assessed by R. Williams, 'The Select Committee on Science and Technology: the First Round', *Public Administration*, vol. 46 (1968) p. 299.

ized parliamentary committees was mounting pressure on Members of Parliament, which became acute in mid-1968. At that time experiments with morning sittings and similar devices to expedite government business were also at their height and Members found that they could not meet all the demands made on them.[1] Also, the number willing to spend time on relatively unspectacular details of administration in any particular field is likely to be fairly small. Most of the work of the Estimates Committee, for example, is done by sub-committees attended by as few as three members. But a more important reason was the hardening attitude of the Government after the first few months of the experiment.

There was a generally favourable response to the work of the Science and Technology Committee in contrast with the difficulties placed in the way of the Agriculture Committee. These must have been the result of Ministerial decision; no civil servant would take it on his own authority to thwart a parliamentary committee. The Science Committee did not hesitate to tackle questions of policy, but nuclear reactor programmes, oil pollution or even the role of defence research establishments, which was the subject-matter of this Committee's third investigation, are fairly technical matters, outside the mainstream of party politics. They are also relatively self-contained. Similarly, revelations from the Nationalized Industries Committee about Ministerial control of British European Airways are important and receive due prominence in the business sections of the quality press, but they do not raise clouds of parliamentary dust. By contrast, the effect on food prices of joining the Common Market is of considerable political interest. If the Agriculture Committee had discovered weaknesses in the machinery for briefing the Minister of Agriculture it would have been easy for opponents of the Government to make political capital out of it. This sort of investigation poses a much more realistic threat to the doctrine that the Minister is personally accountable to Parliament. It also strikes at the doctrine of collective responsibility, since the views of the Minister of Agriculture may not coincide with the policy that finally emerges from the Cabinet. This seems to have been in Mr Wilson's mind when he told Norman Hunt:

They are supposed to be looking at the administration of a department. I think they have taken the bit between their teeth

[1] See Mr Wilson's statement in *H.C. Debs.*, vol. 762 (11 April 1968) col. 1587, about the difficulty of filling positions.

a little . . . The Committee have decided to interpret their terms of reference as involving an examination of one part of the problem of deciding whether you go into Europe. They are not going to decide the policy. I don't think they wanted to decide the policy, because they know that the policy must be decided on much broader grounds than agriculture alone, however important agriculture may be.[1]

In the United States, specialist committees of Congress are deeply involved in policy. They enjoy status and influence that is hardly conceivable in a parliamentary system. The U.S. Congressman hopes to become chairman of an influential committee, whereas the British Member of Parliament hopes for Ministerial office. But even in the United States the continuous involvement of committees in policy-making seems to have blurred the concept of executive responsibility. In Britain, it is interesting to note that while Mr Wilson at one time envisaged parliamentary 'pre-legislation' committees being chaired by Ministers and thus brought firmly within the government structure, the oldest committee of all – the Public Accounts Committee, set up to assist Parliament to keep an eye on the way Ministers of the Crown spend voted moneys – is chaired by a member of the Opposition. It seems more natural for backbench committees to harry the administration than to try to supplant it.

The main achievement of the new committees has been the publication of papers and evidence submitted to them, rather than in their specific recommendations. The growing practice of holding public sessions has resulted in good press coverage and in more informed public discussion of rather complicated issues. At the same time members of the committees have been able to familiarize themselves with particular topics and to study them more intensively than is possible in a full-scale parliamentary debate. They have been helped by the new practice of appointing experts to assist in organizing their enquiries and assessing evidence.[2] There is, however, a risk of

[1] 'The Prime Minister on the Machinery of Government', *The Listener*, vol. LXXVII (13 April 1967) p. 481.

[2] The Science and Technology Committee sought assistance from Professor Eley, Professor of Physical Science at Nottingham University, for its study of oil pollution, and from Mr C. Harlow of P.E.P. and Mr W. R. Thomas, Chief Scientist of Elliott Automation, on defence research and development. The Nationalized Industries Committee employed Professor Maurice Peston, Professor of Economics at Queen Mary College, to assist its enquiry into Ministerial control. The Estimates Committee appointed Professor Graham Pyatt, of the University of Warwick, for its study of Government Statistical Services (*Fourth Report, 1966–67*, H.C. 246).

overloading both the parliamentary and the administrative machines with the preparation and assimilation of additional material.
The printed evidence now published along with most reports
frequently runs to three or four hundred pages in the close-printed
style favoured by H.M. Stationery Office. It is of course inevitable
that growth in government activity should be accompanied by the
production of more material for control purposes. New techniques
may be needed and existing institutions may need to be modified in
order to handle it and keep it within manageable limits.

ADMINISTRATIVE IMPLICATIONS

The most immediate effect of these developments is to create more
work. Papers for a committee have to be prepared and witnesses
have to be briefed. Both have to be done with some care, in the
knowledge that written and oral evidence will be published.
Parliamentary investigations are not likely to be so demanding as
the Fulton Committee, for which the Treasury and the Civil
Service Commission prepared over a thousand pages of text and
statistics, all of which was published, but they can still involve a
substantial amount of work. Thus the Committee on Race Relations
started its work by calling for evidence from the Home Office, the
Department of Education and Science, the Department of Employment and Productivity, the Department of Health and Social
Security, the Ministry of Housing and Local Government, the Race
Relations Board and the Community Relations Commission.[1]

Time and effort are also needed to deal with complaints referred
to the Parliamentary Commissioner for Administration, whose own
staff numbers about sixty. The Commissioner has described in detail
his method of conducting investigations.[2] His first step, after confirming that a complaint is not clearly outside his jurisdiction, is to
ask the Permanent Secretary of the department concerned for
comment, which usually contains 'a full statement of the facts known
to the department and of the department's view of the case, often
with supporting evidence'. Even in cases that are taken no further,
there is a good deal of work involved in assembling details of a
perhaps complicated history going back a year or more. But in

[1] *Special Report from the Select Committee on Race Relations and Immigration 1968–69*
(H.C. 62).
[2] *Fourth Report of the Parliamentary Commissioner for Administration 1967–68*, pars.
12–15.

most cases this is followed by an examination of departmental files, discussion with the officials concerned, and discussion of a 'results' report with the Permanent Secretary, who has to consider at that stage whether to advise the Minister to prohibit the publication of any information contained in the report. Any official mentioned in the original complaint must also be given the opportunity to comment. Nor need that be the end of the matter, since M.P.s can still question the Minister about the Commissioner's findings. Since the complaint may concern advice given informally or on the telephone (a characteristic of many cases in Social Security or Inland Revenue) it may be difficult to recall incidents of which there is no record. A secondary effect of the investigations may therefore be to make departments keep more detailed records of trivial occurrences against the possibility of an inquisition by the Commissioner.

Detailed record-keeping is already a feature of public departments and the new requirements are additional to the work involved in dealing with M.P.s' correspondence, material for parliamentary debates (always painstakingly voluminous, since it covers all points that Members are thought likely to raise, and largely consigned, unused, to oblivion after the debate) and answers to questions in the House. In the first month of the 1965–6 session 756 questions were asked – an increase of 50 per cent on the previous average. Oral questions were costing, on average, £10 10s. 11d. to answer and written questions £7. 11s. 4d. in the summer of 1965. The cost of *finding out* the cost was over £2,000 in the Treasury alone. Kingdom has recalled the saying:

> A civil servant's time divides into three parts: doing his own work, interfering with other people's work, and saying what he is doing . . . The last is a very necessary part of democracy but one feels it is on the increase and it can seem to take up a lot more than a third of the time . . . What happens, one wonders, if it rises to a point where there is no time for anything else – when your whole doing consists of saying what you are doing. Is it something like the curious problem of what happens in the end when two snakes start swallowing each other by the tail?[1]

The first two years' work of the Parliamentary Commissioner suggests that the gain in public confidence and the correction of

[1] T. D. Kingdom, 'The Confidential Advisers of Ministers', *Public Administration*, vol. 44 (1966) p. 272.

some minor injustices may have to be weighed fairly carefully against the costs in administrative time, disruption of normal work during an enquiry and possibly greater reluctance on the part of staff dealing with the public to step outside safe limits in the effort to be helpful.

The second effect of increased parliamentary scrutiny will be to focus more attention on the kind of factors that interest Parliament (consistency, impartiality, and integrity as well as the currently fashionable topics of parliamentary interest). On the whole, this will reinforce the Minister's control of his department, since he is concerned with much the same factors and is equally concerned that his department's activities should be defensible by political standards.

It may seem paradoxical that changes designed to strengthen political control of the administration should be introduced at a time when other reforms are being aimed at improving its technical quality and at giving more autonomy to the individual adminis-trator. But changes in British administration can occur only to the extent that they can be accommodated within the current frame-work of political assumptions – which means, in this country, only to the extent that they will be tolerated by Members of Parliament. Within this context, it is inevitable that arrangements to strengthen executive administration should be felt to create a need for compen-sating improvements in the machinery for political accountability.

The political framework has not altered since 1918, when the Haldane Committee said:

> It would, we think, be generally felt that any improvement in the organization of the Departments of State which was so marked as substantially to increase their efficiency should have as its correlative an increase in the power of the Legislature as the check upon the acts and proposals of the Executive.[1]

The Committee went on to commend specialist parliamentary committees, which would, they thought, by making members more informed about departmental problems, encourage officials 'to lay more stress upon constructive work in administering the services entrusted to them for the benefit of the community than upon anticipating criticism which may, in present conditions, often be

[1] *Report of the Machinery of Government Committee,* Cd. 9230 (1918) p. 14, par. 48.

based upon imperfect knowledge of the facts or the principles at issue'.[1]

[1] Ibid., p. 15, par. 54. For a useful discussion of the Fulton recommendations in their political context see W. Plowden: 'The Failure of Piecemeal Reform', *New Society*, vol. 12 (18 July 1968) p. 82. Similar points were made cogently by Nevil Johnson in his evidence to the Committee (*Fulton Report*, vol. 5, p. 946, par. 23 *et al.*). By contrast, James Robertson, whose evidence evidently carried much weight, argued that a completely fresh look needed to be taken at all our political institutions (ibid., pp. 1025–42). He was particularly doubtful about the wisdom of reforming Parliament in a way that allowed members to concentrate more of their attention on matters of detailed administration (ibid., p. 1076, par. 167 (a)).

PART TWO: Theory

VI. People and Organization

We have now outlined the main features of the British system of central administration as it is at present. Its evolution has been related to changes in the work it has been asked to do. Some parts of its task (for example some aspects of the parliamentary system of control) have hardly changed at all over the last century. Other parts have altered a great deal, and continue to alter at an increasing rate. The administrative system has to cope with many new problems in the fields of planning and management, while some of the old ones have become much more complex, particularly those of co-ordinating a growing area of government control and influence. They have not all been successfully overcome.

If the demands of the job are not being met, and cannot be altered, it may be possible to improve the organization. There has been no shortage of suggestions over the last few years. They centre on (a) the relationship between structure and function in various parts of the administrative machine and (b) such factors as recruitment and training, which are thought to influence the quality of major decisions. They would all, if adopted, alter the existing balance of forces within the system of public administration by strengthening one element in it and so causing a shift in priorities.

It is not enough for the reformist to show that the part of the task in which he is interested is not being well done and would be done better if his proposals were adopted. He must also be able to answer the objection that any gain would be cancelled by adverse effects elsewhere. If the system as a whole has failed to adapt spontaneously to meet changing demands, adaptation may have to be forced upon it. But even successful adaptation will not necessarily ensure the optimum performance of any particular job taken in isolation. Nor should it be assumed that all failures are caused by administrative deficiencies. No amount of restructuring will avoid the need for unpleasant decisions about the claims of increased personal consumption, expanding social services and overseas commitments on a limited national purse.

How can such questions be analysed? Academic students of public administration have tended to interest themselves mainly in questions about the powers of public bodies, the status of public servants, legal safeguards for the citizen and the constitutional relationship between administration and politics. They have used the methods of the historian and the constitutional lawyer and have, until recently, rather neglected the less formal aspects of administration. Public discussion of the actual workings of the machine tends, at the time of writing, to be dominated by businessmen or by economists with recent experience of Whitehall who have become interested in the administrative structure within which economic policy takes shape. Valuable though their contributions are, their experience is naturally limited to economic departments and they have tended to judge the quality of administrative machinery rather narrowly by the extent to which it produces policies oriented to economic growth or to industrial enterprise.

A more hopeful approach is to treat the problems primarily as ones of organization and to relate them to the ideas of people who have made a special study of such problems as a class. In principle, this approach has much to commend it. There is now a vast literature about organization. Much of it is American, although more British and European writers are appearing and some of them have made distinguished contributions. Many of the most important works are immediately concerned with the problems of industry. Some are by practical administrators reflecting on their own experience, but the most important contributors are engineers and the 'behavioural scientists' – sociologists and psychologists. In studying a problem it is clearly sensible to see what has been learned about similar problems elsewhere. It is also sensible, so far as it is possible to do so, to describe problems in the language and concepts that have been found useful by others, so that common elements in different situations can be identified and related to each other. Some general discussion of organization theory is a desirable preliminary to the examination in Part Three of specific problems in British public administration.[1]

---

[1] This chapter does not attempt to provide more than a very broad introduction to organization theory. There are now many comprehensive surveys of the field.

CLASSICAL THEORIES OF MANAGEMENT

A generation ago there was a wave of optimism that some of the problems of public administration would yield to scientific analysis. In 1941 the Select Committee on National Expenditure looked at the small beginnings of what is now the Treasury Organization and Methods Division. Its report complained that the years between the wars had been marked by 'almost complete failure to foster the *systematic study of organization* as applied to government depart-ments'[1] (my italics). It suggested that O & M should be the supreme arm of Treasury control and that the remit of O & M officers should cover the distribution of functions at the top of the civil service hierarchy as well as the discharge of routine business at the bottom. A few years later the theme was taken up again by the Estimates Committee. It defined the purpose of O & M as 'to secure maximum efficiency in the operation of the government's executive machinery and, *by the expert application of scientific methods to organization*, to achieve economy in cost and labour'. It also sug-gested that more attention should be paid to the higher levels of administration: 'The part played by O & M techniques and know-ledge must be that of planning the structure and machinery of government rather than that of attending to its plumbing and maintenance'[2] (my italics).

Members of the Select Committee were aware of the impact in the United States of the Brownlow Committee on Administrative Management. This expert, three-man committee had been appointed by President Roosevelt to examine the chaos of adminis-

Perhaps the best general introductions are to be found in R. Stewart, *The Reality of Management* (London, 1963) or J. Luptar, *Management and the Social Sciences* (London, 1966), both of which are by British authors, or in A. Etzioni, *Modern Organizations* (Englewood Cliffs, N.J., 1964). More comprehensive surveys, mostly American, include: J. G. March and H. A. Simon, *Organizations* (New York, 1958); A. Etzioni, *A Comparative Analysis of Complex Organizations* (Glencoe, Ill., 1961); P. B. Applewhite, *Organizational Behavior* (Englewood Cliffs, N.J., 1965); P. M. Blau and W. R. Scott, *Formal Organizations* (London, 1963); B. M. Gross, *The Managing of Organizations* (London, 1966); N. P. Mouzelis, *Organisation and Bureaucracy* (London, 1967). All these authors present their own distinctive points of view, as well as reviewing the field. Any one survey may therefore give an unbalanced picture.

[1] *16th Report of the Select Committee on National Expenditure, 1940–41* (H.C. 120) 'Organisation and Control of the Civil Service', par. 81.

[2] *5th Report of the Select Committee on Estimates 1946–47* (H.C. 143) 'Organisation and Methods and its effect on the Staffing of Government Departments', par. 49.

trative agencies created to carry out the New Deal programme. The successful implementation of many of their recommendations was hailed as a victory for analytic reasoning in a field previously dominated by politics.[1] The Committee claimed to be applying universal principles:

> The foundations of effective management, in public affairs no less than in private, are well known. They have emerged universally wherever men have worked together for some common purpose . . . Stated in simple terms, these canons of efficiency require the establishment of a responsible and effective chief executive as the centre of energy, direction and administrative management; the systematic organization of all activities in the hands of a qualified personnel under the direction of the chief executive; and to aid him in this, the establishment of appropriate managerial and staff agencies.[2]

In this it was echoing the founders of the two (rather ill-assorted) streams of what is now often termed the classical school of management theorists.

Frederick W. Taylor (1856–1915) and his followers adopted the title 'scientific management' for the critical approach to production methods which they developed and recommended. In essence their method consists of careful study and pre-planning of repetitive operations in order to find the 'one best way' of doing a job. Under names like work study, O & M, and production engineering, their techniques have provided a foundation for modern mass-production methods in the factory and in the office. Allied to the modern computer, they have developed into an impressive range of management tools for simulating and pre-programming expensive operations before taking final decisions. Critical path analysis, operational research, statistical decision theory and cost-benefit analysis all belong to the same family. They have been extensively used in public administration and need not be discussed in detail here.[3]

[1] E.g. L. Urwick and E. F. L. Brech, *The Making of Scientific Management* (London, 1957) vol. I. Similarly grandiose claims for a 'scientific' approach were made in *Papers on the Science of Administration*, edited for the Committee's use by L. Gulick and L. Urwick and published separately by the Institute of Public Administration (New York, 1937).

[2] *Report of the President's Committee on Administrative Management* (Washington, 1937) Introduction.

[3] In 1967 and 1968 the Treasury (later Civil Service Department) O & M teams saved £1·2 m. in 37 assignments. *O & M Bulletin*, vol. 24, no. 2 (May 1969), Supplement.

Taylor claimed, quite reasonably, that his methods were equally applicable in all spheres of life from government to the domestic kitchen, and that their general adoption would make great achievements possible.[1] But his 'scientific method' is relevant, whether in production or in administration, only to the selection of means for securing an agreed end. Politics (like many aspects of industrial management) is often more concerned with the choice of objective. The weaknesses of the British system of government relate mainly to the identification of problems, or to the ordering of priorities, and only incidentally to the means of carrying out decisions. Here Taylor cannot help. As Professor Mackenzie has put it, Taylor's theory is 'not the science *of* management, but science *for* management, an ambiguity neatly concealed by the phrase "scientific management"'.[2]

The other stream of thought is associated with the name of Henri Fayol (1841–1925), a successful general manager of a French mining company. Fayol attributed his success to the application of 'principles of administration'. He believed that some such principles were valid in any field and that a body of administrative theory could be developed, partly from the reflections of successful administrators, and could be taught. After retiring at the age of 77, he reviewed the organization of the French post and telegraph service and took part in an enquiry on the tobacco monopoly, attributing their deficiencies to failure to apply sound administrative principles. He also founded an early Centre for Administrative Studies in Paris.[3]

Fayol's own principles were intuitive generalizations. They are concerned with the kind of formal structure that the head of a firm should develop as an instrument of his will. There are principles concerned with the need for specialization, stability in post (to which Fayol felt political leaders gave insufficient attention), unity of command, a hierarchical chain of command, and so on. As administrative proverbs they appeal to common sense if they are

[1] F. W. Taylor, *Principles and Methods of Scientific Management* (New York, 1911) Introduction.
[2] W. J. M. Mackenzie, 'Science in the Study of Administration', *The Manchester School*, vol. 20 (1952) p. 8.
[3] H. Fayol, 'The Administrative Theory in the State' in Gulick and Urwick (eds.) *Papers on the Science of Administration*; also *General and Industrial Management* (tr. Storrs) (London, 1949). There is a general account of his work in M. B. Brodie, *Fayol on Administration* (Administrative Staff College Monograph) (London, 1967).

not examined too closely. They are very popular with management consultants who find them clinically useful, in a somewhat refined form, as a check-list of possible organizational diseases. It was essentially Fayol's principles that guided the American Brownlow Committee. But they have no real coherence. Like most proverbs, they come in contradictory pairs (for example, centralization and initiative; specialization and unity) and often fail to fit the real situation.[1] Like Taylor's methods, they are concerned with means and give no guide to the choice of ends. Consequently they offer, at best, prescriptions for abstract problems of organizational engineering without taking account of the social and political problems faced by the members of real organizations. Even in industry, the freewheeling tycoon at the head of Fayol's ideal organization probably no longer exists. He has certainly no equivalent in public administration.[2]

Some of these objections can also be made to the work of Max Weber. His writings on bureaucracy, however, have had a tremendous influence on other writers and contain important insights on the internal workings of large organizations.

BUREAUCRACY

The word 'bureaucracy' has many meanings. Some are pejorative: in *The Bureaucratic Phenomenon* Crozier is looking specifically at organizations that are too inflexible to learn from their own mistakes. To a political scientist 'bureaucracy' can mean a system of government by bureaux of officials. To a student of organizations the word refers to the structure found in modern large organizations, whether they are government departments, business firms, armies or organized religions. It is 'a continuous organization of official functions bound by rules'.[3]

[1] The most convincing empirical demonstration of their inadequacy has been a study of 100 Essex firms, some of whom had worsened their position by trying to apply principles in inappropriate circumstances. J. Woodward, *Industrial Organization: Theory and Practice* (Oxford, 1965).

[2] Crozier shows how severely rules and precedents can in practice restrict the power to give leadership and direction. The French *prefect* appears to enjoy considerable delegated power in his *département*. But his ability to provide dynamic solutions to problems is so limited that his real function becomes one of maintaining order and balance. M. Crozier, *The Bureaucratic Phenomenon* (London, 1964) ch. 8.

[3] Max Weber (tr. A. M. Henderson and T. Parsons), *The Theory of Social and Economic Organization* (Glencoe, Ill., 1947) p. 330.

The members of a bureaucracy are career officials, who are selected, controlled and as far as possible promoted according to impersonal rules. They occupy positions in which they carry out prescribed functions. The authority which they exercise (on behalf of the head of the organization) belongs to their office, not to themselves. They are expected to approach their work impersonally, regardless of their own feelings. Senior positions are filled by promotion. The security of a salary and a life career protects them from any personal consequences of their decisions, so long as they have been taken in accordance with the rules.

Such a system has many advantages beyond the obvious ones of continuity and orderliness. The clients of large (and particularly public) organizations expect fair, and therefore uniform, treatment which can best be secured by a system of centralized authority implemented according to rules. In public administration a bureaucratic form of organization is closely associated with political accountability. A new Minister inherits an organized staff of officials ready to implement his will, with no personal commitment to the policies of his predecessor. Through them his personal charisma can be widely diffused.[1] Weber thought that bureaucratic organization was the most rational means of deploying power in any setting.

The model implies that the person at the apex of the hierarchy is completely responsible for the organization and has its resources at his entire disposal, subject to any external constraints on his own authority. Since he cannot discharge this responsibility personally, he preserves certain key decisions to himself and, after deciding in broad terms how the organization will work, delegates limited discretion to his subordinates. They in turn reserve certain questions to themselves and delegate the rest, with slightly narrower terms of reference, and so on down the line. In a large organization like a government department, the model becomes intelligible only in terms of roles. It is inconceivable that a single person should decide consciously what to delegate and what to retain over the whole field of work. In practice, a new head would learn, fairly slowly, the delimitations of the role that had been evolved by his predecessors, while gradually modifying it to suit his own interests

---

[1] In Britain administrative decisions are usually attributed to the Minister personally. While no serious student of politics takes this very seriously, the man in the street has no reason to doubt the authenticity of a letter or even an advertisement which appears to have been prepared by the Minister himself.

and abilities. In the meantime, junior staff have to keep their work moving and use their discretion in dealing with new problems. In many ways their staff work defines the problems that will later be considered higher up.

Weber's model has been severely criticized, partly for its inability to accommodate the problem of change.[1] If initiative is taken within the bureaucracy, in response to changing circumstances or perhaps the self-interests of the bureaucrats, effort may be deflected from fulfilling the intentions of its head. On the other hand, if officials develop the habit of waiting for initiative to come from the top, the organization can become very inflexible. The system of rules can itself stifle initiative. An apathetic official may be tempted to take the easy course by rigidly following precedents, even when it is obvious that they are no longer appropriate. Even if he is not apathetic, he may feel that it is inappropriate or unnecessary for him to challenge the rules. Crozier identifies a 'bureaucratic personality' with the belief that any necessary change will be encompassed by the rules themselves.

The hierarchical element in a bureaucracy supplies career rewards and sanctions, since an official's superiors can grant or withhold promotion. It also provides a chain of accountability. Does it therefore lead to efficiency? In theory, it is likely that senior officials will be more proficient than subordinates who have not yet earned promotion; the most knowledgeable members of the organization are also the most powerful. But this argument is sound only if the career structure is completely closed, if the relevant techniques are of a sort that can be learned only within the organization (as in, perhaps, the administration of a defined code of law) and if the work is not too specialized for a superior to be able to draw on his own experience in guiding his juniors. There may be some corners of older government departments where such conditions apply, but they are becoming rare, as more people with special skills are brought in to the administration and the work itself becomes more 'professionalized'. Senior posts may be filled by outsiders with no direct knowledge of the work at lower levels. Junior staff may have special qualifications or experience not shared by their nominal superiors. In such circumstances too much emphasis on supervision and control may lower the efficiency with which

[1] This is a very brief summary of the argument. The question of innovation is dealt with more fully in Chapters VIII and XII below.

work is done. Most real hierarchies include fairly sharp discontinuities, with an abrupt change in character and outlook at a particular level. Posts below this level are concerned solely with the efficient performance of a defined block of work. Above it, interest shifts to the value of the activity and its relationship to others. The higher group cannot effectively supervise the lower, since it is concerned with a different type of problem.

Weber himself described his model as an 'ideal type' which would not be fully realized in any actual organization. Nevertheless, his work is valuable as an exploration of the logic of a modern large scale organization, whose members are supposed to be the impersonal instruments of another's will. In practice, of course, they never can be. And the attempt to treat them as if they were may involve unexpected side-effects.

HUMAN RELATIONS

There must be some control over the work of subordinates if a bureaucracy is not to disintegrate. Detailed day-to-day supervision may not be possible. It can often be replaced to some extent by general sanctions, or by selection and training arrangements which allow superiors to take certain skills and attitudes for granted among their staff. But there are usually some direct controls. One method of control is to keep statistics of output or other measurable aspects of performance. Another is to file periodic reports on the general qualities of individual subordinates. These systematic controls are often supplemented by intermittent control of detail, when senior officials look into the details of their subordinates' work (and judge it by their own system of values) either on a random programme of 'administrative audit' or when their interest is stimalulated by a complaint or breakdown. Some writers argue that all forms of control are intrinsically damaging to the individual, and that this one, which they style 'managemnt by crisis', is particularly wasteful and demoralizing. It leads subordinates to keep j.i.c. ('just in case') files and to cover up remediable faults in their routines in order to avoid the dislocation of an inspection.[1] The more committed staff are to their work, the more resentful they are likely to be of what they regard as uninformed external criticism.

[1] E.g. C. Argyris, in a series of books of which *Personality and Organization* (New York, 1957) is the best known.

Underlying these arguments is a belief that the demands made by bureaucratic organizations conflict with the human needs of their members. People need social and psychological rewards, like status and self-fulfilment, as well as a salary and economic security. Moreover, organizational standards differ from those of the outside world. In society at large, people are respected for their integrity, their self-reliance, their home-centredness and their ability to plan ahead on a fairly long time-scale. By contrast, a bureaucrat is expected as part of his work to carry out the instructions of others and to subordinate his own values and needs to those of the organization. His career is planned for him and he is expected to accept abrupt changes in function and status without complaint when the organization requires it.

The first important recognition that failure to take account of these conflicts might affect performance on the job came about forty years ago after a famous series of experiments in the Western Electric factory at Hawthorne, near Chicago.[1] Social psychologists began to think about factors affecting the satisfactions men obtained from work. They noted that many 'human needs' – for recognition and social esteem – were satisfied through the working group which interposed itself between the individual and the organization and conditioned his attitude to it. They suggested that managements should take account of these social aspects, and that management itself was essentially a social skill. It was thought that factors leading to high job-satisfaction – like a participative rather than authoritarian pattern of supervision – would lead to greater involvement in work and to higher output.

The original findings have proved to be naïve. Many exponents of a 'human relations' approach were excessively optimistic about the effect on productivity of involving workers more in their work. It has become clear that in some cultures workers are conditioned to expect substantial differences between their roles at home and work, and do not mind work that is intrinsically unsatisfying, so long as it is adequately paid. But meantime, the original theories have inspired a great deal of useful research about 'group dynamics', the effect of different leadership styles, motivation and attitudes to work. A fresh dimension has been added to the formal theories of

[1] F. J. Roethlisberger and W. J. Dickson, *Management and the Worker* (Cambridge, Mass., 1939). The experiments and their implications are discussed more briefly by E. Mayo, *The Social Problems of an Industrial Civilization* (London, 1949).

organization discussed earlier, and much of the new material is based on empirical research.

The original work at Hawthorne was concerned with industrial assembly workers, and much of the subsequent research has been directed at this group. But it is probable that 'human relations' factors are more important at senior levels. American studies suggest that the needs for 'self-actualization', creativity and achievement are felt most keenly by managers and professional staff.[1] At these levels, basic material needs are not so pressing, but work as such occupies a more important part of life. Social and geographical mobility weaken the claims of other ties and, for people like senior civil servants, long hours of duty and commuting reduce the opportunities for social contacts outside the work place. In large organizations, where authority is centralized, postings are frequent, and it is seldom possible to take a decision without impinging on the discretion of colleagues, even those near the top are likely to complain about the lack of autonomy and achievement.

In general, the 'human relations' approach has failed because research has shown that human beings are readier to adapt themselves to organizational roles than seems likely on *a priori* grounds. But this does not mean that they acquiesce in all the organization's demands. Explicitly or implicitly, they bargain with the organization. Working groups fix a price for accepting tighter controls and adopting better methods. The price may be too high to be met without modifying the original objectives and the result is a compromise between what the organization wants and what its members want. To take an example from higher levels in the professional civil service, it may not be possible to obtain the services of a prominent architect unless he is given a chance to do some building himself, nor to recruit scientists unless they are given facilities for research that is not strictly necessary. The human relations school forced organization theorists to recognize the importance of private and group objectives. But more recently interest has shifted away from the desirability of reconciling these goals with the needs of the organization to the process of bargaining through which modifications are made on both sides.[2]

[1] The research is summarized in Applewhite, *Organizational Behavior*, ch. 2.

[2] The effects of bargaining within the organization are explored by R. M. Cyert and J. G. March, *A Behavioral Theory of the Firm* (Englewood Cliffs, N.J., 1963), and by M. Crozier, *The Bureaucratic Phenomenon* (London, 1964). Crozier's work is

GENERAL THEORIES OF ORGANIZATION

Most of the early theories were incomplete. Some treated administration as a technological system geared to efficiency; others
regarded it as a social process, in which morale may be as important
as the attainment of objectives; others, to be discussed in the next
chapter, described it as a system for making decisions and formulating policy. Much effort has gone into modifying and improving the
original concepts.[1] Several writers have also tried to integrate all
the approaches into a general theory of organization.

All of them abandon the idea of an organization as a passive
instrument serving ends determined for it from outside. It is a
semi-autonomous system which develops goals of its own. One
goal which all organizations acquire is the desire to survive: there
are, in Simon's phrase, 'conservation' objectives as well as 'performance' objectives.[2] Another is the need to maintain some kind
of equilibrium between the requirements of the organization and
the personal objectives of its members. New goals, and new rules,
emerge within the organization in the process of bargaining with its
members and also allow it to survive in a changing environment.
Very often the goals are mutually inconsistent. Even those imposed
on it from outside may be irreconcilable, in the sense that conflicts
between objectives cannot be resolved by appealing to some over-
riding principle. It is not, therefore, realistic to assess organizations
solely by their effectiveness in achieving particular goals. The real
challenge is not to secure one goal at the expense of others but to

particularly interesting because his field work was carried out in French public
organizations. He concludes, in opposition to the traditional human relations
school, that many employees deliberately try to avoid a high level of commitment.
They train themselves both to give less and to expect less in the working part of
their lives. A well developed bureaucratic system offers a not bad combination of
personal independence and security to people who choose to accept it, at the cost
of an unsatisfying and (in terms of achievement) 'unsuccessful' career. In bargaining, their representatives do not press for more rewarding work; instead they aim
at rules that limit their commitment and protect them from arbitrary demands.
(See Crozier, pp. 203–8.)

[1] For example, Pugh and his associates at Aston in Birmingham have shown
empirically that the characteristics of a Weberian bureaucracy are not mutually
interdependent. Centralized decision-making and the extensive use of standard
rules are not necessarily found in the same organizations. (D. S. Pugh, *et al.*,
'Dimensions of Organization Structure', *Administrative Science Quarterly*, vol. 13
(1958) pp. 65–105).

[2] H. A. Simon, *Administrative Behavior* (2nd edn.) (New York, 1957) pp. 117–18.

achieve and maintain some kind of practicable balance among them. An administrative organization is a self-sustaining social system which has important metabolic and adaptive functions as well as goal-centred ones. Argyris, for example, defines an organization as 'an organic interrelatedness of parts' which has three 'core activities': (a) achieving particular objectives; (b) maintaining itself internally; (c) adapting to the external environment.[1]

From the Labor and Management Center at Yale, E. Wight Bakke offers a wordy but comprehensive definition of such a system:

> A social organization is a continuing system of differentiated and co-ordinated human activities utilizing, transforming and welding together a specific set of human, material, capital, ideational and natural resources into a unique problem-solving whole engaged in satisfying particular human needs in inter-action with other systems of human activities and resources in its environment.[2]

Each word is carefully chosen and the rest of Bakke's paper is a detailed spelling out of the various concepts, all of which are in Bakke's view essential to the functioning of the system. They include the basic resources the organization employs, such as personnel, materials and ideas. They also include the organization's essential activities, for example: the central core of work flow activities; perpetuation activities, covering the supply of materials and the renewal of personnel; the maintenance of internal controls; 'homeo-static' activities which keep the whole organization in 'an evolving state of dynamic equilibrium'.

The system is not completely autonomous. It is interacting with other systems in the environment and constantly needs to adjust its relationship to them. Moreover, changes in any part of the system have repercussions in other parts. For example, changes in the control system may affect the organization's ability to recruit staff and ultimately its capacity to cope with its work.

Stated in this summary form, these theories appear somewhat arid. The persistent reader who penetrates the rather formidable

[1] C. Argyris, *Integrating the Individual and the Organization* (New York, 1964) p. 17. The 'system' approach to organization is discussed by A. Etzioni in 'Two Approaches to Organizational Analysis', *Administrative Science Quarterly*, vol. 5 (1960) p. 257.
[2] E. W. Bakke, 'Concept of the Social Organization' in Mason Haire (ed.) *Modern Organization Theory* (New York, 1959).

jargon in which they are expressed will find many ideas that increase his insight. He is likely to be both impressed at the efforts that have been made to knit various researches and concepts into a single theory and at the same time disappointed at the results. Bakke's elements, for instance, are little more than a list of all the features and processes that an organization is likely to encompass, with the additional statement that they are all interconnected. What is impressive is the sheer comprehensiveness of his list and its value as a reminder to practical administrators of points to which they need to pay attention. A study of any of these models provides a useful reminder that organizational problems have a background and potential repercussions which make it difficult to treat them in isolation.

STATUS OF ORGANIZATION THEORY

In the eyes of practical administrators, writers on organization theory have sometimes spoiled their own case by trying to arrive from first principles at universal laws which apply not only to any conceivable organization, but also to any 'system' from an atom to a galaxy, embracing cells, biological organisms, telephone networks, formal and informal organizations and whole societies on the way.[1] In the process, they have often discovered rich veins of analogy. Some writers have found biological and ecological concepts helpful in describing problems of organizational growth – Vickers uses biological analogies in discussing 'cancerous' growth to a point at which powers of co-ordination begin to fail.[2] Others have applied engineering concepts, like that of 'channel overload' in telecommunications, to the communication system of organizations. But the use of analogy, whose limitations are recognized, is one thing. The attempt to find universally valid laws for all systems is another. The concepts of the general systems theorists are necessarily intuitive and may be either so general as to be vacuuous or, like any other analogy that is pushed too far, positively misleading.[3]

[1] The most far-ranging application of systems theory to political organization is D. Easton, *The Political System* (New York, 1953) and *A Framework for Political Analysis* (Englewood Cliffs, N.J., 1965).

[2] Sir Geoffrey Vickers, *The Art of Judgment: A Study of Policy Making* (London, 1965) pp. 141–2.

[3] There is a useful and fairly optimistic discussion of this topic in W. J. M. Mackenzie, *Social Science and Politics* (London, 1967) ch. 8.

Even within the field of organizations, it is possible to doubt whether statements of any value can be made that will apply equally to organizations as diverse as 'a Soviet *kolkhoz*, General Motors, the British Medical Association, the Roman Catholic Church, a handful of grocery stores in Iceland, the University of Rome, a Japanese shipping line, a Swiss mountain hotel, the Police Department of a Swedish town, or a government department in the Sudan'.[1] It may be useful to start by distinguishing what Mouzelis calls 'conceptual framework' and 'content' theory.[2] The former is concerned with the conceptual tools of analysis; it provides a common framework through which empirical observations can be related to one another and 'constitutes a more or less useful guide which tells the researcher how to look at organizational reality and what to look for'.[3] By contrast, 'content' theory is concerned with sets of hypotheses about particular problems of organization. Unless the framework concepts can be made reasonably unambiguous and applied on a fairly general scale it is difficult to see how there can be any meaningful discussion of organizations at all. But this does not mean that it is also possible to arrive at 'content' theories that are universally valid. There is no reason to suppose that a statement about the relationship between the control system and the efficiency of General Motors will also be true of a government department in the Sudan, without regard to differences in purpose, technology or cultural setting.

It is probably fair to claim that framework theory has developed at least to the point at which there is a common language for describing problems that occur in very different sorts of organizations – like the relationship between hierarchical control and specialization, or the effect of professionalism on innovation. Developments in theory are also helping to link the study of organizational problems to general developments in the social sciences, particularly sociology, social psychology and political science, to the enrichment of both sides. Moreover, the attempts of Bakke and others to develop unifying concepts have made it easier for students of particular organizations to avoid over-simplification and to keep in mind the idea that an administrative organization is a social system whose parts are so

[1] W. A. Robson, 'The Managing of Organizations', *Public Administration*, vol. 44 (1966) p. 276.
[2] N. P. Mouzelis, *Bureaucracy and Organisation*, p. 178.
[3] Ibid., p. 3.

interconnected that changes in one part have repercussions, favourable or unfavourable, in others. For example, the introduction of a new technology, or the establishment of a new research department, involves strains and political threats to existing members of an organization. If they are not recognized, the general loss in morale and efficiency (particularly at the higher levels) may outweigh the advantages to be gained from the innovation.

> The problem of relating organizations effectively and stably to the environments in which they operate is one of trying to balance the economic, technological and socio-psychological advantages. The hypothesis proposed is that to optimize any one of these elements does not necessarily result in a set of conditions optimal for the system as a whole. To strive for maximum technical advantage and economic reward might well create social and psychological havoc, which in turn jeopardizes economic goals. Similarly, to attempt to create high job satisfaction might adversely affect the gain to be had from technological efficiency and so on.[1]

The position in content theory is less satisfactory. There is a vast literature of conflicting research results. The organization theorist has to be careful not to make general statements about leadership and inter-group conflict by extrapolating from the results of experiments among ten-year-old schoolboys. He cannot assume that clerical workers in Paris or Newcastle will respond to the same incentives in 1970 as telephone assemblers in Chicago in the 1920s. Too many generalizations have already been proved to hold only for a particular social group in a particular cultural and economic environment. Some well-entrenched theories are not as well supported as their proponents imply. For example, many of the 'laboratory' experiments on group behaviour and on problem-solving have been conducted in rather artificial conditions with students from one or other of half a dozen United States universities. In real organizations things might happen differently.

But this is merely to say that more research is needed on particular problems. The ideal procedure is analogous to that of natural science. The researcher should take a proposition, deduce what should follow from it if it were true, and test it in conditions where the relevant variables can be isolated. When this procedure has

[1] Lupton, *Management and the Social Sciences*, p. 44.

been taken far enough it should be possible to make fairly confident predictions about the effect on human behaviour of adopting a particular organizational form in specified circumstances.

The concepts of administration are simply systematic ways of thinking about the organization of human work and purpose. As principles they remain abstract and as such they are useful tools of exposition and analysis. But these abstract principles take on operational meaning only when they are applied to concrete organizational situations at a particular time in a particular environment. And then the cloth of principles must be cut to fit the form and personality of the organization being examined.[1]

Empirical research is needed to discover at what points, for example, structural changes involving additional stress for senior officials cease to pay off. Some statements cannot be assumed to apply in public organizations, simply because they have never been put to the test, but there are plenty of hypotheses that have been tried out elsewhere.

One of the achievements of organizational research in the last decade has been to offer suggestions about the circumstances in which a particular type of substantive theory is likely to be useful. One aspect of this is Miss Woodward's discovery that different principles seem to apply in industries using different technologies.[2] Another is the critique of bureaucratic structure by Thompson and Tuden, who suggest that a strictly bureaucratic form of organization is appropriate only when there is reasonable consensus about what needs doing and also about how to do it; if there is uncertainty about either means or ends, so that the decisions to be taken are not just computational, some other form of organization is needed. (More specifically, if the objective is clear but there is uncertainty about means, the best solution is likely to emerge from the collective judgement of qualified experts. If the dispute is about objectives, a decision strategy based on the sort of compromise reached in representative assemblies is most appropriate.[3]) Although their paper is theoretical and needs refinement in detail, it is now supported by a

[1] W. S. Sayre, 'Principles of Administration', *Hospitals* (Journal of American Hospital Association) 16 January 1956.

[2] J. Woodward, *Industrial Organization: Theory and Practice*.

[3] J. D. Thompson and A. Tuden 'Strategies, Structures and Processes of Administrative Decision' in J. D. Thompson *et al.* (eds.) *Comparative Studies in Administration* (Pittsburgh, 1959).

good deal of empirical material about the relative strengths and weaknesses of highly structured organizations, including the research by Burns and Stalker on innovation in the electronics industry.[1] More studies of this sort are needed.

In the meantime, here are three examples of the sort of statements about people and organizations that have been tested in various settings and seem likely to prove useful to the student of public organization. The first two are 'framework' theories which generate substantive hypotheses when applied to concrete situations. The third has both 'framework' and 'content' elements.

1. Any method of organizing work generates a social sub-system, imposing its own norms and pressures on members, which may or may not help to achieve the primary purpose of the organization.

2. Decisions are also affected by social structure. The outcome of a discussion is different when some members of the group are hierarchically senior to others; a group reaches different decisions from individuals acting independently.

3. A system of organization that is highly structured and specialized is economical to operate in the short term, but likely to prove difficult to adapt if circumstances change.

These ideas will be used later in examining particular problems of public administration. First, however, it is necessary to develop more fully an important branch of organization theory dealing with decision-making. That comes in the next chapter, leaving to Chapter VIII the question whether any special feature of public organizations makes it unlikely that findings from elsewhere will be relevant to them.

[1] T. Burns and G. M. Stalker, *The Management of Innovation* (2nd ed.) (London, 1966).

VII. Decisions

The most characteristic activity of a government department is reaching decisions; at senior levels, there may be no other output. 'Decisions' in the sense of grand strategic determinations of policy are, of course, infrequent and elusive. But decisions of another sort are being made all the time – whether to consult a committee, how to time a memorandum, what advice to give the Minister, how to deal with a particular case. There are equivalents to these at managerial levels in most organizations. Administration, indeed, is sometimes defined as a problem-solving and enabling process.

Theories about decisions can be divided into two groups. One is concerned with the way decisions ought to be made, the other with the way they are in fact made.

NORMATIVE THEORY

Statistical decision theories are about the way a completely rational decision-maker would analyse a problem and arrive at the best possible solution, given the circumstances and the information at his disposal. The usual problem is to select the strategy which gives the greatest possible chance of maximizing a specified value, like profit. Often this means estimating probabilities. The calculations can become very complicated if the number of factors and the range of uncertainties are increased to approximate to a real-life situation. In games theory, the complication of playing against a calculating opponent is added. In the theory of teams, the object is to find the 'best' decision rules for a number of players, none of whom has complete information. All these branches share an essentially computational approach to decision-making. There is assumed to be a highly structured problem-situation, in which all relevant information is known or knowable and the results of adopting any strategy can, perhaps with difficulty, be expressed mathematically.[1]

[1] There is a useful discussion of this type of theory and its relevance to organization structure, with particular reference to the theory of teams, by J. Marshak,

This approach has many uses. It can clarify the general logic of a problem and accustom decision-makers to look out for aspects that can be quantified. It is now taught to civil servants in the Centre for Administrative Studies.[1] Problems of this type can also be given to groups in 'laboratory' conditions to ascertain the effects of different incentives, working conditions and social factors on the speed and accuracy of their solutions.

But it also has distinct limitations. Real-life decisions are seldom like this. In the first place, the values to be realized are not usually set out clearly and distinctly. Sometimes implicit objectives emerge only in the process of aiming at something else. When they are clear, they often conflict. Consider the complex of considerations facing a civil servant who is asked for advice on the future of a statutory service, employing large numbers of people, which was established with popular support under the party now in opposition to meet a need that has apparently declined in importance in the meantime. If he were to approach this 'rationally' he would have to place relative weights on existing commitments to staff and clients, the financial requirements of some (probably unknown) other service and the risk of political embarrassment for the Minister if a popular service is abandoned. It is not just that it is difficult to establish these values – there is no unique way of combining them.

Secondly, it is not often in fact that the individual decision-maker is able to take a comprehensive view of a whole problem. In real life what at first sight appears to be a deliberate decision is apt to turn out to be the formal culmination of a slow process of commitment over a period of time, in which the range of possibilities has gradually been narrowed as different members of the organization contribute to it in their turn. Decisions can not often be attributed to one person, or even to a group of people consciously acting together at one time.

A third, and most damaging limitation is that most organizations would be paralysed if even a small proportion of decisions had to

'Efficient and Viable Organizational Forms' in Mason Haire (ed.), *Modern Organization Theory* (New York, 1959). The paper in the same volume by A. Rapoport entitled 'The Logical Task as a Research Tool in Organization Theory' is also relevant.

[1] 'The primary objectives are to develop an understanding of the contribution to decision making in the public service of techniques based on mathematics, statistics and economics, together with an appreciation of the role of the present and the next generation of computers in this field of management.' H.M. Treasury, *Civil Service Training 1966–67*, 1968, par. 27.

await the outcome of such a process. Decisions often have to be taken in a hurry. Only the really important ones justify the expense and delay of setting up a computer programme to analyse them. An essential part of 'effective' decision-making involves the use of incomplete data.

DESCRIPTIVE THEORY

If we are looking for a more generally helpful approach to decisions, it is fruitful to turn from normative theories to theories which try to explain how decisions are actually reached in real-life situations:

> The role of decision-making in behavioral science is to describe how people make decisions under conditions of imperfect information – that is, where complete information as to the present state of affairs, possible courses of action, and consequences is not available. Decisions are influenced by individual differences, social pressures, leadership differences, communication structures, etc. Social scientists are interested in how individuals and groups reach a decision; how much information is necessary, who influences the outcome the most, how disagreements are resolved, what procedures are used and how choices are made.[1]

Unfortunately, it is difficult to study the normal processes of decision-making. There are practical difficulties, including confidentiality, about observing senior people in their normal settings at all. It is also difficult to isolate a 'decision' from the incessant stream of consultations, committee discussions, authorizations and initialling of papers that makes up the normal day. Many experiments, therefore, have been made with college students – or with administrators when they are on courses, away from their normal work – and can be criticized as artificial. This in itself is not a ground for dismissing theories which appeal to common sense and experience, which provide insight into the way administrators'

[1] P. B. Applewhite, *Organizational Behavior* (Englewood Cliffs, N.J., 1965) p. 54. The discussion in this chapter borrows heavily from the work of Cyert, March and Simon at the Carnegie Institute of Technology in Pittsburgh. The main sources are: H. A. Simon, *Administrative Behavior* (2nd edn.) (New York, 1957); J. G. March and H. A. Simon, *Organizations* (New York, 1958); R. M. Cyert and J. G. March, *A Behavioral Theory of the Firm* (Englewood Cliffs, N.J., 1963). Other (including more recent) work on decision-making is summarized in Applewhite, op cit., ch. 4. Detailed references to these primary sources would become very tedious and are avoided as far as possible in the following discussion.

minds work, and which are not apparently contradicted by any research findings so far. But the *caveats* mentioned in the last chapter should be kept in mind.

The main framework concept behind most of these studies is the assumption that any decision is reached in stages, each of which can be analysed and examined separately. First there must be an awareness that the problem exists. A signal must be received which suggests that some change in policy is needed. In a government department, the signal may come through political channels, or through the formal and informal machinery that links the department to the outside world, or perhaps from some internal source in the department, like a research and intelligence section which receives information suggesting that an existing policy is not working as well as it might. However the signal originates, it needs to be interpreted and related to other information so that the nature of the problem can be seen. When it has been structured in this way, there is an exploration stage. Possible courses of action or inaction are listed and a rough estimate is made of the probable consequences, desired and undesired, of each. This is followed by evaluation and by a provisional decision that one policy is preferable to the others. (In Whitehall terms, this is the point at which a 'departmental line' is taken.) There may follow a process of consultation in which the proposals are tested for acceptability (to interested parties and political groups) and feasibility (in the eyes of various sorts of expert), and finally, perhaps after modifications, brought to a higher level for authorization. This might be followed by communication of the decision reached, its implementation and, ultimately, review to check whether the consequences are as expected.

BOUNDED RATIONALITY

If the problem is at all complex (as are most problems in public administration) the range of considerations which this process entails is beyond the scope of a single human mind. The only way it can be tackled at all is by factorization. Different aspects are handled by different people, each of whom is forced, by and large, to take the work of the others on trust. To take a crude example, civil servants who are considering the merits of a proposed increase in a service do not personally have to work out the 'opportunity costs' that would be incurred through spending money on it rather than in an infinity of other ways. They assume, if they think about it at all, that opportunity costs are somehow reflected in the amount of Treasury opposition that has to be overcome. It would be unreasonable to expect them to do more. Similarly, if a proposal entails the use of scarce manpower, they would seek advice about its availability from the appropriate department, which they would not question.

Responsibility for a decision can be divided horizontally and vertically. In a hierarchical system different contributions will be made at different levels. Typically, junior members will not question their seniors' definition of the ends to be served, while the latter will assume that the factual information reported by their juniors is correct. Typically, too, the most senior levels will be concerned with authorization – with the final check that a proposed course of action is consistent with a general system of values – rather than with working out detailed proposals. But they may also take the initiative by setting a broad agenda, or specifying general rules to which their subordinates have to work.

But the factors have to be brought together again. An administrative organization can be regarded as a system of communication which exists in order to link decision-makers and to reassemble information about aspects of a problem that have been settled separately. Its coherence is maintained by specifying rules to guide its members in their partial decisions and by setting limits to the range of acceptable solutions that they may adopt. The limits appropriate to different levels in the hierarchy may be laid down precisely in so many words in terms of the financial or other commitments that an official has authority to incur. More often there is merely an understanding, to which the inexperienced officer may find it difficult to attach a precise meaning, that he ought to 'take his superiors with him' on questions of a certain character. The decision rules say what criteria should influence the decision, what consultations should be undertaken and so on. Again, the rules may be unwritten but this does not necessarily make them less compelling or less rigid.

So far, this is simply a spelling-out, using different language, of the structure of a Weberian bureaucracy. Duties and responsibilities are allocated in order to allow finite human beings to contribute collectively to the rational solution of infinitely complex problems.

Marshak, indeed, suggests that the student of an organization should ask, not for an organization chart, but for a rough description of 'who does what in response to what information'.[1] But while the system tries to be rational, it can never quite succeed. Its rationality is ultimately limited by the capacity of its human members.

In a typical decision situation, an official looks at a number of pieces of information, rejects some and selects others to be rearranged and passed on in the form of information, a recommendation or an instruction to somebody else. Both in what he takes into account and in what he does with it there is an unavoidable element of uncertainty. Even in the most routine cases, when his choice of action is supposed to be completely determined by circumstances, he may not react as expected. He may be insufficiently trained to understand what he has to do or he may mistakenly believe that there is some room for the exercise of his own judgement; this is a frequent cause of misunderstanding. In non-routine matters, where there is room for discretion, the number of factors an official thinks of and the weight he gives to them will significantly affect his performance as a decision-maker. They are influenced – and meant to be influenced – by his personal qualities and by his position within the organization. Rarely will he exercise choice over the complete range of possibilities that is logically open to him. The real situation, even after some aspects of it have been dealt with by others, is nearly always too complicated to be grasped. It cannot be tackled unless some of the detail is removed. 'Rational behavior involves substituting for the complex reality a model of reality that is sufficiently simple to be handled by problem-solving processes.'[2]

SELECTIVE PERCEPTION

The first element of uncertainty is whether the existence of a problem will be recognized at all. If the problem is one that the organization is accustomed to handling there will be programmes for bringing it to the notice of the appropriate people – government departments have well-developed procedures for dealing with the Minister's correspondence, questions in Parliament, and so on. In other cases a good deal depends on the ability of someone in the organization to recognize it as a problem.

[1] Marshak, 'Efficient and Viable Organizational Forms', p. 309.
[2] March and Simon, *Organizations*, p. 151.

Different people will identify a problem in different ways. In an experiment at the Carnegie Institute of Technology some middle-management executives were asked to read a long factual account of a company and its current position and to say what aspect of it they thought should be attended to first. Eighty-three per cent of the sales executives saw the main problem as sales. But only 29 per cent of the executives from other divisions saw it as sales, although both groups were working from identical material.[1] Training and experience help people to structure a problem situation by focusing on one or two main features of it. But the focus will be different for different people.

In administration it is sometimes a sign of immaturity and inexperience to accept complaints and suggestions at their face value. It is not difficult to imagine a penetrating parliamentary question which evokes quite different responses from three officials, one of whom has for some time been advocating a review of the policy under attack, while another is an expert at the political game and knows that the questioner is unlikely to know how well-aimed his question is and a third is mainly anxious to keep the peace until he retires and hands over a tidy block of work to his successor. Each reaction might be predicted from social and psychological information about the official concerned.

People 'rationalize'. They try to structure their experience in ways that are consistent with their previous background, beliefs, prejudices and values. Features that do not fit in tend to be rejected. In an organizational setting an official's approach to a problem will be governed by his experience. He will have developed a repertory of programmes for handling different situations. If the problem looks superficially like ones he has already solved successfully he will be inclined to look for a solution along the same lines. In a large-scale organization experience takes on an extra dimension, since the collective experience of the whole organization over a period of time is, in theory, available to the individual decision-maker. Relevant facts may be ascertainable from the filing system or from colleagues working on similar problems. Problem-solving techniques may be available and some of these may have been elevated into decision-rules. Methods that have been developed for one purpose tend to be used for another. For example, consultative

[1] D. C. Dearborn and H. A. Simon, 'Selective Perception: A Note on the Departmental Identification of Executives', *Sociometry*, vol. 21 (1958) pp. 140–4.

procedures in government departments tend to follow a set pattern, regardless of the subject matter. Once an organization has settled down and developed a memory, precedents are available for many situations and much has to be treated as given that would be left to discretion in a more open situation. All this makes for economy of effort and is fairly commonplace. But there is inevitably a biassing effect on the way problems are perceived and structured. The policies that result may be less than optimal.

Moreover, if collective experience is to be useful, it must be accessible. In large organizations the arrangements for pooling information tend to become very complex. The staff may be unable to use them without special training. We can say that a person's potential contribution depends on: (a) his personal qualities and experience; and/or (b) the total relevant experience that is available in the organization as a whole combined with (c) procedures, channels of communication and filing systems (with the staff to operate them) to make the experience accessible and (d) his own knowledge of the procedures and readiness to use them. Characteristically, a professional will tend to be most at home with (a); a general administrator will tend to rely on (b) to (d). In both cases there is likely to be some distortion.

A different type of distortion appears when decisions are taken collectively by groups or committees. Groups do not necessarily use all the experience that their members possess. It has to be communicated and accepted by a majority as relevant. If most members of the group share certain attitudes, these are reinforced by 'resonance' and are difficult to dislodge. A group that has been successful in the past is particularly inclined to reject unfamiliar suggestions from new members. Even in a 'brainstorming' session, when the group is actively seeking new ideas, it is psychologically difficult for members to produce ideas that deviate markedly from the general consensus. Fewer creative ideas emerge in a homogeneous group, in spite of the ease of communication. Face-to-face groups are inclined to accept the ideas of more senior members, if there are differences in status, or from the most talkative, regardless of their merit. In tackling constructive problems groups seldom surpass the performance of their best individual members: a greater range of creative solutions is likely to be produced by the members working independently for an equivalent number of man-hours. Groups can be more effective than individuals at analytic problems of an arithmetical or 'twenty questions' type, when effort can be saved by division of labour and through the mutual correction of errors. But even this is not true if much time is needed for intercommunication and co-ordination. The utility of group work as a device for achieving consensus, is, of course, another matter.[1]

SEARCH ACTIVITY

The individual decision-maker has different types of considerations at his disposal. There are 'facts', or at least statements supplied by others which appear to describe a real situation. There are 'value-premises' indicating the objectives, sometimes conflicting and sometimes ambiguous, at which he should aim. And there are problem-solving techniques and 'decision-rules' to guide him in integrating and relating these other premises. Some of these will be in the front of his mind, immediately within his span of attention. Normally they will be a small sample, far short of what he needs to make anything approaching an objectively 'rational' decision. If he feels unable to reach an 'adequate' decision on this basis, he will have to search for additional material, in his own memory for personal experience, in his set of office instructions or regulations for decision rules and procedures, in files and consultation with colleagues for information and advice. The search may be intensive or it may be superficial. The more it is extended, the more complete will be the decision-maker's model of the situation, and the closer will his actual decision approximate to a theoretically ideal one (always assuming that he structures his material logically when he has it, since there is a point beyond which additional information does not assist effective decision-making but is merely confusing).[2] The question

---

[1] The research on group versus individual decision-making is summarized in Applewhite, *Organizational Behavior*.

[2] There is a good example of this in L. T. Wilkins, *Social Policy, Action and Research* (London, 1964) app. IV. Wilkins describes an experiment in which probation officers were systematically supplied with items of information, in a sequence determined by them, bearing on a case where they had to recommend for or against probation. At each stage they had to make a provisional decision and say how confident they were about it. Different probation officers called for information (e.g. on home background, previous criminal records etc.) in different sequences. Regardless of the sequence, the probation officers became more confident in their decisions as they received more information in the early stages; but long before all the factors had been taken into account they began to lose confidence and their decisions became erratic. It may be that some such factor

how widely search activity is likely to range is a motivational one, conditioned partly by the prevailing 'ethos' of the organization. It has been illuminated in laboratory investigations at Carnegie.

An individual will not search beyond the point at which he is enabled to make a decision that appears satisfactory to him. If such a solution occurs to him right away, he will not spend time and energy looking for an 'ideal' one. In Simon's phrase, the administrator does not 'maximize', he 'satisfices'. If he does not feel that any of the obvious solutions is satisfactory, he will search for a better one, by calling more and more factors into his span of attention. The search will be sequential; only a few additional factors will be considered at a time and the search will be abandoned when he feels that he has found a reasonably satisfactory answer. His standard of 'satisfactoriness' will vary. If he does not find a satisfactory answer fairly quickly, he may continue searching, or he may lower his standards. Sometimes circumstances may compel him to decide on what he feels to be unsatisfactory evidence. In any case he is likely to stop long before all possible alternatives have been examined. This may be partly because of the way human beings reason. The character of a situation is quickly inferred from a few tentative observations and perhaps only the scientist feels a need to test exhaustively for the unexpected; for others, 'subjective rationality' is enough.

Search-activity may be cut short by time pressure. The number of other problems clamouring for attention is a major factor influencing the quality of decisions. It is also affected by increasing difficulty. As the enquiry extends from familiar territory to more distant parts of the organization it is pursued with decreasing vigour unless it is known from experience that information of a given sort is normally available at a certain point. A participant in a highly complex system tends to be uncertain about how to deal with more remote parts of it and therefore to concentrate on the factors within his immediate range of vision. It is no disparagement of civil servants to say that they are often unaware of information that is relevant to their problems even when it is being collected as a matter of routine in another department. A study of the possible applications

explains the phenomenon described in the *Fulton Report* (vol. 1, par. 54) that generalists (i.e. civil servants who lack a professional technique for structuring large amounts of technical information) may react to uncertainty either by caution *or by rashness*.

of census data or material from the Household Expenditure Survey might reveal many instances of this.

Perhaps this can be summed up by saying that the depth to which it is felt 'reasonable' to take a problem will vary with its importance, the accessibility and adequacy of relevant data, the training and experience of the official dealing with it, and the number of other problems requiring his attention in the time available. These factors may not seem to apply in, say, a research and planning division since such divisions 'are deliberately constructed to enable the organization to continue search activity even when most of the organizations' members are quite satisfied'.[1] But this is simply to say that different conditions may be made to apply in different parts of the same organization.

UNCERTAINTY ABSORPTION

Much of the information reaching an official will already have passed through a similar process at the hands of colleagues. In an organization of any size information may be used as a basis for decision many removes away from the point at which it enters the system. As it is transmitted it is progressively structured and simplified. One consequence may be that material which was initially highly ambiguous tends to become more and more precise. Decision-making is impeded if there are inconsistencies in the information relating to the same situation. 'Official' figures are developed so that conflicting information can be ignored. 'The greater the need for co-ordination in the organization, the greater the use of legitimized facts.'[2] This is how interest groups become committed to policies that may have originated in marginal choices by a bare majority of their members. To selective perception and rationalization, we have to add uncertainty absorption as the third main source of distortion in the simplified picture of reality with which decision-makers work.

This is one reason why it is so difficult to say who 'makes' a decision; filtering at each stage successively reduces the range of possibilities that is available to be considered. Once proposals have been formulated the range begins to decline quite sharply. Ultimately, only one possibility may be presented for approval. There

[1] A. Etzioni, *Modern Organizations* (Englewood Cliffs, N.J., 1964) p. 31.
[2] March and Simon, *Organizations*, p. 166.

is also an important difference between formulating proposals and considering them. Experiments have confirmed the common-sense observation that once concrete suggestions have been put on paper (for example to a Minister or a committee) it is less likely that fresh ideas, independent of the set framework, will come to mind.[1] This means that great power is wielded by those at the point where the greatest amount of uncertainty is absorbed, since they can considerably influence the decisions that will finally be made by others. Such a position may be filled by an 'expert' who is nominally quite junior in the hierarchy or by an 'adviser' who can be appealed to on matters of difficulty that cannot be resolved by rational analysis.

STRUCTURAL INFLUENCES

The decision-maker emerges from this analysis as a sort of human computer, with limited storage capacity and a partially random input. Up to a point, he can be programmed. Organizations influence their members by structuring their environment, that is, by controlling the information supplied to them and, through training and other means, conditioning the way they react to it. The extreme case of a fully programmed decision, in which all the ingredients are supplied and also rules for dealing with them, is a clerk dealing with routine cases according to the rule-book. Programmes allow central but recurring problems to be handled as routine. Hence the paradox noted by Mackenzie and Grove that 'on the whole the least qualified members of the service must do one of the most difficult parts of the business, that of meeting the public as individuals'.[2]

Organizations also try to control the framework of experience which their members bring to problems. The main instruments are recruitment, training and career policies.

It is not always easy to predict what sort of personal experience will be most appropriate. One factor is the amount of experience that is already available in the organization's memory. Many problems which face civil servants involve the application of general administrative principles to a concrete situation. What bodies should be consulted? Should Treasury be brought in? Should the

[1] Applewhite, *Organizational Behavior*, p. 65.
[2] W. J. M. Mackenzie and J. W. Grove, *Central Administration in Britain* (London, 1957) p. 450.

matter be cleared with the Cabinet? How should any decision be made public? A great deal of experience has been accumulated on such matters, so that new problems can often be handled effectively and economically as examples of a familiar type. Internal experience of precedents and procedures over a wide field may then be most useful. Hence the case for recruiting people of general ability and transferring them frequently from one post to another, assimilating 'organizational wisdom' and learning how to use it as they go.

No amount of mutual laundering, however, will create expertise that does not already exist. If the problem contains substantial new elements, additional experience may have to be imported by recruiting staff with special qualifications.

The relative emphasis on personal or 'organizational' experience implies different types of career structure. Personal experience can be kept at a high level by avoiding frequent changes of post. But long periods in specialized posts may not help officials to accumulate the general knowledge of the system that they need in order to exploit its resources of information. Specialist knowledge of a professional type is less relevant to problems which are too complex for the individual specialist to grasp.

Training has a number of functions. Training courses can supply a repertory of programmes for solving problems. By making people familiar with the organization's resources and its communication system, training can develop self-confidence and make them more ready to search fairly widely for relevant information. Sometimes training courses have a 'staff college' function. They provide an opportunity for colleagues to meet and develop a common outlook. This helps communication, since the usage of communication channels is affected by the ease with which they can be used and this in turn is influenced by the compatibility of the users. Channels that are socially rewarding tend to be used while others are neglected: one effect of the long courses at the Centre for Administrative Studies has been easier communication between departments, since at any one time their private offices are staffed by a cohort of Assistant Principals who got to know one another at the Centre. Generally speaking, decision-making becomes more predictable if participants share a common culture of beliefs, norms and aspirations. Training courses, therefore, often focus on certain values and beliefs about the system and its objectives in the hope that the trainee will make them part of his own frame of reference. One aim of this sort of training is to sensitize the official to certain aspects of problems and to guide his choice of priorities.

Perhaps the most effective instrument of orientation is departmentalization. If officials are grouped so that over their careers they are constantly exposed to the same kind of information and value systems, and interact with others in the same position, all the findings about selective perception, role-concept and group resonance point to the emergence of a characteristic departmental philosophy.

PRIORITIES

Administrators have finite spans of attention. They also have finite amounts of time at their disposal. Can we say anything about the way they allocate their priorities? How do they decide to which problem, or to which aspect of a particular problem, they should pay most attention?

The administrator tends to give his attention first to tasks for which a programme exists ready to hand. In another laboratory experiment at Carnegie subjects were made responsible for managing an inventory control system. They had to pass on to clerical staff some routine information about inventory levels in various warehouses; at the same time they were responsible for adjusting the allocation of clerks to warehouses so that each group of clerks had a comparable work-load; finally, they were to suggest changes in procedures. They were told that all three jobs were equally important and should receive equal attention. All the subjects spent considerably more than a third of their time on the routine part of their job even when the flow of information was kept light. As the amount of information was increased, the time they spent on planning was consistently reduced until virtually no planning was done at peak loads.[1] This is 'Gresham's Law' of planning – that daily routine drives out planning. Staff at all levels tend to get the easy jobs out of the way first and there is a risk that long-term ones never get done at all. Many observers have commented on the perfectionism which higher civil servants in Britain bring to matters of detail, especially the niceties of drafting. Penmanship comes easily to the British type of generalist. Stylistic weaknesses, when they occur, are an easy target for criticism in Parliament and the press, and there is every temptation to spend a disproportionate

[1] J. G. March, 'Business Decision Making', *Industrial Research*, Spring, 1959.

amount of time trying to eliminate them. This means, of course, that difficult questions of substance are, perhaps unconsciously, pushed into the background.

When activities are not programmed there is an apparently random element about the way priorities are determined among them. Similarly, if no technique for analysing a problem is ready to hand, decision time tends to be short and the outcome is likely to be influenced more by the order in which alternatives are presented than by any serious attempt to find a common yardstick. This seems to apply particularly to problems of allocating uncommitted resources. If some additional money suddenly becomes available, it will go to those who are quick off the mark. The beneficiaries are likely to be those whose strategic position in the communication system enables them to time their bids rather than those who have a good case on merit.

An important part may be played by external cues. Fire precautions will receive more attention than normal if there has been a fire recently. Safety precautions will be tightened up after an air crash. There is likely to be a spate of instructions on even minor aspects of security (to an extent that may seriously interfere with normal performance until it is felt safe to ignore them) after a prominent espionage trial. Sometimes it is impossible to restore the previous balance because a system of priorities becomes institutionalized, for example by appointing a security inspector to report breaches of regulations. Similarly, an active training department may succeed in making a whole department training-minded, even if this entails a loss in productive time.

There are various ways in which the organization can influence the individual's choice of priorities. Through training and programming some kinds of jobs can be made easier to tackle. A common device is to provide a formula which enables easy computational problems to be substituted for difficult qualitative ones. This may entail giving excessive attention to aspects of a problem that can be measured. Professor Eckstein thought that the use of formulas significantly reduced the rationality of decision-making in the Ministry of Health.[1]

Priorities can be attracted for some questions by the use of deadlines: a letter from a Member of Parliament has to be answered within a given number of days; a parliamentary question is given

[1] H. Eckstein, *The English Health Service* (Cambridge, Mass., 1958) ch. 9.

top priority because of the tight timetable for preparing a reply. Considerations thought to be important can be 'cued-in' to the administrator's frame of reference by constant reminders (like the annual reference to economy in the Treasury's letter inviting departmental estimates – although this particular line has perhaps lost its punch!). They can be institutionalized by building pressures into the structure – for example in an advisory committee – and instituting procedures to ensure that they are brought into play. The tendency to give priority to the short-term can be counterbalanced by creating a special unit which is concerned solely with long-term planning and innovation.

The problem of priorities is no less acute for the organization as a whole. It is seldom possible to attend to all its objectives simultaneously. They may be inconsistent – fresh commitments are acquired over time without always being related to existing ones. Separate units develop their own goals, which may be mutually incompatible. The goal of the training branch is to develop training schemes; the finance officer is concerned with economy; the establishment officer is interested in the efficient use of personnel; administrators in executive divisions are at various times concerned with all of these, as well as with carrying out the wishes of Parliament, placating pressure groups, sponsoring new legislation and furthering their own careers. In normal times an organization manages to survive with inconsistent goals by the simple expedient of failing to attend to more than a few of them at any one time. Lord (then Sir Edward) Bridges unwittingly emphasized this point in an address which he gave to the Royal Institute of Public Administration at Exeter in November 1954. 'However complicated the facts may be – however much your junior may try to persuade you that there are seventeen arguments in favour of one course and fifteen in favour of the exact opposite, believe me, in four cases out of five there is *one* point and one only which is cardinal to the whole situation. When you have isolated that one point, and found the answer to it, all the other things will fall into place. And until you have done that, you have done nothing.'[1] Lord Bridges would no doubt agree that the 'one essential point' may differ from time to time.

But sometimes inconsistencies cannot be ignored and an apparatus is needed for resolving disputes. One of the functions of a hierarchy is to provide a court of appeal.

[1] Bridges, *Administration: What is it? and How can it be Learnt?*

The important difference between the formulation and the authorization of policy has already been mentioned. There is a stage at which the various components of a decision can be brought together and integrated in a workable set of proposals. The proposals may have to be referred to higher authority for approval but this is often a formality. Usually, the 'level of integration' is kept as low as possible to ease the burden at the top and to increase the speed of decision-making. Occasionally a deliberate attempt is made to keep the options open by making it impossible for the various strands to be woven together except at the top. Senior members of the hierarchy may also be forced to review matters of detail if they have to resolve conflicts among their subordinates. This is one of the ways in which they keep in touch.

But those at the top have value-systems of their own which they apply in giving judgement. Consequently a centralized system of authority is one means of securing priority for these values. Junior staff learn what considerations will rank as most important if their work is reviewed. If, for example, the formal structure allows conflicts to be resolved only at 'political' level (perhaps because two departments have strong opposing interests in a question which neither of them can settle independently) officials try to anticipate their Minister's (or the Cabinet's) frame of reference when they are deciding whether a particular point of view is worth pursuing to the limit. In the late 1960s, when responsibility for economic policy was divided between the Treasury and the Department of Economic Affairs, some journalists alleged that the object was to ensure that the Prime Minister's view prevailed on certain issues. This would have been achieved even if no disputes were in fact referred to him, so long as those involved kept in mind how he would decide if he had to.

CONCLUDING COMMENTS

The theories discussed in this chapter are concerned with the supply of information, including information about other people's ideas, to the decision-maker, and the use he makes of it. The model of the organization as a communication system makes it possible to judge a procedure, an arrangement of functions, a rceruitment policy or a training scheme by its contribution to good decision-making. If these are well devised, they will make it more likely that the 'relevant' considerations will be taken into account by the right people at the right time. Decision-making is not the whole of organizational life, but it is a very important part of the life of government departments. It is worth taking some trouble to see how it can be improved.

As in Chapter VI, there are no universal prescriptions. If the head of a department knows what kinds of decisions he wants, he can be shown how to design an organization to increase the chances of getting them. Often he will not know too clearly what he does want. He may be persuaded to say in broad terms what relative weights he places on particular elements in decision-making, like accuracy, speed, economy, flexibility, good co-ordination and various sorts of expertise. It is certain that he will not be able to get an organization in which all these elements are maximized. Compromises are unavoidable, because there are limits to what human minds can assimilate and because there are limits to what a communication system can handle. Moreover, there is no absolute standard of 'relevance'. The requirements change with time. What is relevant to 'good' Treasury decisions today may be relatively unimportant next year. But it is some help to see what is involved.

It is especially useful to have a model which interprets the general theories of the last chapter in terms of individual performance at decision-making. What emerges is the now familiar point that every conceivable arrangement carries costs as well as advantages. If decision-makers are trained and equipped to focus sharply on A, their vision of B inevitably becomes a little bit distorted. The cumulative distortions that result can to some extent be balanced within the overall organizational structure, but never completely, because of communication and co-ordination problems.

In aiming at the best available balance the organization cannot control the perceptions of its participants. But it can influence them through training, recruitment, the structure of authority, communication links and so forth. The mechanisms at work are largely cognitive. In a bureaucracy ignorance is usually a structural problem – the official does not know what he has not been told, or had a chance to learn, nor can he remember everything all the time. But motivational factors are important too. The bureaucrat can sometimes be induced to try a little harder, given reasonable conditions and a modicum of encouragement.

VIII. Administration and Politics: A Model

In this chapter and in Chapter IX the analysis is taken further into the British political framework. Before applying concepts from Chapters VI and VII to public administration, it seems necessary to start by asking how great are the differences between public and other organizations. This leads to an examination of policy-making in a political setting and of the contributions made by different participants. Traditionally, one of the main problems of public administration has been taken to be the relationship between permanent officials and elected politicians. In order to understand this relationship, some discussion is needed of the place of lay judgement in policy-making.

PUBLIC AND PRIVATE ADMINISTRATION

The hypotheses discussed in the previous two chapters have often been illustrated with an example from a government department. But perhaps this has been premature. It may be argued that the characteristic problems of an organization are intimately related to its purpose. The purpose of a public department is very different from that of a business organization designed primarily to secure profit for its owners. It is not, therefore, realistic to extrapolate from one to the other. Blau and Scott argue that the characteristic problems facing an organization depend on whether its primary beneficiaries are its owners, its members, its clients or the public at large. The crucial problems of a business firm are thus concerned with efficiency and profit; those of a mutual-benefit association with internal democracy; those of a service organization with balancing the professional service ethic against administrative procedures; and those of a commonweal organization with the retention of political control. The differences, however, are only of degree: commonweal organizations have to face the problems of internal efficiency as well as of accountability.[1]

Certainly, if the whole field of government activity is taken into account, there are important qualitative differences between it and private enterprise. In his evidence to the Fulton Committee, Professor Self suggested that the following were particularly relevant:[2]

(a) Government disposes of coercive powers which do not arise in the private sector.

(b) Partly for this reason, administrative decision-making is bound by rules of consultation, objection and appeal which have no parallel.

(c) Management accounting cannot be applied within government (unless in very modified form) to yield tests of efficiency.

(d) Government undertakes or sponsors speculative ventures in defence and technology which have no close equivalents.

(e) While business management is strongly orientated to market innovation, public administration can be said to be more concerned with market compression – with the limitation of demands which cannot all be met.

(f) Government co-ordination of economic action occurs at a much higher level, yet in more limited form, than is true of decisions made by top managers of even the largest firms.

Not everybody would accept every item on this list. For example, the Treasury has been trying with some success to encourage the application of management accounting techniques even in the social services – although some feel that it is artificial to look for a substitute for 'profitability' in this way. Others would attach greater significance to the direct effects of political control. Through the Minister, the work of civil servants is almost always open to detailed criticism in Parliament. The need to justify decisions retrospectively means that the process of reaching them has to be unusually conscious and articulate. Great weight has to be given to integrity and impartiality, since the parliamentary system spotlights and magnifies any lapses that may emerge. Apart from that, however, there are no stable criteria by which senior civil servants can judge their own effectiveness. Their work is successful in so far as it is not challenged. Sometimes decisions that are technically sound are

[1] P. M. Blau and W. R. Scott, *Formal Organizations*, pp. 42–57.
[2] *Fulton Report*, vol. 5, p. 1121, par. 69.

difficult to explain or defend in political terms. Whether they are acceptable or not may be influenced by the unpredictable movement of stray political currents at a particular time. A special element of instability is introduced to departmental decision-making by the fact that it takes place in the arena of party politics.

After an exhaustive survey of the literature, Parker and Subramaniam came to the conclusion that the main difference between government and private activity was its 'allocative' and 'integrative' character.[1] Society is made up of a great number of interlocking sub-systems. A firm, a club or a family group is itself a system of members who carry out an economic or social function. They interact with other systems from which they obtain resources in return for providing goods or services. No system of this sort is self-sufficient: its continued existence depends on maintaining satisfactory relationships with the other systems in the environment (that is to say the higher level system of which it is a sub-system). The relationships between sub-systems are often regulated by the market. Alternatively they can be regulated by conscious political decision. The characteristic function of government is to control or influence the distribution of resources among the sub-systems of a society and to integrate their activities in the interests of the whole. Government departments and agencies provide the necessary apparatus. In addition, a government may itself take over direct control of some activities as an alternative to manipulating the market.

From this can be inferred the essential characteristics of public administration:

> The public administrator, by the very nature of Government's integrating function, must look at *all* the organizations in society and integrate different interests into something like a general interest. Different forms of polity may shift the stress given to different interests as well as affect the process of working out a general interest, but the need to *consider* every interest always remains a corollary to the need to integrate all sub-systems in society. The Government administrator must take account of the whole where the private administrator representing a single part can restrict his field of vision.[2]

[1] R. S. Parker and V. Subramaniam, 'Public and Private Administration', *International Review of Administrative Sciences*, vol. 30 (1964) pp. 354–66.

[2] Ibid., p. 365.

Hence the exceptional problems of co-ordination which cause so much difficulty in the public sector. Hence too the centralization of decision-making and the prevalence of 'Treasury' methods of control: purely governmental bodies have to bargain for resources within a framework of what is supposed to be best for society as a whole. The emphasis on rationality, consistency and justifiability is extended to the internal operations of the departments themselves and also, to a lesser extent, to government-sponsored agencies, even when their activities are not primarily integrative or allocative but are directed to the production of goods and services. It explains the convention that the managers of nationalized industries accept Ministerial suggestions even when they lack statutory as well as commercial force.

It is not, of course, possible for the individual public administrator to take such a comprehensive view. He has to be placed in a framework (another sub-system) which obliges him to take into account a limited number of 'integrating' factors in making his own, partial, decisions. The general interest is represented by the political environment in which he works. Parker and Subramaniam are not concerned with any particular type of political system. But clearly, in a democracy, the ultimate criteria for decisions about integration and allocation are supplied through the channels of political representation. The organizational problem is to make sure that the administrator pays attention to these criteria. This can be done by the elaborate machinery of structural devices and attention-directing cues that we call political accountability. The rather obvious conclusion follows that the public administrator must be sensitive to public opinion, as expressed through orthodox political channels, and that the traditional questions of the political scientist about the constitutional devices for maintaining political control over the administration are as important as ever.

THE GENERAL INTEREST

But the concept of 'control' is far too narrow for analysing the complex relationship that now exists between, say, the Home Office, the House of Commons and the Home Secretary. It suggests a division between policy (reserved for politicians) and administration (which can safely be handled by properly controlled officials) that hardly anybody now believes to be useful. High officials are not mere instruments of a political will. They have knowledge and values of their own which are applied not only in executing policy but in arranging for the policy to be changed. Their views on what should be done complement, rather than compete with, those of politicians. The word 'control' suggests recurrent conflict which has to be settled by the exercise of power. The Home Secretary controls the Home Office because he has the power to override its advice and to prescribe what its members will do.[1] Parliamentary control, on the other hand, is alleged to be weak because in practice, under party discipline, the House of Commons lacks the comparable power to override the Home Secretary. 'Today,' said Mr R. H. S. Crossman, then Leader of the House, in 1966, 'not only the House of Lords has been shorn of most of its authority. The House of Commons too has surrendered most of its effective powers to the Executive and has become in the main the passive forum in which the struggle is fought between the modern usurpers of power, the great political machines.'[2] The alleged loss of authority causes much frustration to Members of Parliament and some anxiety to political theorists.

The relationship between Parliament and the executive can be analysed in a different way. The integrative and allocative functions of government imply a need for some procedure for bringing specialized activities before a court where they can be tested for consistency with the welfare of society as a whole. Very roughly, the perspective widens as the level rises. The National Coal Board may be concerned only with the most effective use of coal. The Ministry of Power may try to relate coal to other fuels, perhaps by means of tax discrimination. The Cabinet will be more concerned with the overall effects of taxation and fuel policies on the standing of the Government at home and overseas. Members of Parliament will be concerned, as individuals, with the impact of alternative policies in their constituencies and, collectively, with their effect on the outcome of the next election. There is a shift from the specific to the general, from the technical to the political, from fact to value.

This is not because Members of Parliament are wiser and better than Cabinet Ministers and the Chairman of the National Coal

[1] There is a marginal question of *vires* (since the Home Secretary's powers and duties are partially limited by statute) which acquires practical importance only when raised by an offended outside body or, if the Home Secretary orders illegal expenditure, when the departmental Accounting Officer seeks to protect himself with a written explanation to the Comptroller and Auditor General.

[2] *H.C. Debs.*, vol. 738 (14 December 1966) col. 479.

Board, but because the House of Commons is designed to reflect a broader range of opinion than the leadership of the ruling party, and so on back down the line. The problem is differently perceived at different points. Left to themselves, the coal experts might settle for a policy that was best from their industry's point of view, but not well related to the other needs of society. On the other hand, a policy based on general political preferences might be very unsound technologically. If coal has been brought under public control, the public expects the industry's activities to be co-ordinated with those of other public bodies and to be integrated in the general interest. But this does not mean that technical aspects are unimportant.

The example, of course, is an artificial one. Experts have their ideals and politicians have their sectional interests. But a more realistic illustration would obscure the logic of the situation. Professional experts, civil servants, Ministers, Members of Parliament, all contribute to the consideration of a policy. So may academic thinkers and research workers, members of pressure groups and journalists in the press and television. Their contributions can be arranged along a spectrum, with experts and pressure groups near the specific-technical-fact end and politicians and journalists nearer the general-political-value end. It is helpful to see the system of accountability not as a hierarchical filter in which those at the top are superior people controlling those lower down, but as a set of procedures for ensuring that new policies are considered from various points of view along the spectrum. It suggests that meaningful organizational questions can be asked about: (a) the kind of contribution to be expected at different points; (b) the most effective way of dividing the labour; (c) the order in which contributions can best be combined to avoid wasted effort.

All this is another way of saying that Parliament is only one of several specialized channels through which ideas, information and pressures are legitimately applied to the development of public policy. It is at the 'general' end of the spectrum and therefore of distinctive importance in public administration. But on any specific issue, the contribution of Parliament may be very small and over-shadowed by professional expertise, material from surveys, and so on. This can be spelled out in terms of what we know about decision-making to arrive at a model for analysis. (The word 'model' is used here to mean an analytic representation of what actually happens. It will be argued later that this particular model is also prescriptive, in the sense that it describes how the system *must* work if different sorts of contributions are to be combined effectively.)

INITIATION OF CHANGE

In a well-established service, existing policies may be reviewed in the light of routine reports and statistics, provided that the information they contain is in a useful form and that it is somebody's job to study it. But routine feedback is more likely to suggest minor modifications than real changes in direction. More substantial innovation within the service itself implies a readiness to consider new ways of doing things – a more active search for alternatives than is normal when things are apparently going smoothly. It seems to need time for reflection and a sort of psychological emancipation that is often denied to members of busy hierarchies, watching their deadlines and conscious of the need to reach a consensus quickly. For this reason, special 'thinking' units are sometimes set up and freed from the pressures of day-to-day business. But there is then a problem of preventing the thinkers from getting out of touch and of bringing their ideas to the notice of those able to apply them.

In a service which employs professional staff, changes in policy may be suggested by those who provide the service. Professor Donnison and his colleagues have described how professional field-workers played the major part in the development of local social services:

> The providers of service usually take this initiative . . . in an attempt to meet in a more appropriate or satisfying way the actual or potential demands they perceive. Thus their perceptions of the needs to be met and the standards of service they regard as fitting are crucial. These perceptions depend largely on the education and previous experience of the staff, and the climate of opinion they establish amongst themselves.[1]

Their case studies suggest that developments in services of this sort, which necessarily leave a good deal to the discretion of professional workers, are quite likely to be implemented before approval is sought from the authority nominally responsible for the service – possibly in order to secure additional resources. 'Formally approved

[1] D. V. Donnison and V. Chapman, *Social Policy and Administration* (London, 1965) pp. 237–8.

"changes in policy" announced by the governing body may simply recognize and codify a process worked out over several years by people at humbler levels.'[1] Their analysis is probably equally applicable to national services whose development is stimulated by lobbying from professional groups like teachers, doctors or admirals. Such pressures, coming from the best-informed source, naturally reflect the commitments and aspirations of the profession involved and are, in a very important sense, sectional. A similar role may be filled by academic experts who have specialized in a particular field and are interested in its development.

It sometimes happens that innovation comes mainly from political levels. The Labour Government of 1945 offers the most conspicuous examples in recent times of major acts of policy – the decision to grant independence to India, the final shape of the National Health Service, the creation of nationalized industries – stemming from a decisive political initiative (although technological imperatives also came into play, for example in reports from expert working parties on the problems of key industries). Most governments come into office with a programme of sorts. The commitments of the 1964 Labour Government to re-nationalize steel and to remove prescription charges were almost entirely political; prescription charges had to be restored, by the same Government, for financial reasons three years later. Really radical change probably comes most easily from political levels – from a Minister looking at problems with a fresh eye, from the election manifesto of a new government, or from a pressure group whose case commands more political sympathy than administrative logic. Such initiatives are unpredictable and may have a wanton element about them. Radical change is costly. Procedural devices, and the need to consult advisers, may prevent it being introduced too easily.

IMPLIFICATION

If a new idea falls on fertile soil, it has to be made 'operational' by translating it into workable proposals. The range of thinking must first be widened and then narrowed again. The widening process means placing the proposal in the context of existing schemes and policies and searching as widely as possible for information about

[1] Donnison and Chapman, *Social Policy and Administration*, p. 246.

its repercussions. In the case of a public service, since nearly all problems interlock and the immediate range of possible repercussions is therefore very wide, the theoretical limits to this search are set by the whole boundary of actual and possible public policy. In practice, a minimum field of consultation will be defined by formal instructions and departmental habits. It may be extended by the personal knowledge and interests of the staff directly concerned. The Treasury will normally be involved and perhaps an advisory committee or two.

When enough data has been collected it has to be structured. The range of considerations has to be narrowed down to one or two broad alternatives that can reasonably be put to other bodies and to the person who will take formal responsibility for the decision.

It is in this process of simplification that one finds what Donnison and Chapman have called the 'major junctions' in policy at which decisions are taken to select one route and exclude many others potentially available up to that point.[1] Lord Bridges makes a similar point:

> The experience of anyone who has worked in Whitehall is that there is an early stage in any project when things are fluid; when, if you are in touch with those concerned and get hold of the facts, it is fairly easy to influence decisions. But after a scheme has been worked on for weeks and months, and has hardened into a particular shape, and come up for formal decisions, then it is often very difficult to do anything except either approve it or throw it overboard.[2]

Nothing that is done at this stage is irrevocable, since formulated proposals have to clear other hurdles before they become policy. But if they fail, they come back to the same crossroads to start on another route.

Clearly much depends on the people who are involved in the process at this stage. Their ideas about what is relevant will be influenced by personality, background and training. They will also be influenced, particularly in the amount of trouble they are prepared to take, by the atmosphere in which they work – how much credit is given for personal initiative, how much pressure there is to

[1] Ibid., pp. 35, 246.
[2] Lord Bridges, 'Whitehall and Beyond', *The Listener*, vol. LXXI (25 June 1964) p. 1016.

reach amicable compromises, and so on. In a government department, Ministers are unlikely to be involved in most matters at this
stage, even if the policy originated with them, unless they have a
strong personal interest in it, simply because of pressure on their
time. In a department which employs them, professionally qualified
officers and members of the Inspectorates will be involved very
closely. A vital part, including 'procedural' decisions about whom
to consult and what use to make of their advice, is played by
generalist civil servants in the higher executive and middle administrative grades, up to the level of Assistant Secretary.

The process of formulation becomes rather easy (perhaps
dangerously so) if there are mechanical means of resolving uncertainties and ambiguities. Favourite devices include a majority
recommendation by a committee, the report of an Inspector or
Tribunal, the results of a cost benefit analysis, a categorical opinion
from an authoritative source – and precedent.

LEGITIMATION

Before a final decision is sought on a new policy it nearly always
has to be discussed with other interests that are going to be affected.
This means that it will be put in the form of a proposal to a number
of other government departments and consultative bodies in the
hope or expectation that they will endorse it. A policy on, say,
health service reorganization might be formulated entirely by a
working party within the Department of Health but might have to
be cleared with the Ministry of Housing and Local Government,
the Home Office, the Department of Education and Science and
the Treasury, not to mention external interests like the Society of
Medical Officers of Health and local authority organizations, before
being put up for final approval. A primary function of permanent
advisory bodies is to provide a touchstone for policies drafted in the
appropriate Ministry. Most of the papers considered by the Central
and Scottish Health Service Councils, for example, are prepared by
professional staff in the Health Department, and presented by civil
servants who attend Council meetings. Meetings tend to be short
and agendas long. It is rare for a paper to be rejected, or even
exhaustively discussed. But papers are prepared with possible
reactions in mind. In other words, the known views of the interests
represented on the Council have been taken into account at the

'simplification' stage, which will often have included a more open-ended discussion on a sub-committee or working party of the Council itself.

The habit of consultation is very strong in British administration; indeed the ease with which affected interests and relevant expertise can be co-opted into the decision process has largely compensated for lack of subject-specialization in the permanent administrative machinery. The process of being consulted on a proposed policy, however, is not unlike that of being asked to authorize it. The policy is already there in draft. It may be difficult to discuss in detail and it is often possible only to confirm that it is not objectionable or to ask for it to be reconsidered. If objections are raised at this stage and the policy goes back for a remould, there is likely to be great pressure to salvage the effort already invested in it by reaching agreement on a compromise which may smother some of the disagreements. The effect may be to blunt the cutting edge of the policy, some conflicting interests can often best be accommodated by not making a policy too explicit. There are occasions when a policy has to be modified substantially after consultation – but this suggests that it has been formulated too hastily or, if it happens too often, that the administrative structure needs attention.

AUTHORIZATION

In our system of government, no change of any substance can be made without the agreement of the responsible Minister and often of a Cabinet committee. A very large number of questions have to be considered by a small number of very busy people. Most of them can be considered only in terms of bare essentials. By the time a question has reached the Minister it is usually in a form in which it is really only possible to say 'yes' or 'no' and it is usually easier to say 'yes'. What the Minister does is decide for himself the general principles on which he will intervene personally in the stream of business flowing across his desk: 'Part of the art of being a good or successful Minister is to know what the subjects are that require one's personal attention.'[1] What he cannot do is to work out a new policy himself, partly because he has not the time, partly because he lacks the knowledge and partly because he cannot get involved in detail if

[1] J. E. Powell, 'Whitehall and Beyond', *The Listener*, vol. LXXI (26 March 1964) p. 505.

he is to stand back and look at things politically. It is extremely difficult to do such a job well. A British Minister, of course, has some of his interventions chosen for him by the fluctuating interests of Parliament.

Parliament itself exercises something like a 'Ministerial' function when it is considering draft legislation or major items of government business. The mechanics are different, if only because there are so many individual M.P.s, and the pattern is complicated by Parliament's other functions as a sounding board for individual grievances and as a court of appeal for dissatisfied pressure groups. It is always possible, when a proposal is presented for statutory authorization, for individual Members of Parliament to represent interests that were overlooked or overridden in earlier discussions. Parliament's role in legislation thus involves elements of legitimation as well as authorization. In fact, as is well known, only a tiny proportion of the detailed matters coming formally before Parliament are even discussed, let alone seriously reviewed. But the possibility of challenge is more important than the fact. When this latent power *is* exercised, policies are criticized from a 'political' standpoint, that is, in terms calculated to appeal to public sympathy by reference either to the general welfare or to supposedly general principles like equity and good faith. Parliament links public departments to the political interests of the public at large, and parliamentary accountability obliges Ministers and their civil servants to keep in mind how their policies will look if they are challenged from that point of view. We shall see in the next chapter what kinds of factors seem to be significant in this context.

A SYSTEM WITHIN A SYSTEM

A government department is only part of a larger social and policy-making system with which it merges at the edges. The larger system includes Ministers, Parliament and the electorate, and it is conventional to speak of the department's relationship to them in terms of control: Parliament controls Ministers who in turn control their departments. But the department touches other parts of the larger system in its contacts with pressure groups, in its dealings with the public and in its arrangements for securing expert advice, to say nothing of its own recruitment needs. In order to survive (that is to say, to avoid dislocating criticism and review) it has to preserve some sort of equilibrium in all its relationships. The political relationship does not even supply the department's main contact with the external world. But it is qualitatively different from the others because it provides a higher court of appeal. Its total effect, although not necessarily felt in any particular instance, is to supply a general pressure towards integration and rationality and it is the directly experienced strength of this pressure that distinguishes a government department from a private firm.

Formally, the department is designed to respond to pressures from the political sub-system, if they are forthcoming. And pressures are in fact being applied all the time, directed almost randomly through the Minister at different sections of its work. But it is misleading to describe the department as an instrument of its political head. He does not (like the head of Weber's bureaucracy) specify broad objectives which are progressively broken down into divisional and branch assignments, except on the rare occasions that involve major questions of party policy. No more does the Permanent Secretary. Any part of the department can best be described as a self-sustaining machine, organized generally on bureaucratic lines, which has the capacity to generate improvements within the broad policy directions given to it and will continue to do so until stopped. It continues in operation without much regard to a change of government. It has elaborate adaptive mechanisms through which information is processed and translated more or less automatically into requests for authority to modify the prevailing policies. Its methods of working are influenced by the pressures exerted on it by all its neighbours, not only the political environment. If any of these forces were to alter, or to be removed, the work of the department would also alter in character.

ORGANIZATION THEORY AND PUBLIC ADMINISTRATION

We can now look again at the question raised at the beginning of this chapter. How far are the theories of organization discussed in Chapters VI and VII relevant to the problems currently facing public administration in Britain?

Chapter VII was concerned with decisions. It touched on the limitations of human rationality and their consequences for individual and collective decisions. Since people have limited reasoning capacity, the way they perceive and analyse problems is biased by their previous experience and by their position in the communication system. Different people respond to different cues. Their response is always incomplete, whether they are politicians, professional advisers or potato-merchants.

This framework seems likely to prove helpful in analysing the contributions of all those who take part in making public policy. Civil servants are influenced in their choice of priorities partly by the way they perceive the demands of the political system. But those demands are in turn governed by the way politicians interpret the material coming before them, and by their motivation to pursue one aspect of a question rather than another. Similar questions can be asked about the impact of pressure-groups on government departments, and indeed about the way members of the public perceive issues and the effect on their voting behaviour. Altogether, the application of Simon's theoretical framework seems likely to provide sensitive instruments for analysing a wide range of political and administrative behaviour.

But the most important questions are about the way policies emerge from the *combination* of incomplete perspectives. We are led back to the questions about organizational design discussed in Chapter VI. Towards the end of that chapter, the main point of the discussion was seen to be the suitability of different types of organization for getting different sorts of work done. Relevant considerations included the readiness of organizational members to participate and the need to balance social, economic and operational factors in arriving at the best pattern of organization for a given purpose. These are the kind of questions we raise about the organization of individual departments or of the civil service as a whole.

When these structural theories are viewed from a wider perspective, it seems that they are really about relationships and about relating the structure of a department or agency to its function in the total system. What is a department (or the whole service) required to do? What resources are available to it and on what conditions? Which of its objectives are primary and which problems is it most important should be tackled effectively? On any particular set of answers to these questions some advice can be given about the type of organization that will probably be most appropriate.

As part of this advice, there is a place for simple recipes about the way to maximize efficiency. But it is likely to be a small one. The chief functional problems of a government department are more likely to be concerned with its arrangements for formulating policy and with its relationship to the rest of the policy-settling machinery. Any discussion of organization in the public sector must take account of three overriding factors:

1. The need to ensure, through administrative structure and consultative procedures, that policy is not settled on too narrow a base.

2. The need to secure a place for 'lay' thinking, even on the most technical issues, *before* policy is hardened up.

3. The need to secure, largely through the order in which different aspects of a problem are considered and the priorities in people's minds at each stage, that a reasonable balance is kept between expert and non-expert contributions.

Organization theory can help to show how these aims can be achieved in a way that is compatible with the recruitment and retention of enough public servants of calibre to do the work (a factor sometimes ignored by hostile critics of the civil service) and with the limited cognitive capacity of all the human participants in the system. A department can be structured, and its members trained, so that more attention will be paid to one set of considerations than to others. For example, the relative weight given to political and technical factors in formulating policy is likely to be a factor, among other things, of the relative positions of general administrators and specialists in the hierarchy.

In an illuminating article Subramaniam contrasts the specialist and the generalist in terms of the relationship between fact and value in decision-making. He accepts Simon's analysis that every decision is a conclusion derived from a value proposition combined with several relevant facts. Any major decision involves (a) more than one value, (b) not each of which is clearly postulated, (c) several facts, it not being always clear what facts need to be assembled, (d) nor easy to assemble those needed. Subramaniam suggests that the specialist is particularly good at assembling the facts in his field (d). But he will be less alert to the explicit and implicit values involved in (a) and (b) and may consequently lack skill in identifying all the factual material that is relevant at (c). By contrast, the general administrator (or the politician) is sensitive to the scope and value implications of a decision but unable to explore factual areas without specialist help. The main weight of decision-taking can be placed either on the specialist or on the generalist according to the relative importance and difficulty of value-elements and factual-elements in the decision.[1]

There are important choices to be made, not only in the extent to which administration is entrusted to specialists but also in the extent to which politicians are involved in detail, in the weight that is given to continuity, and in the economic, political and human costs that it is felt reasonable to incur in order to maximize some other value. We are a long way from the universal 'canons of efficiency' quoted from the Brownlow Report in Chapter VI. But the basic assumption in the Brownlow Report, that the method of analysis is the same for public departments and private organizations, holds up fairly well. The position was summarized neatly in a 1964 Treasury report:

> The basic principles, tools and techniques of management are common to both Civil Service, Industry and Commerce. But the difference in motivation and background will compel differences in application.[2]

The 'differences in application' have been over-emphasized in the past because the teaching of administration has been fragmented. Until recently the different fields of administration have tended to be taught separately in Britain to different groups of people and to stress different concepts. Courses in 'public administration' have been mainly about the history and legal powers of public authorities and have emphasized the problems of control and accountability. 'Social administration' has been concerned with the functions and aims of social service organizations and their success in terms of welfare output. 'Business administration' has been firmly rooted in the economics of profit while 'industrial administration' has tended to stress efficiency and to use engineering principles. Only recently can it be said that common concepts have begun to appear in all these fields. It is now reasonably likely that a university course under any of these titles would include some of the material discussed in the previous two chapters. As a result, some of the traditional differences have become less stark and have faded into shades of emphasis. For example, it is often suggested, rather crudely, that

[1] V. Subramaniam, 'Specialists in British and Australian Government Services: a Study in Contrast', *Public Administration* (1963) pp. 357–73.

[2] *Report of a Working Party on Education and Training for Management in the Civil Service* (H.M. Treasury, 1964, unpublished). Appendix III ('Differences between Industrial, Commercial and Civil Service Management').

the accountability of a government department to Parliament is not very different from the accountability to shareholders of a board of directors. If behavioural rather than legal concepts are used to analyse each relationship, it becomes obvious that the analogy is misleading in some respects (because the 'sense-making' tendency of parliamentary intervention is more obtrusive and less consistent than the 'profit-mindedness' of shareholders) but helpful in others (for example, the conditioning effect of accountability on executive decisions).

The differences of emphasis are, of course, important. Even when a common 'organizational language' is employed, some of the basic questions of organizational choice in the public sector – accountability versus flexibility: centralization versus initiative – are very old friends to the political scientist. Their very familiarity argues that they could usefully be explored more systematically than they have been in the past, with a clear framework against which to calculate the losses and gains. Some of the more acute points of controversy will be examined in Part Three, after some further discussion in the next chapter on the significance of 'lay' control as an integrative and allocating factor in public administration.

IX. Administration and Politics: An Illustration

A distinguishing feature of public administration is the part played in it by lay politicians. What kind of contribution do laymen make to policy? How does it differ from the contributions of experts and administrators? Is there any special significance in the order in which it is combined with other elements in policy formulation? The discussion will be illuminated by an illustration.

THE POLICE WIDOW'S GRATUITY[1]

The case concerns a proposal to pay a gratuity to certain police widows. In its original form the proposal provoked such opposition in the House of Commons that it was withdrawn and a more generous one substituted.

The story begins in 1961 when the Police Federation (representing the lower ranks of policemen) took the initiative by asking for a change in the Police Pensions Regulations which would allow a £4,000 gratuity to be paid to the widow of any policeman who lost his life in the course of duty. A policeman's widow is normally entitled to a pension, which is paid on a higher scale if her husband died after a murderous assault (but not, for example, after an accident incurred while patrolling a motorway in the fog). The new gratuity was to be additional to the increased pension.

The claim was discussed, under the usual procedure, by a committee of the Police Council for Great Britain. This is a Whitley-

---

[1] Details of the incident can be traced in issues of the *Police Review* (official journal of the Police Federation) and *News Summary* (official journal of the Local Authorities' Conditions of Service Advisory Board) between 1961 and 1964, and in parliamentary papers. These sources do not reveal the exact part played by individuals. Consequently, as is usual in such case-studies, we cannot distinguish the personal contribution of the Home Secretary from those of his civil servants, nor clearly determine the parts played by different elements on the official side of the Police Council.

type body which settles questions of police pay and conditions of service. It consists of a 'staff side' representing various grades of policemen and an 'official side', consisting of representatives of the local authorities, which employ the majority of policemen, in addition to representatives of the Home Office and the corresponding Scottish department. The local authority representatives on such a body are occasionally professional officers but more often elected councillors or aldermen who have no special technical knowledge. They may express general views from time to time, but on the whole they take their lead from the civil servants and from the secretary to the official side, who also acts as chief negotiator. The civil service members, in turn, are bound by general government policy on public expenditure, and it is well known that they look to the Treasury for guidance. This was the body that had to 'structure' the problem.

The official side was quick to reject the claim as it stood. It pointed out that it could lead to a flood of claims for the payment of gratuities to widows whose bereavement could be attributed to public employment. The repercussions would be excessively costly – one can see Treasury influence here in widening the frame of reference. It would, however, be prepared to consider on the merits a less generous scheme which could be limited to policemen.

The Police Federation then modified its figure to roughly £2,000 (two years' pay for a constable). It also agreed to exclude from the claim the widows of colleagues whose husbands had been killed on point duty, or had lost their lives in saving life from drowning or from burning buildings, since special treatment for such cases could clearly run up against the objection about repercussions. It made a fresh proposal which was limited to three categories of widow: those whose husbands died as a result of a murderous assault; those who sustained fatal injuries while trying to effect an arrest (for example, by falling off a roof during a chase); and those who were killed while trying to prevent an escape (for example, through an accident to a pursuing vehicle).

The official side felt able to agree to a scheme covering the first category but not the other two. The problem had thus been simplified into a choice between the revised Federation proposal and the narrower one which was acceptable to the official side.

There followed nearly three years of stalemate in which all parties became increasingly embarrassed at the possibility that their continuing disagreement might deny a gratuity to the widow of a murdered policeman, since there would be no provision in the regulations to cover it. Changes in the police pensions code can be made only by amendment regulations which require the approval of both Houses of Parliament. By statute, amendments are proposed only after 'consultation' (which normally means agreement) with the Police Council. In this case the procedure for legitimizing and authorizing a change was nearly (but not completely, since it contained no reference to the Treasury) defined exhaustively in the statute.

The Home Secretary (then Mr Henry Brooke, later Lord Brooke of Cumnor) finally decided to seek parliamentary approval to regulations covering the point that *had* been agreed. Draft regulations[1] appeared on the Order Paper of the House of Lords for 7 July 1964 and of the Commons for the following day. In the ordinary way they would have gone through, like hundreds of other regulations every year, without discussion and perhaps without even being read by more than a handful of members. Like most superannuation codes, police pensions regulations have become increasingly complicated over the years. Amending regulations are usually technical and difficult to understand, even with the help of the explanatory memorandum which is appended to all statutory instruments to explain their purpose and effect. At any rate, they seldom attract much parliamentary attention. Approval is often given formally and few M.P.s are really aware of what has been done.

In this case, there was in fact a short debate in the House of Lords in which Liberal and Labour spokesmen both expressed doubt, on general social policy grounds, about treating some widows more generously than others with the same financial needs. The draft regulations were, however, approved.[2]

In the meantime, the Police Federation was directing a campaign at members of the lower House. Every M.P. received a broadsheet urging him to ask for the regulations to be withdrawn and replaced by more comprehensive ones. Since M.P.s receive many such appeals, it is unlikely that many of them studied it very carefully. But constituency pressures are another matter. On the day of the debate itself, each M.P. received a telegram from the local branches of the Federation in his constituency. They all read alike: 'Members

---

[1] *Police Pensions (Amendment) (No. 2) Regulations, 1964.*
[2] *H.L. Debs.*, vol. 259 (7 July 1964) cols. 931–8.

of the —— Police Federation ask you to oppose Police Pensions (Amendment) No. 2 Regulations 1964. Proposals provide for officers who die after an attack but not for officers who are killed while attempting to make an arrest.'

It is worth describing in some detail the course of the debate on the Home Secretary's motion to approve the draft regulations.[1] His opening speech was interrupted by five Opposition M.P.s who flatly condemned the proposals as inadequate, without offering any arguments. After Mr Brooke sat down, Mr James Callaghan, declaring his interest at that time as consultant to the Police Federation, gave a reasoned exposition of the Federation point of view and criticized the Home Office for acting unilaterally. He was interrupted by two Conservative M.P.s who complained about being 'bombarded' by telegrams without being given time to find out about the problem and understand it. In the rest of the short debate there were four Conservative and three Opposition speakers. On the whole they made conventional points expressing sympathy for widows and hoping that the Home Secretary was not being niggardly. There was, however, a deeper undercurrent. Sir Spencer Summers (Conservative) said that this was 'one of the rather rare occasions when backbenchers bring an influence to bear on the front bench'. Mr Robert Mellish (Labour) said: 'Let the House of Commons prove itself just once in a while.' Finally, the Home Secretary said: 'I might not yield to the Opposition; but I will certainly yield to the House.' He promised to ask the Police Council if it would agree to widen the category of widows to whom the special gratuity would be paid.

The official side evidently agreed without difficulty (although the Federation Secretary later complained rather ungraciously that the Home Secretary had violated a constitutional principle by not consulting the staff side too!) A few days later, fresh draft regulations were presented which gave the police all they had asked for (and indeed rather more, since they extended the higher pension as well as the gratuity to widows in the two additional categories).[2] They led to some mutual congratulation in Parliament but no real discussion on the merits of the issue.

[1] *H.C. Debs.*, vol. 698 (8 July 1964) cols. 543–77.
[2] *Police Pensions (Amendment) (No. 3) Regulations, 1964,* approved in the Commons on 27 July 1964 (*H.C. Debs.*, vol. 699, cols. 1176–86) and in the Lords on 28 July (*H.L. Debs.*, vol. 260, cols. 967–70).

This case is interesting because it was argued throughout in terms of principle. There was no question of party discipline and the financial effects were unimportant: the additional cost of accepting the modified Federation proposal was estimated at a maximum of £20,000 a year. The question was a fairly simple one of deciding at what point a generally accepted principle, that the needs of widowhood should normally be met through universal comprehensive schemes, should yield to the moral claim of a policeman's widow for selective treatment. The main protagonists were the Police Federation, pressing the sectional case, and the Treasury officials behind the scenes who, as experts in this branch of social policy, represented the general community interest and stimulated the official side's resistance. (It is not always appreciated that the Treasury, now succeeded in some respects by the Civil Service Department, is the main source of expertise in many matters like this. The Treasury is usually thought to be concerned only with saving money; in this case it appears as the 'sense-maker' which opposes sectional interests that cannot be reconciled with a general system of values running through a whole field of policy.) The Home Office officials seem to have acted mainly as intermediaries. The interesting question is the role of the lay participants, since it is on this kind of value issue that lay judgement might be supposed to come into its own.

The official side of the Police Council included a majority of local authority laymen (who, as employers, also had a minor interest in economy). They seem to have been content, as laymen often are on such bodies, to acquiesce in what the administrators proposed to them (that is to say, in the Treasury point of view until the Home Secretary himself abandoned it). They had the voting strength to reject the official line. But this strength, normally latent, remained so on this occasion.

The other lay body involved was Parliament. The Members of both Houses were invited to acquiesce in a minor piece of policy determined by the executive. The Lords did so. In the normal way the Commons would also have approved the draft regulations without difficulty even when the Home Secretary had drawn their attention to the value-questions involved. This time, the broadsheets and telegrams triggered off some of the latent forces. But when the interests of Members were aroused, they did not go on to discuss the value-questions in detail. Nobody said: 'The issues here are so and so; they are pretty finely balanced, but on the whole x is preferable for these reasons.' The points raised were apparently much more gross – 'political' rather than analytic. What they conveyed was, approximately: 'Hold on! There must be something wrong or the Police Federation would not be going to all this trouble. Take it away and think again.' When the Home Secretary came back, having re-thought, nothing tripped the wire and perhaps only those immediately involved were fully aware of what had been done.

This is a minor case and it is untypical in many ways. The Home Secretary could have forced his original proposals through the House had he so wished. Although he referred to 'the feeling of the House', only thirteen members spoke apart from himself. What seems to have happened is that the Federation's lobbying coincided with a particular mood among backbenchers, possibly anxious to demonstrate their independence, and struck a particular chord in representatives of both parties and perhaps in Mr Brooke himself. Major constitutional struggles are not settled in this way, at least not overtly.[1]

LAYMEN IN POLITICS

But it suggests some general hypotheses about the way lay 'control' works when it is not overshadowed by power factors and by party discipline. Although the M.P.s successfully resisted a government proposal, it was not on substantive grounds. They did not consciously oppose general to sectional values on the particular issue. There was a broad assumption that this unpopular job would be done anyway within the government machine – as indeed had been the case. The lay members were apparently concerned with a more abstract point – whether the job of formulating balanced proposals had been well done, with proper attention to the usual patterns of consultation and procedure. They were afraid that the balance of consideration had become distorted and produced a result that was not self-evidently acceptable. This is essentially a 'Ministerial' approach.

Sometimes, no doubt, lay politicians do have to apply their judgement and experience in settling difficult questions on their

[1] Mr Humphry Berkeley mentions this incident as one that gave backbenchers an unusual lift to the spirits, soon to be deflated by more three-line whips. *The Power of the Prime Minister* (London, 1968) pp. 18–19.

merits after considering all the available information. One tends to think of nineteenth-century government in these terms. It may be that some small local authorities still work in this way. Royal Commissions, usually with a lay chairman and at least a majority of lay members, are set up for this very purpose. But such bodies are the exception and even in these cases members do not work in a vacuum. They are exposed to pressures of various sorts and have to take a minimum of factual material into consideration. As the volume of political and technical factors increases, their ability to handle it comprehensively declines and their scope for manœuvre is restricted. They are almost forced to find some rational strategy for limiting their role.

For a Member of Parliament the difficulty is correspondingly greater because of the number and complexity of questions competing for his attention. He cannot hope to become involved in more than a fraction of them, nor to inform himself completely about those that do attract his notice. What sort of strategy can he work out to cope with such a responsibility? Three principles seem to apply fairly generally:

1. Latency Since in practice he can intervene so little, he can maximize his influence by stressing what he might do rather than what he actually does. He will press for procedures that give him the *opportunity* of intervening – like regulations requiring an affirmative resolution and statutes that have to be renewed annually – and will resist any encroachment by the executive on the rights and privileges of Parliament. He is encouraged by journalists and possibly by constituents who expect him to defend his ability to defend their interests. So far as he is successful, the effect is to keep the possibility of review constantly in the minds of administrators and departmental Ministers.

2. Sensitivity to pressure. He will not (or not very often) actively seek out matters to investigate. He has no need to. Party whips are looking for speakers and trying to man committees. Various interest and cause groups are seeking his alliance. Constituents are pressing him to take up various issues on their behalf. His problem is to choose to which pressures he will respond. Since he is a politician, and depends for success on his ability to persuade others, he tends to take up issues that look most likely to command popular support, at least in his own constituency. A miners' M.P. is likely to be fairly deaf to the clean air lobby. Part of his job as a politician is precisely to identify the relevant political issues. If he mistakes his role, or misjudges his support (like some Members who have followed their consciences or defied the party whip on what they saw as a moral issue), he may be disowned by his constituency association before the next election. The effect here is to give him an integrative and mediating role, closely connected with the grievance-settling function of Parliament, which can counteract departmental tendencies to work from too sectional a frame of reference.

3. Non-competition with experts. Conscious of his own ignorance, he will not try to dispute with experts on their own ground. He is more likely to press for the appointment of additional specialists when he suspects that there is some deficiency in the way decisions are reached. Occasionally, he may feel that a specialist has exceeded his competence – for example if the results of expert advice are producing unpalatable results in his own constituency – but this is rare. He is, however, ready to exploit a difference of opinion between experts. He will then make jurisdictional points – suggesting that a particular school of thought ought to be represented in the advisory system, or that more weight ought to be given to the views of a particular pressure group. His incentive is again political. There is no political kudos in challenging the views professed by an established group of experts – whether they be doctors, economists or what have you – so long as they are generally held within the specialism. But reputations can be made by espousing the interests of emergent new groups whose strength is currently under-represented in the machinery of government. The effect of intervening in this way is obviously 'allocative', and also partly integrative, since jurisdictional settlements can recognize new movements and alter the general direction of development. But it can leave an entrenched body of opinion without challenge even when (as perhaps in both medicine and economics) it embodies or obscures important value-elements. In this context, 'expert' implies membership of a recognized discipline or profession. Administrators are not experts in this sense and do not enjoy the same immunity.

Members of Parliament are not the only laymen in central government. Ministers are still politicians, although they experience pressures in a slightly different way when they attain office. Civil service administrators are also trained to anticipate and respond to such impulses. After a time in the machine, even professional advisers tend to become attuned to political realities, although less so than the administrators. There is a gradual shading from the completely lay to the almost completely specialized. In one sense this is a continuum of responsibility and political accountability. In another sense it is a continuum of different approaches to a particular issue – from precise but narrow specialism to the intermittent and sometimes badly aimed evaluations of the complete generalist.

Price has described the pattern, as it applies in the United States, in terms of the mediaeval relationship among estates.[1] He distinguishes four estates – the scientific, the professional, the administrative, and the political – which form 'a spectrum from truth to power'. At one extreme the scientist (including the social scientist) is remote from actual power and not on the whole interested in practical applications of his work. Professionals – doctors, engineers and so on – use the work of scientists to achieve particular purposes for which they are accountable. In doing so, they have to find compromises between what is technically possible and what is politically and economically acceptable.

It would be possible to eliminate nearly all cases of any particular epidemic disease, or nearly all transportation casualties, or for that matter nearly all professional crime, if we were willing to pay the price, in money or freedom or both. How far we go in any given case depends in part on scientific and technical considerations and in part on the opinion of the average citizen. But it depends, too, on the degree to which scientific and professional people are permitted to act on their own and the degree to which they are subject to administrative and political control.[2]

Administrators are more concerned with the general purposes of the State and with the organization and management of power. They have their own forms of expertise, but in terms of policy they are too close to their political superiors to have even the limited autonomy of the professionals.

Politicians are at the other extreme from the scientists.

The men who exercise legislative or executive power may make use of the skills of administrators and engineers and

[1] D. K. Price, *The Scientific Estate* (Cambridge, Mass., 1965) chs. 5, 7.
[2] Ibid., p. 124.

scientists, but in the end they make their most important decisions on the basis of value judgements or hunch or compromise or power interests. There can be no common discipline or body of established principles to guide them, for their business is to deal with problems in which either the inadequacy of scientific and professional data, or the conflict of expert opinion, makes it necessary or possible to come to decisions that are based on judgement and must be sustained by persuasion or authority.[1]

The balance between truth and freedom is maintained by checks and balances among the estates.

This analysis is valuable (bearing in mind that the elected Congressman has a more direct influence on policy than the elected Member of Parliament). But it would be misleading to try to draw rigid dividing lines between the respective contributions of the professional and the generalist, or between the roles of the permanent official and the elected politician. Too many people move easily from one side of the line to another – from professional to amateur status as it were. The careerist and the politician have their own clearcut brands of loyalty and commitment, but the differences are not reflected sharply in the way they approach policy, certainly not in any sharp distinction between 'fact' and 'value' or between 'administrative' and 'political' frameworks. After studying county government in Cheshire, Lee found the similarity between the chief county officials and the key elected representatives so great that he grouped them together as 'a kind of ministerialist party'.[2]

STRONGER LAY CONTROL

It is natural for Members of Parliament to complain that they lack the opportunities, the information and the expert assistance to make their 'control' of the executive more effective. This is an expression of the 'latency' principle discussed earlier. There is enthusiastic support, within Parliament as well as from outside, for specialist committees and other devices through which the M.P. can inform himself about the work for which Ministers are theoretically accountable to him. Some recent developments have been described in Chapter V. But M.P.s have not shown themselves over-zealous to

[1] Price, *The Scientific Estate*, p. 134.
[2] J. M. Lee, *Social Leaders and Public Persons* (Oxford, 1963) p. 214.

use their opportunities when they have had them. Many important debates are sparsely attended and not many members in fact seem prepared to put a great deal of work into something like the Estimates Committee.[1]

There are also administrative implications. Given the current attitudes of most M.P.s, a successful attempt to involve some of them more deeply in technical and administrative details is likely to have several effects on the development of policy. The first is that the few Members who do play an active part (particularly as chairmen of sub-committees) can acquire a great deal of influence. Because of the 'latency' principle, any parliamentary recommendation carries some weight in government departments. A comment in a Select Committee report is less weighty than a decision reached by the full House under party discipline. But it is studied carefully, and many changes in policy can be traced to, say, a recommendation from the Estimates Committee.[2] The reports themselves are seldom debated in the full House. Since the number of members on each committee is small, and few of these play a large part in the proceedings, the views of a single person may virtually pass unchallenged as the embodiment of parliamentary thinking on a particular matter.

On major issues, of course, this cannot happen, because major decisions have been processed in the Cabinet machine and perhaps brought before Parliament as a whole for ratification. (Committees

[1] This view is taken by Nevil Johnson in his discussion of the Estimates Committee (*Parliament and Administration*), e.g. pp. 144–5. On the other hand, after a study of the Select Committee on Nationalized Industries (*The Member of Parliament and the Administration*), David Coombes took a more optimistic view about the availability of members for service on such committees. Events seem to have supported the gloomier view, which may of course simply reflect the habits and other commitments of the present generation of M.P.s.

[2] Johnson (op. cit., ch. IV) doubts whether these recommendations can be said to have a decisive impact on departmental behaviour. But this may not be a very good criterion: a department may need time to persuade its special 'public'. The real yardstick of a committee's influence on departmental thinking would be the extent to which its recommendations affected the department's initial position in bargaining with these interests. There is a remarkably close connection between Estimates Committee recommendations and the institution of departmental enquiries, with other interests participating, as the first step towards reformulating policies in the desired direction. The most conspicuous examples were the *Sixth Report of the Estimates Committee, 1957–58* (H.C. 254–I) on 'Treasury Control of Expenditure' which led to the influential Plowden Committee on Control of Public Expenditure, and the *Sixth Report of the Estimates Committee, 1964–65* (H.C. 308) on 'Recruitment to the Civil Service' which led to the Fulton Committee on the Civil Service.

are supposed to avoid 'policy' issues of this sort.) And even on minor questions a committee that chooses to review settled policy is likely to find a department defensive and inclined to appeal to a higher political court. But when it engages in discussion with departmental witnesses on an embryonic issue where policy is still fluid, the views embodied in its report can be very influential, simply because they appear in a parliamentary document. (The influence of Dr Jeremy Bray on official thinking about the structure of the civil service and the organization of government statistical services in the mid-sixties was attributable very largely to his chairmanship of the sub-committees which prepared Estimates Committee reports on these subjects.[1])

When a committee takes expert evidence, the effect is even stronger, because (at least in some circumstances) more attention is paid to the views of a witness who has gained the ear of a parliamentary committee than he might have received in the normal processes of departmental consultation. It may be unfair to cite the influence of three academic witnesses on the 1964–65 Select Committee on Procedure whose fourth Report[2] recommended the establishment of specialist committees, since this was an exclusively parliamentary matter. But even in this case it is fair to claim that the outcome might have been different if different witnesses had been consulted or if the distribution of presentational skills had been different. Quite apart from the principle that the layman does not directly criticize the expert, it is, of course, difficult for a parliamentary committee, or its chairman, to assess the whole balance of considerations on a particular matter. A committee has to select the evidence on which it will base its recommendations and its selection is bound to be influenced by the personal views of its expert adviser.[3]

Independent assessments can be a useful addition to the regular machinery for preparing policy. The personal contributions of individual Members of Parliament may be (and in many of the instances that come to mind undoubtedly have been) of considerable value. But this has been because the M.P. is a knowledgeable and intelligent person. The fact that he is a member of a representative assembly does not seem to be relevant.

[1] *Sixth Report 1964–65* (H.C 308) and *Fourth Report 1966–67* (H.C. 246).
[2] (H.C. 305).
[3] See p. 111, note 2.

A second effect may be to *weaken* the most useful part that laymen can play in the process. The special value of parliamentary review lies in the M.P.'s place in the communication system which links departments to various publics. It cannot be delegated to a few members who happen to be knowledgeable and interested in a particular subject. Indeed, too much knowledge may be a disqualification. Special knowledge tends to imply a commitment and committed laymen become relatively less sensitive to other pressures. To retain a balance, they may need to be made accountable to other laymen who are neither knowledgeable nor involved. Since Parliament cannot handle all the business with which it is charged, it is inevitable that some of its work should be delegated to committees, and in practice to the small number of active members on each committee. The older, non-specialized, committees probably approach their task of reviewing proposals and procedures in much the same spirit as Parliament as a whole. But it does not seem that the newer, specialized, committees will serve the same purpose. It may be necessary for their reports to be discussed by uncommitted laymen as critically as the older sort of committee discussed the work of departments. And pressures on parliamentary time (as well as the reluctance of relatively inactive backbenchers to criticize their more active colleagues) make it unlikely that this will be done.

THE BALANCE OF CONTRIBUTIONS

The intermittent, amateur character of the present parliamentary system seems remarkably appropriate in the light of what is *distinctive* about politicians' contribution to policy. It is already the function of Ministers and general administrative civil servants to undertake a continuous and relatively knowledgeable review of the demands made by technical experts and special interest groups in order to relate them to other pressures and commitments. It is their business to take as broad a view as they can, to assemble as much information as possible about conflicting technical views on a problem and to formulate policies that have a reasonable chance of being acceptable to the special interests concerned and to the public at large. Their job is to achieve a kind of balancing act among facts, pressures and assumptions. Part of the job of politicians outside the government is to make sure that they do. If the policies that emerge from this process are repeatedly found to be unacceptable, the process is clearly deficient and perhaps the structure needs revision. But Ministers and civil servants, in their respective ways, are still in the best position to put matters right. It is not functional for those at a more general level in the system to try to do it for them. Granted that politicians are not supermen, the opportunist, random, way in which the attention of M.P.s is directed to particular subjects may well offer the most effective means for injecting their pressure for rationality – for consistency and integration – into the policy-making system. They are bound to complain at the lack of access to special advice and information. But it might not be an unmitigated blessing if their requests were granted. Price speaks of the risk in the American system that Congress 'will surrender its powers to its own committees, and that they will be too obsessed with new technological toys to deal with broader issues of policy'.[1]

A further point of importance here is the order in which different contributions can most effectively be combined. At what point can pressures for integration most effectively be related to technical aspects of policy? We have noted the difficulty of modifying policies once they have been formulated. There is constant pressure to involve lay interests at an earlier stage so that they (the public, Members of Parliament, Ministers, general administrators) can influence the direction of technical thinking.

This question will exercise us from several points of view in Part Three. One or two preliminary points can be made briefly. A political decision tends to be more difficult to alter than a technical one. Since it is supposed to be based on *all* relevant considerations it is hard to admit later that an important point has been over-looked; the only real court of appeal is the still less expert one of public opinion. It is also quite easy for experts to make technical judgements without taking political factors into account. But it is very difficult to make defensible political decisions without taking account of such technical information as is available. The model outlined in the last chapter is in fact functionally correct: as policy develops, the framework of consideration moves sequentially from the technical to the general. If the 'integrative' and 'allocative' elements in public administration are to be attended to by finite human minds, it must normally be near the end of the process rather than the beginning, unless it is the process itself that is being

[1] Price, *The Scientific Estate*, p. 81.

scrutinized. Civil servants have a number of perfectly respectable reasons for wanting to keep Ministers 'out of their hair' until the right moment. Ministers are concerned with their reputations, and are interested in action. On the other hand, they find it difficult to change their minds in public without embarrassment. Sir Edward Playfair has described how when he was at the Treasury he had, after intricate manœuvring, nearly reached a solution to a minor but long-standing problem when the then Prime Minister heard about it and started asking questions, with the result that everybody else fell back into inflexible bargaining positions.[1] Ministers feel the same about exposing their preliminary ideas to Parliament before they have been firmed up. This does not, of course, exclude the role of political *initiative* in defining objectives that subsequently have to be converted into workable policies (see Chapter VIII, p. 162). And on questions such as comprehensive secondary educa-tion, or selectivity in the social services, where feelings run high but factual evidence is absent or ambiguous, the politician will often take the burden of decision upon himself in matters of detail also.[2]

This model, which gives politicians a primarily apellate and mediating role, assumes that in Britain, at least, society has many purposes which are often in conflict. Within the framework of the social services, for example, the objectives of the health and teach-ing professions cannot ultimately be reduced to a common denom-inator. Even the various branches of medicine are competing for re-sources and prestige rather than mutually supporting in the pursuit of a common goal. The task of administrators and politicians is primarily one of integrating competing elements and allocating resources to them. An Act of Parliament or an annual budget repre-sents a compromise among the conflicting interests of, for example, doctors, patients and taxpayers. The special function of elected politicians is to symbolize a 'general good' which can be opposed to more sectional goods. But in the last resort this is only a device to provide a focus for the allocative and integrative activities: in reality the 'general good' has no meaning apart from the sum of sectional interests. It is useful only so long as it is left inexplicit.

[1] Sir E. Playfair, 'Minister or Civil Servant?' *Public Administration*, vol. 43 (1965) p. 268.
[2] Rather similar conclusions are reached by Walkland, who has discussed the policy-making process from a more legal and formal point of view. S. A. Walkland, *The Legislative Process in Great Britain* (London, 1968). See especially his analysis of proposals for parliamentary reform in ch. VII.

There is one other point to be made at this stage. It concerns the effect on the general administrator's frame of reference of strengthening the political part of the spectrum. It is almost impossible to over-stress the weight which the present system gives to parliamentary considerations. Parliament may look weak to the reader of *Hansard*. But the civil service still acts as if it were not so. Its preoccupation with Parliament is a major factor in the way policy is at present formulated. It may be excessive for modern conditions. Clearly, parliamentary pressures will be less 'appropriate' in some areas of decision-making than in others. Fairly substantial areas of public action have been (or are being) taken out of the area open to parliamentary scrutiny. Shielded from this form of pressure, the responsible administrators will be freer to concentrate on commercial or other aspects of the problems before them. It seems likely that as the public sector grows large sections of it will be 'depoliticized' in this way. The criterion in each case must be the effect of one or the other type of structure on the balance of considerations in the mind of somebody contributing to decisions and to the formulation of policy. If there is less opportunity for Parliament to intervene, integrative and allocative pressures will have less impact and internal technical considerations will therefore carry more weight.

We are again faced with the problem of balance. If we know what we want to achieve, we can devise an organization suitable for the purpose. In public administration weight has to be given to co-ordination and integration as well as to internal efficiency and technical adequacy. More emphasis on one of these aspects means less on another. In Part Three we shall examine a number of specific questions about the structure of public administration from this point of view.

PART THREE: Problems

X. The Machinery of Government

ADMINISTRATIVE INNOVATIONS IN THE TWENTIETH CENTURY

Questions about the machinery of government seem to attract public interest only at times when governments are taking on new kinds of responsibilities that cannot be absorbed along familiar lines and there is a period of experiment before they are fully digested. Three such periods can be identified in the present century. The first was prompted by the great increase in government activities, including new social services and the temporary control of industry, about the time of the First World War. The Ministry of Labour (1916), the Department of Scientific and Industrial Research (1915), and the original Ministry of Health, which looked after local government and the Poor Law as well as the Health Insurance Scheme (1919), date from this time. The relevant controversies can be traced in the famous Haldane Report.[1]

The second period was immediately after the Second World War. First the Coalition and then the Labour Government accepted responsibility for full employment, for new and expanded health and insurance schemes, for large sections of the transport and fuel industries and, with the help of the local authorities, for new schemes of housing, welfare and town and country planning. Controversy about the most appropriate machinery for government supervision and control of nationalized industries stimulated a considerable academic literature. The new relationships between central and local government also led to controversy and to the important reports of the Local Government Manpower Committee.[2] An

[1] *Report of the Machinery of Government Committee*, Cd. 9230 (1918). The Committee's terms of reference were 'to enquire into the responsibilities of the various Departments of the central executive Government, and to advise in what manner the exercise and distribution by the Government of its functions should be improved'.

[2] *First Report of the Local Government Manpower Committee*, Cmd. 7870 (1950); *Second Report*, Cmd. 8421 (1951).

authoritative study of changes in central government organization which was originally commissioned by the Royal Institute of Public Administration during this period has become a standard text-book.[1] The main departmental innovations dating from this time were the Ministries of Housing and Local Government (1950), National Insurance (1946), and Fuel and Power (1942).

The third period of administrative innovation is the present. It began in 1962 with important changes in the machinery for financial and economic planning: the Treasury was reorganized to give more weight to forward planning of public expenditure and the National Economic Development Council was established as a joint government-industry-union organization to seek agreement on ways of improving the United Kingdom's economic performance. The relatively unsuccessful National Incomes Commission, boy-cotted by the unions and ultimately to be replaced by the far more powerful Prices and Incomes Board, was also set up at this time. In the following year the President of the Board of Trade was specially charged with the co-ordination of policies related to economic development in the regions. In April 1964 the Office of the Minister of Science was combined with the old Ministry of Education (initially on federal lines, with two Cabinet Ministers and two Permanent Secretaries) into a strong Department of Education and Science which also took over from the Treasury the responsibility for university development.

The process was accelerated after the Labour victory in October 1964. Science was divided into pure and applied, and the latter became the sole responsibility of a new Ministry of Technology. Existing administrative units were elevated into the Ministry of Overseas Development and the Welsh Office. A new Ministry of Land and Natural Resources was created, and looked for a time like taking planning from the Ministry of Housing and Local Govern-ment. The brightest star in the new firmament, however, was the glamorous new Department of Economic Affairs. To D.E.A. went the long-term economic planning functions of the Treasury, the regional development functions of the Board of Trade (soon to be complemented by an impressive apparatus of regional economic planning councils and boards), much of the planning work, as well as many of the staff, of the National Economic Development

[1] F. M. G. Willson, *The Organization of British Central Government 1914–64* (2nd edn.) (London, 1968).

Office, a glittering array of economists and industrial advisers drawn from the whole civil service, the universities and private industry (some of them without government pay), and one of the strongest personalities in the Government as First Secretary and Secretary of State.

The next four years saw almost continuous change and experiment, both in administrative machinery and in the political command. There were four successive Secretaries of State at Education and Science, four different heads at D.E.A., including a spell under the Prime Minister, and as many co-ordinators of social policy. The Ministry of Land and Natural Resources was re-absorbed into the Ministry of Housing and Local Government after setting up a Land Commission. The Ministry of Technology, originally a sort of glorified Department of Scientific and Industrial Research, took on successive responsibilities from the Board of Trade for specific industries and finally absorbed (or was absorbed by) most of the Ministry of Aviation. After the collapse of its first National Plan the Department of Economic Affairs began to lose many of its original staff and functions, culminating in the loss of its responsibility for prices, incomes and productivity to the Ministry of Labour (renamed the Department of Employment and Productivity) in April 1968 and its final demise in October 1969.

By the middle of 1968 it had been decided to create a new Civil Service Department out of the Civil Service Commission and part of the Treasury. Discussions were proceeding about the most suitable parent department for the Post Office when it became an independent corporation in the following year. Other changes seemed bound to follow from reports of the Seebohm Committee (which wanted social work responsibilities to be concentrated in one department)[1] and the Select Committee on Nationalized Industries (which wanted to see a new Ministry for Nationalized Industry).[2] On the other hand, some older departments were being wound up. The Colonial Office had disappeared and a further amalgamation was planned between the Commonwealth Office and the Foreign

---

[1] *Report of the Committee on Local Authority and Allied Personal Social Services,* Cmnd. 3703 (1968) esp. pars. 637–9.

[2] *Report of the Select Committee on Nationalised Industries, 1967–68* (H.C. 371–I) 'Ministerial Control of the Nationalized Industries'. After consideration the Government rejected the proposal for a separate Ministry but agreed with the need to review the existing responsibilities of various departments towards the industries. Cmnd. 4027 (1969).

Office. The Ministries of Health and Social Security were about to be merged.[1]

Away from Whitehall, the Government had established two further semi-autonomous bodies, the Prices and Incomes Board and the Industrial Reorganization Corporation, to extend its influence over the economy. The steel industry had been re-nationalized under the British Steel Corporation and it seemed possible that a National Hydrocarbons Authority would be established to handle North Sea gas. British Railways had been restructured and the financial obligations of the nationalized industries redefined. A new group of public bodies, Regional Transport Authorities, was planned to take over the transport undertakings of some local authorities. Predictably, local government was being reviewed: committees had reported on its staffing and management and a Royal Commission was considering areas and functions.[2]

As in the earlier post-war period, there has been no comprehensive official review of the principles behind the many changes. The main architect seems to have been the Prime Minister himself, and the reasons for various bits of re-structuring have to be pieced together from statements by Mr Wilson and other government spokesmen, and from odd paragraphs in committee reports.

It is tempting to suggest that all this ferment calls for a new Haldane enquiry into the purposes of government and the most appropriate instruments for carrying them out. But the issues have not become any simpler over the last fifty years. It seems very doubtful whether an enquiry of the Royal Commission type would be able to survey such a vast field as the public sector today, even with the support of research, and produce useful conclusions. Opinions about the best division of responsibility between the public and private sectors, or between central and local government, or between conventional government departments and public boards for whose activities the Minister is only broadly accountable, reflect

[1] The Foreign and Commonwealth Office came into existence in October 1968 and the Department of Health and Social Security on 1 November. The latter, like the Department of Education and Science in 1964, was a federal department with two Ministers and two Permanent Secretaries under the Secretary of State for Social Services (see pp. 211–12 below).

[2] *Report of the Committee on the Management of Local Government* (Maud Report) Ministry of Housing and Local Government, 1967; *Report of the Committee on the Staffing of Local Government* (Mallaby Report) Ministry of Housing and Local Government, 1967; *Report of the Royal Commission on Local Government in England*, Cmnd. 4040 (1969).

broad political choices about the kind of society we want to live in, and cannot be resolved by an 'impartial' enquiry. But political choices could be much better informed that they are now.

In the remainder of this chapter, the ideas in Part Two will be applied, tentatively, to one small part of the problem – the distribution of functions between the departments of central government. General discussion of the principles involved in some recent developments is followed by a detailed study of the special field of social welfare administration.

Political Factors

Some changes can be attributed largely to the personal qualities of various leading politicians at the time. Thus, Mr Quintin Hogg (Lord Hailsham) is a key figure in some of the reshuffles before October 1964, just as the personalities of Mr George Brown and Mrs Barbara Castle became important afterwards. The Prime Minister has to keep party strengths and loyalties in mind when exercising his patronage over Ministerial posts.

Other innovations may have been prompted mainly by the Government's desire to be seen to be doing something about a particular problem. Between February 1961 and July 1963 the Prime Minister was asked in the House of Commons if he would appoint Ministers to take charge of the following subjects: Disarmament, Sport, Overseas Aid, Welsh Affairs, Economic Planning, Civil Defence, Shipping and Ship-building, Government Information Services, Housing in Scotland, Development in Scotland, Location of Industry, Overseas Trade, Security, Satellite Communications and United Nations Affairs.[1] In each case, at least one M.P. felt the subject sufficiently important to require the attention of a full-time Minister. (Many of the suggestions were in fact adopted over the following five years, often by simply adding a new title to an existing post or attaching a new junior Minister to an existing department without necessarily giving him any supporting staff.) Lord Hailsham's title of Minister of Science seems to have been purely symbolic when it was bestowed in 1959: the research councils already reported to him as Lord President of the Council and he was given no additional duties. Similar motives seem to have inspired the Ministry of Technology in its original form: presenting

[1] I am indebted for this list to Mr James Robertson.

the enabling bill in the House of Lords, Lord Snow admitted that its practical objectives could be met in other ways, but said that it was desirable to mark the Government's commitment to technological progress by creating a new department with a Cabinet Minister (Mr Frank Cousins) at its head.[1] The elevation of the Department of Technical Co-operation into the Ministry of Overseas Development under Mrs Barbara Castle is in the same category.

It is almost impossible to judge the success of such 'symbolic' changes. Responsibility for pure science was given to the Department of Education and Science in 1964 largely in the belief that a strong departmental Minister would be in a better position to obtain the resources needed for scientific development. It was not long before aggrieved critics were claiming that both science and the universities were suffering because the Secretary for Education and Science was giving most of his attention to school problems. As there is no means of determining what resources would have been secured under alternative arrangements, it is impossible to prove or disprove the allegation. The only test of a political move is political; do the new arrangements generate more confidence than the old ones?

Meeting New Needs

The new Department of Economic Affairs was not just the product of reshuffling existing functions. It was intended to provide a focus for work that was not being done at all within the existing framework, notably national planning for faster economic growth and the restructuring of British industry. The same kind of thinking inspired the 1968 proposals for new departments to promote efficient management in the civil service and in the nationalized industries; it was believed that a new driving force would be generated by bringing a number of existing activities together in a department that had no distracting functions, like the Treasury's interest in short-run economy or the Board of Trade's interest in persuading the air corporations to buy British. Again, it is almost impossible to say whether D.E.A. achieved more than would have been done by, say, the Treasury and the Board of Trade under equivalent political direction and leadership. But we can say something about the organizational mechanics involved. First, we need to digress and

[1] *H.L. Debs.*, vol. 262 (4 February 1965) cols. 1298–9 (Second Reading of Science and Technology Bill).

explore the problems of co-ordination and specialization in the public sector.

PROBLEMS OF CO-ORDINATION

The work of government departments can be broken down into a large number of more or less self-contained tasks which have to be co-ordinated. In isolation each task presents its own technical problems calling for special knowledge and techniques in anything from office management to operational research. But each task also has to be related to others. If it is instrumental to some broad aim of policy it has to be controlled and kept under review, so that the means does not become an end in itself. Primary co-ordination is normally achieved by grouping tasks in departments. Moreover, some devices are needed to ensure that tasks are not carried out in ways that prejudice the welfare of society as a whole, or the current framework of beliefs about the way the State should conduct its business – rules about economy, assumptions about the weight to be given to private rights, and so on. These external factors again have to be injected into the work of individual sections, perhaps by indoctrination training, or by superimposing financial controls, appeals systems and formal consultation procedures upon them. The difficult question (indeed the real question about administrative machinery) is what weight to allow in the structure to each of the competing pressures with a claim on the attention of those carrying out basic tasks.

Let us start with a few examples. In the Department of Education and Science groups of administrators are concerned with the negotiation of salaries, pensions and conditions of service for teachers. Similar groups in the Home Office and the Department of Health are engaged on almost identical problems affecting policemen, firemen, doctors and nurses. In their day-to-day work they are applying common principles about consultation, national incomes policy and public service conditions of employment. Their knowledge and techniques have far more in common with one another, and with the divisions in the Civil Service Department that supervise these things, than with those of colleagues in their own departments. They are, of course, applying departmental policy as well – the problem of providing incentives to aid recruitment in difficult areas, for example, is viewed differently in the three departments.

But they specialize in remuneration rather than in education or health. Other divisions in the same department will similarly be applying inter-departmental techniques to building programmes, the control of revenue expenditure, routine servicing for technical committees, and the application of cost-benefit analysis to operational problems.

Nevertheless, the work they are doing is only a means to the provision of an education service employing staff of a certain quality, deployed over schools of certain types, bearing certain ratios to the numbers of children in each area. It is under the control of a Minister and senior staff who are concerned with the service as a whole and will have its broad objectives in mind in reviewing problems that come up (for example after parliamentary challenge) from the remuneration division. The staff in the division will have acquired a fair amount of personal experience of the problems facing other parts of the department. Through constant exposure they will also have picked up some of the department's characteristic ethos. Departments develop inbred habits and attitudes, both internally and in relation to outside bodies. They differ, for example, in their attitudes to professional expertise, and this attitude tends to permeate all their dealings with experts. (In his evidence to the Fulton Committee, Trevor Smith argues that whole departments can be classified along a scale of 'modernity', on the basis of the complexity of their decision-making process and hence the status enjoyed by the specialists who understand it.[1]) They have characteristic patterns of consultation and of delegation. Whatever the pattern is, it tends to become entrenched in a social system, with its own norms and pressures, to which newcomers have to conform if they are going to fit in smoothly.

Some features of this social structure may be irrelevant to the way tasks are performed. Others may be beneficial. For example, it was claimed that specialists and administrators (half of them qualified in economics) in the early D.E.A. comprised 'a small highly-integrated group working intimately with other departments and more or less wholly engaged in policy-making'[2] and generated a commitment to economic growth and national planning that would

---

[1] *Fulton Report*, vol. 5, pp. 1135–6. (Trevor Smith on behalf of the Acton Society Trust.)

[2] Sir Eric Roll, 'The Machinery for Economic Planning: the Department of Economic Affairs', *Public Administration*, vol. 44 (1966) p. 6.

have been very difficult psychologically in the Treasury. The Minister of Technology has made a similar point about his department:

> I think what has justified the establishment of the Ministry of Technology, and it is a reason which is hardly ever mentioned, is that there is now a government department whose top echelons are manned more or less equally by engineers, scientists and administrators and whose job it has been to get close enough to industry to understand what industry was trying to say to government – to go to industry with a microphone to pick up what it was saying, rather than with a megaphone.

Mr Wedgwood Benn went on to say:

> I am sure . . . that it was right to divide technology from academic science. With science, you should take a lump sum – however much you can afford – and you should invite the scientists to divide the money for you. With technology, we ought not to have a lump sum. We ought to have to justify the money we spend in terms of its likely return.[1]

The argument here is that the department as a whole develops a technology, as well as a collective attitude, which is valuable throughout its work. Similarly, the Select Committee on Nationalized Industries thought that specialization in efficiency methods would develop most naturally in a department which was solely concerned with the economic performance of the industries.

In such a case, departmental grouping may facilitate administrative specialization. But these may be the exceptions. In most cases, the tasks of a department are heterogeneous, and it seems less likely that its characteristic technology will be equally useful throughout its sections. The techniques and mental approach appropriate for the control of local education authority expenditure may be a serious handicap if applied to forward planning of education policy A departmental basis for career planning may prevent individuals from acquiring specialized techniques – without *necessarily* giving them a compensating awareness of common purpose, since most departments embody more than one purpose and departmental boundaries may in any event alter considerably in the course of an individual's career.

This was certainly the view of the Fulton Committee. It recom-

[1] 'Mintech – Myth and Reality', *The Times* (London) 29 March 1968.

mended that administrators should specialize in an area of administration, and suggested economics and finance on the one hand and
social administration on the other, with a number of sub-specialisms
on each side, as a provisional basis for career planning. It found that
it was not possible to link these careers to individual departments.
In the Department of Education and Science, for example, although
this was predominantly a 'social' department, it found groups of
administrators dealing with questions of departmental efficiency,
finance, general science policy, and technical aspects of building
projects, each of which, according to the Committee, required its
own form of expertise. The Committee recommended accordingly
that career patterns should be related to the subject-matter of the
work and not, as at present, to particular departments or even
groups of departments. The 'economic and financial' administrators should have 'appropriate qualifications, experience and
training in such subjects as economics, finance, business administration and statistics' and therefore 'should be employed in any
department in posts that are mainly financial or concerned with
economic administration and management'.[1] Similarly the 'social
administration' group should move among departments in posts
that develop 'the basic concepts and knowledge relevant to their
area of administration . . . The basic principle of career management should be a progressive development within a specialism and
between fields of activity that are related to each other.'[2]

Jobs can be analysed to see what knowledge and techniques they
require. Posts could then be allocated on a basis of individual
qualifications and suitability for them. For example, there must at
some point in the central administration be a person who deals
with, say, teachers' pensions and is a focal point for enquiries,
negotiations and the preparation of statutory instruments to give
effect to changes. The superannuation code is a complicated one.
In one sense, responsibility for pensions is clearly part of a general
responsibility for the education service and some provisions of the
code arise specifically from the special nature of the teaching force
(for example the problems of part-time married women). On the
other hand, some of the most complicated parts of the code arise
from the application of general government policy on public sector
pensions (such as their relationship to the National Insurance

[1] *Fulton Report*, vol. 1, par. 9.
[2] Ibid., par. 115. (But see ch. 3, p. 56 above for reactions to these proposals.)

scheme and the implementation of the Pensions (Increase) Acts), and are similar to provisions in the superannuation schemes for nurses, policemen and others. If the officers responsible for teachers' pensions have spent their careers largely on various pension schemes, they will be able to handle problems arising from the general policy fairly quickly; but it may take them quite a long time to sort out what lies behind a point that is specific to teachers. It is a matter of trial and error to discover which kind of question is likely to arise most frequently and to measure the time saved or lost by arranging career progression so that an officer develops familiarity with one rather than the other.

The problem here is a simple one of operational economy, of discovering which combinations of tasks produce the greatest savings because they use the same information, techniques or working methods. At higher levels, the quality of decision-making becomes more important than operational economy. The important factor there is the relevance of the ideas that are in the minds of administrators and politicians when they are preparing material for decision.

The Haldane Committee concluded in 1918 that departments should be organized on a basis of the service provided (for example health or education). Its argument was couched in administrative terms:

> . . . the acquisition of knowledge . . . and the development of specialized capacity . . . are obviously most likely to be secured when the officers of a Department are continuously engaged in the study of questions which all relate to a single service and when the efforts of the Department are definitely concentrated upon the development and improvement of the particular service which the Department exists to supervise.[1]

But an administrative case could be made out just as well for specialization by process (public building, finance or conditions of service), by place (Scotland, Wales or English regions), or by special clienteles (children, pensioners, the poor). The Haldane argument is really a political one, related to the political needs of its time. It was desirable, in the eyes of Beatrice Webb, Robert Morant and other members of the Committee, to get away from the degradations of pauperism by creating preventive social services, a policy

[1] *Report of the Machinery of Government Committee*, p. 8, par. 20.

that seemed most likely to succeed if there were distinct departments separately committed to the various services.

Political needs, however, change. We shall see in the next section that current thinking on social policy tends to be orientated to clienteles rather than to services. There are also many examples of minor changes in emphasis. Early in 1966 a junior Minister with special responsibility for immigration was transferred from the Department of Economic Affairs to the Home Office, which administers immigration controls. The original appointment had been made at a time when the National Plan was under preparation and immigration policy was closely related to what was then seen as an emerging shortage of manpower. By early 1966 the main problem was seen to be the administration of controls and the orderly assimilation of immigrants into the community. In another field, the Ministry of Aviation, as partial successor to the wartime Ministry of Supply, employed very large numbers of scientists and spent substantial sums on scientific research and development which was primarily related to defence. In the changed conditions of 1966 it was clearly desirable that the fruits of this work should be applied wherever possible in civilian industry. The Ministry's purchasing power was also seen to be an important weapon which governments could use to encourage innovation and modernization in key industries. It was a logical step to bring most of the Ministry's staff and functions under the political direction of the Minister of Technology.

The effect of such a change is, ultimately, to mesh together two previously disconnected pieces of policy. A Minister usually sees a sample of the work carried out in different parts of his department. His mind is likely to fasten on common elements, if only because considerations that came up in connection with problem A are still at the back of his mind a few minutes later when he looks at problem B from the other 'side' of his department. If he feels that an important connection is being missed, he has the authority to ask for a review. Or he may simply ask questions that in Laski's phrase 'inject a stream of tendency' into developments. The combination of functions under a single Minister is a sound and elegant way of implementing political ideas about the primary context in which certain problems should be regarded. The parliamentary system, moreover, places Ministers under some pressure to be consistent over the whole field for which they are accountable. While it is always hazardous to speculate about the way these things work in practice (and much of the foregoing argument is necessarily *a priori*) it seems possible that even the unlikely association of child care with crime prevention under the Home Secretary encouraged the policy assumption that juvenile delinquency and deprivation were different aspects of the same problem.[1]

What goes for the Minister also goes for senior advisers and administrators who prepare material for his decision and take decisions on his behalf. At top policy levels, political arguments about the machinery of government make sense. But they make much less sense lower down the line. In the extreme case, the scientist in his government laboratory may be very little concerned in the uses to which his work may eventually be put. For him, a change of responsible ministry may mean a good deal of irrelevant and meaningless disturbance. There will be trivial and possibly irritating changes in designations and filing systems. Professional contacts may be unable to find him in the *Imperial Calendar*. More seriously, he will have to learn how to win resources from a new establishment and organization division, who may play the game according to unfamiliar rules. The scientist may, in practice, be screened from much of this disturbance. But his administrative colleagues will not, and may well suffer the extra dislocation of a physical move to a new departmental building.

The fallacy is to assume that only one type of co-ordination is important. Unification by primary political purpose may be achieved at the expense of other unities – by administrative technique or by the relationship to other purposes. It does not usually make political sense to divide functions among Ministers according to the administrative techniques involved. But technical specialization could be furthered by finding a better basis than departmental boundaries for administrative careers. The problem of devising machinery that will relate one purpose to others is more difficult. The operations of the coal industry can be linked with fuel policy, with employment policy, with economic planning or with import-replacement, to name only a few. One of these relationships must predominate at any one time. But the others do not cease to be relevant. Ultimately (because ultimately the function of government *is* indivisible), all arguments of this kind finish by advocating

[1] Reflected, for example, in the White Paper, *The Child, the Family and the Young Offender*, Cmnd. 2742 (1965).

one huge super-department. The nearest practical alternative is to let one purpose (perhaps operational efficiency) determine the primary departmental affiliation, and to provide links with departments which represent the others. One link could be supplied by appointing senior administrators with experience of these departments to the coal division. Or there could be rules that certain decisions were to be taken only after consultation. A supervising department whose main interest was in efficiency might be required to consult the Department of Employment before approving a pit closure. If agreement was not reached, the question would have to be resolved in discussion between the two Ministers, or at Cabinet. Financial discipline (that is to say, attention to the economy goal in public administration) is secured throughout the service by securing to Treasury a right of objection over nearly all expenditure proposals and by planning careers so that a proportion of staff in spending departments have personal experience of Treasury work.

It is now possible to return to the argument about a separate Department of Economic Affairs. Any basis of departmentalization implies a system of priorities. This may reflect a balance of forces within the department – perhaps the relative seniority of those who are accustomed to favour one set of factors over others. In a hierarchical organization, pressure for consistency at the top can lead to a monolithic outlook in which one set of considerations is permanently suppressed because someone has expressed a marginal preference on a normative occasion, for example when a leading case is settled at high level. Sir Edward Boyle has written about the tendency of civil servants to assume that the Minister's mind was much more firmly set than in fact it was.[1] Thus in a department which was responsible both for economy and for industrial redevelopment, it could happen that redevelopment schemes were always put aside because of the inherent reluctance of senior officials to incur expenditure in the short term. The argument is a theoretical one, but it has been supported by the Prime Minister:

MR BRUCE-GARDYNE Now that the D.E.A. has lost the prices and incomes policy, what other purpose does it serve, apart from providing the member for Stepney with a car, office, and a fat salary?

[1] Sir Edward Boyle (with others), 'Who are the Policy Makers?' *Public Administration*, vol. 43 (1965) p. 258.

MR WILSON The short answer is that he has an extremely important portfolio that ensures by the co-ordination of the industrial administration that the real resources are available to meet the requirements of the Chancellor's policy, both as regards productivity, exports and import replacement. It is an important function that could not be left in the Treasury.

MR THORPE Why is it that jobs discharged by the D.E.A. cannot be discharged by the Treasury?

MR WILSON The Treasury has an extremely full time job to do with not only the general financial policy, budgetary policy, expenditure and international liquidity policy. We have found over past years when the Treasury was also responsible for industrial co-ordination that the work was not done and was always sacrificed to purely financial considerations.[1]

The point has been made that policy-makers can focus only on a limited number of factors at once. If a department serves only one purpose there is no risk of that purpose being neglected. Hence more disputes will arise between it and other departments and will have to be settled at political level. The options will be kept open and, if the choices are fairly marginal, a more balanced run of decisions may result. It may be that a department committed exclusively to export policy and import replacement will at some stage become a liability and distort the balance of some future argument about trade expansion. In that case, political forces should secure its demise. But sometimes it is more important to get the balance of forces right *within* a department. The Economics Editor of *The Times* argued that it was wrong to strip the Treasury of responsibilities for management and long-term planning because, isolated from these pressures, it tended to revert to an old-fashioned (and very hampering) Ministry of Finance.[2] The Conservative Party has maintained throughout the existence of the D.E.A. that it was better to have a single department (that is to say, the Treasury) covering all economic functions.

To sum up so far, any administrative task, such as the negotiation of teachers' superannuation or a cost-benefit study of road-pricing devices, can be viewed from at least three points of view: (a) its technical content, (b) its relationship with a major political

[1] *H.C. Debs.*, vol. 763 (23 April 1968) cols. 27–8.
[2] Peter Jay, 'Don't Split the Treasury', *The Times*, 1 August 1968.

purpose, (c) the need for consistency with other major purposes. These are separate dimensions and it is unlikely that the same structural arrangements will serve all three. Technical expertise can best be secured by the selection and training of staff who pursue an integrated career in the field. Subordination to a major goal implies locating it in a department whose senior echelons are committed to the pursuit of that goal. Consistency with other goals implies inter-departmental co-ordination procedures and a supra-departmental authority to resolve disputes. According to the political and administrative needs of the time, any activity can be slotted into place along each of these three dimensions. The first is independent of the other two (although it has not been recognized as such in the past) and presents mainly career and training problems. The other two are much more closely inter-connected, since it must be a matter of judgement whether any particular goal-conflict is too important politically to be resolved by the internal processes of a large department at any particular time. In a very few cases, the relative advantages and disadvantages of different groupings could be compared systematically if research workers had access to the files of government departments in different parts of the United Kingdom. For instance, the School Health Service comes under the Health Department in Northern Ireland but under the Education Department in England.

The question of intra- or inter-departmental co-ordination has been obscured by another current trend, that of amalgamating departments in order to simplify and strengthen the political chain of command. It is often suggested that Cabinet government would work more effectively if instead of a score or more independent departments the number could be kept down to about half a dozen, each presided over by a Cabinet Minister, to cover huge fields like Economics and Finance, Defence, External Relations, Trade and Industry, Home Affairs, Local Government and Social Services. (Even these overlap.) A tendency to amalgamate and combine existing departments has succeeded the tendency to proliferate new ones in 1964. Hence the general support given to the abolition of the Colonial Office, the Commonwealth Office, the separate service departments (a process started with the creation of the Ministry of Defence in 1946 but not completed until nearly twenty years later), the Ministry of Aviation, the Ministry of Land and Natural Resources and the separate Ministries of Health and Social Security.

SOCIAL WELFARE ADMINISTRATION

Most of these points can be illustrated from changing ideas about the administrative structure most appropriate for social security, health and family welfare.

In July 1948 three of the main post-war welfare services came into operation. The National Insurance scheme was designed to provide universal subsistence benefits as a right in return for compulsory weekly contributions. National assistance was intended to provide relief, without contribution conditions but subject to a means test, mainly for those whose incomes failed before they had qualified for insurance benefits. The National Health Service was, with minor exceptions, free to the user but financed partly from a weekly contribution collected along with insurance payments. Family allowances, payable without means test or insurance conditions, had already been operating since 1946.

The Beveridge Report recommended that family allowances, national insurance and national assistance should be administered by a new Ministry of Social Security, which might also take over war pensions, employment services and the regulation of voluntary insurance schemes.[1] In fact, we had a Ministry of National Insurance which was initially made responsible only for family allowances and the National Insurance scheme. It was amalgamated with the Ministry of (War) Pensions in 1955, when both schemes had settled down and it was thought that a merger would produce economies. To administer the assistance scheme, an independent National Assistance Board was set up on the model of the earlier Unemployment Assistance Board. Although the Minister of National Insurance handled the Board's parliamentary business, he was not answerable for its actions in individual cases. This was partly to prevent the affairs of the Board's clients from being raised in Parliament; the Board was very jealous of its confidential status. It was also felt that assistance and insurance were different sorts of services and were best administered in watertight compartments. The main problems of the insurance scheme were maintaining contribution records and checking claims for benefit against entitlement in the light of a complicated code of regulations. The National Assistance Board also had its scales of entitlement; but in addition

[1] *Social Insurance and Allied Services*, Cmnd. 6404 (1942) pars. 385–98.

it had to administer a means test humanely to applicants who were often in need of other social services; its staff became increasingly involved in 'first-aid' social work and referral. The Board and the Ministry both took their responsibilities to the public seriously. They developed impressive and highly specialized training arrangements for their staff, who worked with little overlap from different local offices. On the Insurance side, also, a great deal of effort was spent on streamlining office methods, with consequent savings on administrative overheads.

By the 1960s, however, the original financial distinction between the two schemes had collapsed. An attempt was made to keep the insurance fund in balance, but benefit rates had been increased to keep up with the declining value of money and the amounts paid out were not actuarially supported by what the recipients had paid in. Even so, the rates did not always cover subsistence needs: many of the elderly and unemployed needed to look to the National Assistance Board to supplement their insurance benefits. Those who were entitled to supplementation did not always seek it. A survey disclosed that a fifth refrained from applying because they wished to remain independent, while another three-tenths were prevented by ignorance or misconceptions.[1] The Government decided that an administrative merger between the two schemes would make for simplification and eliminate stigma. In February 1966 Mr Douglas Houghton announced the Government's intention to create a new Ministry 'in which the old distinction between national insurance and national assistance officers will disappear and the name National Assistance will disappear for ever'.[2] Six months later the necessary legislation had been passed: the Minister of Pensions and National Insurance became the Minister of Social Security; the National Assistance Board was wound up and a Supplementary Benefits Commission set up to assist the Minister to run equivalent services; a number of minor changes were made in forms and nomenclature; and the process of integrating the two services was begun.

The primary object of the merger, therefore, was to present a better image to potential clients. (It was not only that. The Estimates Committee had criticized the cost as well as the inconvenience of parallel chains of local and regional offices for different

[1] *Financial and other Circumstances of Retirement Pensioners.* Report on an Enquiry by the Ministry of Pensions and National Insurance with the co-operation of the National Assistance Board (1966).

[2] *H.C. Debs.*, vol. 725 (23 February 1966) col. 432.

government services, and had been assured that the question was under review.[1] Ministers also claimed that the change would make it easier to co-ordinate policy over the whole field; but it is hard to see how this could follow from a measure that did not alter political responsibility.) It is difficult to judge its success. There were half a million new claims for non-contributory benefits, but these could have been due to an intensive publicity campaign that was launched at the same time. The intention of combining local offices was certainly not carried out quickly. By February 1968 there were only 131 combined offices, against 607 specializing in insurance and 297 in ex-N.A.B. work, although it was claimed that they all provided a complete service.[2] By July the Treasury *O & M Bulletin* claimed that amalgamation had gone as far as it could at national and regional headquarters level; progress at local office level had been slow, although O. & M. staff had made an unsuccessful attempt to find the best way of introducing a combined service.[3] At that time, too, separate training courses were being maintained for staff on each side of the work, and local officers still identified themselves with one or the other. It seemed likely that the functional requirements of the two schemes were incompatible; they called, for example, on different areas of special knowledge and demanded a different approach to the client. In other words, the merger was misconceived because it did not reflect realities at the crucial field level. Any improvement in services might have been achieved more easily without the upheaval and the expense of formal realignment.

The offices involved in this reshuffle provided basically 'cash' services. The main 'care' service, the National Health Service, was given to the Ministry of Health, and became its main responsibility after the transfer of housing and local government to another department in 1951. The Ministry also supervised local authorities' welfare functions for the old and the handicapped. The social care of deprived children, however, was supervised by the Home Office. School welfare, the School Health Service, and school milk and meals came under the Ministry of Education. The Ministry of Labour was involved in welfare services connected with unemployment, including vocational guidance, the settlement of disabled

---

[1] *Fourth Report of the Estimates Committee 1964–65* (H.C. 274.) 'Ministry of Pensions and National Insurance'; *Fourth Special Report 1965–66* (H.C. 32).

[2] *H.C. Debs.*, vol. 758 (15 February 1968) cols. 423–4 (written answer).

[3] 'O and M in Social Security', *O & M Bulletin*, vol. 23 (1968) p. 61.

persons and the administration of unemployment benefit on behalf of the Ministry of National Insurance.

One of the main objectives in the 1940s had been to get away from the all-purpose Poor Law and appoint separate agencies on Haldane lines for separate services. It was not long, however, before the disadvantages of specialization began to appear. Special arrangements had to be made to co-ordinate services for multi-problem families. Charges were made for some 'care' services, with exemptions for persons with low incomes, and eventually the theoretical distinction between exemption from payment and a cash grant was seen to be unrealistic. When prescription charges were reintroduced on a selective basis in 1968, the division of responsibilities between the Ministries of Health and Social Security is thought to have increased the difficulty of settling the basis for remission. (In the scheme that was abolished in 1965, persons with low incomes had been able to obtain a refund of prescription charges from the National Assistance Board. In the 1968 scheme exemptions were also allowed for certain age groups and for those suffering from certain diseases. The social security machinery could not handle these categories and eventually it was decided to waive charges at source.) Meanwhile, the Inland Revenue Department was gradually seen to be part of the redistributive machinery of the Welfare State. Its tax allowances and rate differentials were as much an instrument of social policy as the provision of cash grants and free services, and could no longer be treated virtually in isolation from the social welfare services. Income tax child allowances were thus reduced in 1968 to cancel out the benefit of higher family allowances for tax paying families.

In the 1964 Labour Government, Mr Houghton, who had vast experience of tax and insurance problems, was appointed to the Cabinet as Chancellor of the Duchy of Lancaster (later Minister without Portfolio) and asked to co-ordinate social policy. This meant that he had ill-defined powers to co-ordinate the work of the Minister of Health and the Minister of Pensions and National Insurance, who remained responsible to Parliament for the work of their departments. Mr Houghton established an inter-departmental committee of officials, including Inland Revenue, to discuss the possibility of combining income tax and social security payments (negative income tax) into a single system based on a single assessment of needs and resources. After he had left the post Mr Houghton explained the lines on which he was working in a paper published by the Institute of Economic Affairs.[1] He was defeated by technical difficulties. But the problem was still being examined, with groups of officials looking at possible developments in the computer field on the one hand, and studying discrepancies among the hundreds of different means tests administered by local and central government departments on the other. When these studies have progressed enough, there will be scope for a departmental reshuffle which: (a) simplifies and improves services to the public; (b) achieves administrative economy by cutting out duplication at the operating level; (c) makes policy co-ordination easier by bringing related problems on to the desk of the same group of Ministers and officials at the head of a unified department.

It is seldom that the advantages of reorganization are as clear as this. We have seen that they were not at all clear in the minor alteration in the administration of assistance in 1966. Nor are they clear in the case of the creation of a Department of Health and Social Security in November 1968. In the previous March, the Prime Minister had been reorganizing and in some respects streamlining the central Cabinet machinery with an Inner Cabinet of nine, called the 'Parliamentary Committee', meeting much more frequently than the full Cabinet, which remained twenty-one strong but still excluded the Ministers of Health and Social Security. One of the members of the Inner Cabinet, Mr Richard Crossman, was appointed Lord President of the Council, made chairman of the Social Services Committee and asked to bring about an amalgamation of the Ministries of Health and Social Security.[2] Mr Crossman subsequently became the first head of the combined department.

It is difficult to know what this merger will achieve, beyond a reduction in the number of Ministers separately accountable to Parliament. A merger had been suggested by the Conservative Opposition in their policy statement *Putting Britain Right Ahead* of October 1965, as a necessary step towards making social services more selective. It was claimed that in the new department 'the constant use of research would enable policies to be adapted or

[1] D. Houghton, *Paying for the Social Services*, Institute of Economic Affairs Occasional Paper 16 (London, 1967).
[2] J. P. Mackintosh, 'Mr Wilson's revised Cabinet system' *The Times*, 21 June 1968. The 'Parliamentary Committee' was replaced in April 1969 by a true Inner Cabinet of seven (*The Times*, 6 May 1969).

introduced to meet changing and new needs. There would be administrative savings, too.'

At the operating level, however, the overlap between the services is at present very small. The former Ministry of Health is essentially a large executive headquarters for the various branches of the health service. Except for a few highly specialized services such as artificial limb-fitting, and a special hospital for the criminally insane, day-to-day operations are left to a complicated network (currently under review) of hospital boards, executive councils and local authorities. The central administrative divisions are engaged in planning new hospitals and health centres, applying professional advice to the operation of special services, and the remuneration and deployment of health service employees. An extensive programme of research is geared primarily to producing as much medical care as possible with the enormous sums spent on the service. The former Ministry of Social Security on the other hand manages a chain of over a thousand local offices and employs over 60,000 mainly clerical staff, some of whom also have social welfare responsibilities. Apart from internal office management, its main headquarters activity is the maintenance and application of a code of law, involving a good deal of case work. Major questions of policy are probably infrequent and settled at political level. Its research programme is slightly remote from its day-to-day activities, being concerned with the incidence of poverty and the impact of social security on the community. It is hard to see what administrative economies can arise from combining the activities of such diverse departments. This is a question that would repay study, which should include the arrangements in Northern Ireland where there has for some time been a combined Ministry of Health and Social Services; it may be significant that a federal pattern of organization has been adopted both in Belfast and in London.

The case for a merger may be stronger at policy level, especially if the basis of health finance is altered so that the incidence of charges becomes a major preoccupation of Ministers and their senior advisers. There are already a number of areas, such as the care of the elderly, in which a balance has to be sought between financial and institutional means of meeting need. Again, experience of the social security approach might make health administrators relatively more sympathetic to consumer-orientated rather than service-orientated research. Arguments like this can be found to support almost any combination of functions and should not obscure the point that so long as the health service remains roughly in its present form the main preoccupation of its administrators must be the partnership with the health professions. But so far as there is any functional argument for combining the departments it must be in terms of common purpose.

A final complication should be mentioned. The Seebohm Committee recommended that local social services should be strengthened by combining a number of local authority functions related to children, the elderly and the handicapped in a single Social Service Department. These services at present fall variously within the fields administered centrally by the Department of Health, the Home Office, the Department of Education and Science, and the Ministry of Housing and Local Government. They are also closely related to the work of the Supplementary Benefits Commission. The Committee felt that:

> . . . it would be no use altering the organization of the local authority services unless the organization of central government was changed to correspond with it . . . There must be one central government department responsible both for the relationship between central government and the social service departments which we have proposed, and to provide the overall national planning of social services, social intelligence and social research.[1]

There seem to be three arguments here. There is the now familiar point about co-ordination: problems will be considered more adequately by Ministers and administrators who have become aware of related issues through exposure to problems over the whole field. Next, each department tends to have its own style in dealing with local authorities. The Committee does not press this point, but there is ample evidence for it in a study of central and local government relations for the Royal Institute of Public Administration which compares, for example, the slightly paternalistic Home Office way of supervising children's services with the Health Department's more *laissez-faire* approach to local health and welfare authorities.[2] It would be easier for the local departments to deal with people who shared a common departmental ethos.

[1] *Report of the Committee on Local Authority and Allied Personal Social Services*, par. 637.
[2] J. A. G. Griffith, *Central Departments and Local Authorities* (London 1966) pp. 515–28.

Finally, implicit in the argument, is the feeling that a single department would be a more committed sponsor, just as the concentration in the Home Office of most functions relating to deprived children seemed to institutionalize the Government's commitment to that new service in 1948.

The Seebohm Committee did not suggest which department should have these responsibilities nor whether a new department should be created. (The Institute of Social Welfare suggested in 1965 that there should be a separate Department of Social Work and Welfare covering roughly the area surveyed by Seebohm.) At the time of writing, the Government has not announced its intentions. But it seems probable that the Committee's wishes will be at least partly met by transferring some functions from the Home Office to the Department of Health and Social Security or vice versa. In either case, there will be a mixture of gains and disadvantages which may or may not balance out to outweigh the disturbance involved!

CONCLUSIONS

The current spate of administrative experiment is caused by growing pains in the machinery of government. Both political and administrative considerations enter into the best way of allocating functions at any particular time. They may point in opposite directions.

The political aspects command most attention. The grouping of functions around key Ministers will reflect the primary interests of the government of the day. These will necessarily change from time to time. In the current decade, political interest has centred on the modernization of the economy, a more coherent approach to social policy, and the control of prices and incomes. Changing ideas about the most suitable instruments (including the calibre of individual politicians) for pursuing these ends and about their relationship to other concerns of the State have naturally led to changes in departmental responsibilities.

Senior administrators who are underpinning the Minister and working closely with him on policy need to share his frame of reference and to be exposed to the same range of material. Bridges begin to appear between areas of policy that are attended to by the same group of people. But there is no simple relationship between administrative functions and the focal points of Ministerial responsibility. As one moves away from the political battlefield to day-to-day administration and executive management, the need for quite different patterns of specialization begins to appear. The administrator in charge of technical aspects of hospital building needs broad experience of clinical requirements and of project management, but it is relatively unimportant to him whether his Minister has other duties that incline him to regard a new hospital, say, as part of the economic infrastructure or as an instrument for achieving social equality. Some of the worst features of civil service 'amateurism' have been caused by the assumption that the grouping of functions under departmental Ministers was a valid basis for career-planning.

The Fulton Committee's recommendations about administrative specialization are a useful first step towards freeing the administrative techno-structure from subordination to political orientations at a completely different level. A logical development would be the definition of administrative 'bureaux', specializing in particular fields of administration, which could be allocated to different Ministers as political considerations required. Many (but certainly not all) administrators would base their careers on the 'bureau' rather than on the department. The Fulton suggestion about 'hiving-off' functions to autonomous agencies on the Swedish pattern goes further still, since agencies could be shunted around, without even altering their notepaper, as easily as responsibility for B.E.A. and B.O.A.C. was transferred from the Ministry of Aviation to the Board of Trade in 1966.

Finding the best division of functions among 'bureaux' (or whatever the lower administrative units are called) is a more or less objective matter of working out the different economies of different groupings and the relevance of various sorts of experience. There is need for much detailed research and analysis, which would need to be repeated every time there was a substantial change in the major policy assumptions of the government.

The day has, however, passed when a new Haldane-type enquiry, covering the whole structure and functions of government, was likely to be practicable.[1]

[1] The Prime Minister told the Commons that the wider review of the machinery of government which the Fulton Committee recommended 'was and is a continuing process' which it was impossible to refer to an outside body (*H.C. Debs.*, vol. 773, 21 November 1968, col. 1563).

XI. Management

DEFINITIONS

One of the main duties of the civil service is management in the sense of getting things done. In the past it has been the particular concern of the executive class. We have seen in Part One that the Fulton recommendations were largely designed to accelerate the trend, which began with the 1961 Plowden Report on *Control of Public Expenditure*, for senior administrators and professional officers to become more and more involved in management.

The Plowden Committee suggested that management was one of the three main responsibilities of Permanent Secretaries; and hoped that its importance was fully appreciated 'not only by the Permanent Secretaries themselves, but also by the Ministers whom they serve'.[1] From this point on, the word 'management' occurs more and more often in civil service papers. The Treasury set up management divisions and produced a series of reports on management training. The Fulton Committee was asked to examine the 'structure, recruitment and management including training' of the Home Civil Service. It was suggested that the administrative and executive grades should be merged into a 'general management group'.

The change is partly a shift in nomenclature: the civil service use of 'secretary', 'administrative' and 'executive' to describe posts at decreasing levels of seniority is confusing and contrary to normal industrial practice. In its memorandum to the Fulton Committee the Treasury did not seem to envisage any substantial change in the role of the service and explained that its use of 'management' covered policy-making as well as executive functions.[2] But the use of the word also reflected a real interest in managerial skills. New methods of handling data and new techniques of economic and statistical analysis were becoming available. New types of specialist

[1] *Control of Public Expenditure*, Cmnd. 1432 (1961) pars. 44–7.
[2] *Fulton Report*, vol. 5, p. 1 'The Future Structure of the Civil Service' (H.M. Treasury).

had to be brought into the machine to handle them, and administrators had to learn something of their language. Senior civil servants began to feel that it was essential for their subordinates to be at home in this new world. Administrators were also becoming uncertain about their traditional role. The secretarial and judicial work at which they were most skilled no longer seemed to be understood or required. They felt increasingly vulnerable as generalists in an age of specialization. Training in management offered a basis of professionalization that would at least be recognizable by specialist colleagues and a critical public.

The Fulton Committee was very critical of management in the service. Its recommendations made management the most important single element in administrative training; it wanted to 'professionalize' the administrator by making him a specialist in particular fields and techniques of administration; and it wanted to restructure departments in order to give more weight to managerial efficiency ('a structure in which units and individual members have authority that is clearly defined and responsibilities for which they can be held accountable . . . [and there are] recognized methods of assessing their success in achieving specified objectives').[1]

The word 'management' has several meanings. The Fulton Committee's management consultancy group defined it as 'the formulation and operation of the policy of the enterprise' and distinguished 'four aspects which make up the total management task of the Civil Service: (a) formulation of policy under political direction; (b) creating the machinery for implementation of policy; (c) operation of the administrative machine; (d) accountability to Parliament and the Public'.[2]

This list seems to comprise all the work of government below political level. It closely resembles the formal definition of administrative class duties.[3] Indeed the consultants blamed administrators for neglecting part of their duties:

> Their primary interest is in being advisers on policy matters to people above them rather than in managing the administrative machine below them. The process of selection, training and movement from job to job is designed to produce generalist administrators familiar with the processes of policy making, Ministerial

---

[1] *Fulton Report*, vol. 1, par. 145.   [2] *Fulton Report*, vol. 2, par. 303.
[3] See ch. I above, p. 11.

cases and the system of financial control. It does not, however, equip them to handle the total managerial task nor to develop the specialist knowledge or techniques required by Departments for their particular policies and activities. Yet as Departments have grown, sometimes to the size of whole industries, so the management task in all its four aspects has increased in importance until today it demands professional management of the highest order.[1]

But although these sentiments were echoed in the main report, the word 'management' there seems to have a more limited meaning: managers are 'responsible for organization, directing staff, planning the progress of work, setting standards of attainment and measuring results, reviewing procedures and quantifying different courses of action'.[2] Much of the work of the administrative class 'is not managerial in this sense'. The criticisms of 'management', therefore, seem to be aimed at weaknesses in the second and third of the items on the consultants' list – in the structuring and operation of the administrative machine. (This interpretation is supported by an odd comment about the undesirability of staffing the new Civil Service Department with 'officers who have spent most of their careers in the Treasury, and can thus have little experience of direct responsibility for management';[3] on the wider definition, this statement is clearly absurd.)

When the Committee came to discuss the structure of departments, it concentrated on four main elements in the work for which the top-level direction of each department had to provide. These were: (a) the management of executive activities; (b) administrative work of a non-executive character, such as high-level case-work concerned with the operation and adaptation of existing policies; (c) day-to-day work on internal organization and personnel; (d) the formulation and review of policy under political direction.

It is noticeable that this list does not include arrangements for parliamentary or public accountability. It does include policy work; the Committee's recommendations on policy and planning will be reviewed in the next chapter. For the moment, let us look at the need to improve what we may call 'executive management' in departments and the probable effects of introducing the Fulton proposals.

In the previous chaper it was suggested that any particular block of work can be fitted into the machinery of government from several

---

[1] *Fulton Report*, vol. 2, par. 324.   [2] *Fulton Report*, vol. 1, par. 18.
[3] Ibid., par. 255.

points of view. Any activity embodies a particular administrative technique and can be grouped with other tasks employing similar techniques; it serves a major political purpose and can be brought under the control of a Minister who is accountable for that purpose; through career-planning and procedural devices it can be co-ordinated with other political purposes. These arrangements affect individual decisions by limiting the information supplied to those involved in the decision-process and by influencing the frame of reference within which they interpret it. More emphasis on one set of considerations implies less on others. What Fulton is saying is that, at least in some government activities, excessive emphasis on co-ordination was costing too much in terms of individual responsibility and technical efficiency. Generalists were unlikely to take bold initiatives, since civil servants who were too conscious of possible repercussions in Parliament and in other departments were inclined to caution and to over-insurance. A more dynamic approach was needed, and it was more likely to come from task-centred administrators who specialized in particular fields. The Committee does not use this language: its recommendations are couched in terms of making good deficiencies in civil servants who 'are more at home with the machinery of administration than with its content'.[1] But it is less emotive and more helpful to think in terms of altering a balance.

'HIVING-OFF'

The Committee was aware of the constraints imposed by Ministerial accountability to Parliament. There is an excellent statement in the management consultants' report of the impact of parliamentary controls on administration – the high degree of centralization, the emphasis on equity and on the avoidance of error, the elaborate record-keeping and the displacement of long-term planning by short-term political pressures at the top.[2] So the Committee looked very sympathetically at the possibility that some large-scale executive operations should be 'hived-off' to autonomous public bodies, carrying full responsibility within the powers delegated to

[1] Ibid., par. 54.

[2] *Fulton Report*, vol. 2, pars. 20–7, 305–15. Perhaps these tendencies reflect cultural expectations (such as the current vogue for egalitarianism) that are felt just as strongly in non-parliamentary systems like those in Eastern Europe. But in this country it is the fact of Ministerial accountability that gives them such emphasis.

them. The day-to-day operations of such bodies would not be controlled by Ministers (and would not therefore be subject to parliamentary scrutiny), but Ministers would have power to give directions on particular matters and would presumably be accountable to Parliament in these respects.[1]

There is at present a bewildering variety of government organizations, at various removes from parliamentary control:

1. Closest to the parliamentary system are the conventional Whitehall departments, headed by a Minister and under the immediate policy direction of the Cabinet.

2. Then there are executive departments which do not come directly under Ministerial control but are headed by boards or individual officials. Examples are the Board of Inland Revenue, the General Register Office, H.M. Stationery Office and, until November 1968, the Civil Service Commission. The National Assistance Board, although its members were not career civil servants, came into the same category. So does the Land Commission. Although these departments (or 'bureaux') are subject to policy direction from Ministers, their semi-autonomous position on day-to-day matters avoids political intervention in individual casework unless, like some of the work of the Land Commission, it raises major questions of principle.

3. A rather similar group of bodies, including the National Board for Prices and Incomes, the Monopolies Commission and the Industrial Court, relieve Ministers of responsibility for investigations and policy recommendations of a quasi-judicial nature.

4. Next are a number of agencies, such as the Research Councils, the University Grants Committee and the Arts Council, through which the spending of public money is entrusted to experts in the relevant field. Detailed questions of scientific, academic or artistic judgement which govern the distribution of funds in these areas are thus removed from the political arena. The national museums and grant-aided bodies like the Centre for Environmental Studies carry out similar functions, although on a somewhat different legal basis. The Industrial Reorganization Corporation offers a parallel in industrial management: its existence allows public money to be used to promote rationalization (which may involve such intensely

[1] *Fulton Report*, vol. 1, pars. 147, 188–91.

political issues as local unemployment) without parliamentary intervention.

5. Finally, there are all the *ad hoc* bodies engaged in commercial or quasi-commercial activities. They range from the nationalized industries proper (British Rail, regional Gas Boards and so on) through the Forestry Commission and the Atomic Energy Authority to the B.B.C. and the Bank of England.

There is no general principle governing the allocation of functions to one type of body rather than another. There has been a trend in the last decade to 'hive-off' commercial functions like airport management, the development of atomic energy and postal services to *ad hoc* bodies, but to integrate non-commercial activities, like national assistance and policy towards the arts and higher education, more closely with central Ministerial control. But there are many exceptions on both sides and there seems no good reason why there should not be further moves in one direction or the other. The Fulton Committee had in mind the possibility of hiving-off a wide variety of activities, from the work of the Royal Mint and air traffic control to parts of the social services. Other possibilities suggested in evidence to the Committee included overseas aid programmes, management of the national research and development effort, administration of civil service personnel and the preparation of budgets and accounts on the same basis as the U.S. Bureau of the Budget. 'The object of arrangements of this kind would be to push out of the Ministries all work which is primarily of a professional, technological and non-political character and to bring it into the public light of day.'[1]

Another range of possibilities is suggested by the proposed reorganization of local government.[2] Although the Redcliffe-Maud Commission was not empowered to recommend the transfer of functions from Whitehall, its proposals about local government structure offer the hope of creating local authorities strong and efficient enough to take over additional responsibilities and relieve congestion at the centre. An obvious field, if financial problems and professional resistance could be overcome, would be the National Health Service.

The effect of such a transfer cannot be predicted with any precision. Some authorities enjoy the appearance of autonomy but

[1] See *Fulton Report*, vol. 5, pp. 1069–70 (evidence from Mr J. H. Robertson).
[2] *Report of the Royal Commission on Local Government in England*, Cmnd. 4040 (1969).

not the reality. The nationalized industries are not free from Ministerial pressure, even on questions of commercial management. On the social service side, it seemed for a time that Hospital Boards, which are wholly financed by the Health Minister and legally his agents, enjoyed more independence from detailed controls than the nominally autonomous local health authorities. It is possible, however, to indicate what type of machinery is most likely to achieve any desired balance. Thus, one would expect more weight to be given to political factors in a conventional Whitehall department, headed by a politician with a supporting staff of generalists, than in an independent board with its own staff and a distinguished industrialist as chairman. In theory, one would expect local government services to be politicized, although in terms of local rather than national purposes. For some local authority services, like housing, this may be true; but others are organized in such a way that technical factors predominate. Some again are so tightly controlled from Whitehall that their administration reflects a Whitehall rather than a local frame of reference. Another important influence in value-setting may be the existence of an independent source of finance: organizations that are dependent on Treasury money are more ready to accept 'public authority' standards of equity in spending it and may be more preoccupied with budget-balancing than with the development of services.[1]

It is not enough to know the legal status of an authority. The decisions made in its name are affected by the previous experience – and to some extent by the career outlook – of its staff and by the frequency with which different factors are brought to their notice. Even within government departments, there are areas where political factors intrude so seldom that staff specializing in, say, management services get into the habit of working from purely technical premises. Some of the independent agencies for scrutinizing the administration, notably the offices of the Comptroller and Auditor General and the Parliamentary Commissioner for Administration, are staffed by conventional executive class civil servants. If they were members of an independent corps, they might be less knowledgeable about departmental administration and perhaps less sympathetic with a department's difficulties; in practice the principles involved in their work are so clear and consistent that they appear to identify themselves with it without difficulty. Neverthe-

[1] Vickers, *The Art of Judgment*, ch. 13, 'Internal Criteria of Success'.

less, the most effective way to 'technologize' a block of work may be to entrust it to staff whose careers are limited to the application of a particular technique to a particular objective and to put them into an independent agency subject to the minimum of Ministerial and parliamentary control.

It may also be easier for such a body to experiment with new administrative methods and with different organizational patterns. There are, for example, various techniques for decentralizing authority and responsibility to unit managers, giving them discretion to find the best way of achieving an agreed objective within a given budget. (This provides them with an incentive to concentrate on efficiency and to have less regard for incidental repercussions: thus a site manager who is trying to build a new factory in a development area is not concerned about the long-term effects on the local economy of paying high wages to labourers during the operation.) They are more easily applied within an organization which is devoted to a single measurable goal and whose detailed operations are not likely to be challenged by higher authority because of their incompatability with other goals.

Another dimension along which organizations differ is the fluidity of their management structure. Organizations that are run on highly 'mechanistic' lines, with hierarchical patterns of control and the duties of each post clearly set out in an organization chart, seem to be efficient in stable conditions, but cannot respond quickly and flexibly to change. In conditions of rapid change organizations with a collegiate system of responsibility are more successful: instead of a new problem having to be referred to the head of the firm so that he can decide how to adapt the organization to meet it, everyone becomes involved and gaps are automatically filled as managers try to clarify the implications for their own ill-defined areas of discretion.[1] It would obviously be easier for an autonomous agency

[1] T. Burns and G. M. Stalker, *The Management of Innovation* (London, 1961; with revised introduction, 1966). Burns and Stalker identified the polar types of 'mechanistic' and 'organic' forms of organization after a study of firms adapting to changing market and technological conditions, mainly in the electronics industry. Since this study has been widely misquoted, it is perhaps worth making the point that managers in the 'organic' firms were *not* happy, creative people reacting favourably to the absence of control. The ill-defined structure in which they worked was deliberately brought about by the head of the firm; those involved were forced to interact at the expense of getting on with their own specialized jobs, and found the permanent uncertainty rather uncomfortable; they were not being 'creative' but adjusting themselves quickly to changes in the external world.

to adopt the internal structure most appropriate for its own situation. (One rather assumes that a government department will be 'mechanistic' and it is true that there are mechanistic elements about the chain of accountability necessary to implement the Minister's will. Nevertheless, day-to-day relations among administrative colleagues tend to be collegiate rather than hierarchical. The Fulton proposals about personal accountability would almost certainly make relationships *less* fluid, except at top management levels and in planning units.)

But the creation of an *ad hoc* body of this sort implies the existence of a goal that can be institutionalized – getting coal, recruiting personnel, or relieving poverty. Price has shown how, in the United States, the existence of the Atomic Energy Commission made it difficult to ask proper questions about the cheapest way of meeting certain objectives, since officials of the Commission saw it as their duty to promote the use of nuclear fuel and used sympathetic Congressmen to advance their claims; a development like the nuclear submarine was taken beyond the point that the Department of Defence would have chosen or the President's Science Advisory Committee recommended.[1] The British Atomic Energy Authority may similarly have 'over-egged the atomic pudding'. The more subject-centred the agency is, the more necessary it will be to alter it drastically if political needs change. Once a chain of such bodies has been set up, each with a body of staff who are committed to a particular goal, changes may be difficult to introduce. With conventional government departments, given a staff of reasonably interchangeable generalists, it is not difficult to set up a Department of Economic Affairs or a Land Commission very quickly after a change of government: if the next Government has different ideas, the staff can be redeployed. It is far more difficult to wind up a nationalized industry – or to reorganize existing industries so that, for example, there is one Area Light and Power Board supplying the most appropriate mix of coal, gas and electricity to a neighbourhood instead of three different boards confusing the customer with claims based on their own fuel.

CONSTRAINTS

The creation of separate agencies, then, may involve a new kind of inflexibility. Another difficulty is finding some means of relating

[1] Price, *The Scientific Estate*, p. 224.

their activity to other national objectives. In conventional Ministries the ultimate sanction for consistency and attention to general values not related to the task in hand is the constant threat that any action will be exposed to parliamentary criticism. In the case of nationalized industries (and for a time in the case of national assistance) detailed operations have been deliberately removed from this sort of political audit. It has been reintroduced in other forms: by allowing a Select Committee to review the work of a whole industry and by the use of Ministerial powers of direction (for example, the instruction to British European Airways to buy British aircraft instead of American and the direction to the National Coal Board to slow down pit closures). The uncertain touch with which Ministers have used their powers of direction suggests that it is not easy to reconcile managerial autonomy with the need to co-ordinate a huge public industry with other political objectives.

There is an inherent absurdity in a Select Committee complaining that Ministers interfere with the commercial judgement of nationalized industries. One of the really valuable functions of Parliament is the pressure it generates to reconcile conflicting goals within the public sector. The strongest argument for a separate Minister for Nationalized Industry is that such a Minister might protect an industry from excessive pressure from other Ministers more concerned with the political effects of, say, short-term unemployment or rising prices than with the long-term development of the industry, and thus force the conflict to be recognized and resolved after public discussion. But this argument seems to underestimate the role of Cabinet in suppressing public confrontations between Ministers. Nor is it clear why a government department should be thought likely to press more strongly for purely commercial efficiency than the managers of the industry itself.

Autonomous boards must be subject to some constraints, with sanctions to ensure that they are applied in practice. It is easy to devise sanctions: annual reports can be debated in Parliament and Ministers given reserve powers – in the last resort to sack a recalcitrant chairman. It is not so easy to find constraints that will adequately and permanently reflect the public interest in the way operations are carried out. For a revenue-earning public corporation using capital borrowed from the Treasury, it is obviously sensible to require a stated level of return on investment. Major changes, like closing a branch railway line, can be made subject to a procedure which allows public debate and perhaps public subsidy. But minor changes in policy have no less serious consequences. A selective fares policy could have important social repercussions if it encouraged too many (or too few) people to commute long distances to work. An electricity board can strike a commercial bargain with a housing developer that prevents householders from cooking with gas if they wish to. A fuel industry can adopt policies that increase or decrease employment, encourage or discourage developers, provoke claims for wage increases, and so on. It is difficult to see how consideration of repercussions such as these can be 'cued-in' to the attention of decision-makers whose primary objective is to increase sales and run efficient services, except by requiring political approval or through Ministerial 'interference' in a rather unsystematic way.

In social services there is the more fundamental problem of defining basic objectives. What is the equivalent of profitable return on investment for an Area Health Board? What terms of reference should be given to an autonomous social security organization: should it be compelled to structure its schemes so as to encourage redeployment or to discourage voluntary cessations, to favour the needy or to reward the thrifty, to cut down on overheads or to provide advisory and 'convenience' services for the public? These are primarily political questions to which there is no unequivocal answer. They can be resolved only through changing political judgements about the correct balance of priorities in the circumstances of the moment.

It is easier to ensure the consideration of 'external benefits' within a government department. Political direction by a Minister, overall accountability to Parliament, the unwritten assumptions that underlie bargaining with the Treasury and (above all) the ethos of the administrative class all tend to set ill-defined but well-understood limits on the extent to which a particular goal will be pursued without regard to its repercussions elsewhere. Formal procedures, particularly those concerned with financial control and parliamentary scrutiny, play a part in this, but it is a relatively small one.

It would be useful to test the effect of locating a function in a government department rather than elsewhere if a suitably controlled situation could be found. For example, government departments, local authorities, hospital boards and nationalized industries all purchase large quantities of equipment and place large-scale contracts for goods and services. A comparative study of something as simple as tendering procedures might indicate how far purely managerial considerations were affected by wider considerations (employment given to disabled persons, the technological development of the industry, local employment situation in the supplier's area etc.) in the different types of organization and through what machinery. In another field, decisions about cash grants to relieve poverty used to be taken by officers of an *ad hoc* agency (the National Assistance Board). The same decisions are now taken largely by the same people (although this may not be so where national insurance and 'supplementary benefits' are now administered from combined offices) in the Department of Health and Social Security, which is a conventional government department. Similar decisions about entitlement to clothing grants and school meals are made by officials employed by local education authorities. It would be valuable to have an empirical study of the factors entering into discretionary decisions by officials in each of these situations. If no perceptible differences emerged, the *a priori* case for hiving-off would have to be re-examined.

'ACCOUNTABLE MANAGEMENT' IN WHITEHALL

The Fulton Committee suggested that many of the advantages of 'hiving-off' could be secured by establishing clearer lines of authority within departments. It thought that civil servants engaged on executive management could, on certain conditions, be encouraged to place as much emphasis on immediate goal-achievement as could members of autonomous bodies. The conditions were:

1. Executive and policy work should be separated by distinguishing 'those within departments whose primary responsibility is planning for the future, from those whose main concern is the operation of existing policies or the provision of services'.[1]

2. Departmental organization should permit the 'principles of accountable management' to be applied to executive activities.

3. Cadres of 'professional administrators', specializing in particular areas and techniques, should be available to staff posts in the accountable units.

All these points can be traced to the management consultancy group, whose general approach was that the purely management

[1] *Fulton Report*, vol. 1, par. 191.

functions of the service should be handled in ways as similar to those of industry as possible.[1]

The first condition corresponds very roughly to the distinction made in 1920 between the duties of the administrative (policy-making) and executive classes. That distinction had become obscured and unsatisfactory in many ways, not least because it did not take account of the place of the professional classes. The Committee suggested a different basis of differentiation which, in principle, has much to commend it, although it also presents a number of difficulties that will be examined in Chapter XII. Condition (3) has already been discussed.[2]

By (2) 'accountable management', the Fulton Committee meant 'identifying or establishing accountable units within government departments – units where output can be measured against costs or other criteria, and where individuals can be held personally responsible for their performance'.[3] The Committee thought that output could be measured against cost in any case where large numbers of similar operations were performed, such as dealing with applications, handling individual employment problems at local offices or handling stores or supplies. Those in charge of such units 'should be given clear-cut responsibilities and commensurate authority and should be held accountable for performance against budgets, standards of achievement and other tests'.[4]

An important part of accountability in this sense would depend on identifying the cost of an activity. Public accounting in Britain is fairly primitive. Departments prepare estimates and statements of expenditure under sub-heads related to the service being administered; Parliament is not normally provided with budgets for particular objectives. (The difference is between having an estimate for the running costs of hospitals, broken into staff, equipment and supplies etc., and an estimate for the cost of dealing with maternity cases or special services for immigrants.) Some activities have been specifically costed for internal purposes, although there is plenty of room for development.[5] The Ministry of Defence has, for obvious

[1] *Fulton Report*, vol. 2, pars. 344–80.
[2] See ch. III, pp. 53–6 above and ch. X, pp. 197–206.
[3] *Fulton Report*, vol. 1, par. 150.
[4] Ibid., par. 154.
[5] For an account of the recent position see K. E. Couzens, 'The Management Accounting Unit' and other papers in *O & M Bulletin*, vol. 32, no. 2 (February 1968).

reasons, been under pressure to cost some of its more expensive activities and has copied the technique of 'Planning–Programming–Budgeting' from the Pentagon. The detailed activities of this Ministry are perhaps less subject to day-to-day parliamentary control than those of any other department and it is interesting that two early experiments in 'accountable management' were both in defence (one in a Royal Ordnance Factory and the other in the R.N. Transport and Supplies Service).

The Committee saw that over a large part of government activity it would be difficult to relate output to costs in this way:

> One cannot lay down in advance how long it should take to review effectively the investment programme of a nationalized industry, or to study and make a sound recommendation on the acceptability of a proposed company merger.[1]

Administrative work is difficult to assess because of the unpredictable demands that arise from the Minister's accountability to Parliament and the unique character of much new policy-making. Even here, however, the Committee felt that the principles of 'management by objective' should be applied. The head of a branch engaged in non-executive work (the adaptation of existing policies, the formulation of new policies, or research) should work to an agreed programme of objectives, with priorities and deadlines. Progress would be regularly reviewed. Each individual would know the extent of his responsibilities and the limits of his authority. 'The effectiveness of the branch and the contribution of its individual members could then be more effectively assessed.'[2]

In these recommendations the Fulton Committee was more emphatic than the management consultancy group, which was content to stress the desirability of experimenting with some industrial practices if the difficulties could be overcome. The consultancy group saw that the authority of a line manager in the civil service, unlike some of his counterparts in business and industry, was limited by the centralization of personnel and finance and by political factors beyond his control. It also saw that authority could not be delegated unless there was a system of controls and safeguards and suggested that management research programmes should be set up to identify key tasks and devise new organizational forms in

---

[1] *Fulton Report*, vol. 1, par. 155.   [2] Ibid., par. 156.

which management controls and delegation to individuals would have their place.[1]

The first problem is whether it is practicable to decentralize authority over resources in the way suggested. In industry it is often possible to delegate wide powers over staff and money, subject to overall budgetary control and to assessment of performance after the event. The Accounting Officer of a government department may have to satisfy the Public Accounts Committee not only that money has been wisely spent but that it has been properly spent in minutest detail. It is true that parliamentary control of supply is in need of radical overhaul, but Members of Parliament are not selected for their financial sophistication and it is hard to imagine any system of parliamentary review of expenditure that will satisfy Members if it does not allow them to discuss whether departmental letters should go by first or second class post. It seems inevitable that civil service managers should have less than full discretion over the use they make of their budgets. On the staffing side, salaries are negotiated centrally. There are rules about increments and promotion. Postings are arranged centrally in order to make best use of the staff available to the department as a whole and also in order to even out career opportunities for individuals. The Fulton Committee, moreover, seemed to be arguing two ways about personnel policy: on the one hand it seemed to be thinking in terms of giving the line supervisor more authority over his subordinates; on the other hand it felt that central personnel departments should take a stronger hand in career planning. It is not practicable to decentralize much authority over personnel to a line manager so long as the civil service takes responsibility for offering most of its employees a lifetime's career and so long as it takes the responsibility for putting trained staff into new, and possibly temporary, departments to suit the needs of different political administrations.

It is not that the civil service has failed to make easy and obvious arrangements like those sometimes found in industry, but that it has found a different type of solution (and perhaps in some ways a better one) to a common problem. There are two different approaches to managerial responsibility also. One approach is to

[1] *Fulton Report*, vol. 2, pars. 360, 366–74. There is a very fair account of the problems, but a perhaps unduly optimistic view of the advantages, of introducing 'management by objective' in a paper by two members of the group. J. Garrett and S. D. Walker, *Management by Objectives in the Civil Service*, C.A.S. Occasional Paper no. 10, H.M.S.O., 1969.

find a man able to do a job, give him the resources he asks for and leave him to get on with it. The other is more subtle: it involves appointing a man to fill a niche in an on-going organization, inheriting a set of practices and a group of staff who will go on doing what they did under his predecessor until stopped. It may take the second man longer to make his mark, but work flows on in the meantime and there is likely to be less disruption if he turns out to be a misfit or has a breakdown.

It is also difficult (although not necessarily impossible) to work out formal systems of controls and sanctions which provide incentives for efficiency without too much damage to central administrative discipline. In industry it is usually possible to define constraints fairly clearly in financial terms and to measure results unambiguously in terms of profitability and growth. The effect of setting up accountable units is to institutionalize particular purposes. But the standards of success in public administration are more ambiguous. Since political currents are unpredictable – and the effects of a change of government are particularly so – it seems very difficult in practice to formalize the 'external factors' to which civil service managers should pay attention. The traditional system was to rely on the political sensitivity of a general administrator who viewed specific problems in the light of possible political repercussions and judged his success by his ability to avoid raising political trouble (in other words, by the extent to which his policy was achieved without detriment to other policies that were of concern to politicians). In areas of activity that are close to current centres of political interest, the traditional system seems better. Indeed, one might say that 'management by objective' is most likely to be practicable in areas remote from politics.

POLITICAL CONTEXT

Authority and responsibility could hardly be delegated to individual civil service managers without an accompanying change in the relations between administration and Parliament. The principle of accountable management implies that a Minister would normally decline to intervene in a matter where a civil servant was acting within his delegated authority. It is almost impossible to imagine Ministers – especially new Ministers anxious to show the world that they were not pawns of their departments – accepting this degree of self-restraint. And once the political head of the department has intervened, it would be extraordinary if his civil servants did not give priority to meeting his desires. Nor could they well be penalized for failing to meet strictly managerial objectives because they had spent their energies dealing with political inquests.

Managerial efficiency is important. The majority of junior civil servants are doing work to which normal efficiency techniques can be applied. There is a good case for developing and extending an already impressive range of work-measurement, method study and cost-effectiveness units in the Civil Service Department and in the larger operating departments. This is, however, going ahead so fast that it is hard to see the need for a new pattern of incentives to encourage middle and senior administrators to use the new techniques. Indeed, the administration of non-commercial operations by, say, Inland Revenue or the old Ministry of Social Security offers outstanding examples both of efficiency and of adaptability to necessary change. When the advantages are so doubtful and the difficulties are so great, the case for introducing 'accountable management' to conventional Whitehall departments begins to look very weak. The Civil Service Department's reaction to this set of Fulton proposals was distinctly doubtful and cautious.[1]

It would have been more realistic for the Fulton Committee to accept that political needs rule out any fundamental change in the top management of central departments, except perhaps in special fields like defence and management services which are protected from detailed parliamentary review by security considerations or by sheer lack of political content. Otherwise, the more important a field of administration is, the less likely it is that the administrative technologists working on it will be left in peace. The best hope for a single-minded approach to the efficient management of particular services is through the creation of various forms of *ad hoc* bureaux (including non-Ministerial departments) whose day-to-day operations are protected from parliamentary scrutiny. In many departments management in the narrower sense is in fact relatively unimportant: the execution of policies is already left to outside agencies (hospital boards, local authorities, public or private industrial corporations) and the internal problems of managing headquarters staff are marginal compared with the effect of decisions outside.

[1] Civil Service National Whitley Council, *Developments on Fulton*, pars. 61–4.

Institutionalizing administrative activities in bureaux carries the disadvantages already discussed. Functional bureaux have to be linked to the rest of the system by formal constraints. It is more difficult to reshuffle established bureaux when needs change than it is to reallocate functions among departments of a unified civil service. The tendency of staff to identify with their organization, especially if they have no other career outlet, may be a prescription for dynamic administration or a form of organizational disease, according to the circumstances and your point of view. The disadvantages can be tolerated if they are exceeded by the gains.

Conventional government departments are not the best places to build up purely managerial expertise – they are too exposed to political turbulence and the political requirements of the Minister are bound to take precedence over routine administration. There are some important exceptions to this rule. Tremendous strides have been made with the application of quantitative techniques of control in fields ranging from the day-to-day operations of schools and hospitals to more complex problems in transport and defence. In these areas there may indeed be a risk of obscuring political choice by the sheer weight of computer hardware. But the honeymoon period between Parliament and the computer is likely to be brought to an end by constituency pressures sooner or later and it may be better to take positive steps to identify areas of executive management that can be 'technologized' and protected from political interference.

A further reason for taking the 'hiving-off' idea seriously is that our attempts to process a great deal of matter through the central machine seem to have become self-defeating. As the Fulton investigations showed, the price of co-ordinating minor acts of executive government through the central Cabinet-cum-Treasury resource-allocating machinery, serviced by generalist administrators, has been frustration and delay for those who want to get on with their jobs. And many able administrators have been so busy co-ordinating that they have been unable to find time for reviewing policy and making necessary changes.

This does not mean that the activities of *ad hoc* bureaux can be left free-floating. As instruments of political purpose they have to be tied in with other Government activities. Control techniques have to be devised which limit their autonomy in key areas. There are some precedents, worth studying for their experimental value, in the changing relationships between Treasury and other central departments, which were considerably simplified for a time after the Plowden Report. Others may be found in the more recent attempt to divide town and country planning functions between central and local government in a way that compels local authorities to pay some attention to the national interest but does not swamp the central department (and ultimately perhaps the Parliamentary Commissioner for Administration) with detail. The ultimate test of any organizational device is its effect on decisions. Perhaps the most important test is how an official would decide a marginal question under pressure – when he has little time for reflection and has to decide on a basis of the considerations that come first to his mind.

CONCLUSIONS

So far as the management of executive activities is concerned, there is a case for some alteration in the present institutional arrangements. The sector of the economy which is under direct government control is far too large for its management to be left open to disturbance every time there is a need to find staff for new departments or to deal with an unexpected avalanche of parliamentary discussion. Nor is it right that responsibility for executive management should rest with a group of administrators whose interests are primarily in policy and political work. Some very effective work is done in this area by executive and professional class civil servants, but the future quality of both these groups is affected by problems of morale and by recruitment difficulties.

The Fulton answer was to 'managerialize' the civil service. A more stable solution (and one that would relieve overloading at the centre) would look to the creation of more autonomous bureaux subject to proper constraints and under ultimate political direction.

There are disadvantages either way and it is important to make choices with as full as possible a knowledge of the losses and gains. More organizational research would help.

XII. Planning

The previous chapter was about getting things done. We now need to look at the processes through which policy goals are determined.

The British system has not been conspicuously successful at sorting out priorities and evaluating policies. Or perhaps not until recently. The Plowden Committee proposed in 1961 that public spending should be brought under proper control by looking ahead, reviewing existing policies and forcing the Cabinet to take collective decisions on priorities instead of dealing with specific schemes piecemeal.[1] Most of the Plowden recommendations have been implemented. After a faltering start, techniques have been developed for forecasting expenditure and enabling politicians to make better-informed choices on key developments. The visible sign of this has been a succession of White Papers on public expenditure, including the unfortunate National Plan of 1965, which tried to relate public expenditure to changes and growth (that did not in fact materialize) in the rest of the economy.[2] Less visible has been the annual Chequers weekend at which groups of Ministers try to thrash out the competing merits of their departments' expansion schemes. At the same time economists and other specialists have been brought in to help with evaluation.

The planning exercise has been made particularly necessary by pressure of growing social services on a relatively stagnant economy. The acceptance of a plan inevitably restricts the freedom of action

[1] *The Control of Public Expenditure,* Cmnd. 1432 (1961). The report should be read with authoritative commentaries, e.g. U. K. Hicks, 'Plowden, Planning and Management in the Public Sector', *Public Administration,* vol. 39 (1961) p. 299; D. N. Chester, 'The Plowden Report: Nature and Significance', *Public Administration,* vol. 41 (1963) p. 3; W. J. M. Mackenzie, 'The Plowden Report: a Translation', reprinted from *The Guardian,* 25 May 1963, in R. Rose (ed.) *Policy-Making in Britain* (London, 1969) p. 273.

[2] Cmnd. 2235 (1963); Cmd. 2764 (1965); Cmnd. 2915 (1966); Cmnd. 3515 (1968).

of future governments; this has raised new problems about the civil service. The Fulton Committee noted that while civil servants had to be ready to serve under governments of any political complexion, they also had a special responsibility to show initiative and far-sightedness in working out the needs of the future and how they might be met. They had been relatively unsuccessful, in the eyes of the Committee, and had failed to recognize the need for new kinds of specialism quickly enough, particularly in fields like economics, statistics, accountancy and research. The administrative class were not only bad managers, they were also unable to provide the dynamic innovation that circumstances demanded.[1]

These criticisms are not new. Fifty years ago the Haldane Committee was complaining that 'adequate provision has not been made in the past for the organized acquisition of facts and information, and for the systematic application of thought, as preliminary to the settlement of policy and its subsequent administration'.[2] The Haldane Committee made a number of proposals for improving this situation. It proposed the development of government-sponsored research, the extended use of advisory committees, a separation of planning responsibilities from day-to-day administration, and encouragement for all senior officials to spend more of their time on 'enquiry, research and reflection'.[3] With the exception of the last, these ideas have passed into current orthodoxy.

There are three main questions. First there is the problem of ensuring that the material most relevant to a policy decision – information about facts, political opinions, future possibilities – is available. Then there is the problem of sifting this information and presenting the essential factors in manageable form to the group who are concerned with the final decision. Third there is the problem of ensuring that they are not prevented by other preoccupations from evaluating and using the material.

SOURCES OF DATA

There are four main sources from which the raw material for new policy can come: (1) the conventional political system; (2) the system

[1] *Fulton Report*, vol. 1, pars. 10–15, 31, 36, 54, 172. The Committee's recommendations about the future of the administrative class have been described in ch. III above.

[2] *Report of the Machinery of Government Committee* (Haldane) Cd. 9230 (1918) p. 6, par. 12.

[3] Ibid., pars. 13–14.

of non-parliamentary pressures and consultative machinery within which departments operate; (3) internal feedback from the operation of existing policies; (4) research and intelligence. The categories overlap and some channels convey material of more than one type. Thus advisory committees may convey information or pressures or both.

1. The part played by the political system has already been discussed in Chapters V and VIII. Criticisms of existing policies and proposals for new ones are continuously reaching Ministers from individual Members of Parliament through letters, questions and debates, from backbench committees, and from the political party machine. Most of these ideas originate with sectional groups outside politics, but they acquire a new significance when they are taken up through political channels.

2. Advisory committees have been popular in British government.[1] The Haldane Committee felt that every department should have an advisory committee 'so constituted as to make available the knowledge and experience of all sections of the community affected by the activities of the Department'.[2] By 1958 there were about 850 advisory committees covering the whole field of government. Sixty-three new ones were added between October 1964 and March 1965. Every major department has some sort of advisory committee structure and a high proportion of policy decisions is taken after a reference to such a body. The current desire for more openness and consultation while decisions are being prepared will presumably be reflected in the creation of more consultative apparatus. The common element to all advisory committees (whatever their title or status) is that they provide a channel through which information and ideas can be fed into the government machine from outside. There is, however, an important difference in function between committees composed mainly of experts and those which represent interested parties. It seems to be difficult to combine both in the one body. The eight professors and a Cambridge Fellow, with a well-known academic geographer in the chair, who were appointed early in 1965 to the Advisory Committee on Natural Resources to assist Ministers in working out principles and objectives to ensure the best

[1] For a full account of the development of the advisory committee system see R. V. Vernon and N. Mansergh, *Advisory Bodies: a Study of their Uses in Relation to Central Government 1919-39* (London, 1940); K. C. Wheare, *Government by Committee* (Oxford, 1955); P.E.P., *Advisory Committees in British Government* (London, 1960).
[2] *Haldane Report*, p. 11, par. 34.

use of resources, might be expected to make knowledge and experience available in finding solutions to practical problems. On the other hand, some advisory bodies made up of professional representatives (at least in the social services field) are frankly political rather than expert. They meet to consider papers prepared by civil servants and their real function is perhaps to tell the Minister what their constituents will or will not stand. Committees of this sort are doubtful sources of new ideas, but there are exceptions. The Central Advisory Council for Education has produced a series of penetrating reports (Crowther, Newsom, and Plowden) which have been major contributions to educational policy. A recent trend is for committees of enquiry to commission research, which is published alongside the main report. It is not clear whether the availability of research simply sets limits to the range of bargaining among interested parties that goes on in such committees or whether it can provide a basis for a real shift in their understanding. The Fulton Committee seems to have made hardly any use of even the limited amount of research published in Volume 3 of its report.

3. A possible function of the professional committee is to channel information about the way a policy is working out in the field. In practice, the institutionalized pressures at work on such a body tend to distort any feedback. Internal statistics may provide a better indication of the need for adjustments within the framework of existing policy. Sir Geoffrey Vickers describes the 'cybernetic' collection of information that can lead automatically to a correction in course. For instance, chief education officers use information about a changing child population as a basis for continual modification in school building and maintenance programmes.[1] Similarly, the Treasury has channels for supplying information about the state of the economy as a matter of routine to those responsible for economic policy decisions. There is a less obviously cybernetic (or 'homeostatic') element in many other routine statistics that departments collect. Danger signals do not always lead to action, but at least the figures are there to be interpreted. Another, perhaps more effective, source of information about a service is the number of complaints it generates – that is to say the amount of attention it receives from politicians in their capacity as grievance-settlers. But radical change is not likely to be prompted by information about the operation of existing policies.

[1] Vickers, *The Art of Judgment*, ch. 1 *et passim*.

4. The Haldane Committee thought that 'a Minister in charge of an administrative Department must have at his disposal, and under his control, an organization sufficient to provide him with a general survey of existing knowledge on any subject within his sphere'.[1] This may have been less utopian in 1918 than it is today; the world of knowledge is no longer so manageable.

Since the early fifties there has been a revival of interest in research and intelligence bearing on departmental policies. To take one example out of several, the Ministry of Health appointed its first statistician in 1955 after parliamentary criticism. The department now has a strong staff of specialists and administrators working on statistics, research and intelligence which provides the sort of underpinning for committees enquiring into particular problems, as well as for the routine work of the department, that the Haldane Committee had in mind. The Ministry has also sponsored a substantial programme of external research on subjects as diverse as decision-making in hospital committees, the pre-symptomatic detection of disease, the sociology of nursing and the career intentions of young doctors. There are similar problem-orientated programmes in the Home Office and the Department of Education and Science and also in some of the non-social service departments like the Ministry of Transport. All this activity is fairly recent, and has been stimulated by the Heyworth Report on Social Studies.[2]

Slightly further away from departmental policy centres are the projects carried out in government research establishments such as the Road Research Laboratory and the Royal Aircraft Establishment. Research in science and technology, particularly research geared to defence, has been a government responsibility since the First World War. Further away still are the research councils, sponsoring research in their fields under the general auspices of the Department of Education and Science. The research council arrangements were reorganized in 1965 when the older Medical Research Council and the Agricultural Research Council were joined by the Science Research Council, the Natural Environment Research Council and the Social Science Research Council, all except the last being loosely co-ordinated by the Council for Scientific Policy and ultimately by the Central Advisory Council for Science and Technology, whose terms of reference are 'to advise the

[1] *Haldane Report*, p. 32, par. 60.
[2] *Report of the Committee on Social Studies*, Cmnd. 2660 (1965).

Government on the most effective national strategy for the use and development of our scientific and technological resources'. The Haldane Committee had foreseen much of this, and envisaged a two-way flow of requests for help from departments and suggestions from the research councils about the practical application of research discoveries. What it could not have envisaged was the increasing trend towards 'pure' research that has little direct application to the immediate problems of industry and government; nor the difficulty of ensuring that potential applications of it are identified and explored, perhaps by people who have little understanding of the original research.

ASSIMILATION

The real problem is how to assimilate all this material in decision-making. It is easy to spot gaps in information. For example, the Home Office procedure in reaching decisions about police establishments, described in Chapter IV, could be considerably improved by studies designed to show the marginal value of a policeman. The Home Office Police Research and Planning Branch has in fact made some progress with relevant studies. But on any major question of social or economic policy the amount of information already available somewhere in the system is formidable. The problem is how to bring it to bear, in time, on actual decisions that are being taken at or near Ministerial level. If research and expert advice are to be useful they must be assimilated by those making policy decisions and carrying them out. This is not easy and there are grounds for pessimism about the ability of the policy-making system to cope.

We need to be clear about the nature of the difficulty. It is not a question of giving the Minister or any other single decision-maker all the information needed to reach a rational decision. No individual could cope with the complexity involved. Indeed, it is likely that his decisions would become wilder as the material grew beyond his handling capacity. We need a structure which allows major problems to be factorized – in departments, or sections of departments – and then, after processing, brought together again at Ministerial or Cabinet level.

We are only slowly learning the necessary techniques. The Haldane solution of finding an administrator of quality and giving him more time to think is at best incomplete and at worst a blind alley. First, no amount of thinking in a padded room will do the job: the information theoretically relevant to any major decision is so vast that it has to be sifted several times before the range of considerations has been reduced to a scale on which the individual can take it in – he must be part of an efficient communication system. Second, there is no real evidence that administrators with additional time at their disposal would spend it by increasing their range of decision-premises. The evidence reviewed in Chapter VII suggests the opposite – that given a choice between short-term and long-term pressures the administrator will give priority to meeting short-term ones, perhaps more adequately, even if the total pressure is reduced. In Britain senior civil servants are under such pressure to meet immediate demands arising from the public and parliamentary duties of the Ministers whom they serve that longer-term planning and evaluation are simply crowded out. A reduction in their load would not overcome the effects of habit and the priority (indeed the deference) that they give to servicing the political machine.

Consequently, excessive weight has been given at top policy-making levels to considerations presented through (a) the macro-political system and (b) the micro-political consultative structure of pressures and interests surrounding each major field of activity. Not enough weight has been given to (c) internal feedback or (d) research and intelligence, nor to evaluating all the factors and preparing material for a balanced decision. This goes a long way to explaining what has been lacking in the British system of government decision-making. The machine has been limited both in the range of information to which it reacts and in its capacity for fundamental change of direction after assimilating it. Both deficiencies reflect on politicians as well as on civil servants. Both can be dealt with only by attending to overall structure.

RESPONSE

A particularly disturbing feature of recent years has been the tendency to wait for pressure from an outside source before making full use of information already available within a department. To take examples from civil service personnel administration (of all fields the one most amenable to initiative from within the service), the reasons for a shortage of red brick candidates for administrative class competitions were accurately described in the Civil Service

Commission's Report for 1960–1. It was not until the Estimates Committee reported on the problem four years later, basing its comments on an independent survey by the Acton Society Trust, that the Commission took serious steps to deal with the problem. Again, the case for amalgamating the executive and administrative classes in the light of changing responsibilities has been discussed within the civil service since the early 1960s. No proposals emerged from the Treasury until evidence was required for the Fulton Committee's review of civil service structure. The Fulton Committee itself was established only after the Estimates Committee had taken up suggestions from university witnesses that a review was needed.

When the machine does respond to a stimulus it is often too timid. The reaction to a parliamentary criticism might be to institute a wholesale review of the policy that has been brought into question. Often the reaction is a minimal one, conceived in terms of political tactics to safeguard the Minister's reputation. When a procedural change or a new statistical service is proposed, the service has often adopted the suggestion literally without applying its experience to see if the suggestion can be improved and developed. (But its critical and eclectic reaction to the changes proposed by the Fulton Committee is an outstanding exception.) In the field of economic management, the failure to take a view of even middling length until the Plowden investigation (itself suggested by an Estimates Committee report) is an egregious example. Finally, reactions have often been slow and ponderous when consultation with outside interests is involved or hasty and ill-considered when it is not.

Political demands take priority because the departmental structure, with a politician at the apex, secures priority to whatever interests or concerns the head of the department, and because senior civil servants are trained in habits of loyalty from their earliest days in the Minister's private office, around which a great deal of the top level work in the department revolves. This would not matter if the demands reflected through this system truly reflected a balanced assessment of priorities. We have argued in Chapter VIII that in the last resort the acceptability of a policy to a representative lay assembly is not a bad test of its consistency with widely held community values. But a lay assembly cannot plan. Planning (as Professor Beer pointed out in 1957)[1] is essentially an administrative activity; even Ministers are temperamentally unsuited to it. Because

[1] S. H. Beer, *Treasury Control* (2nd. edn.) (Oxford, 1957).

of the mechanics of lay intervention – its latency, eccentricity and subservience to professionalism – M.P.s are well equipped for assessing and criticizing developed policy proposals – or for initiating the consideration of new ideas – but badly equipped for making coherent and workable suggestions for new policy. Normally, ideas coming from Parliament need to be considered against a planning background as well as a political background and should not be given an emphasis that they do not deserve on their merits.[1] Fears that the latter was only too likely to happen led Shonfield to write about the need to restrain Parliament from *tinkering*[2] and the then leader of the Liberal Party to argue that Parliament was incapable of handling the real problems of modern society.[3] In organizational terms, to rely for initiative on the political system may be to put the power of decision in a blind spot, where authority is not matched by knowledge and attention tends to be unstable.

The imbalance described above could in theory be rectified in a number of ways, but not all of them are viable in practice:

1. The quality of parliamentary intervention could be improved, by providing more information to Members and educating some of them through service on specialized committees. Most proposals to improve the quality of parliamentary work seem to depend on the employment of specialist advisers to challenge specialists in the administration – an arrangement which involves a prodigal use of scarce resources. The general question of parliamentary committees has been discussed in Chapter V. It is difficult to reconcile strong policy-oriented committees with Ministerial responsibility or with the essentially 'long-stop' character of ultimate lay control. It is also wishful thinking to expect the parliamentary election process to throw up several hundred representatives who are willing or able to think in administrative terms. In the work of the Select Committees dealing with science and nationalized industries, there are signs that a fruitful relationship could develop between departments and a small group of interested Members of Parliament. But there is not

[1] It is not intended to convey the impression that civil servants are uniquely able to determine what the merits are. The merit of a proposal, in the sense used here, is the merit it would be given in the judgement of knowledgeable laymen, such as M.P.s, when they had been made aware of the full background. Civil servants should be able to anticipate from experience what that judgement would be.

[2] *Modern Capitalism* (London, 1965) Part IV.

[3] Jo Grimond, 'Whitehall and Beyond', *The Listener*, vol. LXXI (12 March 1964) pp. 415–16.

much sign, so far, that the work of these committees will have much impact on the relationship between departments and non-participating Members. The Fulton Committee could offer no more than qualified optimism on the whole subject: 'It would be deeply regrettable, however, if these committees became an additional brake on the administrative process. We hope, therefore, that in developing this closer association with departments, Parliament will concentrate on matters of real substance and take fully into account the cumulative cost (not only in time but in the quality of administration) that the raising of minutiae imposes upon them.'[1]

2. The distraction caused by parliamentary interest in trivia could be reduced by limiting parliamentary rights to question Ministers and to raise individual cases. But the tendency is to strengthen parliamentary powers, through the establishment of specialist committees and the office of the Parliamentary Commissioner, in order to protect individual rights. The Minister and his immediate advisers cannot dissociate themselves from the performance of their department as revealed in the reports of such bodies. Nor, in a country with our political traditions, does it seem likely that a Minister would wish to refuse to investigate cases raised with him privately by M.P.s.

3. Administrators could be trained, through managerial orientation and greater 'numeracy', to be less sensitive to political impulses than they are now. To some extent this argument (implicit in some parts of the Fulton Report) has already been answered. The system of pressures near the top is very hard to resist. Even a 'Fultonized' administrator is likely to have his management training offset by spells in the private office and other quasi-political work, unless a career-path can be devised that excludes these normative elements.

4. Those responsible for planning could be separated from those responsible for day-to-day administration and thus shielded from the direct impact of parliamentary influence. This was the Haldane solution: the Committee drew attention to the 'proved impracticability of devoting the necessary time to thinking out organization and preparation for action in the mere interstices of the time required for the transaction of business' and said that responsibility for 'enquiry and thinking' should be placed 'in the hands of persons definitely charged with it'.[2] It is also the Fulton solution. But if

---

[1] *Fulton Report*, vol. 1, par. 281. [2] *Haldane Report*, p. 6, par. 13.

specialist planning branches are too divorced from the regular political work of the Minister and the department, it becomes difficult to ensure that they are not ignored in a crisis and thus fail to confront political pressures with others at crucial moments.

5. Purely political influences can be counteracted by institutionalizing other pressures, orientated to long-term planning, in the top structure of the department. It is not enough, as we have seen, to have facilities for research and intelligence. The difficulty is to ensure that they are obtruded on the attention of top decision-makers at a time when these people may also be under political pressure to give priority to inadequate, short-term solutions. The answer may be to give sufficient status in the department to a special unit, or a specialist adviser (see Chapter IV), whose whole function is to proffer advice about longer-term considerations at a level where it can hardly be ignored.

PLANNING UNITS

The Fulton Committee proposed that a planning unit headed by a Senior Policy Adviser should be set up in each department to look after major long-term policy planning. The unit was envisaged as fairly small:

> Its main task should be to identify and study the problems and needs of the future and the possible means to meet them; it should also be its function to see that day-to-day policy decisions are taken with as full a recognition as possible of their likely implications for the future. The planning unit should not carry any responsibility for the day-to-day operations of the department. [It should be] equipped to assemble and analyse the information needed for its planning work.[1]

The Senior Policy Adviser should have direct access to the Minister and should share collegiate responsibility with any other top specialists and with the Permanent Secretary. The latter would no longer act as chief adviser on policy but would retain overall responsibility, under the Minister, for all the affairs of the department except one: the Senior Policy Adviser would decide (after consulting the Permanent Secretary but subject only to the approval

[1] *Fulton Report*, vol. 1, pars. 172–7.

of the Minister) what problems the planning unit should tackle. The adviser should be 'an authority in the department's field of activity', he should 'know the other experts in the field, both inside and outside the Service, at home and abroad; he should be aware of all the important trends in new thinking and practice that are relevant'. He might with advantage be a relatively young man. (Here the Committee was influenced by the comparative youth of key officials at policy levels in France and Sweden.) Normally he would be a career civil servant, specializing in the department's field, but 'on occasions he might be appointed by the Minister from outside the Service to give a new impetus to its forward thinking'. It must also be possible to replace the Senior Policy Adviser 'when a new Minister finds the current holder of the post too closely identified with, or wedded to, policies that he wishes to change; or when an adviser's capacity for producing and making use of new ideas declines'. His exact rank would 'depend on the way the Minister wishes to organize his top-level activities' but would normally be at least Deputy Secretary. As a member of the senior policy and management group, his salary would be determined by an annual review of his performance.[1]

Junior posts in the planning units should also be held by comparatively young men, sometimes career civil servants, sometimes appointed from outside on short-term contracts or temporary secondment. They should expect to move back, either to 'operating sections' of the department or to work outside government, at least by their mid-forties. Some of them would be research officers. Although not stated directly in the report, it seems intended that most economists and similar specialists, as well as 'temporary experts' appointed by the Minister to assist him on a personal basis, should be concentrated in planning units. But some of the best career administrators will also spend substantial periods in them at a relatively early stage of their careers. All the staff 'should develop close contacts with the appropriate experts . . . They should be aware of, and contribute to, new thinking in their field. They should also be trained in, and have the capacity to use, the relevant techniques of quantitative analysis.' The planning units should 'provide an environment in which those who possess qualities of imagination and foresight can be identified and developed'.[2]

[1] *Fulton Report*, vol. 1, pars. 182–7, 229 and 286.
[2] Ibid., pars. 52, 129, 174–6 and app. D III.

The Fulton concept seems to have been influenced partly by the view of the management consultancy group that there would be merit in making an organizational distinction between the management of existing policies and the forward planning role of examining and evaluating new policy options. The group seem in turn to have had in mind the role of advisory staff groups in industry and to be thinking in terms of techniques like 'costed options', which is becoming a feature of public expenditure planning. Partly it seems to have been influenced by the existence of something like a planning unit in the Ministry of Defence, whose Permanent Secretary (Sir James Dunnett) was a member of the Committee. Partly, also, it seems to have been motivated by a desire to reduce the Minister's dependence on his Permanent Secretary. The Permanent Secretary appears in the report as a rather dull stick-in-the-mud who cannot be discarded because of his part in securing continuity and financial accountability but who needs to be prevented from fielding the bright new ideas of the young whiz-kids in the planning units. This is a rather unrealistic picture and it is, of course, impracticable to separate the Permanent Secretary's overall responsibility for expenditure from the evaluation, in expenditure terms, of short- or medium-term policy options.

Whatever the motives for it, the proposal is based on a realistic understanding of the difficulty of combining long-term thinking with meeting immediate deadlines. It has three outstanding merits:

(a) By taking some of the ablest staff away from day-to-day pressures (at some inevitable cost to the adequacy with which the department meets these pressures) the planning unit should institutionalize a commitment to forward thinking and appraisal that has hitherto been done too peripherally or not at all in most departments.

(b) By placing the unit under a senior adviser, with direct access to the Minister, the proposals ensure that the ideas developed in it will be inserted at an appropriate level in top-level decision-making. The really important thing about planning machinery is that people at the top should believe in it, and the question of direct access may be a red herring. But it also seems necessary to ensure that planning considerations are not overlooked.

(c) The planning unit should provide an environment in which people of different skills and backgrounds can work together in a more flexible pattern of relationships than normal discipline and accountability will allow in operating divisions.

But the proposals as they stand in the report leave a number of questions unanswered. By blurring several important distinctions, they would permit departments to adopt quite different arrangements in putting them into practice, some of which could cause the main value of the reforms to be lost. The main points of uncertainty are: (a) whether the main purpose of the units is to be centres of creative thought or to provide a bridge between the creative ideas of others and the executive activities of the department; (b) the exact relationship between the unit and the rest of the department; (c) the extent to which the units themselves will be politicized.

CREATIVITY OR INNOVATION?

A hierarchical decision-making and career structure tends to encourage consensus and conformity at the expense of creativity. One of its functions is to integrate centrifugal tendencies.[1] For normal operational purposes, the ability to compromise is an important virtue. Conversely it is difficult to accept conflict as legitimate. A really creative idea is likely to disrupt the smooth flow of business and therefore leads to faction. Those who are primarily concerned with resolving disputes will usually find it easier to turn down an unorthodox idea than to approve it. It is easy, too, to get into the habit of regarding time spent in discussion and research as wasted except when directly related to the achievement of immediate goals. This tendency will be accentuated in a production-orientated organization whose administrators are assessed against norms of output.

Consequently, proposals for radical change are most likely to come from staff who are insulated from the normal pressure to get on with the job and are put into a special environment where unorthodoxy is not only tolerated but approved. It seems essential that those involved should not be too inhibited by the consciousness of infinite ramification. They should be a bit irresponsible. In such an environment differences of status and rank are likely to be relatively unimportant compared with the ability to produce exciting new ideas. These new conditions are most likely to be achieved if the thinking unit looks outward rather than inward

[1] V. A. Thompson, 'Bureaucracy and Innovation', *Administrative Science Quarterly*, vol. 10 (1965–6) p. 1.

(possibly by employing mobile professionals whose loyalties are wider than a single organization) and is detached from the main organization. Dubin suggests that contacts between a research and development unit and the main organization should be reduced to a single highly selective channel.[1]

But the ideas that emerge from such an anarchic group of licensed rebels have to be assessed realistically before being put into practice. If consensus, co-ordination and commitment are inhibiting to the production of new ideas they are essential for their evaluation and implementation. Hence there is room for another sort of thinking unit, made up of people who have a foot on both sides as a bridge (or buffer) between ideas and the authority to accept them. Their task calls for open-mindedness, imagination and communication skills, but not necessarily for originality. Theirs is the task carried out by managers in Burns and Stalker's 'organic' firms,[2] specializing in communication and in co-operative adjustment to change, whereas the main qualities needed in the research unit proper are perhaps stubborn independence and refusal to abandon a line of thought too readily.

Various committees have seen a particular need for bridge-building partnerships between specialists and administrators in this context. Thus the Trend Committee on Civil Science argued the need for scientists to be closely associated with policy-makers in research-using departments.[3] The Heyworth Committee on Social Studies was even more explicit on the subject of social scientists, and deserves quotation at length:

> Anyone engaged in administration in central or local government, or in the institutions of the welfare state, or in education, or in commerce and industry, is engaged in fields which social scientists study. Whether he knows it or not, he is using methods and techniques to help him deal with his work and solve problems that a social scientist would recognize. Rules that he uses may well be years out of date. Of course, much administration is concerned with day-to-day business, but unless an attempt is made to identify long-term problems or penetrate behind the curtain of everyday decisions, the decisions taken will be based on

[1] R. Dubin, 'The Stability of Human Organizations', in Mason Haire (ed.) *Modern Organization Theory* (New York, 1959) pp. 246–7.

[2] Burns and Stalker, *The Management of Innovation*, see ch. XI above, pp. 223–4.

[3] *Report of the Committee on Civil Science*, Cmnd. 2171 (1963) pars. 44, 97–8, 118–19.

wrong or inadequate data. That is why research in the social sciences is important to the administrator . . .

There are two needs. The first is for administrators and managers to be familiar with the scope and value of the social sciences, not only as direct aids to administration, but also as disciplines which are able to limit the uncertainties within which decisions have to be taken, and to evaluate their outcome. But these steps will not be enough to ensure the fullest value is obtained from research in the social sciences. Problems in government or industry do not usually present themselves to administrators in a fashion which at once shows how they could be clarified by research in the social sciences. The second need, therefore, is for social scientists to work at points where problems first emerge and to help identify and deal with them. In order to carry out this intermediary function, social scientists would need to have a foot in both camps: on the one hand they would work closely with administrators as members of the functional team; they would also need to maintain professional contacts with each other and with the outside world.[1]

The Heyworth arguments are clearly sound. The research worker needs to be kept away from the day-to-day pressures of administration or he will not produce any research. The administrator is no longer in a position to attempt long-term thinking, but he must be able to deploy long-term thinking in his daily business. The full-time expert is also, these days, too close to the machine to attempt much long-term work. It is unrealistic to expect one man to carry the weight of human knowledge on any subject, but he should be sufficiently aware of what is going on in his field to know where to go for more detailed advice when it is needed. He must also be reasonably knowledgeable at a superficial level in order to provide advice off-the-cuff in a crisis. So we need a sort of interpretative process which shades into executive administration at one end and into pure research (including departmental research units) at the other.

The Fulton Committee's planning units will be near the executive end of this process. They are not sufficiently detached from the main responsibilities of the department to take a completely fresh view. And they are too small to be doing fundamental research. Their structure – and the analogy with central policy units in Sweden and

[1] *Report of the Committee on Social Studies*, Cmnd. 2660 (1965) pars. 19, 123.

France – suggests that they are more like a forward planning group of the top board, commissioning the real backroom boys to produce new strategic models and exploring the viability of those they have already produced. They are inspired brokers, who really know their market, rather than inventors. The difference is important, because it calls for a different sort of social structure within the units. In the 'boardroom' type of planning unit it is necessary for someone to have the ultimate power of decision. Relationships can be fairly flexible, since each assignment will be unique and it will be more important to use each member's unique experience to best advantage than to allocate duties in a rigid and 'mechanistic' way. But their activities are too close to action to dispense with an underlying discipline. The Fulton Committee does not appear to have appreciated the difference: it argues that research officers should be brought more into the mainstream of policy and not confined to a backroom role, but does not see that this involves giving preference to usefulness over originality. Its report, indeed, drew attention to the need for some central co-ordination, by the Cabinet or the Treasury, of departmental planning units to ensure that 'the emerging problems of the country are to be tackled systematically and comprehensively and on the basis of common major hypotheses.'[1]

In a sense the planning unit is a natural development from the diarchy (or 'joint hierarchy') of administrator and expert adviser that has existed for a long time in, for example, the Health Departments, where many administrators are paired with medical officers who have left clinical practice to become experts in a branch of administrative medicine. Sometimes a committee will have a medical secretary as well as an administrative one. The administrator provides a link with the main policy-making and executive system while the doctor is at the operational end of a chain of increasingly specialized professional expertise that may well end in a university laboratory, perhaps linking serum research to public health policy. In this sort of partnership the professional provides continuity and many of the ideas, the administrator deals with political crises, and a one-to-one relationship works fairly well within limits.

But a sound public health policy these days is likely to require more than medical expertise. It may well involve cost-benefit analysis, social research and demographic forecasting. The medical adviser needs to be replaced by a team of doctors, sociologists,

[1] *Fulton Report*, vol. i, par. 177.

economists, statisticians, demographers, each at the terminal point of a chain of fundamental and applied knowledge. An executive administrator can no longer rely on such a team to speak with one voice to tell him what needs to be done. The team needs a co-ordinator, a sense-maker, someone to find common ground among the different disciplines, to bring its ideas into focus and to subject them to the appraisal of an uncommitted layman. Such a component cannot be supplied by the administrator who is busy with day-to-day crises; it calls for someone like the specialized and knowledgeable administrator who emerges from other Fulton proposals.

RELATIONSHIP WITH EXECUTIVE DIVISIONS

The planning unit's functions are thus closely associated with the main political direction of the department. It follows that there can be no sharp cut-off point between the operation (and explanation) of existing policies and the elaboration of new ones. If short-term decisions pre-empt the future, there is not much point in planning at all. Similarly, if the planners (as distinct from the researchers) are too isolated from the problems facing the department in its day-to-day work their ideas may lack immediate utility.[1] Excessive detachment may be prevented by putting a reasonable leavening of career administrators in the planning units. The Fulton Committee also recommended that the Senior Policy Adviser and the unit as a whole should be responsible for seeing that day-to-day decisions take long-term implications into account. This will hardly be possible without some mechanism for keeping the planning staff in touch with the day-to-day work of the department and making them aware of impending decisions. And on the other side of the fence the Permanent Secretary, retaining overall responsibility for running the office, will not be able to leave longer-term implications of current policies entirely to the planners.

The most natural way of keeping planners in touch is by giving them a vetting function and a seat on committees where decisions are being taken. (This mechanism again fits the 'planning group of directors' concept better than the 'ideas and research' concept.) The risk is that they will spend so much time keeping in touch that they

[1] Lord Bridges felt that the pre-war Economic Advisory Council was in this position: *The Treasury* (London, 1966) p. 90. See also p. 10 above.

will again be swamped with the short term. There is also a risk (although the status of the Senior Policy Adviser should provide some protection) that they will be expected to lend a hand in a crisis. It will be a nice problem of balance: if they are too close to the machine, they may be forced to neglect long-term work; if they are too detached from it they will not be able to influence pragmatic short-term decisions. Badly handled, the institution of planning units could lead to divided responsibility for regular operations, with the planners arguing for decisions to be postponed to await research while the managers want to get on with the job. Or the units could become a fifth wheel, like the Department of Economics Affairs on a smaller scale. A good deal of trial and error will be needed to establish whether the separation of high-level planning from executive responsibility is practicable in the different circumstances of different departments.

There is a special difficulty in the Fulton model. The Committee clearly recognized the amount of political secretarial work falling on the civil service, but in its anxiety to managerialize executive functions and to technologize planning ones, it does not seem to have made any administrative provision for such work. It may have been assumed that the detailed demands of political and parliamentary accountability would be reduced, or at any rate would command a less deferential response than at present. It seems unlikely that either assumption is correct. Another possibility is that Ministers will appoint substantial personal staffs to man their private offices and help them with their political work. It is far more likely that a Minister's needs would somehow be accommodated within the Fulton structure. The Minister would look for help where he could get it, either by diverting the managers from management in order to write speeches and deal with parliamentary criticisms (one of the main weaknesses in the pre-Fulton civil service) or by using the new planning units as a personal staff to underpin his political performance. This would be a most unfortunate (but all too easy) perversion of what is basically one of the best ideas in the Fulton Report.

In some departments, such as those concerned with economic planning and the regulation of industry, nearly all the work *is* planning and parliamentary criticism would probably be concentrated on the work of the planning unit itself. Moreover, there is a risk that planning units will become particularly vulnerable to inquisition by specialist parliamentary committees. The possibility of such probing may prejudice their ability to range freely over policy options, popular and unpopular alike. Their creation does not avoid the difficulty of reconciling technological thinking with the British system of parliamentary accountability.

PLANNING AND POLITICS

Planning cannot, of course, be divorced from politics. The ultimate choice among options is a political choice, not to be avoided by greater use of research and statistics. But the analysis of options preparatory to political choice also involves political as well as administrative elements, except in the rare cases where planners are concerned only with the examination of alternative means, themselves valuationally neutral, of achieving a clearly defined political objective. Normally, the choices of lines to pursue, the weighting given to advantages and disadvantages that emerge and the final selection of a limited number of viable choices all involve value assumptions that are political in nature. The current vogue for cost-benefit analysis tends to overlook the qualitative judgements that have to be made if 'chalk and cheese' comparisons are to be made at all. There may be a tendency at the time of writing for planners to make inexplicit assumptions about the priority of economic factors, that can be measured, over social factors that can not. Samuel Brittan pointed out in 1964 that considerable technical knowledge may be required to ascertain what the real political choices are. He argued the case for a new class of adviser, politically committed as well as an expert in his field, who can examine the whole framework of assumptions on which policy is based and open up the options for Ministers.[1] Many of Brittan's ideas were widely shared and were put into effect by the Labour Government after the 1964 election, particularly in the field of economics, where several government sympathizers were put into key advisory positions. Clearly such men would have to be in the planning unit, and the Fulton proposals allow for this. (Indeed, given what Fulton has said and what the Labour Government has done, there is a real possibility that the Senior Policy Advisers in some departments would always be political appointees.)

[1] S. Brittan, *The Treasury under the Tories*, ch. 10.

As always, there are risks. Career civil servants are trained to be impartial. That does not mean that their policy proposals are not based on value-premises. It means rather that the premises are (or are assumed to be) widely shared, or else reflect such views as the Minister may have made explicit. Although it is an over-simplification to distinguish between the 'objective' formulation of policy alternatives and the 'political' choice among them, it still makes sense to draw a broad distinction between the preliminary assessment of evidence with a view to listing viable courses of action, and the final decision that one course of action has fewer unacceptable side-effects than another. If a distinctively political choice is made too early in the formulation process it may close options rather than open them. Perhaps the dangers are less in a technological department, where development planning is on the whole politically neutral, than in a social service department where political beliefs are likely to be fundamental to one's approach to, say, the development of secondary education or graduated pensions.

The lesson seems to be that planning units could usefully include political appointees to challenge the existing framework and open up new lines of thinking, but that these must not be powerful enough to usurp by suppression the Minister's function of making a final decision among carefully considered alternatives. But this demands considerable restraint both on the part of the adviser and on the part of the Minister who appointed him, especially if the latter is anxious to see the speedy implementation of his favourite schemes. Indeed, one drawback about the whole system is the amount of patronage it places in the hands of an unscrupulous or impatient Minister. The Fulton Committee accepted the need to safeguard the political neutrality of the higher civil service, including, apparently, the Senior Policy Adviser, but it is also clear that the growth of direct appointments was seen as a means of improving a Minister's control over the formulation of policy in his department.[1] It is difficult to reconcile these lines of thought.

The politicization of planning carries an inevitable risk that long-term plans, with effects beyond the life of the current government, will be influenced by a Minister's desire to gain a tactical advantage in the House of Commons through leaks, promises and assurances. But this danger is already present and is probably inseparable from any system of parliamentary government.

[1] *Fulton Report*, vol. i, pars. 285–6.

CONCLUSIONS

A weakness of the traditional Parliament-Minister-civil service structure is the low priority it secures for appraisal and for the application to policy of the fruits of research and intelligence. It is necessary to devise a structure which encourages research and ensures that the resulting data are properly weighed in the consideration of new policies.

Research suggests that radical rethinking is easiest for staff who are insulated from the ordinary routines, who have a low commitment to the traditional way of doing things and who work in an atmosphere where unorthodoxy is highly valued. It is also likely that innovation occurs most spontaneously in units which are reasonably isolated and in which hierarchical discipline is not oppressive. These requirements are incompatible with those of a conventional executive system, designed to foster loyalty, predictability and co-ordination.

The establishment of more planning units, on the lines suggested by Fulton, will serve the rather different function of ensuring higher priority for long-term planning. Although freed from immediate executive responsibility, planning units will be too closely associated with executive action, under political direction, to carry out much fundamental research (which might be better 'hived-off' to *ad hoc* agencies or to universities). Their purpose is primarily the examination of practical policy options and the appraisal of new ideas which are fed into them along open lines of communication. Members of the planning units should be interpreters. On the one hand, they can select relevant material from on-going research and present it in a form which the executive administrator can use. On the other hand, they should be in a position to restate administrative problems as questions to which (so far as our present state of knowledge allows) research may provide at least partial answers. They will provide the final link in a chain of knowledge and ideas extending from research units to the headquarters of administrative departments, in which members of advisory committees and research councils, their assessors, part-time consultants, professional civil servants of various sorts and specialist administrators all play a part.

XIII. The Generalist in Public Administration

REVIEW OF ARGUMENT

In earlier chapters, the present structure of the British civil service and its relationship to the political system have been described. We started by looking at the changing task of public administration, and saw that the essential problem was one of meeting incompatible demands. The administrative structure and individual public servants have to serve different purposes at the same time. It is partly a clash of goals – the expansion of health services and of road building programmes somehow have to be reconciled with one another and with the overall economy goal. But it is also a clash of operating modes – different parts of the total job demand different standards of relevance and a different administrative approach. The qualities needed to streamline a school building programme are not those needed to negotiate an incomes policy nor to help a Minister deal with criticism in Parliament. There is a tension between a Minister's need for loyal servants and the need for those concerned with a developing service to take forceful initiatives; between meticulous attention to detail and the courage to take entrepreneurial risks; between central co-ordination and flexible, speedy decision-making.

The brief survey of administrative theory in Part Two helped to clarify the problem by demonstrating the need for organizational choice and compromise. Within an organization, individual decisions can be slanted by controlling staff selection, training and career development and also by modifying the administrative structure so that appropriate factors are given prior attention. Human limitations make it impossible to achieve more than a limited amount of sensitivity in any one group of people. When too much is expected of a single piece of administrative machinery, there must be compromise. If a compromise is not reached deliberately, a point of equilibrium will be determined by the strength of competing pressures. (For example long-term planning will inevitably take second place to parliamentary business if the same people are responsible for both.) Alternatively, tasks can be divided and different aspects allocated to different parts of the machine, but in that case some co-ordinating mechanism is required. We saw that political accountability is an important co-ordinating device in the public sector – to the extent that less accountability means less integration – but that lay control has certain characteristics, both useful and potentially harmful, which compel attention to the exact part played by a lay assembly in the policy-determining system and to the stage in policy-formulation at which it is exercised.

We have also examined some particular problems in British public administration. The scope of government activity has increased so much that the administrative structure appropriate to an earlier day is clearly due for review and possibly for overhaul. A good deal of adaptation has been taking place within the system as a more or less spontaneous reaction to changing circumstances. Ministers have learned how to focus their attention on politically strategic points, leaving the rest to permanent officials. There have been experiments in the grouping of functions among departmental Ministers and in the internal organization of departments. New techniques of administration have been developed, particularly in quantitative analysis and in forward planning. New specialisms have been introduced along with new training schemes to equip administrators to make proper use of them. A greatly improved status has been given to specialist advisers and to technical managers.

But some of these changes have not gone far enough: specialists still feel deprived of their place in the sun; administrators are overburdened and frankly ill-equipped to discharge some of the functions that come their way in the course of a generalist career; training has been concentrated on economic analysis, perhaps to the neglect of social and political understanding. And some of the basic problems remain unsolved: the historical methods of parliamentary control manage to divert a great deal of energy to trivia without offering much satisfaction to anybody; we have not discovered techniques for reconciling managerial initiative over run-of-the-mill matters with co-ordination and accountability in areas where they really matter; an acute shortage of managers is inevitable in the next decade unless recruitment patterns are altered to take account of educational changes; we have not managed to divert enough time and resources to long-term planning.

With this background, we have touched on the recommendations of the Fulton Committee on the civil service and looked at some of the post-1965 changes in arrangements for parliamentary supervision of the administration. The Fulton investigation was hailed as the most fundamental review of the civil service since the Northcote-Trevelyan Report. When the report appeared, it turned out to be an almost political document, written in so polemic a style that its more extreme attacks on the civil service were disowned by one member of the committee (Lord Simey), by the Prime Minister and by the leader of the Opposition.[1]

Its 158 recommendations included almost every suggestion made over the previous ten years by critics of the social structure, recruitment methods and managerial style of the service. On analysis, and stripped of the extravagant language, the recommendations turned out for the most part to be concerned with the acceleration of trends that were already at work, such as the greater use of specialists, the development of management accounting techniques, better training schemes, and the modification of pension arrangements to allow more movement in and out of the service. More fundamental recommendations concerned the creation of a new Civil Service Department, the institution of departmental planning units, the managerialization of departments into 'accountable units' and the replacement of fairly predictable career structures for different 'classes' of civil servants by a more competitive pattern of post-entry selection and job-evaluation of individual posts. In the last chapter of this book, the probable effects of some of these changes on civil service morale will be discussed. In this chapter the most fundamental recommendation in the Report – the proposal to destroy the unity, philosophy and characteristic strengths of the administrative class – will be taken as a focus for a final general discussion on the administrative process.

FULTON REPORT IN PERSPECTIVE

The Committee's report nowhere recognizes the problem of organizational choice that has been outlined in this book. In a nutshell, it

[1] For parliamentary discussion of the *Fulton Report*, see *H.C. Debs.*, vol. 767 (26 June 1968) cols. 454–65 and vol. 773 (21 November 1968) cols. 1542–1681; *H.L. Debs.*, vol. 295 (24 July 1968) cols. 1049–1194.

proposes strengthening the managerial efficiency of government departments (including forward planning, where the approach is still essentially managerial) in a way that is bound to affect other aspects of departmental performance, without clarifying the cost involved. At times it seems to be saying that there will be no cost in public accountability and in service to the Minister and the public – we can have it both ways. In other passages one can detect an assumption that the problems of reconciling conflicting aims have already been solved, that we have learned how to co-ordinate the work of public departments without impairing the freedom of action of their staff and that we have learned how to exercise democratic control of the administration without holding detailed and inhibiting inquests on minor errors of judgement.

In the 1960s those working in public administration were faced with new problems of perception, assimilation, evaluation and integration. The public expected the Government to extend its activities and to co-ordinate them more purposefully in the interests of economic planning. The knowledge explosion was at the same time adding to the number of factors that had to be taken into account in any important decision. The new demands had to be met initially within the existing framework of political and governmental institutions – Treasury methods of financial control, detailed Ministerial responsibility to Parliament and central co-ordination of policy through the Cabinet.

On the one hand, the government machine became more accessible to new skills and knowledge through the appointment of new specialists, the establishment of internal research and development units and substantial programmes of sponsored research. The proliferation of committees brought many able people and fresh points of view into the business of government. On the other hand all of this material had to be assimilated, brought into some sort of balance and related to the current framework of political assumptions and the economic resources currently available. There was more need for expertise at the periphery, but there was also more need for co-ordination and integration at the centre.

The traditional administrative pattern was partly a help and partly a hindrance. The system worked well as a sensitive and loyal instrument in the hands of a Government that knew what it wanted done, as efficiently and with as little trouble as possible. General administrators, arranged hierarchically under a Minister, provided a ready channel for the transmission of political impulses. Their expert knowledge of administration facilitated inter-departmental co-ordination and the translation of political ideas into workable schemes. But if political initiative was lacking or (in the face of increasing complexity) uncertain, the interlocking ramifications of the administrative machine tended to stifle initiative and innovation.

TRADITIONAL ROLE OF THE GENERALIST

In the traditional pattern, the administrative all-rounder played a crucial part by linking the broad objectives of the politician to the more specific or vocational orientation of sectional and specialist interests, in or out of the department. Some of his functions have been touched on in earlier chapters, but it is worth recapitulating and reformulating them here:

1. The general administrator is in the first instance a *facilitator*. If the politician (or the expert) provides ideas and motive force someone has to ensure that decisions are properly recorded, processed and implemented. This is partly a secretarial function. It becomes more complex when implementation involves securing financial allocations, obtaining formal authority from Cabinet committees, preparing amending regulations for approval by Parliament and perhaps referring proposals to interested parties. Such a role calls for knowledge of the system and some sense of what is possible. It does not demand sympathy with political objectives, nor does it call for a great deal of technical knowledge of the field. But some professionals, particularly engineers and architects, are able and willing to take on much of this work themselves; others are glad to be relieved of it.

2. A more demanding role for the general administrator is that of *mediator*. It becomes especially important when political or financial constraints have to be placed on technical initiative. The task of the mediator is to link the specialist to the rest of the system by discovering what the limits are and trying to persuade him to work within them. Conversely, if the specialist finds the limits intolerable, the mediator will try to have them eased. In defence or the social service departments, this mediating role is sometimes filled by Ministers who find themselves acting as buffers between the Treasury (and sometimes heads of rival departments or critical backbenchers) and their professional advisers. It requires, again, a knowledge of the

machine and also a fairly sophisticated understanding of different value systems. The good mediator can talk several languages simultaneously and this is not a task in which the professional civil servant will easily feel at home. But any particular mediator will tend to be concerned with a particular professional or sectional interest. The most suitable candidate will often be the departmental administrator who is attuned to his Minister's wishes, is aware of the interests of other departments and has moved from post to post often enough to avoid an excessively narrow or specialized commitment. It is probably helpful if he thinks of himself as a member of a service-wide class with common traditions and training.

3. Somebody, however, has to take decisions. There is a need for *arbiters*. Ultimately, this is a political function, but the time of political heads is limited – they need assistants to take decisions on their behalf, to narrow the field and sharpen the issues involved in questions coming to them for decision. This role demands the ability to compare and reconcile conflicting priorities. Some problems are insoluble in the sense that the 'optimal' answer in the political and financial climate at any time is not a 'satisfying' one. There is a place here for a critical mind, trained in scientific methods of evaluation and conscious of the requirements of a scientific proof. This is perhaps why so many have stressed the suitability of the economist for such work. But economic skill is not enough. The politician, or his adviser, must be able to use quantitative measures and at the same time remain sceptical of 'formulae' and stereotyped methods of appraisal which can outlive their usefulness. He must have the courage to choose between objectives that cannot be reduced to common terms and on occasion to sacrifice consistency to flexibility. In short, he needs the power of 'judgement'. Unfortunately this is a quality we know little about. But it seems likely to be distorted by excessive specialization. Perhaps the best candidate for such a post is still the all-purpose administrator of outstanding calibre who combines political flair with an ability to use appraisal techniques where they are appropriate.

THE FUTURE OF THE GENERAL ADMINISTRATOR

These functions are all catered for in the selection, training and recruitment of the administrative class. The Civil Service Selection Board tests are related to a job-analysis of an Assistant Secretary carried out soon after the war which suggested that administrators needed a mixture of academic and pragmatic ability: they had to be able to sense, isolate and define problems; to formulate solutions to them; to accomplish these solutions through people and through paper; and 'to persist in so doing'.[1] General knowledge of the machine and the acquisition of administrative wisdom have been developed through a fairly mobile career, in which administrators could pick up bits of experience from one branch and apply it in another. Communication between departments has been facilitated by inculcating, through common training and cross-postings, a shared set of values against which administrators could interpret the changing requirements of a complicated co-ordinating machine, part legal, part administrative and part political, whose conventions are nowhere codified and are constantly being modified, without serious breakdowns in communication. This sort of mixed experience has in the past helped administrators to develop a political sense and an awareness of the possible. They have become quasi-politicians, dealing with Ministers as informed laymen communicating with the slightly less informed. Mr Powell, as a former Minister of Health, argued that senior civil servants had to be laymen in order to reduce problems to terms in which a lay Minister could exercise his judgement upon them.[2]

The Fulton Committee recognized that administrators selected and trained in this way were highly proficient at operating the government machine and serving Ministers. But it felt that this was achieved at the price of relative weakness at quantitative evaluation and lack of familiarity with the subject-matter of administration. The Committee suggested that these weaknesses should be overcome by more specialized training schemes and by a career-pattern that would allow specialization in a field of administration.

The arguments for specialization are very plausible. Different posts call for different sorts of experience and also perhaps for different personality characteristics. Lord Bridges has described the different qualities needed for what were then different functions of

---

[1] Civil Service Commission, *Memorandum on the Use of the Civil Service Selection Board in the Reconstruction Examinations*, 1950.

[2] J. E. Powell, 'Whitehall and Beyond', *The Listener*, vol. LXXI (26 March 1964) p. 505. Peter Shore had a similar point in mind when he wrote about 'the need to strengthen the power of the "temporary politicians", the Ministers, against the "permanent politicians", the civil servants'. *Entitled to Know* (London, 1966) p. 156.

the Treasury: O & M calls for patience and attention to detail, staff management for negotiating ability and a sense of judgement on when rules can be modified without making a nonsense of them, while expenditure control work requires common sense, all-round experience and an ability to synthesize.[1] In a study of non-civil service managers, Rosemary Stewart found 'writers', 'emissaries', 'trouble-shooters' and 'committee men', each group calling for its own mixture of skills, personality and background knowledge.[2] But the Fulton scheme leaves a gap in another part of the system. It is not realistic to expect all individual civil servants to become equipped as specialists (a) in the problems of a specific service, (b) in management techniques *and* (c) in operating a highly complex piece of machinery for taking, justifying and co-ordinating political decisions. The bias towards (a) and (b) implies a relative weakness in (c). Moreover, the development of specialization is bound to weaken the sense of unity, transcending departmental or subject boundaries, that the administrative class has had in the past.

As a facilitator, the administrator who specializes will be in a better position to grasp the essentials of a particular problem in his field. He will probably have an expert knowledge of the relevant parts of the legislative machine and he will still presumably have been selected partly for his fluency on paper. He may, however, be less able, because of his narrower career, to see the value of an administrative procedure that has worked well in a different field and his lack of breadth may prove a handicap in a Minister's private office.

As a mediator he will, of course, know the rules governing the extraction of money from Treasury and the grant of powers from the legislature. In bargaining over these things he will probably argue strongly on behalf of a service to which he is committed and be slow to accept external disadvantages to what he proposes. The central co-ordinators in Treasury and the Minister's office will find him a difficult adversary – perhaps too difficult for a well-integrated public policy. An administrator who is brought up exclusively in a specialist field is bound to identify with it. Already there is a risk that a civil servant in, say, the Ministry of Agriculture, his shoulders bowed with years of patient negotiation with the National Farmers' Union, is so acutely sensitive to the farmers' probable reactions to

[1] *The Treasury*, pp. 51–3, 102–3, 123–7.
[2] Rosemary Stewart, *Managers and Their Jobs* (London, 1967).

any conceivable development that he becomes incapable of a fresh approach to agricultural problems.

It is as an arbiter that the specialist administrator is likely to be least effective, because all his experience and training has been biased towards a special group of interests. At the level of departmental planning units this may not matter – the economic administrators in the Ministry of Transport will apply cost-benefit analysis to transport policy, while the social administrators in the Department of Health and Social Security will use social survey techniques to ascertain the most advantageous way of dealing with problems of health and poverty. But it looks as if the politician is going to be very much on his own in taking an overall view of questions that have both social and economic implications – a task in which he at present looks for support from his general administrative adjutants. The effect of fragmenting the administrative class would be to place a greater load on the political administration for overall appraisal. It may also deprive them of some secretarial support in their political duties.

VERTICAL SPECIALIZATION

Some would see it as an advantage that the system should compel Ministers to play a positive role – for example in evaluating expert advice from a Senior Policy Adviser, or in settling inter-departmental disputes. But it is always a matter of luck if there are enough Ministers of quality to man all the positions and their load is already so great that it seems unwise to reduce the quality of their support unless the demands reaching them can somehow be reduced. With a weak Minister, there could be an unpleasant vacuum between the political and executive systems which is at present filled by the permanent civil service.

Part of the difficulty about the Permanent Secretary's role in the past has been his need to be a confidential adviser, an economic chief of staff, a chief administrative technologist, financial director and general manager of the department, and a top secretary. It is impossible for one man to do so much and it is also wrong that the careers of so many junior administrators have been geared to training Permanent Secretaries for the future. It is right to divide these roles but it does not help to pretend that some of them will cease to exist. The Fulton Committee's picture of a government department seems to comprise a number of executive management divisions, a small policy and planning group and a top management board chaired by the Minister. But Ministers also need competent staff to help them with their political duties. Especially in the main co-ordinating departments, moreover, their main requirement may be not so much a board of top directors as a large number of staff assistants, relatively uncommitted to particular policies, possessing broad experience of Whitehall, highly sensitive to changes in political climate and possessing outstanding qualities of judgement and incisiveness.

POLITICAL SECRETARIAT

There are really two gaps in the Fulton scheme of things; one is a central co-ordinating staff of generalists, the other is a secretarial staff for Ministers.

In France Ministers appoint *cabinets* of personal staff who bridge the gap between politics and administration. They help the Minister with his political relationships, providing the sort of support that in Britain would come from junior Ministers and Parliamentary Private Secretaries sitting in the House of Commons. They provide a link between the Minister and the quasi-independent 'directorates' that make up a French department. In this respect they combine some of the non-managerial functions of the British Permanent Secretary (who does not exist in France) with those of a British Minister's private office staff. They also serve as a permanent brains trust at the immediate disposal of the Minister. Members of a *cabinet* are personal supporters of the Minister's policies and relationships among them are fairly intimate. There are ten members or fewer except in the Prime Minister's Department, and the Ministries of Foreign Affairs, Finance and the Interior. Although *cabinet* posts are outside the normal civil service career pattern, their holders are paid from public funds.[1]

There have been some enthusiastic supporters of the *cabinet* system in this country, mainly from those who start from the assumption that the Minister is heavily outbalanced by the civil service and needs some independent support. This argument takes

[1] The French system is described in the *Fulton Report*, vol. 1, app. C. See also F. Ridley and J. Blondel, *Public Administration in France* (London, 1964) pp. 65–7 and A. Dutheillet de Lamothe, 'Ministerial Cabinets in France', *Public Administration*, vol. 43 (1965) p. 365.

two forms. One is that anonymous and faceless secretaries, with no political commitment, are incapable of taking initiatives and leading a Minister towards dynamic new policies. The other version is that senior members of the civil service *élite* have strong political views of their own, which condition the advice they choose to give to Ministers. (In *Entitled to Know*, Peter Shore, who was then Parliamentary Private Secretary to the Prime Minister, achieved the difficult feat of arguing both at once.) But the implications are the same in both cases. The Labour Party, for example, suggested to Fulton that Ministers should be able to make temporary appointments of experts, who had been involved in the preparation of party policy and were committed to it, to top level posts to help with its implementation.

In fact, a number of appointments of this sort have been made since 1964. Thus, when Anthony Crosland was Secretary of State for Education and Science he appointed a left-wing sociologist, A. H. Halsey, as Research Adviser to his department – a situation which led the retiring Director of the National Foundation for Educational Research to express fears about political interference with research.[1] Some appointments of senior economists to temporary posts in 1964 were also quasi-political.[2] So, according to the First Division Association, were some of the fifty temporary appointments made to the administrative class shortly after the 1964 election.[3] Perhaps one example of this was Tony Lynes, who became a temporary Principal in the Ministry of Pensions and National Insurance (as it was then called) but resigned, saying he could do more good outside the service than in it, to become secretary of the militant Child Poverty Action Group. If there were too many appointments of this nature (if say a quarter of the posts above Assistant Secretary level in certain departments came to be filled by political patronage) there would be a serious departure from the Northcote-Trevelyan ideal of a career service, open to competition, in which senior posts were filled by merit. But there can be no serious objection to a limited number of such appointments, for example in planning units, provided they are distinguished from ordinary career posts, and the Fulton Committee recommended accordingly.[4]

The Labour Party also suggested that a Minister might appoint 'a

[1] W. D. Wall, *Educational Research and Policy-Making* (London, 1968).
[2] See ch. IV above, pp. 77–9.
[3] *Fulton Report*, vol. 5, p. 125, par. 16 (evidence from First Division Association).
[4] *Fulton Report*, vol. 1, par. 129.

limited number of personal assistants (perhaps up to four) with direct access to him and to all the information in his department. These would form his personal *cabinet*. They would take no administrative decisions themselves . . . [Their function] would be to act as a political brains trust to the Minister, to act as an extra pair of eyes and ears, to stimulate him.'[1] It was tentatively suggested that this group should keep the Minister in touch with what was going on in his department and also liaise with similar groups in other departments. In other words, it would create a new tier of co-ordination between the official and the political level.

Superficially the proposal is an attractive one. If the administrative class becomes technologized in the way the Fulton Committee propose, the case for a Ministerial *cabinet* will be very strong indeed. But there are a number of obvious problems. A temporary *cabinet* would not be able to provide the continuity and experience of the administrative machine which is now available to a Minister in his private office. Then there is the question of calibre. The relationship between a Minister and his political assistants would presumably have to be confidential and it is hard to see what attractions such a post, lacking both public recognition and a career outlet, would offer to candidates of experience and ability. The most likely candidates would be young and inexperienced, possibly more of a handicap than an asset to the Minister and certainly a fruitful source of pointless friction in the administrative machine. On balance, the necessary qualities of loyalty, self-effacement and administrative and political wisdom seem more likely to come from a group of dedicated career administrators. It is significant that two-thirds of appointments to French *cabinets* between 1955 and 1965 were from the ranks of career civil servants. Even in Washington, a good many theoretically political posts are in fact filled by career men.[2] The Fulton Committee advised against the appointment of a *cabinet* of personal assistants.[3]

CENTRAL CO-ORDINATION OF POLICY

Apart from quasi-political secretarial duties, three fundamental requirements have to be met by the central administrative machine

[1] *Fulton Report*, vol. 5, p. 664, pars. 60–9 (evidence from Labour Party).

[2] Dean Mann, *The Assistant Secretaries: Problems and Processes of Appointment* (Washington D.C., 1965) ch. 2.

[3] *Fulton Report*, vol. 1, par. 285.

as a whole: (a) effectiveness and economy in the pursuit of particular goals (without prejudice to the pursuit of other goals); (b) some means of injecting political values, and a respect for other goals, into (a); (c) an apparatus which allows major political decisions to be taken by bringing disparate goals together, evaluating them and where necessary suggesting changes of direction.

The first two requirements have been discussed at length. The first calls for the institutionalization of goals in agencies and departments with specialized staff, some of whom work on long-term questions in planning units. The second is provided through the mechanisms of political accountability. The third requirement presents the greatest challenge to planning – it raises questions about the machinery of government, the distribution of functions between departments, the role of the central co-ordinating machine, and the staff who work it.

The crucial problem is to achieve co-ordination and strategic planning without overloading the central machinery. The task is much more difficult in public administration than in managing a business or directing an army, where there is an over-riding purpose and a clear criterion of what is important. It is not so easy to determine the key issues in steering a balance among the competing goals of a nation.

We have noted that any major decision emerges from a series of dialogues to which different contributors add their piece in accordance with the information selected for them by earlier contributors, their personal frame of reference, and the prevailing 'tone' and values in the part of the machine where they work. The way functions are divided and grouped affects the form in which questions are put, and the order in which the answers are combined affects the outcome. The relevance of this to our problem can be seen from a fairly straightforward example. The classic co-ordinator is money, controlled by the Treasury. In order to get money, 'spending departments' have to expose their ideas to Treasury scrutiny, which means putting them in a form that will be intelligible to the Treasury 'layman' and justifying them in a way that allows comparison with projects or programmes from other departments. In the past this has not worked very well. In the late 1950s the Treasury was still trying to control departmental expenditure in great detail and there was no effective means of comparing projects within the Treasury itself; such co-ordination as there was depended more on the dissemination from the Treasury of shared beliefs about the standards relevant to the spending of public money. Since the Plowden Report and the rehabilitation of planning, this system has been partly replaced by a more strategic approach. Groups of Cabinet Ministers meet at the end of each year to consider global allocations for up to five years ahead against departmental bids on the one hand and the political and economic constraints on the overall level of expenditure on the other. This exercise is conducted on figures prepared by the Treasury. Gradually departments are being given a freer hand to determine their spending within a global allocation, subject to special arrangements on such matters as public sector salaries and capital investment.

The effects of the two sorts of control are likely to be different. If detailed controls are exercised by Treasury, the same kind of control must be exercised by departmental finance branches, so that special interests have to be explained and defended several times before their claims are accepted. Also schemes are less likely to be put up if they are thought likely to cause embarrassment in discussion with Treasury. Thus 'Treasury standards' become general, possibly at the expense of managerially optimal policies in departments. But if departments are free to spend within an allocation, project managers are likely to enjoy much more freedom from *any* routine lay control, since there is no incentive for departmental finance branches to introduce tension into their relationships with technically qualified colleagues. The ultimate effect may be that longer intervals elapse before a particular objective is called in question by anyone who is not professionally committed to it.

The illustration can be extended by imagining two similar areas of policy – say plans to increase the quality of police and of nursing services. Imagine that in one case a detailed scheme is worked out by a team of officials, led by a general administrator, as a preliminary to being presented for financial approval to the Treasury and cleared with an advisory committee on which special interests are represented. Imagine that in the other case a similar team, with a professionally qualified administrator as chairman, is left a free hand within overall financial limits specified by the Treasury and within a broad framework of objectives defined by the advisory committee. The elements in both situations are the same, but differences in the way they are combined are likely to lead to very different policies in detail.

These are cases in which the effect of structural and procedural changes can be predicted and allowed for. It is not so easy to predict the outcome if specialist views are able to influence policy without being 'processed' at all. Imagine (to take a hypothetical example) an Education Department where the main policy branches are staffed by administrators, paired with H.M. Inspectors of Schools recruited from the teaching profession with a fairly conventional attitude to school organization. Suppose the junior administrators to have received special training in economic appraisal and to have access to the results of commissioned economic research. Suppose, too, the senior officials of the department to be expert 'arbiters', accepting briefs that embody these various viewpoints and scrutinizing them from a financial and political viewpoint before passing what they consider a balanced recommendation to the Minister. Suppose, finally, that the Minister has a habit of dining regularly with a group of sociologists with rather unorthodox views about education and that he discusses his policy with them before taking decisions (sociological factors not having been taken into account in the departmental briefs). Clearly the outcome would depend fortuitously on the amount of weight the Minister placed on his friends compared to the departmental machine. It could only be arbitrary. This is doubtless the kind of situation envisaged by Mr Wilson when he spoke of the need to integrate experts properly into the machine and not have them 'floating about in a somewhat irresponsible way'.[1]

Treasury scope for co-ordination is now largely limited to financial and (in conjunction with the Department of Economic Affairs) economic matters. Before 1968 the Treasury also co-ordinated certain matters of administration, for example policy on the political activities of civil servants, civil service training, statutory instruments procedure and the machinery of government, most of which are now handled by the Civil Service Department.

There are two other main devices for co-ordination in the British system. One is Parliament: if a department wants new powers rather than more resources it has to put up a case that Parliament can (at least in theory) understand. There is probably no real abuse of legislation; civil servants are well disciplined to seek specific legislative cover for what they want to do. But in spite of fairly

[1] H. Wilson, 'Whitehall and Beyond', *The Listener*, vol. LXXI (5 March 1964) p. 381.

elaborate arrangements for scrutinizing new legislation and statutory instruments, the amount of detailed reports, accounts and proposals passing through the parliamentary machine is far too great for M.P.s to exert their power of scrutiny and debate more than occasionally, when triggered off by a pressure group or one of the party machines.

Finally, there is the Cabinet. The Cabinet is the apex of the policy-making system and for most practical purposes is the final arbiter of political choice. One has a feeling that Cabinet does not do this very effectively, partly because its members have many other preoccupations, partly because of the way issues are presented to them, and partly because they are not supported by appropriate central machinery. The Cabinet Office is more concerned with the smooth movement of paper than with policy evaluation.

The Cabinet secretariat has lately been strengthened by the addition of Economic and Scientific Advisers and by an improved Central Statistical Office. It is an attractive point at which to build up the service necessary for a proper elaboration of political choices on the broadest possible scale.[1] Some (perhaps most) political decisions are primarily about the use of resources, where the Treasury is the appropriate centre for co-ordination. Others (say about divorce reform) are relatively self-contained and can be handled by one Minister in consultation with colleagues. But there are also some over-riding questions on which co-ordination is required at political levels that do not seem appropriate to the Treasury. Cabinet committees, for example, decide which measures shall take priority in the legislative timetable. Others review policy proposals from groups of departments (for example home affairs). There is also a need to build up machinery, for which there is no obvious place outside the Cabinet, for considering, say, the effect of social welfare on productivity or (to take an American example) the influence of military policy on the economy. There is a risk of confusion if there are too many co-ordinating departments outside cabinet – as there were in 1968–9 in economic affairs.

The administrative structure is bound to become more complex, particularly with the development of more special expertise at the periphery. It will be necessary to experiment a good deal with different patterns of administration, involving political changes as

[1] For a discussion of the role of Cabinet today see J. P. Macintosh, *The British Cabinet* (2nd edn.) (London, 1968).

well as changes in the executive machinery, before finding a system suited to the needs of modern Britain. It is above all necessary to prevent those who should be at the apex of the system from being overloaded with parliamentary trivia, while at the same time not restricting too severely the ability of lay representatives to stumble on issues of principle by investigating matters of detail. It seems unlikely that parliamentary rights to scrutinize the acts of central Ministerial departments will diminish. The tendency is the other way and the tradition of Ministerial responsibility to Parliament fits British political habits very much better than the obvious alternatives – the open system of Swedish government, the articulation of administrative law in a Conseil d'Etat, or what is in effect the division of executive authority between government and parliament as in the United States. But since there is a limit to what Parliament can handle, there is a strong case for decentralizing powers to an invigorated local government or, where suitable constraints can be devised, for 'hiving-off' executive functions to autonomous bureaux.

STAFFING THE SYSTEM

In this complex system different kinds of bodies will need distinctive kinds of staff, bringing appropriate brands of experience and loyalties. Already some departments are like large-scale businesses; others are concerned with the enforcement of a code of law, or with the reconciliation of conflicting interests through negotiation, or with central policy appraisal. For a time it seemed that the main functions of the Department of Economic Affairs and the Ministry of Technology were to inspire others, and this may be the key role of the Civil Service Department.

In some agencies it may be appropriate to leave administration entirely to a corps of specialized administrator-engineers, administrator-lawyers and so on. In others it may be more suitable to rely on general administrators of a managerial type, following a fairly specialized career within a particular agency or a group of related agencies, on the Fulton pattern. In conventional 'purpose' departments, there seems to be a need for at least three main categories of administrators: (a) one or more groups of managerial specialists to work in executive divisions, including internal personnel and organization; (b) a group of equally specialized administrators, but perhaps younger, perhaps more highly trained and certainly more mentally supple and temperamentally suited to team work, for the departmental planning unit; (c) a political secretariat.

Finally, the central co-ordinating departments, the Treasury, the Cabinet Office, the Civil Service Department, and possibly others, seem to need personnel not so very different from the present administrative class, able to communicate easily with non-expert politicians, politically sensitive, strong in what Lord Simey called 'more general qualities of judgement and decisiveness, and the ability to understand how the reshaping of values may be embodied in and implemented by public policy'.[1]

One of the main functions of this group would be to keep an eye on the need to review activities that had become too institutionalized in specialized agencies for self-criticism to develop naturally. For such people, experience in depth within a specialist field, while perhaps useful early in training, could be far too confining; since the main requirement, apart from basic ability, is wide experience of quasi-political work in different contexts, even the traditional departmental career is perhaps too narrow. A group such as this would be a disciplined and highly cohesive *élite*, rather like the present administrative class but smaller and relieved of some of the more specialized work now carried out by that class. Its members could be selected after entry in much the way high-fliers are selected from the present administrative entry and given appropriately wide experience.

There would be a place for a representative of this group in the planning unit of every major department, acting as a listening-post and relating departmental ideas to broader streams of techno-political thinking (just as a finance officer acts as a middleman between his department and the Treasury now within his own field). The most appropriate model for the organization of such a group (but not necessarily for its selection and training) may be the French administrative *corps*. It is a pity that the Fulton Committee, which saw so clearly the need for horizontal forms of administrative specialization, was prevented by its anti-*élitist* bias from recognizing the need for 'vertical' specialization in this very subtle and difficult form of policy-integration.

ADMINISTRATIVE RESEARCH

The main purpose of this essay has been to examine some current problems faced by British central government in the light of recent

[1] *Fulton Report*, vol. 1, p. 102 (reservation by Lord Simey).

developments in organization theory – or in other words to expand the field of discourse about public administration to include sociological and psychological concepts about human behaviour in organizations.

The outcome may be disappointing to the reader. Some familiar problems have been restated in relatively unfamiliar language. It will not surprise the student of public administration to learn that it is difficult to reconcile managerial initiative with public account-ability; that co-ordinating machinery ceases to work if it becomes overloaded; that there are communication barriers between the specialized professional and the lay politician; that planning does not get done unless special provision is made for it. And it will be disappointing that few positive answers have been offered to urgent problems. All that we have been able to do is to clarify the need for organizational choice and to suggest how the consequences of change can be assessed and implemented. By relating organizational demands to human limitations, we may have gained a clearer idea of the range of the possible in public administration and to show that any method of working carries costs (sometimes very obscure ones) as well as advantages.

Clearly this is not in itself very much. We need to apply this framework to a programme of applied research which can measure the items on any particular balance sheet and allow organizational choices to be made, by governments and by public administration specialists, in a fuller knowledge of what is involved. It should gradually become less possible to incur major organizational costs for the sake of a political gimmick.

In Britain there has been plenty of discussion and plenty of experiment with new patterns of public organization. Hardly any of it has been systematically examined and appraised from an organizational point of view. Substantial programmes of research have been mounted in various fields administered by the Govern-ment, but there has been very little work on internal problems of government structure. The Civil Service Commission's research unit has attempted to validate selection procedures; efficiency studies relating effectiveness to financial cost are widespread and invaluable in their way; a limited number of social investigations on human factors have been carried out for or in connection with the Fulton enquiry.[1] What is needed now is a fairly massive attempt to discover

[1] *Fulton Report*, vol. 3. The findings with a bearing on job-satisfaction and morale are discussed in ch. XIV below.

the precise effects of different recruitment, training and structural arrangements on problem-solving, political sensitivity, responsiveness to technological change and operating efficiency in various contexts. We do not, for example, have any very precise idea of what 'Fultonization' would cost in terms of the dedication, humanity, integrity and capacity for improvisation which the Committee admired in the unreformed civil service.

The Committee itself called for an on-going programme of research, based on the Civil Service Department and the proposed Civil Service College, to be concerned with new methods of organizing work and the machinery of government.[1] The study and implementation of its report is already being accompanied by the systematic investigation of various aspects of departmental organization and of the job-content of posts held by certain grades.[2] There are many wider questions about the political and administrative machinery that could usefully be studied. What are the precise effects of grouping functions in different ways under departmental Ministers? What is the impact of different methods of Treasury control? How far has the influence of Treasury been a by-product of financial control, and how far of the status of Treasury Ministers in the Government? How will this be affected by the separation of financial control from central responsibility for civil service management; is experience in other countries relevant? How can the work of the Central Statistical Office be most effectively brought to bear on Cabinet decisions? Is there any relationship between departmental organization and the attention paid to the views of pressure groups? What sort of contribution to policy is made by members of different sorts of advisory committees – or by Members of Parliament – and when is it likely to be effective? Could some of the contributions be made more effectively and more cheaply in some other way, for example by market research and social surveys? And so on.

All these questions can be studied by the methods of social science and particularly by those of the 'behavioural' sciences, using the concepts outlined in Part Two. Research of this type can show fairly precisely the strengths and weaknesses of present arrangements. Most useful of all, it can suggest the probable effects of new arrangements before they are made. Until more research has been done it is risky to apply generalizations based on experience in other countries

[1] *Fulton Report*, vol. 1, pars. 102, 248.
[2] *Developments on Fulton*, pars. 20, 25, 48, 63–8, 77.

and in the very different world of business enterprise to problems of the British civil service. Nevertheless, there are already plenty of signposts showing the way to more detailed investigation. Many of them have been mentioned in earlier pages. Some detailed suggestions are brought together in Appendix II. It would be appropriate to end this chapter on a speculative note with another example.

One of the obvious roles of the traditional administrator is that of staff assistant to a Minister. There is an interesting study by Whisler of the role of staff assistants to the heads of various American public organizations. Whisler found that such assistants were most essential in organizations that regularly rotated their managers; incoming managers needed immediate access to information which the assistant could supply. But in organizations facing rapid change the assistant was less useful – the crucial information was changing so rapidly that the head could get it himself as quickly as the assistant could handle it. In these conditions, the head had to become more directly and personally involved.[1] There is no need to go into detail to make the point that Whisler's study suggests a number of hypotheses that are relevant to the British situation. Ministers are birds of passage and depend on permanent administrative staff for continuity and experience. On the other hand we are experiencing rapid change in many fields of administration and both Ministers and experts are impatiently demanding to communicate directly. Perhaps this is a transitional phenomenon and we may expect the claims of continuity and stability to reassert themselves after the current phase of change has exhausted itself. If so, it would be a pity to mortgage the needs of the future by introducing irreversible changes into the structure in order to satisfy the immediate pressures of the moment.

[1] T. L. Whisler, 'The Assistant-to in Four Administrative Settings', *Administrative Science Quarterly*, vol. 5 (1960) pp. 180–216.

XIV. Morale in the Civil Service

The previous four chapters have been concerned mainly with problems of structure. Organizational design may also affect people's enjoyment of their work. We should not perhaps assume too readily that enthusiasm and commitment are essential to make a structure work. But, to put it no higher, the civil service cannot do its job unless it offers sufficient rewards to attract and retain staff of appropriate quality. The purpose of this final chapter is to look at the main features of civil service work as they affect the individual and to examine the probable effects on job-satisfaction of adopting the relevant Fulton proposals. There is no point here in confining discussion to the senior policy groups – the canvas will be broadened to include clerical and executive grades.

This is a field in which the social science approach outlined at the end of the previous chapter seems particularly likely to pay dividends, since it is the human aspects of change that are often the most subtle and the most difficult to evaluate. The main theoretical concepts have been outlined in Chapter VI. The way work is organized affects the pattern of rewards and sanctions, sometimes unpredictably, and generates a social system with norms of its own. In order to survive, an organization has to compromise between aiming directly at the achievement of its goals and satisfying the economic, social and psychological needs of its members.

INCENTIVES: PROPOSALS AND ASSUMPTIONS

The Fulton Committee recommended a number of changes in the framework described in Chapter III. They can be rehearsed briefly:

1. While the civil service should remain essentially a career service, there should be more mid-career movement in both directions, the outward movement including those who are unsuitable as well as those who wish to leave without loss of pension rights.

2. Promotion should not depend on seniority within a class, but partly on past performance and partly on the possession of suitable qualifications and experience for a higher post.

3. Individuals should, wherever possible, be given clear-cut responsibilities and held accountable for performance against norms. Their achievement should be assessed regularly and reflected in their salary (by granting or withholding increments) and career prospects.

4. The convention of anonymity should be modified and unnecessary secrecy got rid of.

5. Careers and training should be planned with more regard to the personal wishes, interests and aptitudes of the individual and with a view to developing his expertise in a special field of administration.

The Fulton Committee was in no doubt that the adoption of these suggestions would improve the efficiency and the working tone of the service.

It believed that 'established' status bred an atmosphere of comfort and complacency. The closed career pattern protected the inefficient and locked in some able people who wanted to move. The Committee's feelings were influenced by the contrast with industry, which is mentioned repeatedly in the evidence it received. Thus the Confederation of British Industry suggested that:

> This almost complete security of tenure cannot be good for effectiveness or for morale: there should be greater rewards for success and greater penalties for failure (including errors of omission as well as of commission).[1]

Similarly the Conference of the Electronics Industry:

> Industry and commerce have their own ruthless methods of eliminating from their ranks those who for one reason or another cannot meet the demands placed on them . . . But the Civil Service offers a safe and progressive career to all who qualify and enter without regard to their future capability and performance. This may be humane; it is undoubtedly a factor in ensuring the integrity of the Civil Service but it cannot under modern conditions be conducive to high efficiency.[2]

[1] *Fulton Report*, vol. 5, p. 511.   [2] Ibid., p. 529.

The Principal of the London Business School did not believe 'that any organization in which security of tenure is a condition of employment can remain fully effective for very long', partly because the mere existence of groups of ineffective personnel would have a depressing effect through the whole organization.[1]

There were both negative and positive arguments in favour of a more open and competitive promotion system. The Committee's management consultancy group had found an underlying dissatisfaction and frustration among Experimental Officers, Scientific Assistants and similar classes who were often doing work similar to that of the higher classes but enjoyed much inferior promotion opportunities. Brighter executive officers were frustrated by the long wait for promotion.[2] The Committee felt that a system of promotion by results would provide a powerful incentive at all levels and that the constant competitive challenge would favour the most able, improve the development of talent, and lead to greater efficiency.[3] Again, its reasoning was supported by evidence from outside the public service. The British Institute of Management argued that the Civil Service must be able to offer its recruits:

> tangible incentives not only of a working life with full security and a pension but also 'job-satisfaction' and – particularly at the senior level – a clear view of progress towards promotion with its status and rewards. A long, slow haul along the path of promotion must inevitably act as a disincentive, if not a deterrent, to many an able and active mind.[4]

And the Institute of Personnel Management commented that:

> The prospect of many years of slow predictable progression must have a considerable demoralizing effect, particularly on the junior staff.[5]

The Committee thought that a more rigorous pattern of staff assessment, linked to promotion and to the award of increments, would improve performance. This seems to have been intended largely as a stick for the idle: 'Fixed annual increments, in our view, do not give enough incentive to effort, and make possible too easy a progress for those who do not pull their full weight.'[6] Increments,

---

[1] *Fulton Report*, vol. 5, p. 854.   [2] *Fulton Report*, vol. 2, pars. 88, 158, 377.
[3] *Fulton Report*, vol. 1, pars. 193, 234.   [4] *Fulton Report*, vol. 5, p. 480.
[5] Ibid., p. 629.   [6] *Fulton Report*, vol. 1, par. 299.

therefore, should be withheld where they have not been earned in relation to the appropriate 'norms'. Even in the highest posts, salary should be determined by an annual review of performance. The Committee seems to have thought that this would not only increase efficiency but also enable men and women 'to get the greatest satisfaction from their work'.[1] The consultancy group also felt that civil servants needed a clearer picture of how they were getting on.[2]

The evidence about anonymity is naturally concerned with accountability rather than with morale. But Dr Arthur Earle thought that it would be good for morale if civil servants had more opportunities for explaining in public what they were doing.[3]

The Committee believed that more coherent career planning would avoid waste of human potential and reduce the frustration felt by people who were given too little responsibility. Rather to its surprise, the consultancy group found that the administrators it spoke to welcomed the variety provided by frequent postings and believed in the implied principle of equipping them with broad experience.[4] But it found few civil servants who believed that postings were planned systematically or reflected their personal aptitudes and abilities.[5] The Institute of Personnel Management commented that the lack of freedom of choice of work might have a harmful effect on morale.[6]

Underlying all these arguments are certain assumptions about motivation and incentives. It is assumed that effort (and probably, although this is not always clearly stated, job-satisfaction) would be increased throughout the service by the introduction of a system of sticks and carrots which related achievement more reliably to reward. It is assumed that the most effective rewards are economic ones: the Committee never mentions any other sort specifically, although promotion carries status as well as monetary rewards and various passages in its report refer to the development of talent in

---

[1] Ibid., para. 147.

[2] *Fulton Report*, vol. 2, pars. 234–9.

[3] *Fulton Report*, vol. 5, p. 852 (misprinted as p. 853).

[4] *Fulton Report*, vol. 2, pars. 66–75.

[5] Several cases were cited in which aptitudes and preferences had clearly been ignored, such as the H.E.O. with a main interest and experience in social work who was posted to investment appraisal. (Ibid., pars. 239, 244.) It is not clear whether this posting was a necessary condition of promotion: executive officers in the Supplementary Benefits Commission, for example, may have to transfer to another department to avoid a long queue for a limited number of vacancies.

[6] *Fulton Report*, vol. 5, p. 628.

terms that suggest this too might provide an incentive. Finally, it is assumed that unless the pattern of rewards is altered along the suggested lines, the civil service will be a haven for the inefficient and fail to attract its share of ability.

It is therefore surprising to discover how well, even in the Committee's eyes, the present system works. Thanks to the development of good staff relations through the Whitley Council machinery, morale is high, industrial disputes are rare, and the staff have shown a co-operative and constructive attitude to changes which may work against their immediate interests, such as the introduction of computers.[1] The Committee commented on the integrity, the humanity, the impartiality and the devotion of the service, its capacity for improvisation and the ability, vision and enthusiasm of some of its members.[2] The consultancy group was evidently surprised at what it found. The 'underlying dissatisfaction and frustration' among the 'lesser' scientific classes did not affect personal relationship at a day-to-day level.[3] In spite of many criticisms, the service has developed 'an approach to personnel work that in total is unique and in some ways impressive'; the 'generally high standard of morale' is largely due to the existence of uniform and well understood procedures and the genuine desire to apply them with fairness.[4] And although centralized personnel procedures have deprived managers of the usual means of encouraging their subordinates, who on the face of it have 'little encouragement . . . to do anything other than avoid mistakes or inaction so serious as to call for an adverse annual report', nevertheless, 'It is surprising that such a system has called forth the dedication, conscientiousness and enthusiasm that we so often saw.'[5] It looks as if there may be something wrong with the theory.

ATTITUDE SURVEYS IN THE CIVIL SERVICE

We may do well to leave the largely *a priori* reasoning of the Committee and study what is known about the motivations of existing

[1] *Fulton Report*, vol. 1, par. 270.
[2] Ibid., pars. 22, 302, 306. It is, of course, not inconsistent to praise the civil service for these qualities while attacking it, in ch. 1 of the report, for amateurism, poor organization and remoteness from the public it serves.
[3] *Fulton Report*, vol. 2, par. 158.
[4] Ibid., par. 294.
[5] Ibid., par. 336.

civil servants and of likely recruits to the service. Fortunately some relevant material is now available. Some of it was collected in 1966–7 for the Fulton Committee itself, notably a study by the Treasury of ability, efficiency and job-satisfaction among executive and clerical officers[1], a study of wastage from the same grades,[2] and an independent questionnaire-cum-interview survey of administrative class Principals.[3] The results can be compared with those obtained by Nigel Walker in a private survey in 1959[4]; they are remarkably consistent.

In all attitude surveys there are problems of interpretation. A group of respondents may rate 'pensions' low among the attractions of their job either because pensions are not important to them or because the pensions scheme is not in fact very good. Or an item like 'interest of work' may appear higher on one list than another because features (e.g. 'long holidays') that might have been rated

[1] 'Study of Ability, Efficiency and Job Satisfaction among Executive and Clerical Officers' (*Fulton Report*, vol. 3(2) pp. 242 ff.). The survey covered 1,507 executive officers and 1,982 clerical officers in eleven government departments. 86 per cent of those approached completed the job-satisfaction questionnaire, which was voluntary. This, in conjunction with the survey of wastage, is referred to in the text as 'the EO/CO survey'.

[2] 'Report on Survey of Wastage of Executive and Clerical Officers'. This survey covered established executive and clerical officers who left the civil service in the year beginning 1 September 1966. Officers who died or who retired at or above the normal age, or for reasons of ill-health, or who were dismissed for misconduct, inefficiency or redundancy, were not included. Nor were women who 'resigned' but continued to serve in an unestablished capacity (i.e. having drawn their super-annuation entitlement in the form of marriage gratuity). The survey covered 639 executive officers (90 per cent of the men and 92 per cent of the women who left 'voluntarily' during the survey year) and 1,154 clerical officers (40 per cent of the men and 15 per cent of the women, the intended proportions having been 50 per cent and 20 per cent evenly distributed among departments). 89 per cent of those approached completed the questionnaire. An interim report, covering wastage during the first four months of the survey year, was published in *Fulton Report*, vol. 3(2), pp. 194 ff. The complete (unpublished) report was kindly made available by the Civil Service Department, and is quoted in the text where appropriate.

[3] 'Profile of a Profession: the Administrative Class of the Civil Service' (*Fulton Report*, vol. 3(2) pp. 1 ff.). This survey by Dr R. A. Chapman covered the 40 men and women who had entered the administrative class as Assistant Principals in 1956. Thirty of the 32 who were still serving completed a questionnaire and were interviewed in late 1966. Of the 8 who had left in the meantime, 3 failed to reply; the other 5 completed the questionnaire and 3 were also interviewed.

[4] N. Walker, *Morale in the Civil Service: a Study of the Desk Worker* (Edinburgh, 1961). Chs. 6, 8, and 9 describe the preparation, administration and results of a questionnaire completed by 1,090 civil servants (380 clerical, 534 executive, 94 administrative and 82 professionals) in two departments in central London, one large and one medium-sized. The object was a 100 per cent sample; response rates were 79 per cent and 64 per cent.

above it are not present in the reckoning at all. Only detailed cross-analysis can discover whether a relatively high or low rating reflects a difference in the situation or a difference in attitude and whether in either case it affects job-satisfaction. Unfortunately, some surveys have not gone far enough to enable this to be done.

It is also difficult to draw definite indications for action from such material. In any group, for example, there will probably be a minority who are dissatisfied with their pay. It does not follow that a pay increase would remove this dissatisfaction or improve job-satisfaction overall. There is also a tendency for people to wish for more of what they already have. The satisfaction of any demand alters the framework of desires and expectations within which fresh demands will be formulated in the future. In some situations attempts to meet demands, especially from a minority, may lead not only to lower efficiency but also to more dissatisfaction.

There is, nevertheless, considerable value in making comparisons between attitudes expressed by members of different organizations, if errors in interpretation can be avoided.

In order to focus on some of the issues raised by the Fulton Committee, the attitudes revealed by these studies will be discussed under the following headings: (a) economic rewards and sanctions; (b) social aspects of work; (c) psychological rewards, often associated with intrinsic characteristics of the work.

Economic Rewards and Sanctions

In the survey of Principals, only one in six mentioned pay as a reason for liking their job, but none said it was a reason for disliking it. Pay was a source of dissatisfaction for male executive and clerical officers who left the service in 1966–7, and for some young clerical officers who did not. But the majority in the EO/CO survey were content with their pay – female staff (who enjoy complete pay equality) conspicuously so. In 1959 Walker's group of civil servants ranked pay, with prospects, about midway in a list of ten possible attractions of their job:[1] feelings about over- or under-payment had little relation to job-satisfaction.[2]

---

[1] The complete list of factors in order of attractiveness for the total sample was: 'security of job', 'pension rights', 'interest of the work', 'holidays', 'pay', 'hours of work', 'promotion prospects', 'physical conditions of work', 'status in the community', 'social life with colleagues'.

[2] A methodological difference between Walker's study and the EO/CO survey makes them difficult to compare. Walker correlated attitudes to pay and other

Career prospects were not mentioned by the Principals either among their likes or among their dislikes. Twenty-eight out of the 35 thought that career opportunities in the civil service were about the same as with any other employer. In the EO/CO survey, only executive officers under 25 were satisfied with their prospects. Those under 40, however, tended to think that seniority counted for too much in promotion, while those over 40 tended to complain that the promotion system gave poor protection against unfair influence; this group was dissatisfied with the opportunities. (The promotion system may be unimaginative and may possibly favour those who perform well under interview stress, but it does make favouritism virtually impossible. One can readily understand those who were still in the basic EO and CO grades in their forties seeking a scape-goat for their lack of career success.) Walker found that half his respondents rated promotion prospects last or second last among his ten 'attractions'. Two-thirds of them, however, thought that the promotion *system* worked 'fairly on the whole' or 'as fairly as possible'. The percentage who were broadly satisfied with it went down with rank, from 84 per cent among administrators to 52 per cent among clerical officers. Those who were not satisfied with the promotion system tended to say that 'being in the right place at the right time' or 'good relations with superiors' counted for promotion at their levels, as opposed to more respectable factors like seniority, ability and hard work; they also showed low overall job-satisfaction.

Security was not mentioned as an advantage by the Principals; nor had it influenced many of them to enter the service; but 21 out of 32 agreed that the Government was generally 'about the same' as other employers in this respect. Half of them had not, in fact, been considering the service as a lifetime career when they joined. Many were thinking of leaving, largely for personal or 'psychological' reasons, and regretted the inflexibility of a non-contributory pensions scheme. The EO/CO survey did not distinguish security from pay and other conditions of employment. But 63 per cent of Walker's group had put security (and 34 per cent put pensions) first or second among the attractions of the service.

The severity of disciplinary sanctions (which would be tightened

features of employment with independent information about job-satisfaction. In the EO/CO study, respondents were asked whether their feelings about *specific aspects* inclined them to satisfaction or dissatisfaction with their jobs; their answers can therefore be interpreted merely as indicating strength of feeling on each issue rather than as evidence of its genuine association with low job-satisfaction.

up under the Fulton proposals) is an important aspect of job-security. Eighty per cent in the EO/CO survey said that discipline was about right, and a factor leading to job-satisfaction. But over a third of Walker's respondents said that discipline was 'a little easy-going' or 'much too lax'. There were varying views as to how the disciplinary arrangements actually worked. Seventeen per cent of the civil servants (more in the lower grades) believed that incompetents were 'got rid of quickly' or 'given a chance and then got rid of'; they overwhelmingly approved. At the other extreme, nearly 20 per cent believed that incompetents were 'allowed to stay on wherever they are'; this was almost as overwhelmingly disapproved. The remainder, varying from 74 per cent of the administrators to 55 per cent of the clerical officers, believed that they were 'put where they do least harm'; of those who held this belief, 29 per cent approved, 46 per cent disapproved, and the remainder found it 'hard to say'.

Social Aspects of Work

The three main aspects of social satisfaction that can be associated with employment are the pleasures of working with congenial colleagues, the external status the job brings and the quality of relationships with superiors.

Among the Principals, congenial colleagues were the most liked aspect of their work: 24 out of 35 mentioned it spontaneously, and 6 made remarks about 'the absence of rat-race', or 'presence of team spirit', which were essentially on the same point. Eighty per cent of those who took part in the EO/CO survey found a source of satisfaction in colleague relationships and commented favourably on the social climate of the office. Nearly 90 per cent of Walker's civil servants said their colleagues were 'likeable' or 'very likeable'; the proportion was even higher among administrators. However, social life ranked lowest on Walker's ten-point scale, and few of his sample were involved with their colleagues in any out-of-office clubs and societies.

Walker also found that 'status in the community' ranked low with his group. He found a link between job-satisfaction and 'estimated status' and devoted a substantial part of his final reflections to the problem of combating low public esteem. The problem of external status did not seem to bother those in the EO/CO survey, however; roughly one-third thought the public had a high opinion of their jobs as civil servants; another third thought that people were indifferent and the remainder thought that people looked down on it; but three-quarters of the sample said that the public's attitude did not influence their own feelings about their work. (We are not told whether the other 25 per cent were inspired by an admiring public or depressed by its indifference.) The Principals were more unanimous in agreeing that the public did not understand what they were doing; half thought this did not matter, but the others were concerned about the effects of public misunderstanding on recruitment and on internal morale. Several suggested that less anonymity and more public appearances by senior civil servants would help to remove ignorance. Only three out of 35 mentioned anonymity as a feature that they disliked in their own jobs.

Eighty per cent of Walker's sample were satisfied with the amount and manner of supervision they received. But there was less satisfaction with the system of authority as a whole: 57·5 per cent of them described their department as 'impersonal', as opposed to 'friendly'; most (85 per cent) were usually told when they had made a mistake, but over half (52 per cent) said that they were 'hardly ever' told when they had done a good job. There may, of course, be a tendency for unpleasant incidents to displace agreeable ones in the memory. But prejudices are facts to the people concerned and there was a strong connection with job-satisfaction: 40 per cent of the 'generally satisfied' civil servants claimed that they had hardly ever been praised, compared with 60 per cent of the 'generally dissatisfied'. The absence of praise was commented on in the EO/CO survey as a frequent source of dissatisfaction which was particularly upsetting to young women and to those who left the service. Half the clerical officers and nearly two-fifths of the executive officers said that good work was rarely if every acknowledged. Resentment was also expressed by older clerical officers engaged on large blocks of work, whom one might have expected to have become relatively indifferent – as they were to civil service life as a whole; they may have felt the need for substitutes for conventional career rewards.

The same dislike of impersonal aspects of the system was evinced by the Principals. Bad man-management and indifference to individual wishes and preferences was the most frequently-mentioned source of dislike – 19 out of 35 brought it up – and particular examples of impersonal treatment were clearly a source of considerable anger and resentment. The same kind of resentment is evident in much of the individual evidence given to the Committee by former members of the administrative class.[1]

Psychological Rewards

The last two paragraphs have touched on the recognition of the individual, which is perhaps one of the more important psychological aspects of work. Others are: the interest and scope of the work itself; the amount of personal freedom it offers; the opportunities it affords for the development of individual skills.

Twenty-three out of 35 Principals mentioned the interest and importance of their work as one of its main attractions. At the other end of the scale many of the EO/CO leavers complained about lack of interest. Most of those in the EO/CO survey were satisfied with its variety, except younger clerical officers, who would have liked more. Walker found that 32 per cent of his sample put interest as first or second attraction in their work, and he found a strong link with satisfaction. As might be expected, higher grades gave it more weight: 77 per cent of the administrators put interest first or second, but only 26 per cent of executive and higher executive officers and 15 per cent of clerical officers. Of his clerical officers, 32 per cent said that their work lacked variety, compared with 9 per cent of the administrators.

Many of the EO/CO group, especially the younger ones, complained that they were given too little responsibility. This was a cause of dissatisfaction among leavers. The Principals also complained about this, and so did 38 per cent of Walker's sample (54 per cent of the male clerical officers, 29 per cent of administrators).

In the EO/CO survey, 46 per cent of the executive officers and 53 per cent of the clerical officers thought that full use was not being made of their abilities; the leavers were particularly influenced by their opinion of the quality of the work they had been given. Walker found 40 per cent of his male clerical officers, 20 per cent of the executives and 17 per cent of the administrators claiming that they were working well below capacity. This was closely associated with dissatisfaction: 45 per cent of the dissatisfied, but only 21 per cent of the satisfied, felt the work was below their abilities.

These questions are closely tied up with ideas about personal development, and with the opportunity to use one's basic knowledge

[1] *Fulton Report*, vol. 5, p. 929 (P. Jay); p. 998 (W. J. L. Plowden and others).

and extend it through training and a planned career. Many of the Principals stressed the need for more constructive career planning, and a sixth spontaneously mentioned their dislike of the cult of the amateur; many complained about the low intellectual quality of what they were doing – only 10 out of 35 mentioned intellectual challenge as an attraction. They were acutely dissatisfied with training opportunities. (This, however, was a group that had missed both the long course for Assistant Principals and the early 'conversion' courses for younger Principals at the Centre for Administrative Studies.) Most of the EO/CO group as a whole thought that training arrangements were satisfactory, but nearly half the younger members were dissatisfied. Nearly half of them thought that postings were badly planned for the development of their abilities, and this was a cause of dissatisfaction, especially for the leavers.

OVERALL JOB-SATISFACTION

Only 19 of the 35 Principals said that the service had lived up to their expectations. After ten years, 8 of the original 40 had left; 17 of the remainder said that they would seriously consider leaving; 8 had actually been applying for other jobs; another 4 declined to answer the question. The reasons they gave for thinking about leaving suggest that, for these Principals at least, the satisfactions of the job did not counterbalance its demands and frustrations. In this balance-sheet, economic factors seemed relatively unimportant. Over half the total sample included bad man-management and poor working facilities (room-sharing and inadequate secretarial help) among their dislikes and over half mentioned congenial colleagues and the interest and importance of the work among its attractions. No other factors (economic or non-economic) were mentioned by more than a quarter of the sample.

Sixty-nine per cent of the executive officers in the Treasury survey liked their job, 21 per cent were indifferent and 10 per cent disliked it. On the other hand, over 25 per cent of those under 40 said they regretted having joined the service. The attitudes of clerical officers were closely associated with their age: of those under 25, 29 per cent were sorry they had joined, only about half positively liked the job, a third were indifferent and the remaining sixth disliked it; but three-quarters of the women over 25, and of the men over 50, liked the job. The main causes of satisfaction were good supervision, pleasant relations with colleagues and the social atmosphere of the office. For younger people, the main causes of dissatisfaction included the poor quality of work which did not use their capabilities or develop their potential, lack of recognition of the individual, inadequate training and poor working conditions. Pay and conditions of service also caused dissatisfaction for a minority. Older members of the group were more concerned about what they saw as an unfair promotion system.

Among the leavers, half the women were leaving for family or domestic reasons and most of these were satisfied with the service. If they are excluded, the leavers are almost equally divided between those who were satisfied and those who were not. Leavers showed the same general likes and dislikes as the general EO/CO population, except that the dislikes, especially in relation to training, career development policies, and personal interest in the individual, were more strongly marked among the dissatisfied leavers. Among the dissatisfied executive officers who left, there was strong dissatisfaction with career prospects and the interest of the work, both of which were found satisfactory by executive officers generally.

Walker found that 25 per cent of his sample were generally satisfied, 13 per cent dissatisfied and 62 per cent somewhere in between. Satisfaction increased with age, time in post, the interest of the work, estimated status, and rank: 32 per cent of the administrators were satisfied compared with 20 per cent of male clerical officers.

The overall picture is not idyllic, but neither is it on the whole a bad one. It is unfortunate that so many people dislike their jobs, particularly at the lower levels, and that more civil servants do not derive positive satisfaction from their work. It is, of course, the dissatisfied who articulate their grievances to investigating committees. The main causes of dissatisfaction seem to lie in the area of psychological rather than economic rewards – not many would be removed by more competition. In order to put the problem into perspective we must go on to ask three questions: (a) How does civil service experience of job-satisfaction compare with that in other large organizations? (b) Does low job-satisfaction affect efficiency? (c) Can anything in fact be done about it?

JOB-SATISFACTION IN OTHER OCCUPATIONS

The great attraction of Walker's survey is that he did try to collect comparable information from the employees of two private firms.

He found a higher level of job-satisfaction than among the civil servants: 43 per cent came into the satisfied category as against 25 per cent of civil servants.[1] The firms' staff rated interest as the main attraction of their job, followed by security and pay (whereas civil servants put security first and interest third; they also put pension rights and holidays – both of which were in fact better than in the firms – ahead of pay). Only 21 per cent of the firms' staff described their organization as 'impersonal', compared with 57·5 per cent of the civil servants. Fewer of them complained that they were working below their capacity. There were interesting differences in attitudes to promotion and discipline. Nearly half the private office staff believed that incompetents were got rid of (either quickly or after being given a chance), compared with only 17 per cent of civil servants; the overwhelming majority approved. Their attitudes to promotion were less cynical and less critical than the civil servants': only 24 per cent felt the system worked unfairly, compared with 34 per cent of the civil servants, and fewer thought promotion was influenced by luck or by good relations with superiors. (This is a surprising result, since the promotion system in the firms was much less systematic. Walker believed that civil servants were simply more knowledgeable about their promotion arrangements and therefore more prepared to offer criticisms. Also, 'promotion' in the firms included the award of more pay for doing the same job, which the civil service would normally cover by increments. Since individual pay was secret, the firms' staff could not compare their fate with that of colleagues.)

Nevertheless, the answers from private office employees were on the whole remarkably similar to those from the civil servants. The proportions expressing satisfaction with colleague relationships, discipline and supervision were almost identical. So were the numbers complaining about low status, insufficient responsibility, and poor recognition of individual work. There was the same tendency for those at the top to be more satisfied and to enjoy more interest, variety and responsibility (although the differences

[1] From other evidence, Walker regarded the civil service answers as more typical of office workers. The firms may therefore have been unusual in some way; or reactions to this question may have been affected by some special characteristic. Nevertheless, it is a large sample: a total of about 650 employees (60 upper level, 240 middle and 350 lower) comprising response rates of 63 per cent and 65 per cent from two large firms in central London; the firms were both parts of the same even larger organization.

between levels were less marked than in the civil service: 37 per cent of the firms' top men complained of too little responsibility, against 29 per cent of administrative civil servants, but only 51 per cent of the male lower grades, against 54 per cent of male C.O.s). Walker concluded that civil service dissatisfactions are largely endemic to office work anywhere.

Another point of comparison is supplied by Dr Pickering's survey of candidates who took the administrative class competitions in 1951 but did not subsequently enter the service as Assistant Principals.[1] They were asked to rank ten factors contributing to job-satisfaction. They put 'interest in job' first followed by 'earnings' and 'independence of action'.[2] They were then asked to estimate, on a four-point scale, how far these ideals were realized in their current job. A 'score' was worked out for each characteristic on the basis that it scored 100 per cent if all respondents put it in the highest category and 25 per cent if they all put it in the lowest. Scores of 80 per cent and above were obtained for interest (90 per cent), security of tenure (84 per cent), opportunity to use special skills (81 per cent), and independence of action (80 per cent); earnings scored only 68 per cent. (Interestingly, most thought they would have enjoyed less independence if they had joined the administrative class, nearly half thought they would have had less interesting work, only a third said they would have enjoyed more security and they were about evenly divided as to whether their pay and prospects would have been better, about the same, or worse.) Finally, Pickering worked out a specific job-satisfaction index by weighting the satisfactions obtained by each employment group against the values placed on them. The highest overall satisfaction levels were recorded by staff in univer-

---

[1] 'The Civil Service Unsuccessfuls: Fifteen Years Later' (*Fulton Report*, vol. 3(2) pp. 31 ff.). The survey was based on 482 candidates who were unsuccessful in the competitions, withdrew at a late stage, or (in ten cases) were successful but declined to take up an appointment. Some of these had died or were untraceable. Others did not reply. The actual response rate was 68 per cent. By 1966 the 252 respondents were in a wide variety of employments including industry (47), universities (38), schools and further education (45), finance and law (23), civil service (20), research and management consultancy (14) and local government (11).

[2] The other items were, in order of preference, 'contribution to well-being of society', 'promotion prospects', 'sense of vocation' (this was the third choice among those working in universities), 'opportunity to use special skills', 'security of tenure', 'geographical location' and 'contact with members of the public'. In addition, one in ten wrote in 'quality of colleagues' and 4 per cent added 'travel' in the lines provided for additional items.

sities (largely because of high scoring on interest and independence and the low importance given to pay), followed by those in research and management consultancy. High earnings in industry, finance and law did not bring their members out of the middle ranges for job-satisfaction. The lowest scores were by local government officers and civil servants (mostly in grades lower than administrative class). Pickering's conclusion was that morale is likely to be lowest (and the problems of recruiting and retaining staff will therefore be greatest) in occupations where both pay *and* the satisfactions derived from non-monetary rewards are low.

We can compare these attitudes of a reasonably successful group of 'near-civil-servants' with the career aspirations of university students. Here we can draw on a survey of student attitudes carried out for the Fulton Committee by the Psychological Research Centre in 1966–7[1] and a smaller study along similar lines at Hull University for the Estimates Committee in 1963.[2] The Hull students placed personal freedom, the opportunity to use their degree knowledge and the possibility of mid-career transfers among the most important features of a job, and felt that the civil service would be less likely to provide them than some other occupations. Only 7 out of 67 put 'prospects of quick promotion and a high salary at an early age but with little job security' among their first three requirements, but 26 included 'reasonable job-security, with regular and defined salary increases, and slower promotion prospects'. In the larger student survey transferability was described as the most important feature of a pensions scheme: the students felt that it would be more difficult to leave the civil service than some other employments if they wanted to. Many of them (60 per cent of those interested in the administrative class) said they would be attracted to the idea of working in the civil service on a short (for example three-year) contract. But nearly half the arts and social science students felt that security was one of the *advantages* of the service (compared with 31 per cent who felt that about large private industry). They also rated the civil

[1] 'Recruitment of Graduates: Survey of Student Attitudes', *Fulton Report*, vol. 3(2) pp. 309 ff.). The survey covered 2,031 students (an 82 per cent response rate) in a stratified 4 per cent sample spread over the first, middle and final years of first degree courses in fourteen British universities.

[2] *Sixth Report of the Estimates Committee 1964–65* (H.C. 308). 'Recruitment to the Civil Service', pp. 199 ff. (Memorandum by the Acton Society Trust.) This was based on a random sample of 20 per cent of British final year students at Hull aged 28 or under, of whom 69 (62 per cent) responded.

service better than most other occupations, including industry (except for the really large firms), for salary prospects. For many, it seemed more likely than industry to offer interesting work. Many members of both groups, however, had a stereotyped picture of civil servants as a rather grander sort of clerks.

Finally, we have some roughly contemporary material collected for the Mallaby Committee about local government staff.[1] Just over a quarter of the local government officers liked their work 'very much'; one in six was indifferent or actively disliked it. Staff under 21 were less satisfied than their seniors. Their main motives for joining the local government service had been, first, a belief that the work would be satisfying and, next, security and pension. Graduate entrants had been less influenced by security and more by prospects or force of circumstances. But 38·5 per cent (44 per cent of those under 21) said that their expectations had been disappointed. Seventeen per cent were seriously considering leaving, mainly on account of poor pay and prospects, although lack of scope for initiative was often given as a third reason. Thirty-two per cent of the remainder would do so if it were not for the loss of pension rights. Most local authorities had in fact been experiencing losses exceeding 20 per cent of entrants in their first five years of service. Of the total, 39 per cent (49 per cent of those aged 21–5) claimed there was not enough scope for initiative; 27·5 per cent (36 per cent aged 21–5) complained that they enjoyed too little responsibility.

We can at least say, therefore, that the civil service is not alone in failing to offer a satisfying job to all its members, particularly those at the bottom. We can also say that earnings and economic prospects are not the only (perhaps at higher levels not even the main) sources of motivation and job-satisfaction in any of the fields we have studied.

EFFECTS

The effects of staff discontent on organizational performance are conventionally measured by correlating dissatisfaction with absence,

---

[1] *Report of the Committee on the Staffing of Local Government* (London, 1967) app. D. The information was collected by means of a questionnaire sent to every seventh person in every eighth branch of the National and Local Government Officers' Association. The response rate was 80·3 per cent and 2,890 returns were used in the analysis. The circumstances of the enquiry may be criticized as likely to encourage respondents to exaggerate their dissatisfactions, particularly with pay and status, in the hope that the Committee might be induced to recommend improvements.

wastage and inefficiency. Indeed, high absenteeism, high turnover of staff and low output are sometimes taken as *prima facie* evidence of 'low morale'. A fourth effect could be on recruitment, if potential entrants were discouraged by what they knew about the experience of those already in the service. In fact it is doubtful if poor job-satisfaction in the civil service can be associated with any of these on present evidence.

Absenteeism, in the sense of staying away from work without an excuse, is virtually unknown in the service and would be regarded as a serious disciplinary offence. But in common with many other office-workers civil servants are normally allowed to take paid sick leave without a medical certificate for up to four days at a time and up to a ceiling of seven days in any twelve months. The concession can be withdrawn from individuals who are thought to be abusing it. The scheme appears to offer a fairly generous umbrella for those who are unhappy in their work and might well take advantage of opportunities to stay away. If uncertificated sick leave is used in this way, it is on a very small scale. Over 80 per cent of the EO/CO sample had taken two days or less uncertificated sick leave or less per annum over the previous five years; only 6 per cent took four days or more. Those who said they liked their work had taken rather less sick leave than those who said they disliked or were indifferent to it. But the differences were trifling – about a fifth of a day per annum. for men and about a third of a day for women (who take more sick leave anyway).[1] The figures are interesting, partly because they demolish a popular myth about white-collar abuse of privileges. But they do not reveal a major problem. Walker found a similarly significant, but relatively unimportant, connection between job-satisfaction and uncertificated sick leave in his 1959 sample.

Wastage from the civil service is on the whole very low.[2] But such wastage as does occur attracts a good deal of attention.[3] Although

[1] Thus married women C.O.s had taken 1·61 days per annum if they liked their jobs, and 1·94 if they did not. Male E.O.s had taken 0·95 days if they were happy and 1·17 days if they disliked or were indifferent to their work (*Fulton Report*, vol. 3(2) pp. 253–4).

[2] See ch. III, pp. 50–2.

[3] The Treasury studies of wastage and job-satisfaction were inspired by the Estimates Committee report on 'Recruitment to the Civil Service', pars. 42–4 and Evidence, p. 113. The (by civil service standards) alarmist allegation in that report that there was a wastage rate of 21 per cent among executive officers under 30 seems to have been based on a fallacious comparison between the number of resignations and the number of new E.O.s recruited by the Civil Service Commission in the same year. Also the resignation rate of 13·5 per cent among E.O.s

the populations in the two EO/CO surveys were not exactly comparable, there is sufficient in common to allow an estimate to be made of the effects of dissatisfaction on turnover in these grades. In general the leavers were more dissatisfied than the stayers, and felt more strongly about the features of civil service employment of which they disapproved.[1] But the majority of leavers were not dissatisfied with the civil service at all. Apart from those who left for domestic or family reasons one-third of the executives and one-seventh of the clerical officers left to take up a full time education course. Moreover, the leavers as a group seem to have been somewhat below the general standard of their grade.[2]

It is necessary to keep a sense of perspective. About half the leavers had served for less than two years, which does not seem an unreasonable settling down period for young people. Thereafter voluntary resignations are infrequent. Appendix III shows the number of leavers at different ages and with different amounts of seniority in their grade. When the latter figures are used to project the 'fall-out' rate from a cohort of new entrants, they suggest that about 10 per cent of male executive officers and about 35-40 per cent of male clerical officers will resign voluntarily before completing ten years' service in that grade. In these terms, wastage is hardly worth bothering about.

We have no comparable information for other grades and classes. Wastage from the administrative grades, although small, may be significant in terms of quality. Resignations among special or technical groups, like draughtsmen and A.D.P. specialists, may be serious in numerical terms also. More enquiries are needed to establish the extent and causes of wastage in such categories. But it should not be assumed that all outward mobility is undesirable or a reflection on the quality of life in the civil service.

The efficiency of nearly all civil servants is assessed annually on a confidential staff report. Although the criteria used in this

under 20 in 1963, quoted on p. 113, seems to have been incorrect (compare appendix III below).

[1] See the 'Satisfaction Index' for each grade in *Fulton Report*, vol. 3(2) pp. 204, 209. These 'interim' figures are substantially confirmed in the unpublished final report covering the full year. There are one or two odd features: C.O. leavers seem to have been *less* dissatisfied than the stayers with departmental posting policy and training, and they had more *favourable* attitudes to office accommodation and to colleagues. This may be due to different survey conditions, or to distance enhancing the view. At any rate the differences are slight.

[2] Ibid., pp. 201, 206.

assessment were severely criticized by the Fulton Committee's consultancy group (particularly in relation to promotion procedures) it does allow staff to be distinguished according to whether their performance on current duties is (a) above standard, (b) standard, or (c) below standard. For each officer in the EO/CO survey with over five years' service (to eliminate the effects of inexperience) this assessment was compared with his attitude to the job, with the following results.[1]

	Efficiency rating	*No.*	*Percentage who like the job*
Executive Officers	above standard	207	75
	standard	341	71
	below standard	45	49
Clerical Officers	above standard	175	72
	standard	436	68
	below standard	97	58

The differences were not great, except that more of the small number who were judged below standard efficiency disliked or were indifferent to their job.

Walker made a similar comparison and found no association between satisfaction and efficiency ratings, except that those graded very good or very bad tended to have stronger feelings about their job (not necessarily in the expected direction) than those whose performance was more average. Again, there is no suggestion that more attention to job-satisfaction would automatically increase the efficiency of the great bulk of civil service desk grades.

Unfortunately these surveys do not tell us very much about the effect of job-satisfaction on performance at high administrative levels. One reason for the absence of a relationship at lower levels could be that people who are dissatisfied with work which they regard as below their capabilities nevertheless succeed in carrying it out very well. This neutralizing effect is less likely to be felt in work that is challenging by any standard. It is, of course, difficult to find reliable criteria against which performance at these levels could be assessed (although an attempt was made by the Civil Service Commission in order to validate selection procedures).[2] and it is unlikely that the

[1] *Fulton Report*, vol. 3(2) p. 261.
[2] 'Administrative Class follow-up Survey' (*Fulton Report*, vol. 3(2) pp. 135 ff.).

surveys could be replicated realistically for senior administrators. But *a priori* reasoning suggests that strength of motivation is likely to be highly relevant to the extent to which a senior administrator exploits his abilities and applies them to the service of his department. We cannot, therefore, ignore the possibility that job-satisfaction may be vital to efficiency at the levels where it matters most.

Finally, it is sometimes claimed that job-satisfaction is bound to be reflected in recruitment. Presumably this can happen in one of two ways. Dissatisfied members of a service can advise their children and their friends' children against following their own example. Or the unattractiveness of working in it may become obvious to the public that includes potential new entrants. Walker found that only about a third of civil servants would advise a friend with similar qualifications to follow their own career, compared with half to three-fifths of private office staff. (The proportions vary with grade; the executive grades were least enthusiastic.) The results, as might be expected, were strongly correlated with the adviser's own job-satisfaction, although it was not true that all the satisfied respondents would advise favourably:

Advice to a friend thinking of entering their career in the same way with similar qualifications[1]

Job-satisfaction	Against	Impartial	In Favour
satisfied	19·8%	21·3%	58·9%
in-between	41·0%	29·4%	29·6%
dissatisfied	67·8%	18·9%	13·3%

There is no comparable information in the Fulton enquiries, although a third of the Principals said that they would advise their children against entering the civil service if they could not get into the administrative class. These negative influences might affect recruitment from groups within the civil servant's sphere of influence, such as members of his former college. But only one undergraduate in eight hears about jobs through people already in them.[2]

When all the information about potential recruits and their impressions of the civil service in the student surveys and in evidence (mainly concerned with the executive class) from schools and youth

---

[1] Walker, *Morale in the Civil Service*, p. 186.
[2] 'Survey of Student Attitudes' (*Fulton Report*, vol. 3(2) p. 399, Table XXXVI).

employment officers[1] is put together, three general impressions emerge:

1. There is a large number of potential recruits at all levels who know very little about the civil service, whose impressions of it are largely stereotyped (red-tape, close supervision etc.) and who would consider a civil service career only as a last resort. These people might eventually become happy and successful civil servants. But what they need to start them on the road is either more information or direct experience. The effect on them of trying to improve job-satisfaction within the service (with the attendant publicity about current shortcomings) is uncertain.

2. Then there is a group – perhaps a third to a half at undergraduate level – who have a fairly realistic impression of the advantages and disadvantages of a civil service career, and do not like what they see. Some of them do not like big organizations; some are attracted by the more competitive atmosphere of private industry; some rate the satisfactions of a teaching career very highly. Some of these might be induced to consider the civil service if they could be persuaded that it could provide them with the varying satisfactions they want. For some, this might entail changes of a Fulton type in the structure of the service.

3. A third group, smaller than the others, is also reasonably knowledgeable and is attracted by distinctive features of the service – such as the opportunity to take part in important and interesting work, a fairly non-competitive relationship with colleagues, and so on. They consider the service seriously – and their favourable attitudes tend to be confirmed by a Whitehall visit – but reject it in favour of other work (typically university teaching) which offers similar advantages combined with others. In this group, recruitment difficulties are not so much due to the failure of the service to attract as to the greater attraction of other opportunities. Its members are likely to be influenced by the reactions of people already in the service, so far as they are aware of them. But changes in the career structure designed to attract more of the second group may be a discouragement for them.

SCOPE FOR ACTION

It is not really very surprising to find that some people do not like their jobs. Some of the unsatisfactory features about life in the civil

[1] *Fulton Report*, vol. 5, pp. 743–78, 818–25.

service, particularly at the lower levels, are probably inseparable from work in any large organization. The advantages of size are often gained from extreme division of labour which makes many jobs too routine to be interesting while others are extremely frustrating for the independently-minded. It is difficult to do much about this, except marginally, without sacrificing the advantages of large-scale organization. Instead of trying to make jobs artificially interesting, it may be more realistic to accept a high wastage rate from recruits who do not settle down fairly quickly, and to compensate the survivors with good pay and extrinsic rewards.

The most dissatisfied people we have encountered in these surveys have been junior in age as well as in the hierarchy. Their elders have learned to adjust. In an age of full employment we must accept the inevitability (perhaps even the desirability) of some job-changing by young people who are reluctant to settle down in the more humdrum parts of a big administrative machine.

But if dissatisfaction is not a condition peculiar to civil servants, there are some special features of civil service work from which low morale might be predicted. It is subject to unusually close control and review from the top (although not perhaps more than administrative work in local government, where morale is also low). Ministerial accountability to Parliament places a premium on accuracy which makes it difficult to delegate responsibility. The need to insure against crises means that people are placed in posts where their abilities are not fully used for much of the time. The ultimate ramifications of any block of work are bafflingly complex. The official who succeeds in imposing his own order of priorities is likely to have it dislocated by a sudden shift in parliamentary or Ministerial interest. If things go well, the Minister takes the credit – if badly, civil servants are deluged with criticism and extra work in dealing with it. It is difficult to offer civil servants at any level the independence and the opportunities for personal achievement that some undergraduates seek in a job.

These conditions may not make for satisfied staff, but our system of government does need civil servants who will tolerate them. As if in answer to the stresses, a social system has grown up which offers some protection and some compensations. At the top, where civil servants have the almost unbearable task of putting their knowledge and abilities at the disposal of Ministers with differing abilities and philosophies, they have enjoyed the protections of anonymity and of virtual security against dismissal, as well as the satisfaction of belonging to an *élite* whose rather esoteric skills will be needed and valued by the next political administration. (It is only fair to add that both the protections and the satisfactions began to look dangerously weak under the Labour Governments of 1964 and 1966, when the top civil service was also working under severe pressure. Some Ministers spent their period of office in acute mistrust of the motives of their advisers. In two cases, Ministers were reported to have tried to dispose of their Permanent Secretaries for reasons that, though obscure, seemed faintly discreditable to the Minister.)

Lower down the scale, the career structure offers unexpected compensations. A Principal or Senior Executive Officer doing his stint on a particularly trying or unrewarding block of work has known that it would not last for ever and that the system would not allow him to be forgotten, nor to be indefinitely penalized for an unlucky mistake. And he has been able to get on with his work – perhaps losing himself in perfecting arrangements for the more equitable treatment of some obscure class of beneficiary – without having to look over his shoulder at the effect on his promotion ratings: he has had no incentive either to conceal his mistakes or to expand an empire which in a year or two would be inherited by someone else. For all grades, centralized bargaining with staff associations has resulted in procedures for discipline and promotion which offer considerable protection from arbitrariness and 'scapegoating'.

There is nothing inevitable about these arrangements, although they appear to suit the special requirements of public administration remarkably well.[1] In considering possible alternatives, it is necessary to distinguish between reforms that could be implemented without much, or perhaps any, violence to the present system and those that could not be applied without far-reaching losses and gains.

Foremost among the first group are improvements in personnel policy that would increase the chances of overall job-satisfaction without prejudicing the conduct of public business. At present, although consultation is well-developed and conditions of employment are civilized, there are a number of blind spots in civil service

---

[1] Not only in Britain. Professor Chapman has shown that similar arrangements have grown up in many other European countries. In some, the civil service is virtually self-governing in internal matters. B. Chapman, *The Profession of Government* (London, 1959).

personnel work which seem to lead to dissatisfaction. There is the impersonal postings procedure. Within limits, there is no reason for not taking personal interests and preferences into account on the type and duration of postings;[1] and it seems from the EO/CO survey that more could be done to offer other opportunities to those who are unsuited to the work they are doing. Then there is the question of giving civil servants a better sense of personal fulfilment: it would not be difficult to find some means of reassuring individuals who are anxious about their performance and want to feel that they are getting somewhere; for some people, especially young entrants, the absence of regular appraisal generates unnecessary tension and anxiety. Thirdly, there is the question of training. The operational value of training is often disputed. But there is not much doubt about the beneficial effects of training on morale. The position of the generalist is a particularly vulnerable one in a skill-orientated society and almost any training that gives him a sense of confidence is likely to be a good investment, provided that the cost and duration are not seriously out of proportion to the benefit. (A training scheme also seems to be one of the things most recruits expect from a job. It is possible that the old requirement of economic security, based on the organization, has been replaced by a need for 'occupational security', based on the possession of visible qualifications. It is interesting that top-quality graduates in the survey of student attitudes were less concerned about further training than other, presumably less confident, respondents.)[2] Finally, there has been a tendency to over-insure against crisis by over-grading posts – a tendency which can be attacked as a misuse of human resources as well as for its effects on morale and should be checked. Each of these improvements is advocated in the Fulton Report. Their adoption should help to minimize avoidable sources of dissatisfaction and may in the long run have some effect on performance, wastage and recruitment.

Other aspects of the Fulton recommendations cannot be welcomed

---

[1] The limits appear to be: (a) there must be some constraints to prevent civil servants from identifying themselves too closely with the expansion and perfection of activities that may have outlived their usefulness; (b) some civil servants must be required to pursue a fairly broad career path in order to develop an overall view of several fields of policy (see ch. XIII above); (c) some jobs may be so unpopular – or so unattractive to those of above-average ability – that they can be staffed only on a rota system.

[2] *Fulton Report*, vol. 3(2) p. 379.

so unreservedly, because it is not clear what their total effect will be, either on the pattern of rewards and sanctions or, ultimately, on performance.

Several are designed to allow individuals to identify themselves more closely with success and to enjoy specific rewards for specific performance. Taken in isolation, these suggestions are well-based and should improve both the performance and the satisfaction of the individuals concerned – although perhaps less than might be expected. But these advantages have to be set against the cost of lower satisfaction, and possibly lower performance, by the less successful, who on the Fulton proposals will forfeit some of the career prospects they now enjoy, or by those who rightly or wrongly lack self-confidence and are afraid of the possibility of failure. Walker's survey suggested (a) that low morale was associated with a sense of failure and (b) that the optimism of those who felt themselves capable of better things was not universally shared by their superiors. If a system of rewards that is visibly fair (within a class) produces these reactions among the relatively unsuccessful it seems safe to predict that the casualties of a more 'merit-orientated' system will tend to see faults in the system rather than in themselves. It is not valid to reply that Walker found more favourable attitudes to a different promotion system in industry, where 'promotion' carried a different meaning, the career structure was manipulated in a different way and individual expectations were entirely different.

We also have to consider whether the mechanics of the proposed merit system, which is to be based on accurate job-evaluation, will themselves have undesirable side-effects. In a changing situation, job-descriptions may become out of date as soon as they are written. In a study of American managers, Dalton shows how gaps arise between official expectations and the actual requirements of a job; there is never time to legitimize necessary adjustments and short-cuts; the task of the manager is to make loose ends meet by getting the work done while paying just enough attention to the 'official' requirements to safeguard his own position; the *attempt* to put the requirements of the job down on paper, however, diverts attention to the standards by which performance will be assessed, however unrealistic they may be. Too much attention, in particular, may be given to aspects that can be measured (typically quantity rather than quality and speed rather than effectiveness).[1]

[1] M. Dalton, *Men Who Manage* (New York, 1959) ch. 8.

Faced with the stress of meeting incompatible demands, Dalton's managers sought help and moral support from colleagues through the formation of cliques. Civil servants, too, seek support from colleagues, notably from other members of their class and from other staff in their division, in coping with stress and ambiguity. The absence of direct competition makes it easier to develop this mutual help and *esprit de corps*. But this could change. In their more competitive world, Dalton's cliques were defensive and mutually hostile. They existed not only to provide moral support but also to further the interests of their members at the expense of non-members, mainly by collusion to present favourable impressions to those controlling promotion, and to cover up mistakes and unofficial practices. It would be regrettable if such tendencies developed among civil servants, whose ease in vertical and horizontal relationships is important for getting things done in the public service. There is at present no risk that unfavourable information will be used against the informant, and this undoubtedly helps good decision-making. But this openness seems to be closely bound up with the protected career structure.

The reactions of individuals to a more continuous assessment of their performance are not necessarily rational. The sense of being always on probation may lead to a number of side-effects, apart from a more wary relationship between superior and subordinate. Already caution, bred by awareness of the possibility of political review, is one of the main motivational problems in the service. A knowledge that one's work is open to inspection is probably healthy. A preoccupation with the inspector is not. It seems inevitable that there should be some distortion of priorities if controls are made more obvious and the results of inspection are reflected directly in pay and prospects.

Another predictable effect of heightened anxiety is that staff associations will become more powerful. Their members will look to them to regulate competition and to protect individuals from arbitrary decisions. Threats to a cultural pattern that is liked by its participants provoke resistance. One effect of the Fulton report has been the almost unprecedented threat by the Civil Service Clerical Association of strike action if necessary to protect its members against detrimental change.[1] Given the traditions and the balance of forces in the civil service, it is inevitable that staff associations will be

[1] *The Times* (London) 15 May 1969.

actively engaged in protecting the interests of their members while new procedures are being worked out.[1] In a large service it is necessary to develop rules under which individual cases will be handled. The only possible outcome of consultation is thus a set of rules embodying compromises between the staff's desire for protection and security and management's need for order and control. As the Fulton Committee noticed, the existence of standard procedures weakens the direct control of individual managers; and, however desirable a negotiated procedure may appear to a group of staff as a whole, its application in individual cases may be experienced as impersonal and frustrating. The main problem, however, will be to avoid a new form of rigidity.

CONCLUDING REMARKS

In view of the problems and the difficulties involved, it seems unlikely that the Fulton proposals to introduce a more commercial pattern of incentives into the civil service will be taken far enough to harm the supportive relationships associated with the present non-competitive career pattern. That being the case, a slight tightening up to offer special opportunities to the really able and to eliminate the really incompetent (whom existing staff feel are over-protected) might provide no more than a necessary corrective to a system which, left alone, may tend to become more inflexible and rule-bound.[2] Less controversial improvements in personnel management should help individuals by providing support and reassurance of a more personal kind.

It does seem important, however, that changes should not appear unnecessarily threatening or critical. Any change is, to some extent, threatening, and changes prompted by criticism are doubly so.

---

[1] The National Whitley Council set up a Joint Committee as a forum for consultation and negotiation between the Civil Service Department (with other employing departments) and the interests represented on the National Staff Side about the implementation of the Fulton Report (*Developments on Fulton*, par. 80).

[2] Crozier argues that a well-developed bureaucracy, whose internal procedures are governed by the fruits of collective bargaining, becomes so rigid that even minor changes cannot be introduced without 'catastrophic' intervention from outside. (M. Crozier, *The Bureaucratic Phenomenon*, London 1964.) Some of the Fulton arguments depend on the implied major premise that what the British civil service really needs is some sort of shake-up.

They are likely to inspire irrational and possibly destructive resistance. In the civil service, overt hostility is almost ruled out for most grades by the prevailing culture. A more serious risk is indirect damage through diminished self-confidence and heightened anxiety. Even though our analysis has failed to show any important connection between morale and efficiency, it has demonstrated the importance of non-economic factors in civil servants' attitudes to their job. It would be wise to reassure those who feel threatened that changes will not endanger their personal goals and expectations. There is a particular need to restore the self-confidence of the senior ranks in the civil service.

The human effects of any change have to be assessed against other consequences. It may be that there is a net deficit in human terms – the job becomes less rewarding and less satisfying to most of the staff – but that this is outweighed by the gains in functional efficiency. The EO/CO survey suggested that satisfaction was lower among junior staff engaged on large blocks of work which tend to attract the attention of 'O & M' efficiency experts: but this is not necessarily an argument against O & M. What is important is to keep in mind the notion of a system, in which changes cannot be viewed in isolation. The main criticism to be made of the Fulton Committee is its failure to realize that desirable changes in one aspect of an organization cannot be disassociated from other changes, desirable and undesirable, elsewhere. Here are some of the more obvious examples:

(a) One of the strengths of the civil service is the quality of staff relationships achieved through Whitleyism. One effect of Whitley procedures is to weaken control by line management. But it is not possible to introduce stronger line management without losing the main advantage of Whitleyism.

(b) The advantages of a more competitive career structure cannot be achieved without some threat to the solidarity, integrity and self-sacrifice which the Committee admired in the present system.

(c) Specialists bring a more creative approach to administration, and maintain more links with the outside world, partly because they have a more mobile career structure and look outside the civil service for future openings. Those who take these opportunities are lost to the service. But it is not possible to retain specialists by offering them a better internal career without weakening their motivation to maintain fruitful external contacts.[1]

We cannot predict all these ramifications. Here, as in other aspects of the civil service, there is a need for research. Like the Fulton Committee recommendations themselves, personnel practices in the service have grown up as a result of bargaining, or because they were intuitively felt to be 'right', rather than because they have been validated systematically. Many of them (such as the super-annuation code based on the expectation of a lifetime career) are no longer attractive or no longer answer to modern needs. In many respects, civil service establishment work has remained cut off from current thinking, in which social science concepts play a large part, about motivation and creativity. There is a good case for subjecting its assumptions to systematic appraisal.

Proposals for reform need to be examined as critically as the existing system – indeed more so, since the total system being changed embodies the results of a long series of adjustments and compromises between the ideal and the practical, which might have to be begun all over again. The appropriate tools for the investigation seem to be the sort of social science concepts outlined in Chapter VI, combined with empirical data as in the present chapter. Organization theory begins to take on operational value if it enables us to take a clearer view of the probable consequences of adopting or not adopting a specific course of action, such as that recommended by the Fulton Committee. Some practical suggestions for research on motivation and morale are included in Appendix II.

[1] Some readers may think this rather far-fetched. It is the problem of 'local' or organization-centred, compared to 'cosmopolitan' or occupation-centred, professionals analysed by A. W. Gouldner in 'Cosmopolitans and Locals', *Administrative Science Quarterly*, vol. 2 (1957–8) pp. 281–306, 444–80. Professor Mosher suggests in contrast that the American 'in and outer' type of administrator tends to belong to a strongly professionalized cadre whose outlook reflects what fellow-professionals are likely to approve rather than an objective estimate of the public interest. F. C. Mosher, *Democracy and the Public Service* (Oxford, 1968).

XV. Epilogue[1]

RECENT DEVELOPMENTS

A few notes are needed to amplify and in some cases to correct statements in the main text in the light of subsequent developments, particularly those following the change from a Labour to a Conservative administration in June 1970.

SIZE AND COMPOSITION OF THE CIVIL SERVICE (pp. 38–40)

In spite of determined efforts to contain its growth, the non-industrial staff of the civil service increased from 465,000 in January 1968 to 501,700 in July 1970. Even so, it had become clear that the complements in certain grades, particularly in local tax and social security offices, were insufficient to operate current policies effectively.[2] A prominent theme in the first report of the Civil Service Department[3] was the search for ways of making better use of existing manpower. A panel of businessmen, appointed by Mr Wilson to review the need for certain tasks to be performed, did not find room for substantial savings. The panel recognized the special pressures on the civil service for record-keeping and equity, and suggested that 'substantial savings . . . would largely depend upon a general willingness of Ministers, Parliament and the public to accept changes in practices which had been adopted in response to these pressures'. Nevertheless, it was felt useful to compare civil service methods with those of industry.[4] The incoming Conservative Government was committed to reducing the scale of government activity and hence the number of civil servants. An early start was

---

[1] Revised January 1971.
[2] See, for example, *Fifth Report of the Estimates Committee, 1968–69*, Inland Revenue Department (HC 474).
[3] *CSD REPORT 1969*, H.M.S.O. 1970.
[4] Statement published in *Whitley Bulletin*, vol. L, no. 5, May 1970.

made by abolishing the Land Commission and the National Board
for Prices and Incomes.

RECRUITMENT AND CAREER STRUCTURE (pp. 40–56)

During 1969–70 negotiations with the staff side of the National
Whitley Council[1] were leading towards a number of definite
decisions on the implementation of the Fulton report.

(a) An open structure, in which posts would be filled by the best
man available regardless of his 'occupational group' would be
implemented from the start of 1971 for the 650 or so people enjoying salaries of about £6,000 and above and possibly for intermediate
grades later.

(b) The administrative, executive and clerical grades would be
merged into a continuous structure. The Assistant Principal grade
would be replaced by an Administration Trainee grade, to which it
was hoped to recruit a wider graduate intake of 175 and about a
hundred internal candidates each year, and from which a 'fast
stream' would be identified only after several years' performance on
the job. Some of the length of service conditions for internal promotion were considerably eased. Studies were in progress on the
possibility of specialization either by subject or by function.

(c) The scientific and works groups would also be replaced with
one or more continuous grading structures.

TRAINING (pp. 57–61)

The three constituent parts of the Civil Service College (two
residential centres in Sunningdale, Berkshire, and Edinburgh and
a non-residential centre taking the place of the Centre for Administrative Studies in London) came into operation during 1970.
About 8,000 course places, half of them in general management
subjects, were made available at the College in 1970–1.

A major commitment of the College was the provision of initial
courses for Administration Trainees. Initially, this took the form of a
three-stage programme giving one year's training over five years,
starting with a four-week course in quantitative analysis and the
structure of government, followed later by twelve weeks on government and organization and still later (for the fast stream) by

[1] Summarized in *Fulton: A Framework for the Future*, Civil Service National
Whitley Council, 1970.

twenty-two weeks in economic and social administration followed by six weeks in a specialized field.

CONFIDENTIALITY (pp. 98–9)

Some expansion is needed of the second footnote on p. 99. The White Paper on 'Information and Public Interest'[1] recognized that there was often a choice to be made between full consultation and speedy decision making. The more widespread provision of information would involve additional staff time which could be justified only where there was known to be a substantial public interest and the extra work could be undertaken without either an unacceptable increase or diversion of effort from the main job. Moreover, the movement towards more public explanation of administrative processes, while desirable, could not be allowed to prejudice the confidential relationship between civil servants and Ministers by allowing officials to become identified with particular policy views or by revealing respects in which Ministers had rejected their advice.

PARLIAMENTARY COMMISSIONER FOR ADMINISTRATION (pp. 99–104)

A decision to extend the 'Ombudsman' system to other fields was announced in July 1969.[2] The Labour Government's White Paper on local government reform[3] duly announced that up to ten 'local commissioners for administration' would be established to deal with complaints of maladministration in the sphere of local government. A further announcement was expected about a 'Health Service Commissioner'; the advisory service mentioned on p. 101 was to be concerned more with informing the Minister about the malfunctioning of institutions than with specific complaints. Discussions were also proceeding with police representative bodies about independent machinery to replace the 1964 Police Act procedure whereby complaints about the police were investigated by other policemen (and only one in ten was found to be substantiated). The proposed extension of the system was viewed without enthusiasm by both police and doctors, who pointed out the diffi-

---

[1] Cmnd. 4089, 1969.
[2] *H.C. Debs.*, vol. 787 (22 July 1969), cols. 1501–3 (Mr H. Wilson).
[3] *Reform of Local Government in England*, Cmnd. 4276, 1970, pars. 82–7.

culties of trespassing on matters of professional judgement. The scope of the Parliamentary Commissioner had already been extended to Northern Ireland, where it included maladministration on the part of public bodies and authorities as well as of the central Belfast government.

PARLIAMENTARY COMMITTEES (pp. 104–12)

The debate about relationships between Parliament and the Executive was considerably advanced by a report from the Select Committee on Procedure.[1] The Committee, which included some of the most able and perceptive members of the back-benches as well as a former Chancellor of the Exchequer, recommended that the arrangements for Parliamentary scrutiny of public expenditure needed strengthening to provide for three elements: (a) advance discussion of the Government's expenditure strategy and policies; (b) examination of the methods being adopted to carry out the policies on a year-to-year basis; (c) retrospective scrutiny of achievements and value obtained for expenditure actually incurred.

The Government had already developed a system of forward planning of expenditure (see pp. 235–6). What was lacking was some means whereby Members of Parliament could share in the process of policy formulation by debating projections and expressing informed choices between costed alternatives. The Committee therefore argued for a debate on the basis of a White Paper projecting public expenditure over a five-year period. The first White Paper was published in December 1969[2] and was followed by a two-day debate in January 1970.[3]

The debate provided the first real test of the question discussed on pp. 181–4 about the capacity of lay representatives for such an active role in policy development. At a time when Commons membership numbered 624, only 54 backbenchers heard the Chancellor's opening speech and 14 stayed to hear the Opposition winding-up speech at the end of the first day.[4] On the other hand, the quality of

[1] First Report from the Select Committee on Procedure, Session 1968–9 *Scrutiny of Public Expenditure and Administration*, (HC 410).
[2] *Public Expenditure 1968–69 to 1973–74*, Cmnd. 4234, 1969.
[3] *H.C. Debs.*, vol. 794, cols. 523–644 and 723–837 (21 and 22 January 1970).
[4] 'MPs unconcerned over spending of £50,000 million', *The Times*, 23 January 1970.

the thirty or so speeches was recognized to be outstanding and a Conservative M.P. wrote to *The Times* to argue that what mattered was the contribution of those who were able to take part, not the number present: attendance was at least as good as for the debates on the Budget or the Queen's Speech after the main speeches, and Members 'really cannot make themselves constantly available as a perpetual audience in the main chamber of the House. They have a great many other things to do in service of their country and their constituents.'[1]

On the more detailed scrutiny of policy and administration, the Committee's main procedural recommendation was a return to the idea of specialist sub-committees. The Estimates Committee should be replaced by a Select Committee on Expenditure, with sub-committees whose terms of reference would be 'to consider the activities of Departments of State . . . and the Estimates of their expenditure presented to this House; and to examine the efficiency with which they are administered'.[2] A somewhat trimmed version of this proposal was accepted by the Conservative leader of the House of Commons, Mr Whitelaw, in a Green Paper in which it was also suggested that there would be no need for new specialist committees outside the Expenditure Committee framework.[3]

The Committee's other recommendations linked the requirements of political control to the concepts of efficient management which were the main concern of the Fulton Committee. After a full and well-documented discussion of output budgeting and other management techniques, the Committee came to the conclusion that their use was essential for a modern and effective system of control, and that Parliamentary methods would have to be adapted in order to make use of them.

ADMINISTRATIVE INNOVATIONS (pp. 191–5)

There were important changes in October 1969 and again, after the general election, a year later. The first round included the establishment of the Post Office as a nationalized industry and its replacement in Whitehall by a small Ministry of Posts and Telecommunications and a Department of National Savings. It also saw

---

[1] Letter from Mr Kenneth Lewis, M.P., *The Times*, 30 January 1970.
[2] Compare the existing and proposed terms of reference for the Estimates Committee on pp. 105–6.
[3] *Select Committees of the House of Commons*, Cmnd. 4507, 1970.

the final demise of the Department of Economic Affairs and the reallocation of its functions among the Treasury (which thus regained responsibility for long-term economic policy and assessment), the Cabinet Office and a new Department of Local Government and Regional Planning. The last was a small co-ordinating department, attached to the Cabinet Office, which was given general oversight of the Ministry of Transport and the Ministry of Housing and Local Government; the new Secretary of State, who represented all these activities in the Cabinet, was particularly charged with the reform of local government. At the same time the Ministry of Technology absorbed the Ministry of Power and took over most of the responsibilities towards industry of the Board of Trade. It thus acquired oversight of both nationalized and private sector industry. The size of the Cabinet was reduced from twenty-three to twenty-one.

Much of this was to be changed again by the Conservatives. In October 1970, Housing and Local Government, Transport, and Public Building and Works were unified in a single Department of the Environment. At the same time Trade and Technology, along with the productivity functions of the Department of Employment and Productivity, were combined in a new Department of Trade and Industry. The Ministry of Overseas Development became part of the Foreign and Commonwealth Office. The general pattern was for the original department to remain a 'functional wing' of the larger entity under a Minister exercising delegated authority. (The earlier Department of Local Government and Regional Planning had not taken over powers from the departments it was supposed to co-ordinate). The effect, as in the earlier cases of the Ministry of Defence and the Department of Health and Social Security (see pp. 207–12), was to streamline the political chain of command and to allow a further reduction to seventeen in the size of the Cabinet. The opportunity was taken to announce the transfer of children's services to the Department of Health and Social Security (see p. 214).

Although these changes can be read partly as a fresh response to perennial problems of co-ordination between conflicting objectives, the White Paper of October 1970[1] was strangely reminiscent of the Haldane report, written fifty years earlier. Citing the 'functional principle' of organization, it argued that 'government departments

[1] *The Reorganisation of Central Government*, Cmnd. 4506, 1970.

should be organized by reference to the task to be done or the objective to be attained. . . . And policy issues which are linked should be grouped together in organizational terms.' It has been the theme of this book that *all* policy issues are linked; departmental grouping thus reflects the categories of political thought at a particular point of time and cannot embody any final organizational truth. The claim that these structures 'are intended and expected to remain valid for a long time to come' seemed unwise.

LOCAL GOVERNMENT REFORM (p. 221)

The Labour Government announced its proposals for creating fewer and stronger local authorities, broadly on the lines of the Royal Commission report, in February 1970.[1] It was made clear, however, that it was not practicable to bring the National Health Service within local government.[2] The Secretary of State confirmed that the main opportunity for considering the devolution of powers from central government would come later, when the Crowther Commission (see p. 93) reported on the possibility of setting up a provincial tier of government. But local government reorganization would itself reduce the need for central supervision of local authorities and the reconciliation of differences between them. 'The creation of fewer authorities, enjoying greater freedom, will be reflected in a reduction in the tasks now undertaken by central government in relation to local government. This will offer opportunities for reducing civil service numbers in the relevant areas of central government administration. These opportunities will be vigorously pursued.' Although the Conservative Government was not committed in detail to the decisions of the previous administration, both the main political parties had become committed to a measure of decentralization and to accepting the concomitant loss of standardization and accountability at national level.

CENTRAL CO-ORDINATION OF POLICY (pp. 268–73)

Before the general election, the Cabinet Office had begun to emerge as an instrument of policy review and strategic co-ordination.

[1] Cmnd. 4276, op. cit.
[2] Department of Health and Social Security, *The Future Structure of the National Health Service*, 1970.

The offices of the Secretaries of State for Health and Social Security and for Local Government and Regional Planning were attached to the Cabinet Office and the National Economic Development Office reported to it after the disappearance of the Department of Economic Affairs.

The new Government added a further element – a small central policy review staff, headed by Lord Rothschild (a Labour peer with considerable industrial experience) whose task would be to enable Ministers to take better collective policy decisions 'by assisting them to work out the implications of their basic strategy in terms of policies in specific areas, to establish the relative priorities to be given to the different sectors of their programmes as a whole, to identify those areas of policy in which new choices can be exercised and to ensure that the underlying implications of alternative courses of action are fully analysed and considered'.[1] Opposition speakers were quick to suggest that these rather vague objectives were 'a recipe for friction mess and muddle',[2] and certainly there are practical problems about the insertion of an apparently apolitical team of policy analysts between the Cabinet proper and the planning units of the new unified departments. But in essence the new development simply recognized the need, discussed on pp. 235–56 above, and in a pre-election pamphlet by the Parliamentary Secretary to the Civil Service Department,[3] for a long-term policy appraisal on a broad basis by a unit free from day-to-day parliamentary pressures.

The Conservative belief that businessmen had a special talent in this direction had already been shown by the appointment on a full-time basis of a further team of business experts, headed by Mr R. A. Meyjes, Marketing Co-ordinator of Shell International, to the Civil Service Department 'to advise on new approaches to decision-making and the other processes of government'. It seemed that their main function was to help develop the concept of a central policy appraisal unit and also to apply, for example, the experience of Marks and Spencer to Government procurement and purchasing.[4]

[1] Cmnd. 4506, op. cit., par. 47.
[2] *H.C. Debs.*, vol. 805 (3 November 1970), col. 890 (Mr A. Crosland).
[3] David Howell, *A New Style of Government*, Conservative Political Centre, 1970.
[4] *H.L. Debs.*, vol. 768 (22 July 1970), cols. 1053–6 (Earl Jellicoe).

The Administrative Process in Britain

The Civil Service Department showed itself extremely aware of the potential uses of social science research in the management of the central administrative machine. Conferences have been held with the Social Science Research Council and with the Joint University Council for Social and Public Administration.[1] Academics who specialize in public administration have joined civil servants and businessmen in 'thinking sessions' on, for example, the applicability of 'accountable management' in the public service. By the end of 1970, the Department's own research programme, initially limited to *ad hoc* studies concerned with the implementation of the Fulton proposals, included a broad survey of job-satisfaction among most grades of civil servant as suggested in Appendix II below.

There are of course limits to the amount of research that can be accommodated without too much interference with the public service. After reviewing the many areas of civil service management that had been suggested as ripe for research, the Department commented in a paper for the Social Science Research Council that 'to correct the perspective a little, we should perhaps venture the assertion that no organization in the world – whether governmental, industrial, commercial, religious or indeed academic – has ever subjected itself to more than a tiny fraction of the degree of self-examination that is implicit in these programmes'.[2] But after pointing out that it would be necessary to pick from all the possible areas of study those that promised to throw a direct light on pressing problems of management, the Department went on to say that 'much thought is being given to the possibilities of future research especially in the fields of organization, personnel management, selection methods and training'.[3]

Such a statement bodes well for the future integration of administrative theory and administrative practice.

[1] *SSRC Newsletter* (Social Science Research Council, London) No. 7, December 1969, and *PAC Bulletin* (Journal of the Public Administration Committee of the Joint University Council, London) No. 6, May 1969, and No. 8, June 1970.

[2] *Civil Service Management as a Subject for Research*, Civil Service Department, 1969 (available from Social Science Research Council, London).

[3] Ibid., par. 18.

APPENDIX I

Non-industrial home civil servants – numbers by staff groups at 1 January 1968 (including Post Office)[1]

Staff Group	Permanent	Temporary	Total	Per cent of whole
Administrative	2,624	160	2,784	0·4
Executive (general and departmental)	87,907	3,159	91,066	12·0
Clerical officers (general and departmental)	117,308	22,869	140,177	18·5
Clerical assistants	35,419	53,849	89,268	11·7
Typing	11,079	18,880	29,959	3·9
Inspectorate of Factories, Mines, Schools, etc.	2,785	93	2,878	0·4
Messengerial	19,039	16,361	35,400	4·7
Post Office minor and manipulative	182,961	42,090	225,051	29·7
Professional, scientific and technical I (e.g. Accountants, Legal and Medical Staff, Engineers, Architects, Scientific Officers, and various departmental classes)	20,518	6,000	26,518	3·5
Scientific and technical staff II (Specialist classes for which standards of qualification are less exacting than those in the previous group, e.g. Draughtsmen, Librarians, Experimental Officers, Scientific Assistants, Nursing Staff and various departmental classes)	42,343	16,803	59,146	7·8
Ancillary, technical and miscellaneous supervisory grades, etc.	38,085	17,877	55,962	7·4
Total	560,068	198,141	758,209	100·0

[1] *Fulton Report*, vol. 4, p. 12 (Introductory Factual Memorandum).

APPENDIX II

Civil Service Management and Organization:
Suggested Programme of Research

The following programme of research is related to proposals in the
Fulton Report. The purpose of each suggestion is to use social
science methods either (a) to test an assumption in the Report or (b)
to prepare the way for its implementation. Much of the programme
could be based on a Civil Service College and carried out largely by
permanent research staff, supplemented by civil servants on secondment and by course participants, with advice and guidance from
social scientists. Many of these ideas have in fact been taken up by
the Civil Service Department.[1]

DECISION-MAKING

1. Case-studies are needed (dozens of them) to show how real
   decisions are reached. What contributions do different people
   make? What priority do they give to political, financial and
   informational factors? How do these differ according to their
   training and career background, their position in the hierarchy
   and the organizational pattern in which they work?

   Material needs to be systematically collected and discussed in
   order to:

   (a) clarify the present roles of generalist and specialist adminis-
       trators;
   (b) find out what factors are not adequately taken into account
       at present;
   (c) see more precisely what place there is for quantitative
       techniques of decision-making in public administration;

[1] Civil Service National Whitley Council, *Developments on Fulton* (1969); Civil
Service Department, *Report of the Working Party on Material for Training in Government* (1969, unpublished).

(d) appraise realistically the possibilities for administrative specialization.

(e) study and compare the effect on decision-making of different organizational forms.

2. It would be valuable to have some rather wider studies of the effect of pressure group activity on departmental thinking. None of the existing case-studies gets inside the government machine. They do not show how departmental structure compels some civil servants to become spokesmen for special interests while others act as buffers to keep sectional pressures in balance with other aspects of policy.

3. The Fulton Report advocates more 'openness' in discussion of policy. The probable effects could be studied by looking at cases where policy decisions have been reached (for example on the basic unit of decimal currency, the proposal to build an international airport at Stansted, or the regional employment premium) or administrative work has been carried out (for example on aviation contracts) under intensive public scrutiny. It is important to know when the pressure of public opinion leads to more informed decisions and when it leads only to rigidity.

It would be necessary to interview the people concerned in these case-studies, since the files will probably not reveal the full story.

ORGANIZATION

1. Similarly, we need a large number of comparative studies to show the costs and benefits of different organizational forms and their effect on the speed, effectiveness and economy with which work is done. Particular points are:

(a) the merits of different patterns of organization for problem-solving (e.g. the traditional hierarchical structure contrasted with the more fluid pattern in research establishments);

(b) the effectiveness of different structural arrangements for bringing research and new ideas to bear on policy;

(c) a comparison between 'long' and 'short' hierarchies for their effect in different circumstances on (i) the speed and (ii) the quality of decision-making;

(d) the effect on the balance of priorities of including a committee, with or without influential outsiders, in the policy-making system.

2. A study in depth of the amalgamation of two departments (for example the absorption of the National Assistance Board by the Ministry of Social Security or the latter's amalgamation with Health) would clarify its effect on the experience, inter-communication and frame of reference of the staff.

3. How real are the advantages of 'hiving-off'? We can study differences in administrative climate by comparing the way similar work is done in different organizations. For example, how do procurement decisions differ between the Ministry of Defence and a nationalized industry? Are social welfare problems handled differently by officials in a local education authority and in the Supplementary Benefits Commission?

4. Current thinking favours planning branches. It is perhaps time one or two were studied in depth. There are lessons to be learned about their composition, relations with the outside world, relations with policy branches and the qualities needed for working successfully in them.

5. Several 'administrative' functions urgently need a deeper analysis than that in the Fulton Report. For example, when an A.D.P. Division is 'responsible to' an Assistant Secretary, what does the latter actually *do*?

6. Organizational research and re-structuring takes time. Is it worth while in public administration? How long does it take to re-shape a department to meet new tasks, compared with the probable time before the task itself is changed, perhaps after a change of government? Similarly, we do not yet know much about the practicability of career planning in the public service. How far are fragmented careers the result of political 'turbulence' which cannot be cushioned by better personnel work?

MOTIVATION AND MORALE

1. Some Fulton recommendations rest on implicit assumptions about motivation, which need to be tested. Some people may work

better *without* the stress of competition and may have been attracted to the civil service, in preference to industry, for this reason. The application of 'management by objective' and promotion by 'merit' introduces a more stressful relationship between superior and subordinate and between competing peers. In certain circumstances, and for certain types of personality, a loss of security may prejudice the very dedication and loyalty that impressed the Fulton Committee's team of investigators. There is an urgent need for attitude studies among civil servants of different grades and ages before tampering with the existing social fabric of the service.

2. The success of the civil service today depends partly on its ability to introduce change painlessly, especially at lower levels. Good examples are computerization, dispersal of offices and the introduction of new tax or benefit rates. Change involves disturbance. There are various techniques for minimizing resistance to change and for assessing its social cost (which, translated into financial terms, may sometimes outweigh a small technical advantage). A social scientist who is experienced in this field could usefully be involved in the study and implementation of a particular upheaval.

3. Short-term secondments (both in and out) create special problems. A person seconded has to be absorbed before he can be useful. The organization receiving him suffers disturbance. There is now enough experience to allow a study of these problems and methods of overcoming them.

4. Existing studies of job-satisfaction and wastage are on the right lines and should be extended. Priority should be given to an investigation of avoidable causes of apathy and resignation among Assistant Research Officers, Experimental Officers and Assistant Principals. The findings should be interpreted in the light of selection arrangements, the service's need for efficient job-performance and the economic cost of filling vacancies.

5. Some new entrants to the civil service are worried by the lack of any means of measuring their own progress. What special needs do younger staff have for support and encouragement and how difficult would it be to meet them? The best way of finding out would be an attitude survey, accompanied by an assessment of

experiments like the employment of Personnel Officers in the Department of Health.

6. The Fulton Committee suggested a review of current retirement practice. This is partly a human relations problem. How do existing civil servants of varying grades and ages feel about different possibilities? The feelings of potential late-age entrants may also be important: a university teacher of 45 may be reducing his working life by a third if he transfers to the civil service.

7. What would happen if existing staff were encouraged to show preference for different kinds of job? How many would opt, for example, for a career in personnel and organization? Would those indicating a preference for some sorts of work be of such relatively low calibre that it would be better to recruit outsiders?

8. A few case-studies of promotion boards in action, showing the relative weight placed on annual reports, specific experience and interview performance, might alleviate misgivings about the present system. Alternatively, they might underline the case for adopting new techniques.

APPENDIX III

Voluntary Losses of Executive and Clerical Officers (See notes)

TABLE A – *Wastage Rates by Age 1958-67*
Voluntary losses as a percentage of mean number of staff in post.

	Executive Officers						Clerical Officers					
	1958	1963	1964	1965	1966	1967	1958	1963	1964	1965	1966	1967
Men												
50–59	0·3	0·2	0·2	0·3	0·2	0·2	0·4	0·4	0·6	0·6	0·7	0·6
40–49	0·2	0·1	0·2	0·4	0·2	0·2	0·4	0·4	0·7	0·9	0·8	0·9
35–39	0·3	0·3	0·3	0·5	0·2	0·6	0·6	0·9	1·0	1·4	1·8	3·9
30–34	0·7	0·3	0·8	1·0	1·2	1·3	1·0	1·8	2·5	4·6	5·0	6·3
25–29	1·1	2·3	2·7	3·2	2·3	3·6	2·5	3·9	6·5	7·4	7·6	8·0
20–24	5·3	5·1	5·1	5·5	6·8	8·6	11·5	7·3	11·1	11·5	13·0	13·0
Under 20	5·1	4·5	8·2	8·6	7·0	12·3	6·9	5·9	9·9	9·4	11·4	9·9
Under 60	0·5	0·9	0·8	1·1	1·1	1·6	1·3	1·7	2·9	3·4	4·2	4·7
Women												
50–59	1·2	1·7	1·8	1·8	1·5	1·1	1·1	0·9	1·4	1·3	1·5	1·6
40–49	0·8	1·3	1·1	1·1	0·6	0·7	1·2	1·3	1·4	1·5	1·4	1·5
35–39	2·2	2·9	3·5	5·2	2·7	2·2	3·1	3·6	3·7	3·0	3·9	5·3
30–34	2·3	6·0	11·7	5·9	6·2	6·1	7·2	7·7	9·2	8·2	9·2	12·0
25–29	15·4	18·6	17·9	16·4	17·2	13·1	16·1	20·8	25·9	22·6	24·0	22·0
20–24	10·6	14·0	13·7	14·5	16·3	13·9	18·2	16·0	21·4	20·6	20·8	18·2
Under 20	6·3	14·5	18·4	8·3	12·9	14·7	10·0	7·7	9·3	11·8	11·6	11·3
Under 60	2·5	4·5	5·0	5·0	5·5	5·3	4·8	5·8	8·0	8·3	9·0	9·1

TABLE B – *Wastage Rates by Seniority in Grade*
Voluntary losses from September 1966 to August 1967 as a percentage of staff in post on 1 January 1967

Seniority	Executive Officers		Clerical Officers	
	Men	Women	Men	Women
15 years and over	0·1	0·8	0·3	0·7
10–15 years	0·2	0·6	0·8	1·3
7–10 years	0·4	1·9	1·0	6·0
5–7 years	0·6	4·7	3·3	10·0
4–5 years	1·0	3·7	4·8	9·3
3–4 years	0·8	8·7	7·3	12·0
2–3 years	1·7	6·2	8·5	12·0
1–2 years	2·4	7·6	10·5	14·7
6–12 months	4·4	10·0	15·0	18·6
under 6 months	3·1	8·6	16·5	14·7
TOTALS	1·2	4·8	4·3	8·7

NOTES

1. Based on superannuation categories. Include all voluntary losses from 'permanent' (i.e. pensionable) status in the grade concerned, excluding normal retirement. About 16 per cent of all losses between 1958 and 1967 were women 'resigning' and drawing the appropriate gratuity on marriage. Some of these women were re-engaged as 'temporary' civil servants and thus were not strictly 'lost'; those who were re-engaged were excluded from the Wastage Study, and do not therefore appear in Table B.

2. Source: *Report on Survey of Wastage of Executive and Clerical Officers*, H.M. Treasury, November 1968 (unpublished).

BIBLIOGRAPHY

This does not pretend to be a complete bibliography. It includes sources mentioned in footnotes, with the addition of others that the author has found particularly helpful and, for completeness, a few important works that appeared after the main text had gone to the printer. It is divided into three sections, distinguishing (a) British Government reports, (b) books and articles on British government and administration, and (c) more general works on administration. Each section starts with a brief note indicating where more comprehensive bibliographies may be found.

BRITISH GOVERNMENT REPORTS

H.M. Stationery Office, London, publish classified lists of British Government publications in print. New publications are reported by H.M.S.O. in daily, monthly and annual lists, with a consolidated list every five years. The more important publications dealing with public administration are noted in the quarterly issues of *Public Administration*, the journal of the Royal Institute of Public Administration. Since 1968, the Autumn number of the journal has included a survey of administrative developments in the previous year, with appropriate references to official documents. The bound volumes of Parliamentary Debates contain detailed speaker and subject indexes, which are an invaluable aid to research.

The factual evidence to the Fulton Committee (Cmnd. 3638, Vol. 4) is a convenient source of data on many aspects of the civil service; in addition Vol. 3(2) (Memorandum No. 10) contains a summary of reports on the civil service since the Northcote-Trevelyan Report. The history of parliamentary devices for scrutinizing departmental administration is similarly reviewed in the memoranda submitted to the Select Committee on Procedure

(First Report, Session 1968–69). The Redcliffe-Maud Report on Local Government (Cmnd. 4040, Vol. III, Research Appendix 9) contains a summary of reports dealing with the structure of local government.

(a) Command papers (in date order)

Report on the Organisation of the Permanent Civil Service (Northcote-Trevelyan), C.1713, 1854 (reprinted in Cmnd. 3638, 1968, Vol. 1, App. B).

Fourth Report of the Royal Commission on the Civil Service, 1912–15 (Macdonnell), Cd. 7339, 1914.

Report of the Machinery of Government Committee (Haldane), Cd. 9230, 1918.

Report of the Royal Commission on the Civil Service, 1929–31 (Tomlin), Cmd. 3909, 1931.

Report of the Committee on Ministers' Powers, Cmd. 4060, 1932.

Report of the Committee of Inquiry on the Post Office (Bridgeman), Cmd. 4149, 1932.

Social Insurance and Allied Services (Beveridge Report), Cmd. 6404, 1942.

Report of the Committee on the Training of Civil Servants (Assheton), Cmd. 6525, 1944.

Employment Policy, Cmd. 6527, 1944.

The Administrative Class of the Civil Service, Cmd. 6680, 1945.

Report of the Committee on the Political Activities of Civil Servants (Masterman), Cmd. 7718, 1949.

First Report of the Local Government Manpower Committee, Cmd. 7870, 1950.

Second Report of the Local Government Manpower Committee, Cmd. 8421, 1951.

Report of the Public Inquiry into the Disposal of Land at Crichel Down, Cmd. 9175, 1954.

Report of a Committee appointed by the Prime Minister to consider whether certain Civil Servants should be transferred to other duties, Cmd. 9220, 1954.

Report of the Royal Commission on the Civil Service, 1953–55 (Priestley), Cmd. 9613, 1955.

Control of Public Expenditure (Plowden Report), Cmnd. 1432, 1961.

Report of the Royal Commission on the Police (Willink), Cmnd. 1728, 1962.

Report of the Committee on Civil Science, Cmnd. 2171, 1963.

Public Expenditure in 1963–64 and 1967–68, Cmnd. 2235, 1963.

Report of the Committe on Social Studies (Heyworth), Cmnd. 2660, 1965.

The Child, the Family and the Young Offender, Cmnd. 2742, 1965.

The National Plan, Cmnd. 2764, 1965.

The Parliamentary Commissioner for Administration, Cmnd. 2767, 1965.

Public Expenditure: Planning and Control, Cmnd. 2915, 1966.

Departmental Observations on the Report from the Select Committee on Agriculture, (1966–67) Cmnd. 3470, 1967.

Public Expenditure in 1968–69 and 1969–70, Cmnd. 3515, 1968.

Report of the Committee on the Civil Service, 1966–68 (Fulton), Cmnd. 3638, 1968.

  Vol. 1 – Report
  Vol. 2 – Report of a Management Consultancy Group
  Vol. 3 – Surveys and Investigations
  Vol. 4 – Factual, Statistical and Explanatory Papers
  Vol. 5 – Proposals and Opinions.

Report of the Committee on Local Authority and Allied Personal Social Services (Seebohm), Cmnd. 3703, 1968.

House of Lords Reform, Cmnd. 3791, 1968.

Public Expenditure: a New Presentation, Cmnd. 4017, 1969.

Ministerial Control of the Nationalised Industries, Cmnd. 4027, 1969.

Report of the Royal Commission on Local Government in England (Redcliffe-Maud), Cmnd. 4040, 1969:

  Vol. 1 – Report
  Vol. 2 – Memorandum of Dissent by Mr D. Senior
  Vol. 3 – Research Appendices

Information and the Public Interest, Cmnd. 4089, 1969.

Report of the Committee of Inquiry on the Method II System of Selection (Davies), Cmnd. 4156, 1969.

Public Expenditure 1968–69 to 1973–74, Cmnd. 4234, 1969.

(b) Parliamentary papers

Agriculture, Select Committee, 1966–67, *British Agriculture, Fisheries and Food and the European Common Market*, HC 378–XVII. 1968–69, Special Report, HC 138.

Estimates Committee

    1946–47 Fifth Report, *Organisation and Methods and its Effect on the Staffing of Government Departments*, HC 143.

    1957–58 Sixth Report, *Treasury Control of Expenditure*, HC 254–I.

    1961–62 Seventh Report, *Classified Roads*, HC 227.

    1962–63 Eleventh Report, *The Home Office*, HC 293.

    1963–64 Fifth Report, *Treasury Control of Establishments*, HC 228.

    1964–65 Fourth Report, *Ministry of Pensions and National Insurance*, HC 274.

              Sixth Report, *Recruitment to the Civil Service*, HC 308.

    1965–66 Fourth Special Report, *Ministry of Pensions and National Insurance*, HC 32.

    1966–67 Fourth Report, *Government Statistical Services*, HC 246.

House of Commons Debates

    Vol. 530 (20 July 1954) cols. 1284–7

    Vol. 698 (8 July 1964) cols. 543–77

    Vol. 699 (27 July 1964) cols. 1176–86

    Vol. 718 (27 October 1965) cols. 182–5

    Vol. 724 (8 February 1966) cols. 209–14

    Vol. 725 (23 February 1966) col. 432

    Vol. 727 (21 April 1966) cols. 75–9

    Vol. 734 (18 October 1966) cols. 42–61

    Vol. 738 (14 December 1966) cols. 477–94

    Vol. 747 (31 May 1967) col. *33* (written answer)

    Vol. 754 (13 November 1967) cols. 36–165

    Vol. 758 (15 February 1968) cols. *423–4* (written answer)

    Vol. 762 (11 April 1968) col. 1587

    Vol. 763 (23 April 1968) cols. 27–8

    Vol. 767 (26 June 1968) cols. 454–64

    Vol. 773 (21 November 1968) cols. 1542–1681

House of Lords Debates

    Vol. 259 (7 July 1964) cols. 931–8

    Vol. 260 (28 July 1964) cols. 967–70

    Vol. 262 (4 February 1965) cols. 1298–9

    Vol. 295 (24 July 1968) cols. 1049–1194

Miscellaneous Expenditure, Select Committee, 1847–48, Vol. XVII.

National Expenditure, Select Committee, 1940–41, 16th Report, *Organisation and Control of the Civil Service*, HC 120.

Nationalised Industries, Select Committee
1967–68 Special Report, *The Committee's Order of Reference*, HC 298.
Ministerial Control of the Nationalised Industries, HC 371–I.
1968–69 First Special Report, *Subjects of Inquiry*, HC 142.

Parliamentary Commissioner Act, 1967.

Parliamentary Commissioner for Administration
1967–68 First Report, HC 6.
Third Report, HC 54.
Fourth Report (*Annual Report for 1967*), HC 134.
1968–69 Second Report (*Annual Report for 1968*), HC 129.

Parliamentary Commissioner for Administration, Select Committee, 1967–68, Second Report, HC 350.

Police Pensions (Amendment) (No. 2) Regulations, 1964.

Procedure, Select Committee
1964–65 Fourth Report, HC 305.
1968–69 First Report, *Scrutiny of Public Expenditure and Administration*, HC 410.

Public Accounts Committee, 1966–67, Special Report, *Parliament and the Control of University Expenditure*, HC 290.

Race Relations and Immigration, Select Committee, 1968–69, Special Report, HC 62.

Re-organisation of the Civil Service, Papers on, 1854–55, Vol. XX.

(c) Other Government documents

Civil Service Commission
Memorandum on the Use of the Civil Service Selection Board in the Reconstruction Examinations, 1950.
84th Report (covering the period 1941–9), 1950.
86th Report (covering the reconstruction period), 1954, and other post-war reports up to
102nd Report (annual report for 1968), 1969.

Civil Service Department (previously H.M. Treasury)
Centre for Administrative Studies, Occasional Papers, 1967– .
Civil Service Training 1966–67, 1968.

> *Civil Service Training 1967–68*, 1969.
> *O & M Bulletin*, Vols. 23 (1968) and 24 (1969).

Civil Service National Whitley Council, Report of the Joint Committee on the Organisation of the Civil Service, 1920.

> *Whitley Bulletin*, Vol. XLIV (1964), p. 155, 'Review of Civil Service Training'.
> *Developments on Fulton*, 1969.

H.M. Treasury (see also Civil Service Department), Report of a Working Party on Education and Training for Management in the Civil Service, 1964.

Ministry of Health, *National Health Service: the Administrative Structure of the Medical and Related Services in England and Wales*, 1968.

Ministry of Housing and Local Government, Report of the Committee on the Staffing of Local Government (Mallaby), 1967.

> Report of the Committee on the Management of Local Government (Maud), 1967
> Vol. 1 Report of the Committee
> Vol. 2 The Local Government Councillor
> Vol. 3 The Local Government Elector
> Vol. 4 Local Government Administration Abroad
> Vol. 5 Local Government Administration in England and Wales

Ministry of Pensions and National Insurance, *Financial and Other Circumstances of Pensioners*, 1966.

Office of the Minister of Science, Report of the Committee on the Management and Control of Research and Development (Zuckerman), 1961.

BRITISH GOVERNMENT AND ADMINISTRATION

Several books on this subject contain full or lengthy bibliographies. R. M. Punnett, *British Government and Politics* (1968) is particularly full on institutions. There is an annotated bibliography in F. M. G. Willson, *Organization of British Central Government, 1914–64* (2nd edn. 1968). The bibliography in John Palmer, *Government and Parliament in Britain* (2nd edn. 1964), is complete to the date of printing. The Royal Institute of Public Administration has published a *Select Bibliography in British Public Administration* (1963), and there is a longer British Council publication, *Public Administration – a Select*

List of Books and Periodicals (1964). More recent works are usually reviewed in the appropriate journals (e.g. *Public Administration, Political Studies, Political Quarterly*) and mentioned in up-to-date textbooks. For example, R. Rose (ed.), *Policy-Making in Britain* (1969) contains short lists of articles dealing with the policy process and case-studies in public policy.

ABRAMOVITCH, M. & ELIASBERG, V. F. *The Growth of Public Employment in Great Britain*, Princeton, N.J., 1957.

ADAMSON, CAMPBELL. 'The Role of the Industrial Adviser', *Public Administration*, Vol. 46, 1968, p. 153.

ANDERSON, SIR JOHN. 'The Machinery of Government', *Public Administration*, Vol. 24, 1946, p. 153.

BEER, S. H. *Treasury Control*, Oxford, 1957.

BEESLEY, M. E. & FOSTER, C. D. 'The Victoria Line: Social Benefits and Finance', *Journal of the Royal Statistical Society*, Vol. 128, 1965, p. 67.

BELOFF, M. & SHONFIELD, A. 'The Politics of Active Government', *The Listener*, Vol. LXXV (16 June 1966), p. 859.

BERKELEY, H. *The Power of the Prime Minister*, London, 1968.

BIRCH, A. H. *Responsible and Representative Government*, London, 1964.

The British System of Government, London, 1967.

BOYLE, SIR EDWARD and others. 'Who are the Policy-Makers?' *Public Administration*, Vol. 43, 1965, pp. 251 ff.

BRIDGES, LORD. *Portrait of a Profession*, Cambridge, 1950.

'Administration: What is it? and How can it be Learnt?' Lecture, Royal Institute of Public Administration, November 1954.

'Whitehall and Beyond', *The Listener*, Vol. LXXI (25 June 1964), p. 1016.

The Treasury (2nd edn.), London, 1968.

BRITTAN, S. *The Treasury under the Tories 1951–64*, London, 1964.

'The Irregulars', *Crossbow*, October–December, 1966.

Steering the Economy: the Role of the Treasury, London, 1969.

BROWN, R. G. S. 'Organization Theory and Civil Service Reform', *Public Administration*, Vol. 43, 1965, p. 313.

'Research and Policy', *South-Western Review of Public Administration*, March 1968, p. 11.

'Civil Servants – Managers or More than That?' *New Society*, Vol. 10 (10 August 1967), p. 182.

'The Civil Service Examined: the Fulton Report', *South Western Review of Public Administration*, December 1968, p. 33.

BUTT, R. *The Power of Parliament* (2nd edn.), London, 1969.

CAIRNCROSS, SIR ALEC. 'The Work of an Economic Adviser', *Public Administration*, Vol. 46, 1968, p. 7.

CAMPBELL, G. A. *The Civil Service in Britain* (2nd edn.), London, 1965.

CHAPMAN, B. *British Government Observed*, London, 1962.

CHESTER, D. N. 'The Plowden Report: Nature and Significance', *Public Administration*, Vol. 41, 1963, p. 3.

CLARK, W. *Number Ten* (fiction), London, 1966.

CLARKE, SIR RICHARD. 'The Management of the Public Sector of the National Economy' (Stamp Memorial Lecture), London, 1964.

COHEN, E. M. *The Growth of the British Civil Service*, London, 1941.

CONSERVATIVE POLITICAL CENTRE. *Change and Decay*, London, 1963.

COOMBES, D. *The Member of Parliament and the Administration. The Case of the Select Committee on Nationalized Industries*, London, 1966.

COUZENS, K. E. 'The Management Accounting Unit', *O & M Bulletin*, Vol. 23, No. 2, February 1968.

CRITCHLEY, T. A. *The Civil Service Today*, London, 1951.

DALE, H. E. *The Higher Civil Service of Great Britain*, Oxford, 1941.

DEVONS, E. *Planning in Practice*, Cambridge, 1950.

DODD, C. H. & PICKERING, J. F. 'Recruitment to the Administrative Class, 1960–4', *Public Administration*, Vol. 45, 1967, pp. 55, 169.

DUNNILL, FRANK. *The Civil Service: Some Human Aspects*, London, 1956.

ECKSTEIN, H. *The English Health Service*, Cambridge, Mass., 1958.

ELIASBERG, V. F. See ABRAMOVITCH.

FABIAN SOCIETY TRACT NO. 355. *The Administrators*, London, 1964.

FINER, S. E. *The Life and Times of Sir Edwin Chadwick*, London, 1952.

'FORD, JAMES ALLAN'. *A Statue in a Public Place* (fiction), London, 1965.

FOSTER, C. D. See BEESLEY.

FRANKS, SIR OLIVER. *The Experience of a University Teacher in the Civil Service*, Oxford, 1947.

FRY, C. K. *Statesmen in Disguise: the Changing Role of the Administrative Class of the Home Civil Service*, London, 1969.

GARRETT, J. & WALKER, S. D. 'Management by Objectives in the Civil Service', *C.A.S. Occasional Paper*, No. 10, H.M.S.O., 1969.

GILMOUR, I. *The Body Politic*, London, 1969.

GREAVES, H. R. G. *The Civil Service in the Changing State*, London, 1947.

GRIFFITH, J. A. G. *Central Departments and Local Authorities*, London, 1966.

GRIMOND, J. 'Whitehall and Beyond', *The Listener*, Vol. LXXI, 12 March, 1964, p. 415.

GROVE, J. W. See MACKENZIE.

HANSON, A. H. *Planning and the Politicians*, London, 1969.

HICKS, U. K. 'Plowden, Planning and Management in the Public Sector', *Public Administration*, Vol. 39, 1961, p. 299.

HOUGHTON, D. 'Paying for the Social Services', *Institute of Economic Affairs Occasional Paper*, No. 16, London, 1967.

JAY, PETER. 'Don't Split the Treasury', *The Times*, 1 August 1968.

JOHNSON, N. 'Who are the Policy-Makers?' *Public Administration*, Vol. 43, 1965, p. 282.
Parliament and Administration: the Estimates Committee 1945–65, London, 1966.

KELSALL, R. K. *Higher Civil Servants in Britain*, London, 1955.

KINGDOM, T. D. 'The Confidential Advisers of Ministers', *Public Administration*, Vol. 44, 1966, p. 267.

LASKI, H. J. *Reflections on the Constitution*, Manchester, 1951.

LEE, J. M. *Social Leaders and Public Persons*, Oxford, 1963.

MACKENZIE, W. J. M. 'The Plowden Report: a Translation', *The Guardian*, 25 May 1963 (reprinted in R. Rose (ed.), *Policy-Making in Britain*, London, 1969, p. 273).

MACKENZIE, W. J. M. & GROVE, J. W. *Central Administration in Britain*, London, 1957.

MACKINTOSH, J. P. *The British Cabinet* (2nd edn.), London, 1968.
'Mr Wilson's revised Cabinet System', *The Times*, 21 June 1968.
'Failure of a Reform', *New Society*, Vol. 12, 28 November 1968, p. 791.
'Dwindling Hopes of Commons Reform', *The Times*, 13 March 1969.

MANSERGH, N. See VERNON.

MORRISON, LORD. *Government and Parliament* (3rd edn.), Oxford, 1964.

MORTON, W. W. 'The Management Functions of the Treasury', *Public Administration*, Vol. 41, 1963, p. 25.

MUNRO, C. K. *The Fountains in Trafalgar Square*, London, 1952.

NEILD, R. 'New Functions: New Men?' *The Listener*, Vol. LXXII, 27 August 1964, p. 304.

NEWMAN, SIR GEORGE. *The Building of a Nation's Health*, London, 1939.

NICHOLSON, M. *The System: the Misgovernment of Modern Britain*, London, 1967.

PALMER, J. *Government and Parliament in Britain*, London, 1964.

PARRIS, H. 'The Origins of the Permanent Civil Service', *Public Administration*, Vol. 46, 1968, p. 143.
Constitutional Bureaucracy, London, 1969.

PICKERING, J. F. See DODD.

PLAYFAIR, SIR E. 'Minister or Civil Servant?' *Public Administration*, Vol. 43, 1965, p. 268.

PLOWDEN, W. 'The Failure of Piecemeal Reform', *New Society*, Vol. 12, 18 July 1968, p. 82.

P.E.P. (Political and Economic Planning). *Advisory Committees in British Government*, London, 1960.

POWELL, J. E. 'Whitehall and Beyond', *The Listener*, LXXI, 26 March 1964, p. 505.
A New Look at Medicine and Politics, London, 1966.

PUNNETT, R. M. *British Government and Politics*, London, 1968.

REGAN, D. E. 'The Expert and the Administrator: Recent Changes at the Ministry of Transport', *Public Administration*, Vol. 44, 1966, p. 149.

REID, G. *The Politics of Financial Control: the Role of the House of Commons*, London, 1966.

RIDLEY, F. F. (ed.). *Specialists and Generalists*, London, 1968.

RHODES, G. *Administrators in Action*, Vol. II, London, 1965.

ROBSON, W. A. (ed.). *The Civil Service in Britain and France*, Lon don 1956.

ROLL, SIR ERIC. 'The Department of Economic Affairs', *Public Administration*, Vol. 44, 1966. p. 8.

ROSE, R. (ed.). *Policy-Making in Britain*, London, 1969.

SELF, P. J. *Bureaucracy or Management*, London, 1965.

SHONFIELD, A. *Modern Capitalism*, Oxford, 1965.
See also BELOFF.

SHORE, PETER. *Entitled to Know*, London, 1966.

SISSON, C. H. *The Spirit of British Administration: and some European Comparisons*, London, 1959.

SNOW, C. P. *Science and Government*, London, 1961.

SOSKICE, SIR FRANK. Address, *Police Review*, 18 June 1965.

STACEY, F. *The Government of Modern Britain*, London, 1968.

THOMAS, H. (ed.). *Crisis in the Civil Service*, London, 1968.

VERNON, R. V. & MANSERGH, N. *Advisory Bodies: a Study of their Uses in Relation to Central Government 1919–39*, London, 1940.

WALKER, N. *Morale in the Civil Service: a Study of the Desk Worker*, Edinburgh, 1961.

WALKER, S. D. See GARRETT.

WALKLAND, S. A. *The Legislative Process in Great Britain*, London, 1968.

WALL, W. D. *Educational Research and Policy-Making* (National Foundation for Educational Research), London, 1968.

WEDGWOOD BENN, A. 'Mintech – Myth and Reality', interview in *The Times*, 29 March 1969.

WHEARE, K. C. *Government by Committee*, Oxford, 1955.

WHYATT REPORT. 'The Citizen and the Administration: the Redress of Grievances', *Justice*, London, 1961.

WILLIAMS, R. 'The Select Committee on Science and Technology: The First Round', *Public Administration*, Vol. 46, 1968, p. 299.

WILLSON, F. M. G. *Administrators in Action*, Vol. I, London, 1961.
The Organization of British Central Government 1914–1964 (2nd edn.), London, 1968.

WILSON, H. (with Norman Hunt). 'The Prime Minister on the Machinery of Government', *The Listener*, Vol. LXXVII (6 and 13 April 1967), pp. 447 and 481.

WILSON, H., POWELL, E., and others. *Whitehall and Beyond*, London, 1964.

WISEMAN, H. V. (ed.). *Parliament and the Executive*, London, 1966.

WRIGHT, M. *Treasury Control of the Civil Service, 1854–1874*, Oxford, 1969.

GENERAL WORKS ON ADMINISTRATION

This section is closer to a conventional bibliography than the others, although it is still far from complete. Many of the works cited are themselves reviews of extensive fields of writing and research (see p. 120, n. 1, Chapter VI). The best classified bibliography for administrative theory is still perhaps that in P. M. Blau and W. R. Scott, *Formal Organizations* (London edition, 1963). There are others in J. G. March (ed.), *Handbook of Organizations* (1965) and B. M. Gross, *The Managing of Organizations* (1965). There is a much shorter 'introduction to the literatures' in D. V. Donnison and V. Chapman, *Social Policy and Admistration* (1965). On a broader front, Professor Mackenzie offers a very full 'book list' and 'notes on reading', while disclaiming any attempt to produce a bibliography, in his *Politics and Social Science* (1967). The most relevant journals for review articles are *Human Relations*, the *Journal of Management Studies* and the *Administrative Science Quarterly* (U.S.A.).

APPLEBY, P. H. *Policy and Administration*, Alabama, 1949.

APPLEWHITE, P. B. *Organizational Behavior*, Englewood Cliffs, N.J., 1965.

ARGYRIS, C. *Personality and Organization*, New York, 1957.
Interpersonal Competence and Organizational Effectiveness, London, 1962.
Integrating the Individual and the Organization, New York, 1964.

BACCHUS, M. K. 'Relationships between professional and administrative officers in a government department during a period of administrative change', *Sociological Review*, Vol. 15, 1967, pp. 155–78.

BAKKE, E. W. 'Concept of Social Organization' in Mason Haire (ed.), *Modern Organization Theory*, New York, 1959.

BARKER, E. *The Development of Public Services in Europe 1660–1930*, Oxford, 1944.

BLAU, P.M. & SCOTT, W. R. *Formal Organizations*, London, 1963.

BLONDEL, J. See RIDLEY.

BRAYBROOKE, D. See LINDBLOM.

BRECH, E. F. L. See URWICK.

BRODIE, M. B. *Fayol on Administration*, Administrative Staff College Monograph, London, 1967.

BURNS, T. & STALKER, G. M. *The Management of Innovation* (2nd edn.), London, 1966.

CHAPMAN, B. *The Profession of Government*, London, 1959.

CHAPMAN, V. See DONNISON.

CROZIER, M. *The Bureaucratic Phenomenon*, London, 1964.

CYERT, R. M. & MARCH, J. G. *A Behavioral Theory of the Firm*, Englewood Cliffs, N.J., 1963.

DALTON, M. *Men Who Manage*, New York, 1959.

DEARBORN, D. C. & SIMON, H. A. 'Selective Perception: A Note on the Departmental Identification of Executives', *Sociometry*, Vol. 21, 1958, pp. 140–4.

DE LAMOTHE, A. DUTHEILLET 'Ministerial Cabinets in France', *Public Administration*, Vol. 43, 1965, p. 365.

DICKSON, W. J. See ROETHLISBERGER.

DOIG, J. W. See MANN.

DONNISON, D. V. & CHAPMAN, V. *Social Policy and Administration*, London, 1965.

DUBIN, R. 'The Stability of Human Organizations' in Mason Haire (ed.), *Modern Organization Theory*, New York, 1959, pp. 246–7.

EASTON, D. *The Political System*, New York, 1953.
A Framework for Political Analysis, Englewood Cliffs, N. J., 1965.

ETZIONI, A. 'Two Approaches to Organizational Analysis', *Administrative Science Quarterly*, Vol. 5, 1960, p. 257.
A Comparative Analysis of Complex Organizations, Glencoe, Ill., 1961.
Modern Organizations, Englewood Cliffs, N.J., 1964.

ETZIONI, A. (ed.). *Complex Organizations: A Sociological Reader* (2nd edn.), New York, 1969.

FAYOL, H. 'The Administrative Theory in the State' in Gulick and Urwick (eds.), *Papers on the Science of Administration*, New York, 1937.
(tr. Storrs) *General and Industrial Management*, London, 1949.

GOULDNER, A. W. 'Cosmopolitans and Locals', *Administrative Science Quarterly*, Vol. 2, 1957–8, pp. 281–306, 444–80.

GROSS, B. M. *The Managing of Organizations*, London, 1966.

GULICK, L. H. & URWICK, L. *Papers on the Science of Administration*, New York, 1937.

HAIRE, M. (ed.). *Modern Organization Theory*, New York, 1959.

JONES, R. E. *The Functional Analysis of Politics*, London, 1967.

LINDBLOM, C. E. *The Intelligence of Democracy*, New York, 1965.

LINDBLOM, C. E. & BRAYBROOKE, D. *The Policy-making Process*, Englewood Cliffs, N.J., 1968.

LITTERER, J. A. (ed.). *Organization: Structure and Behavior*, New York, 1963.

LUPTON, T. *Management and the Social Sciences*, London, 1966.

MACKENZIE, W. J. M. 'Science in the Study of Administration', *The Manchester School*, Vol. 20, 1952, p. 8.
Social Science and Politics, London, 1967.

MANN, D. and DOIG, J. W. *The Assistant Secretaries: Problems and Processes of Appointment*, Washington, D.C., 1965.

MARCH, J. G. 'Business Decision Making', *Industrial Research*, Spring, 1959.

MARCH, J. G. (ed.). *A Handbook of Organizations*, Chicago, 1965.

MARCH, J. G. & SIMON, H. A. *Organizations*, New York, 1958.
See also CYERT.

MARSHAK, J. 'Efficient and Viable Organizational Forms' in Mason Haire (ed.), *Modern Organization Theory*, New York, 1959.

MAYO, E. *The Social Problems of an Industrial Civilization*, London, 1949.

MERTON, R. K. (ed.). *A Reader in Bureaucracy*, Glencoe, Ill., 1952.

MOSHER, F. C. *Democracy and the Public Service*, Oxford, 1968.

MOUZELIS, N. P. *Organisation and Bureaucracy*, London, 1967.

PARKER, R. S. & SUBRAMANIAM, V. 'Public and Private Administration', *International Review of Administrative Science*, Vol. 30, 1964, pp. 354–66.

President's Committee on Administrative Management (Brownlow Report), Washington, 1937.

PRESTHUS, R. *Behavioral Approaches to Public Administration*, Alabama, 1965.

PRICE, D. K. *The Scientific Estate*, Cambridge, Mass., 1965.

PUGH, D. S. *et al.* 'Dimensions of Organization Structure', *Administrative Science Quarterly*, Vol. 13, 1968, pp. 65–105.

RAPOPORT, A. 'The Logical Task as a Research Tool in Organization Theory' in Mason Haire (ed.), *Modern Organization Theory*, New York, 1959.

RIDLEY, F. F. & BLONDEL, J. *Public Administration in France* (2nd edn.), London, 1969.

ROBSON, W. A. 'The Managing of Organizations', *Public Administration*, Vol. 44, 1966, p. 276.

ROETHLISBERGER, F. J. & DICKSON, W. J. *Management and the Worker*, Cambridge, Mass., 1939.

SAYRE, W. S. 'Principles of Administration', *Hospitals* (Journal of American Hospital Association), 16 January 1956.

SCHEIN, E. H. *Organizational Psychology*, Englewood Cliffs, N.J., 1965.

SCOTT, W. R. See BLAU.

SIMON, H. A. *Administrative Behavior* (2nd edn.). New York, 1957.

SIMON, H. A., SMITHBURG, D. W., & THOMPSON, V. A. *Public Administration*, New York, 1959.
See also DEARBORN and MARCH.

SMITHBURG. D. W. See SIMON.

STALKER, G. M. See BURNS.

STANLEY, D. T. *Changing Administrations*, Washington, D.C., 1965.
The Higher Civil Service, Washington, D.C., 1965.

STEWART, R. *The Reality of Management*, London, 1963.

Managers and their Jobs, London, 1967.

SUBRAMANIAN, V. 'Specialists in British and Australian Government Services: a Study in Contrast', *Public Administration*, Vol. 41, 1963, p. 357.

'Representative Bureaucracy: a Re-assessment', *American Political Science Review*, Vol. LXI, 1967, p. 1010.

'The Relative Status of Specialists and Generalists', *Public Administration*, Vol. 46, 1968, p. 337.

See also PARKER.

TAYLOR, F. W. *Principles and Methods of Scientific Management*, New York, 1911.

THOMPSON, J. D. & TUDEN, A. 'Strategies, Structures and Processes of Administrative Decision' in J. D. Thompson *et al.* (eds.), *Comparative Studies in Administration*, Pittsburgh, 1959.

THOMPSON, V. A. 'Bureaucracy and Innovation', *Administrative Science Quarterly*, Vol. 10, 1965–6, p. 1.

Bureaucracy and Innovation, Alabama, 1969.

See also SIMON.

TRUMAN, D. *The Governmental Process*, New York, 1951.

URWICK, L. & BRECH, E. F. L. *The Making of Scientific Management*, London, 1957, Vol. I.

See also GULICK

VICKERS, SIR GEOFFREY. *The Art of Judgment: A Study of Policy Making*, London, 1965.

WEBER, MAX (tr. A. M. Henderson and T. Parsons). *The Theory of Social and Economic Organization*, Glencoe, Ill., 1947.

WHISLER, T. L. 'The Assistant-to in Four Administrative Settings', *Administrative Science Quarterly*, Vol. 5, 1960, pp. 180–216.

WILDAVSKY, A. *The Politics of the Budgetary Process*, New York, 1964.

WILENSKY, H. I. *Organizational Intelligence*, New York, 1967.

WILKINS, L. T. *Social Policy, Action and Research*, London, 1964.

WOODWARD, J. *Industrial Organization: Theory and Practice*, Oxford, 1965.

INDEX

Date Due